Studies in Celtic History XXXVIII

THE BOOK OF LLANDAF
AS A HISTORICAL SOURCE

STUDIES IN CELTIC HISTORY

ISSN 0261-9865

General editors
Dauvit Broun
Máire Ní Mhaonaigh
Huw Pryce

Studies in Celtic History aims to provide a forum for new research into all aspects of the history of Celtic-speaking peoples throughout the whole of the medieval period. The term 'history' is understood broadly: any study, regardless of discipline, which advances our knowledge and understanding of the history of Celtic-speaking peoples will be considered. Studies of primary sources, and of new methods of exploiting such sources, are encouraged.

Founded by Professor David Dumville, the series was relaunched under new editorship in 1997. Proposals or queries may be sent directly to the editors at the addresses given below; all submissions will receive prompt and informed consideration before being sent to expert readers.

Professor Dauvit Broun, Department of History (Scottish), University of Glasgow, 9 University Gardens, Glasgow G12 8QH

Professor Máire Ní Mhaonaigh, St John's College, Cambridge CB2 1TP

Professor Huw Pryce, School of History, Philosophy and Social Sciences, Bangor University, Gwynedd LL57 2DG

For titles already published in this series
see the end of this volume

THE BOOK OF LLANDAF
AS A HISTORICAL SOURCE

PATRICK SIMS-WILLIAMS

THE BOYDELL PRESS

© Patrick Sims-Williams 2019

All Rights Reserved. Except as permitted under current legislation no part of this work may be photocopied, stored in a retrieval system, published, performed in public, adapted, broadcast, transmitted, recorded or reproduced in any form or by any means, without the prior permission of the copyright owner

The right of Patrick Sims-Williams to be identified as the author of this work has been asserted in accordance with sections 77 and 78 of the Copyright, Designs and Patents Act 1988

First published 2019
The Boydell Press, Woodbridge

ISBN 978-1-78327-418-5

The Boydell Press is an imprint of Boydell & Brewer Ltd
PO Box 9, Woodbridge, Suffolk IP12 3DF, UK
and of Boydell & Brewer Inc.
668 Mt Hope Avenue, Rochester, NY 14620-2731, USA
website: www.boydellandbrewer.com

A catalogue record of this publication is available
from the British Library

The publisher has no responsibility for the continued existence or accuracy of URLs for external or third-party internet websites referred to in this book, and does not guarantee that any content on such websites is, or will remain, accurate or appropriate

This publication is printed on acid-free paper

CONTENTS

List of Illustrations   vi
Acknowledgements   viii
Abbreviations   x

Introduction   1
1. The Book of Llandaf and the early Welsh charter   7
2. The origin of the Llandaf claims   17
3. The charters in the Book of Llandaf: forgeries or recensions?   22
4. The authenticity of the witness lists   32
5. The integrity of the charters   44
6. The chronology of the charters   50
7. The status of the donors and recipients of the charters   59
8. The fake diplomatic of the Book of Llandaf   71
9. The Book of Llandaf: first edition or seventh enlarged revision?   78
10. A new approach to the compilation of the Book of Llandaf   86
11. The evidence of the doublets   93
12. The Book of Llandaf as an indicator of social and economic change   104
13. The royal genealogical framework   117
14. The episcopal framework   157

Appendix I. Concordance and chart showing the paginal and chronological order of the charters   179
Appendix II. Maps of grants to bishops   183

Bibliography   189
Index   199

ILLUSTRATIONS

Maps

A.	South Wales	xii
B.	South-East Wales	xiii
Appendix II.	Maps of grants to bishops (Maps 1–8 from Kathleen Hughes, 'The Celtic Church: is this a valid concept?', by permission of CMCS Publications)	183

Tables

3.1.	Unemended (Fig. 1) and emended (Fig. 2) genealogies	31
4.1.	Sequence i (re-ordered)	36
4.2.	St Dyfrig's disciples in the Sequence i charters	42
8.1.	*Dedit, largitus est*, and *immolauit* paginally (Fig. 1) and chronologically (Fig. 2)	74
8.2.	*Successoribus, omnibus episcopis*, and *presulibus* paginally (Fig. 1) and chronologically (Fig. 2)	76
9.1.	Wendy Davies's archives A–J	79
9.2.	Notifications, Narrations, and Preambles	81
9.3.	*In manu episcopi N* and Sanction formulae	82
9.4.	Further Sanction formulae	83
10.1.	Charters of Bishop Berthwyn	88
10.2.	Doublets and hypothetical single sheets	90
12.1.	Consent formulae	111
12.2.	Narrations paginally (Fig. 1) and chronologically (Fig. 2)	113
13.1.	HG 28 and JC 9 unemended (Fig. 1) and emended (Fig. 2)	123
13.2.	The genealogies according to *EWGT* (Fig. 1) and according to Bartrum's 'Corrections' (Fig. 2)	127

List of Illustrations

13.3.	The female lines in the Jesus College genealogies	130
13.4.	Conflicting patrilineages	134
13.5.	The genealogists' scheme	138
13.6.	A possibly historical scheme	142
Appendix I.	Chart giving a visual impression of difference between the chronological and paginal order of charters	182

The author and publisher are grateful to all the institutions and individuals listed for permission to reproduce the materials in which they hold copyright. Every effort has been made to trace the copyright holders; apologies are offered for any omission, and the publisher will be pleased to add any necessary acknowledgement in subsequent editions.

ACKNOWLEDGEMENTS

I have incurred many debts during the long gestation of this book. It began when I was asked to review Professor Wendy Davies's ground-breaking *An Early Welsh Microcosm* (1978) and *The Llandaff Charters* (1979) in the *Journal of Ecclesiastical History*. The draft of the review rapidly exceeded the required length, so I reduced it to the six-page summary version published in *JEH* in 1982 and reprinted in my *Britain and Early Christian Europe* (1995). A revision of most of the original draft appears in Chapters 1–12 of the present book, but some of it was diverted into earlier publications. One of the latter was the notes and maps which I added to Dr Kathleen Hughes's 1974/5 Oxford O'Donnell Lecture, 'The Celtic Church: is this a valid concept?', for its posthumous publication in *Cambridge Medieval Celtic Studies* in 1981. The inclusion of these additions was approved by Professor Dorothy Whitelock and Dr David Dumville. The maps are reproduced in Appendix II below. As in 1981, I thank Dr David Robinson for his generous help with them. Further material, including more maps, appeared in my *Religion and Literature in Western England, 600–800* in 1990, and in an article about Llan-gors, Brycheiniog, in *Cambrian Medieval Celtic Studies* in 1993.

In 1980 I had a fruitful correspondence with the late Peter Bartrum about the south-eastern Welsh genealogies. The resulting article eventually reached print in a shortened form in *Cambrian Medieval Celtic Studies* in 2017, and now appears in a different, less truncated form as Chapter 13 of the present book. In completing this work I am indebted not only to Dr Bartrum, but also to Dr Ben Guy for further discussion and for a copy of his invaluable Cambridge University Ph.D. dissertation on the transmission of the medieval Welsh genealogies.

An important milestone towards the completion of this research was a grant in 1997–9 from the Leverhulme Trust in support of a project on *Manuscripts of the Old Welsh Period* in the Department of Welsh and Celtic Studies at Aberystwyth University. This had two components, each with its own researcher. Dr Helen McKee worked on the Cambridge Juvencus manuscript. Her excellent work, published in 2000, was not related to the Book of Llandaf, except insofar as the latter's Bishop Cyfeilliog may be the subject of the Juvencus *Cemelliauc* cipher. Directly relevant, however, was the research of John Reuben Davies, which relieved me of the need to complete my work on the Book of Llandaf's twelfth-century context. In 2003 he published *The Book of Llandaf and the Norman Church in Wales* (Volume XXI of Studies in Celtic History). As Dr Davies says in the Preface to this important study, his book and mine are complementary.

While the Leverhulme project was in progress, Dr Jon Coe was working in the Department on a Ph.D. on 'The place-names of the Book of Llandaf' (2001) and soon afterwards Dr Meredith Cane completed her Ph.D. on 'Personal names of men in Wales, Cornwall and Brittany 400–1400 AD' (2003), which is also relevant to the Book of Llandaf. I gained much from working with both of them. Philological aspects of the Book of Llandaf were also discussed in detail in my article on 'Archaic

Acknowledgements

Old Welsh' in the *Bulletin of the Board of Celtic Studies* in 1991. The present book leaves philology to one side, however, and only summarises that article's findings.

It has been a privilege to have known the authors of all the most important works on the Book of Llandaf from 1948 to 2013: Peter Bartrum, Christopher Brooke, Wendy Davies, Kathleen Hughes, Daniel Huws, Kari Maund, Jon Coe, John Reuben Davies, and Thomas Charles-Edwards. Christopher Brooke – whose sparkling 1958 essay on three prelates 'that never existed' ('The archbishops of St David's, Llandaff and Caerleon-on-Usk') kindled my undergraduate interest in 1972 – was always interested and encouraging, and I regret that he and Peter Bartrum did not live to see this book. Over the years a number of other people have advised me on various points. I have tried to thank them all in the relevant footnotes and apologise for any inadvertent omissions. I must also thank the publisher's anonymous referee for helpful comments, and Cath D'Alton for redrawing the maps.

Finally, I am grateful to the series editors, and above all my wife Marged Haycock, for their patience during the long gestation of this book.

Patrick Sims-Williams,
Aberystwyth
April 2018

ABBREVIATIONS

ABT	'Achau Brenhinoedd a Thywysogion Cymru' in *EWGT* 95–110
ABT(E)	ABT, MS E in *EWGT* 95–110
Arch. Camb.	*Archaeologia Cambrensis*
ASE	*Anglo-Saxon England*
BBCS	*Bulletin of the Board of Celtic Studies*
BL	British Library (London)
'Chad'	Charter in the Book of St Chad (the Llandeilo/Lichfield Gospels) cited by number from the edition in *LL* xliii–xlvii
CMCS	*Cambrian Medieval Celtic Studies*, previously, until Winter 1993, *Cambridge Medieval Celtic Studies*
DP	Owen, Henry (ed.), *The Description of Penbrokshire by George Owen of Henllys*, 4 parts (London, 1892–1936)
EA	Davies, James Conway, *Episcopal Acts and Cognate Documents Relating to Welsh Dioceses, 1066–1272*, 2 vols (Cardiff, 1946–8)
EHR	*English Historical Review*
EME	*Early Medieval Europe*
EWGT	Bartrum, P. C. (ed.), *Early Welsh Genealogical Tracts* (Cardiff, 1966)
HB	*Historia Brittonum* in Morris, John (ed. and transl.), *Nennius: British History and The Welsh Annals* (Chichester, 1980)
HG	'Welsh Genealogies from Harleian MS. 3859' in *EWGT* 9–13
JC	'Jesus College MS. 20' in *EWGT* 41–50
JHSCW	*Journal of the Historical Society of the Church in Wales*
LBS	Baring-Gould, S., and Fisher, John, *The Lives of the British Saints*, 4 vols (London, 1907–13)
LL	Evans, J. Gwenogvryn (ed.), with the co-operation of John Rhys, *The Text of the Book of Llan Dav Reproduced from the Gwysaney Manuscript* [1893], facsimile reprint (Aberystwyth, 1979). Arabic numerals are to charter number (cf. below, 5 n. 27) unless 'p.' or 'pp.' is specified
MP	'Miscellaneous Pedigrees' in *EWGT* 121–2
NLW	National Library of Wales (Aberystwyth)
NLWJ	*National Library of Wales Journal*

Abbreviations

PBA	*Proceedings of the British Academy*
Sawyer	Sawyer, P. H., *Anglo-Saxon Charters: An Annotated List and Bibliography* (London, 1968)
SC	*Studia Celtica*
THSC	*Transactions of the Honourable Society of Cymmrodorion*
TYP[4]	Bromwich, Rachel (ed. and transl.), *Trioedd Ynys Prydein*, fourth edition (Cardiff, 2014)
VC	*Vita Cadoci* in *VSB* 24–141 (cited by chapter number)
VSB	Wade-Evans, A. W. (ed. and transl.), *Vitae Sanctorum Britanniae et Genealogiae* (Cardiff, 1944)
WHEMA	Davies, Wendy, *Welsh History in the Early Middle Ages: Texts and Societies* (Farnham, 2009)
WHR	*Welsh History Review*

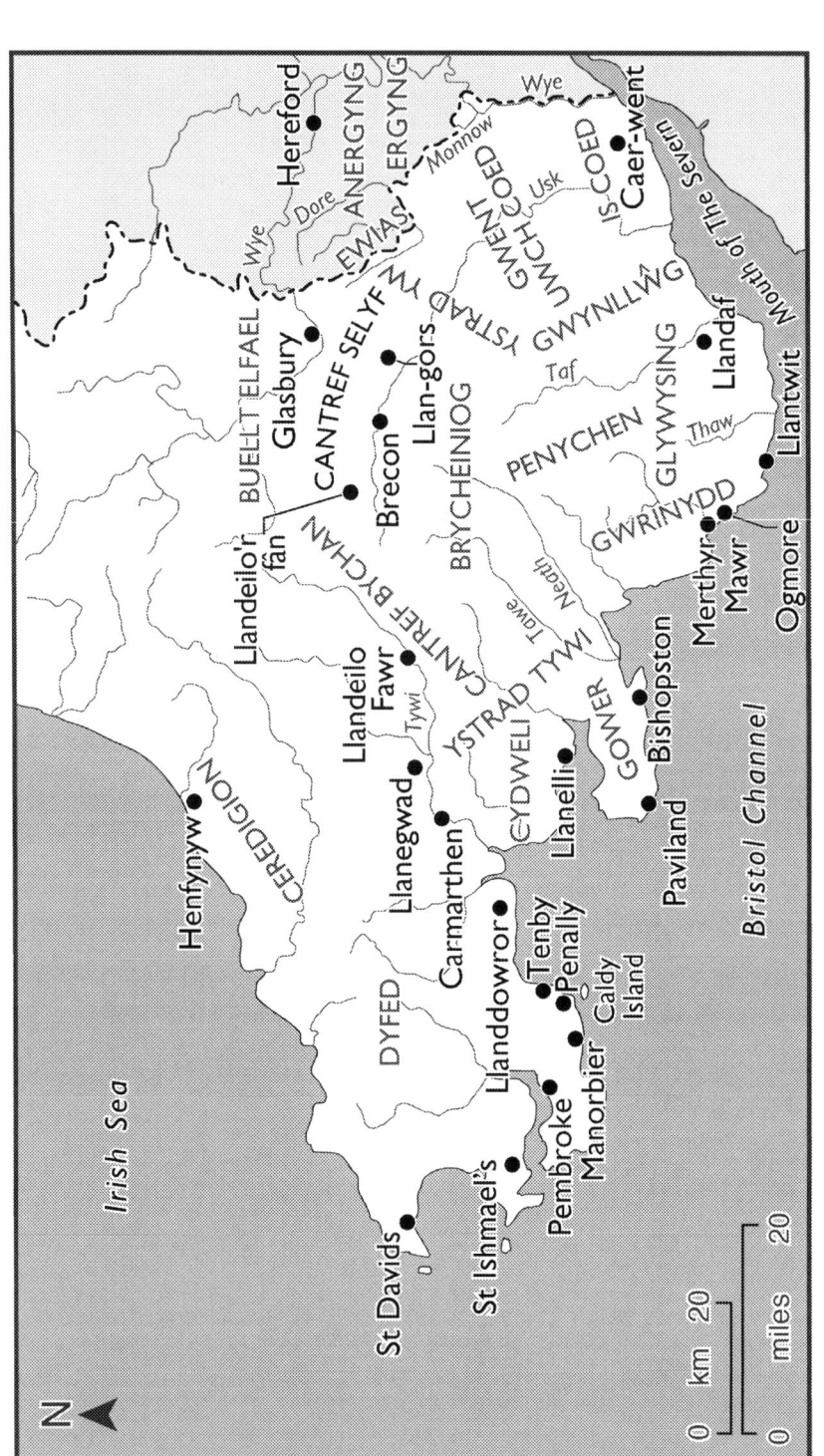

Map A South Wales

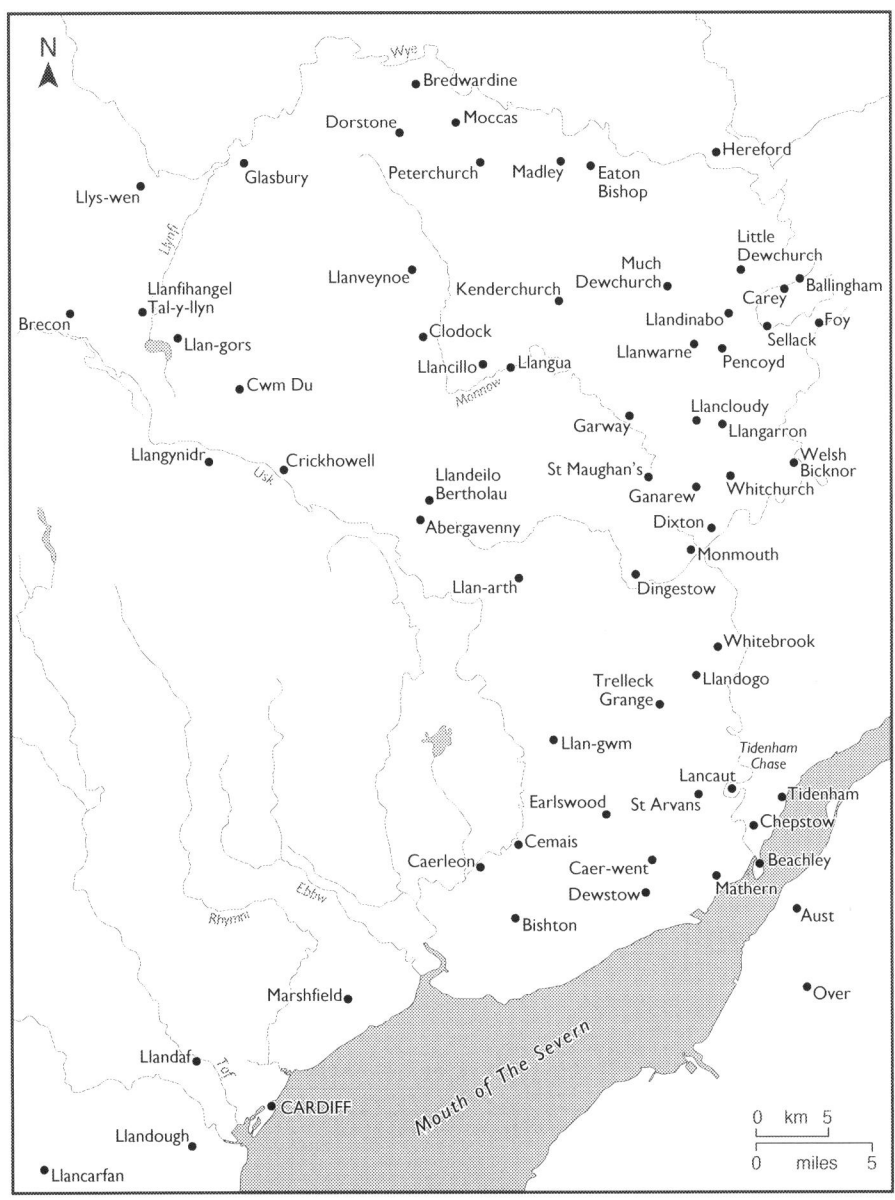

Map B   South-East Wales

INTRODUCTION

Liber Landavensis, the Book of Llandaf (Aberystwyth, National Library of Wales MS 17110E), a Gospel Book cum History cum Cartulary, is at once the most difficult and the most exciting document of the twelfth-century Church known to the present writer. Whether one's interests turn towards hagiography, post-Roman land tenure, ecclesiastical politics, the development of the Welsh language, early medieval diplomatic, or simply forgery on a grand scale, *Liber Landavensis* (hereafter *LL*) is a rich but challenging source. It was justly described by Adrian Morey and C. N. L. Brooke as a 'summit of achievement in the production of bogus documents' in Britain,[1] and therein lies its notoriety and much of its difficulty. Few works better illustrate their contention that in the twelfth century the worlds of the hagiographer, the charter forger, and the historian coincided closely in the service of the spiritual and temporal power and privileges of the churches for whom such men doctored or composed.[2]

In *LL* the saints' Lives, the twelfth-century documents, and the charters are inextricably inter-related, and a full understanding of it and its context will not come until the study of all three elements has been fully integrated. The first two of the three have been studied in detail by John Reuben Davies.[3] His work supplements G. H. Doble's intelligent, but often incomplete, work on the *Vitae*, and J. Conway Davies's and C. N. L. Brooke's interpretations of *LL* in relation to its documents about the struggles of Bishop Urban of Llandaf in 1119–34 against the bishops of St Davids and Hereford, the Pope, and the 'invasion of monks' from houses such as Gloucester and Tewkesbury.[4]

The third element in *LL* is the 159 charters which purport to date from the fifth or sixth centuries to the eleventh.[5] The present book is intended to supplement the two substantial books which Wendy Davies devoted to their evaluation. Her two books, the result of a decade of study,[6] were among the most important works on early Welsh history published in the twentieth century, and in turning attention back to the *LL* charters and their historical uses they performed a timely service. As she was aware, however, they were far from exhausting the potential of the charters. *The Llandaff Charters* was intended as 'a useful guide to their understanding and a coherent framework within which others can approach them' (p. vii). Her attempt to use them as a historical source for early Wales in *An Early Welsh Microcosm* was a pioneering venture into hitherto uncharted territory, and proved quite controversial.

---

[1] Morey and Brooke, *Gilbert Foliot and his Letters*, 128.
[2] *Ibid.*, 141 and 145.
[3] J. R. Davies, *The Book of Llandaf*.
[4] Doble, *Lives*; Conway Davies, *EA*; Brooke, *The Church*. See also Smith, 'The kingdom of Morgannwg', and Cowley, 'The Church in medieval Glamorgan'.
[5] On the number of charters see below, 5 n. 27.
[6] I cite her articles by chapter number from her collected papers, *WHEMA*.

While some scholars were content to accept her assessment of the charters,[7] others were very critical[8] or simply dismissive.[9] The most recent work is constructive and appreciative but not uncritical,[10] and I believe that the present work falls into that category.

To appreciate the importance of Wendy Davies's work one must consider the cloud of opprobrium that descended on the Book of Llandaf from the moment it was published and translated by W. J. Rees in 1840. Since the seventeenth century, when the Book was in England, extracts had been published and passages cited by such reputable writers as Spelman, Dugdale, Ussher, Wharton, and Wilkins, and a few eighteenth-century Welsh antiquaries, including Iolo Morganwg, had been glad to exploit transcripts for their own purposes.[11] Rees's 1840 edition, however, exposed the Book as a whole to criticism. Thomas Stephens, writing anonymously to the *Cambrian* newspaper in 1843, described it as

> a work which, while conducive to no good, is productive of positive injury, by inducing the mind to brood over 'the solitary, vindictive malice of monks.' It is a work purporting to consist of historical documents, but upon the veracity of whose statements the historian, according to the Rev. T. Price, cannot rely.[12]

Even the Dean of Llandaff, an eminent geologist, admitted in 1850 that the Book of Llandaf 'labours under the most serious chronological difficulties, which must throw over the whole a thick veil of obscurity and doubt'.[13] Haddan and Stubbs excluded relevant passages in their *Councils and Synods* in 1869 'as not being contemporary or genuine records', setting the tone for the future, notwithstanding Gwenogvryn Evans's complaints in his 1893 edition about 'the unreasonableness of much of the old criticisms by which the trustworthiness of the *Liber Landavensis* was impugned'. Evans maintained that the true chronology of the charters could be worked out from their witness lists, even if such questions 'would require a volume to discuss them'.[14] Although Alfred Anscombe, secretary of the British Numismatic Society, made a good start on such a programme in articles in the *Celtic Review* (1909–12), these were, and still are, generally overlooked.[15] The normally credulous Baring-Gould

---

[7] e.g. Wormald, Review; Snyder, *An Age of Tyrants*, 46–7.

[8] e.g. Maund, *Ireland, Wales, and England*, 183–206; eadem, 'Fact and narrative fiction'.

[9] e.g. Dark, *Civitas to Kingdom*, 140–8.

[10] Charles-Edwards, *Wales and the Britons*, passim.

[11] See references in Rees, *Liber Landavensis*, x–xxiii, and in *LL*, viii–xii. For Iolo see below, ch. 7.

[12] *Cambrian*, 28 January 1843, reprinted by Löffler and Rhys, 'Thomas Stephens and the Abergavenny Cymreigyddion', 430. The quotation is from the *Letters of Junius*, and T. Price is Thomas Price ('Carnhuanawc').

[13] Conybeare, 'Memoir', 25.

[14] Haddan and Stubbs, *Councils*, I, 125–6, 207–8, 286–8 (cf. 289–96, etc.); *LL* xxiii. E. J. Newell, in his review of *LL* in 1893 (pp. 334–6), tended to agree with Evans, against Haddan and Stubbs and Willis-Bund (cf. Willis-Bund, 'The Teilo churches'). See also Newell, *Llandaff* (1902).

[15] Anscombe, 'Landavensium ordo chartarum', noted in 1946 by E. D. Jones ('The Book of Llandaff', 130 n. 2). When Bartrum undertook the same task in the 1940s he at first had no 'knowledge of Anscombe's scheme' ('Some studies', 286). Extraordinarily, J. W. James ignored both Anscombe and Bartrum in all his articles (from 1955 to 1973). In

Introduction

and Fisher were somewhat dismissive of Llandaf's pretensions in their *Lives of the British Saints* (1907–13) and in 1932 the Revd Arthur Wade-Evans mocked the

> vain imaginings of the Norman-French ecclesiastics, who gave us the Book of Llandaff, a spurious compilation, wherein everything, that is genuinely old, has been farced to bolster up ridiculous claims on behalf of Urban's new cathedral church, for which the Welsh could find no better name than Llan Dâf, 'the Church by the Taff'.

In 1942 the other influential student of the time, Canon G. H. Doble, concluded that the writing of the Book of Llandaf had 'resulted in a huge series of falsifications of history – it will take a very long time before they are all detected'.[16] Almost everybody was against what J. Conway Davies termed the 'pretensions' of Llandaf in his *Episcopal Acts Relating to Welsh Diocese* (1946–8), with the lone exception of J. W. James (1889–1983), who resented Wade-Evans's apparent St Davids bias.[17] Finding the assumptions of his own 1931 Durham D.D. dissertation contradicted at every turn, James published a long series of illogical diatribes from 1955 to 1973 with titles like '*The Book of Llan Dav* and Canon G. H. Doble'. In 1958 Christopher Brooke stumbled unawares[18] into this hornet's nest with his facetiously entitled essay 'The archbishops of St David's, Llandaff and Caerleon-on-Usk', in Nora Chadwick's *Studies in the Early British Church*.[19] This provoked one of Chancellor James's diatribes ('Wrong again, Mr. Brooke ...'), which amused Brooke,[20] and an equally fierce review by John Morris (1913–77) of University College London, who was later to encourage Wendy Davies to start research on the Book of Llandaf.[21] Morris, who called Brooke's 'the one bad article in a good book', ended his review

---

June 1980 Bartrum wrote to me that until Wendy Davies's books appeared he had seen nothing of interest apart from E. D. Jones's 1946 article 'and those by Chancellor James (which I could not take seriously)'. The latter are indeed marred, to quote J. R. Davies, by 'irrational thought processes and partisan prejudices' (*The Book of Llandaf*, 3 n. 12; cf. Sharpe, 'Which text is Rhygyfarch's *Life* of St David?'). By 1993 Bartrum had largely abandoned his 1948 chronology in favour of Wendy Davies's 1979 one (see his *A Welsh Classical Dictionary*, ii and passim).

[16] *LBS* II, 360–2, and IV, 266; Wade-Evans, 'The Llancarfan charters', 160; Doble, *Lives*, 164 (an essay first published in 1942). Wade-Evans's jibe about the name was ill-judged; *Llan* + topographical feature is an old type. See below, 164 n. 59.

[17] *EA* I, 151 and 182; James, 'A history of the origins and development of the Celtic Church in Wales', 231: 'The charge that the Llandaff records are an ex parte statement comes with a bad grace from those who uphold the full and plenary inspiration and inerrancy of Ricemarchus [*sic*] Life of St. David, and of the Vespasian A XIV text of that life'. In this dissertation James's target, alongside Wade-Evans, is the best forgotten Arthur Owen Vaughan.

[18] Personal comment.

[19] Later revised and toned down in 1986 in *The Church*, 16–49 (cf. *ibid.*, ix). By 2005, in his review of J. R. Davies's book, he had modified his views further.

[20] James, '*The Book of Llandav*: the church and see of Llandav and their critics', 7. Cf. Abulafia, Luscombe, and Mayr-Harting, 'Christopher Nugent Lawrence Brooke 1927–2015', 253. James's belief in a single line of bishops is not so wide of the mark (see ch. 14 below) as his notion that they mostly resided at Llandaf.

[21] Davies, *The Llandaff Charters*, vii; cf. Brooke, *The Church*, ix.

with a series of assertions about the Llandaf (and Llancarfan) charters that proved programmatic:

> [T]he grants are anything but uniform. Seventh-century prices are expressed as single objects – a chased swordhilt, a 'best horse', etc.; in the eighth century they are calculated according to a uniform standard of value, the cow, but from the ninth century onward in gold and silver. Early kings consult *cum senioribus Guent et Ercig*, but later kings have *comites*; early bishops are styled *episcopus*, later ones *pontifex* or *praesul*; orthography varies from Iudhail to Ithel, etc. Of the 'elaborate witness lists ... skilfully and plausibly devised', most of the later kings and some of the bishops are named at the right times in both Welsh and Anglo-Saxon contemporary notices, while half a dozen earlier rulers are found in the Cambrian Annals and contemporary inscriptions. But kings and bishops are a tiny fraction of the 1,200 witnesses, who sign over the centuries, father succeeding son, each only in his own ancestral area, without serious chronological inconsistency. So large and cohesive a list has not been 'certainly faked' by any known forger.[22]

These theses were investigated in detail by Wendy Davies in a series of articles from 1972 onwards[23] and in *An Early Welsh Microcosm* (1978) and *The Llandaff Charters* (1979). These books began the rehabilitation of the Book of Llandaf as a historical source for early medieval Wales. The same programme of rehabilitation is further advanced, I hope, in the present work, with various nuances in its favour and against.

* * *

Like all modern studies of *LL*, this book refers to the meticulous text of J. G. Evans, which he published privately in 1893, with the assistance of Sir John Rhys on the Welsh portions and of Egerton Phillimore on topography.[24] Evans's edition unfortunately excluded the early-twelfth-century Gospel of Matthew, which was probably always intended as a solemn inauguration of the codex, as Daniel Huws has shown.[25] Conversely, it included plates of the so-called Lichfield or 'Chad' Gospels, which were mistakenly supposed to be from Llandaf rather than Llandeilo Fawr (*LL* xliii–xlviii). In 1979 the National Library of Wales issued a reprint of the 1893 edition, with new plates of *LL* and the Lichfield Gospels in place of those of 1893. The text of the reprint is identical, except for a brief preface listing some trivial errata and referring to the work of Wendy Davies and the admirable study of the manuscript by E. D. Jones (1946), the codicological and palaeographical aspects of which have now been superseded, however, by Huws's definitive analysis.[26] The whole manuscript can now be seen on the National Library's 'Digital Gallery'. In

---

[22] Morris, Review, 231–2. I will discuss all these assertions without attempting to correct Morris's minor errors.
[23] Reprinted in *WHEMA*.
[24] Birch, *Memorials*, 1, claimed that Evans's edition was 'not immaculate in its readings or extensions of abbreviated words', perhaps over-reacting to Evans's criticism of his own work (*LL*, viii n. 3). On topography see also Egerton Phillimore's notes in *DP* passim, and Coe, 'The place-names of the Book of Llandaf'.
[25] Huws, *Medieval Welsh Manuscripts*, 124–6 (comparing the Sherborne Cartulary).
[26] Jones, 'The Book of Llandaff'; Huws, *Medieval Welsh Manuscripts*, 123–57.

the present work, however, references are by page number to the Evans and Rhys edition (e.g. '*LL* p. 4'), but the charters are referred to by the now standard system (e.g. '*LL* 199a') introduced by Peter Bartrum.[27] References such as 'ii.33' and 'iii.4' refer to the chronological Sequences i, ii, and iii given in Wendy Davies's *Llandaff Charters*.[28]

Readers should note that where possible I have standardised Old Welsh personal names in Modern Welsh orthography, following the conventions of Studies in Celtic History: for example 'Cyfwyre' rather than *Comereg*. Where this is inappropriate, or not feasible, italics are used (e.g. *Comereg*). When there are great discrepancies between old and modern forms, cross-references are given in the Index.

There is no accurate translation of *LL*. Rees's 1840 translation was based on a faulty Latin text, but gives a general idea of the contents, as do the many extracts in Birch's *Memorials of the See and Cathedral of Llandaff* (1912), to which I give some references.

---

[27] Bartrum, 'Some studies'. If this system is ever abandoned much scholarship will become impenetrable! Charters are numbered according to the page on which they begin in the edition by Evans and Rhys, subdivided by letters if more than one begin on the same page (e.g. '199a', '199b'). There are either 158 or 159 charters, depending on whether 199b is treated as a single charter or as two (199bi and 199bii, the latter beginning 'Post multum uero temporis'). 196 is normally counted as a single charter, but is treated as two by Guy, 'The *Life* of St Dyfrig', 5 n. 15. See also below, 22 n. 3.

[28] *The Llandaff Charters*, 35–7, 41–53, and 59–69. I have supplied the Arabic numbers myself.

1

THE BOOK OF LLANDAF AND THE EARLY WELSH CHARTER

In 1107 Anselm, archbishop of Canterbury, consecrated Urban, a priest of the church of Worcester, as bishop of Glamorgan, and Urban made a canonical profession of obedience to Anselm as primate of all Britain.[1] Probably Urban, whose Welsh name was Gwrgan, was a member of a clerical dynasty, most likely that of Llancarfan, and had gone to Worcester, or to Worcester diocese, for his education.[2] For a dozen years after 1107 Urban was preoccupied with shoring up his diocese in the face of the Norman conquest of Glamorgan and the impending competition from his western neighbour, Bernard, bishop of St Davids (1115–48), a formidable opponent with better connections at the English court.[3] According to Bernard, Urban's dispute with St Davids had already begun in the time of Bishop Wilfred (*ob.* 1115), Bernard's predecessor.[4] By 1119, for the first time so far as we know, Urban was styling himself bishop of Llandaf, evidently having fixed his see close to the Norman castle of Cardiff, the *caput* of the new lordship of Glamorgan,[5] where he would enjoy a mutually advantageous relationship with Robert of Gloucester, the lord of Glamorgan.[6] Urban was probably not the first bishop to reside at Llandaf, for the mid-eleventh-century Joseph, whom Urban claimed as his predecessor but one, was described as *episcopus* on what appears to have been his gravestone at Llandaf; moreover Joseph's charters in the Book of Llandaf are clustered around Llandaf itself.[7] Certainly it is difficult to imagine how Urban could have begun to

---

[1] See *EA* I 125–6 and II 612–13, also on his Welsh name *Worgan* (or *Gurgan, ibid.* II 619). According to *LL* p. 280 Urban was previously archdeacon of Llandaf (*EA* I 125). While this claim may be true it could be part of the effort to show that Llandaf had always been 'a properly constituted diocese' (Brooke, *The Church*, 73). Cf. Pearson, *Fasti*, IX, 13 and 17–18.

[2] See Crouch, *Llandaff Episcopal Acta*, xi–xii, and 7 on the connection between Llancarfan and the Llandaf bishops (cf. *EA* II 506–37, Brooke, *The Church*, 38 n. 90, and J. R. Davies, *The Book of Llandaf*, 105 and 142). Note that the 'brothers' (*germani*) of Urban mentioned in a papal letter (Baumgarten, 'Papal letters relating to England', 532) are probably unnamed and distinct from the priest Caradog (*Caratocus*) and the Gwgan (*sic*: *Guganus*) of Llancarfan named in the same letter (cf. Crouch, *Llandaff Episcopal Acta*, xii n. 3, and J. R. Davies, *The Book of Llandaf*, 105). I am grateful to Professor Crouch for discussing this with me.

[3] *EA* I 126–7; Barrow, *St Davids Episcopal Acta*, 2–4.

[4] *LL* pp. 53–4; *EA* II 628; J. R. Davies, *The Book of Llandaf*, 37.

[5] *EA* I 128.

[6] See their agreement in 1126: *LL* pp. 27–9; *EA* II 620–1; J. R. Davies, *The Book of Llandaf*, 51–3.

[7] Redknap and Lewis, *A Corpus* I, 325 no. G39; *WHEMA* IV 67; Davies, *The Llandaff Charters*, 23–4; *An Early Welsh Microcosm*, 21–2, 135–6, and 155. Cf. Brooke, *The*

attempt to foist Llandaf on his contemporaries as an ancient episcopal see if it had no history *at all* behind it.[8] Llandaf need not have been a permanent see, however, for the activities of Herewald (*ob*. 1104), whom Urban claimed as his immediate predecessor, covered a wide area, including Gwent and Ergyng (Archenfield, southwest Herefordshire) as well as Glamorgan; Anselm referred to Herewald only as 'a certain bishop of Wales', not naming any see.[9]

In 1119 Urban launched his great campaign, at first successful, to get the Pope (Calixtus II) to take the church of Llandaf under his protection and to persuade the archbishop of Canterbury to prevent the bishops of St Davids and Hereford, and various monks and Norman nobles, from despoiling it. Duly supported by the archbishop, Urban began building a new church at Llandaf, adding to its allegedly original dedication to St Peter the names of St *Dubricius* (Dyfrig), St *Teiliau* (Teilo), and St *Oudoceus* (Euddogwy).[10] The choice of each of these three Welsh saints advanced Urban's cause in different ways.

The early (seventh-century?) Breton *Vita sancti Samsonis* had associated St Dyfrig with Llanilltud (Llantwit) in Morgannwg and Ynys Bŷr (Caldy Island) in Pembrokeshire, both in areas claimed by Urban.[11] By Urban's day, however, Dyfrig's cult was mainly centred on Ergyng (Archenfield), an area where Bishop Herewald had been particularly active, and this provides a further motive for its adoption by Urban in the context of his dispute with Hereford.[12] In 1120 Urban translated Dyfrig's supposed relics to Llandaf from Enlli (Bardsey Island).[13] Scholars have suggested, on the one hand, that the cult of St Dyfrig was first brought to the Hereford area by Herewald and, conversely, on the other hand, that it was ancient there, and possibly concerned a Dyfrig distinct from the Dyfrig of the *Vita Samsonis*.[14]

Church, 93, regarding Joseph as a 'shadowy figure' and his ordination of Herewald (*LL* pp. 265–6) as 'doubtful'. For other arguments for Llandaf having some antiquity see *EA* I 184–5 and Lewis, 'The *Liber Landavensis* and the diocese of Llandaff', 58–9. There are a few retrospective references in slightly later, non-Llandaf sources to Herewald and Urban as 'bishops of Llandaf' (*EA* II, 612–13, 615, and 649). Note that the Chapter of St Davids, writing to the Pope *ca* 1145, did not deny that Herewald was 'bishop of Llandaf', even while advancing the notion that he had been promoted to that rank by 'Archbishop' Joseph of St Davids (was this a misrepresentation of the role of Bishop Joseph of Llandaf in *LL* pp. 265–6?): see *EA* I 262; Richter, *Canterbury Professions*, xc. MS B of *Annales Cambriae* describes him as *episcopus Landauensis* in his obit, but this may be a modernisation by the late-thirteenth-century scribe, for the Welsh versions s.a. 1045 call him simply 'Teilo's bishop'. Yet, seeing that there are very few Teilo churches other than Llandaf in the area from which Joseph received grants – the three Llandeilos near Abergavenny are the only others (Bowen, *The Settlements*, 56–7, and *EA* I 183) – it seems more likely than not that he was indeed bishop of a church of Teilo at Llandaf.

[8] See J. R. Davies, *The Book of Llandaf*, 10.
[9] *EA* II 610–12.
[10] *EA* II 615–18.
[11] See below, 158–60, and Doble, *Lives*, 56–9. Doble notes that Penalun (Penally), opposite Caldy, is granted to Dyfrig by charter 77 in *LL*. (The fact that 77 is a blatant forgery does not invalidate the point that Urban may have associated Dyfrig with this area.) Cf. Guy, 'The *Life* of St Dyfrig', 10–12.
[12] See Doble, *Lives*, 59–87; J. R. Davies, *The Book of Llandaf*, 84–6.
[13] *LL* pp. 84–6; *EA* II 618.
[14] See below, 160–1.

1. The Book of Llandaf and the early Welsh charter

There was no need for Urban to translate the second patron saint, St Teilo, since, according the Book of Llandaf, a miracle at the time of Teilo's death had created *three* bodies: one for Penally in Pembrokeshire, one for Llandeilo Fawr on the Tywi (Carmarthenshire) – the original centre of Teilo's cult, to judge by its name – and a third – the original, naturally – for Llandaf.[15] Thus Urban could lay claim to the many churches dedicated to St Teilo across south Wales, including those within the sphere of St Davids.[16]

By contrast, the third patron saint, St Euddogwy, seems to have had no previous cult except at Llandogo (*Lann Oudocui*) on the river Wye in Monmouthshire. The chief reason for enlisting him seems to have been the availability, in the archives of Llancarfan and Llandaf, of valuable batches of eighth-century land charters in favour of an identically named Bishop *Eudoce* (a distinct person, Doble supposed, on little evidence).[17]

In 1119 Urban presented Calixtus II with an impressive narrative: according to a chirograph of St Teilo, the church of St Peter at Llandaf had always been paramount in Wales, subject only to Rome (from the time of St Germanus in the fifth century) and to Canterbury and the king of England (from the time of St Augustine in the sixth century). During the reign of King William, however, and in particular during the old age of Bishop Herewald (*ob.* 1104), Llandaf had lost twenty-two of its twenty-four canonries and most of its lands and tithes, owing to lay despoilations and 'invasions' by monks (meaning those of new houses such as Tewkesbury) and by his brother bishops of Hereford and St Davids.[18]

For a while Urban seemed to succeed. In 1129, for example, he went to Rome with 'his privileges and ancient charters' and returned to Llandaf 'with joy'.[19] It is notable, however, that the other side of the argument was often not presented – on this occasion Hereford and St Davids failed to turn up – and that papal decisions had little practical effect. In 1131, when Bernard of St Davids mounted a counter-attack in Rome, Urban was unable to attend, 'prevented by bodily illness', and Innocent II ordered that the dispute should be settled in England.[20] The tide then seems to have turned against Urban,[21] and in 1134 he died on a last visit to Rome, 'having set forth the cause of his journey'. The Pope recommended that the Archbishop of Canterbury leave things as they were and commended Urban's supporters to him, among them a priest Caradog (perhaps the prolific hagiographer Caradog of Llancarfan) and Gwgan of Llancarfan, and also Urban's own brothers (*germani*). Urban's see was left vacant until 1140, and the whole controversy petered out.[22]

Liber Landavensis, the Book of Llandaf, is the embodiment of Urban's case for his church and diocese. Leaving aside various later additions, the codex seems to have reached its first intended form at some time between 1132 and Urban's death

---

[15] LL pp. 116–17. On the Lives of Teilo see Doble, *Lives*, 162–206; Hughes, *Celtic Britain*, 61–3; J. R. Davies, *The Book of Llandaf*, 112–19.
[16] *Ibid.*, 86–9.
[17] Doble, *Lives*, 207–29; J. R. Davies, *The Book of Llandaf*, 89–94. See below, 166 n. 72.
[18] LL pp. 87–8; *EA* I 24, 55, and II 617; J. R. Davies, *The Book of Llandaf*, 63–75.
[19] LL 52–3; *EA* II 625.
[20] LL pp. 66–7; *EA* II 631–2.
[21] The documentation is not preserved in the Book of Llandaf, perhaps not so much because it was unfavourable to Urban as because the compilation of the Book ceased about 1132; cf. J. R. Davies, '*Liber Landavensis*: its date and the identity of its editor', 10.
[22] Baumgarten, 'Papal letters relating to England', 531–2; *EA* II 632–4.

in 1134 (which is not mentioned). It opened with St Matthew's Gospel, followed (in the hands labelled A and B) by saints' Lives, documents concerned with Urban's claims up to 1132, and 159 charters in favour of the supposed 'bishops of Llandaf' from St Dyfrig to Herewald. Hand B may be that of Urban himself, exercising an editorial oversight over the work of Hand A.[23] Whether or not this is the case, it is clear that the codex reflects Urban's intentions. Caradog of Llancarfan must also have had a hand in assembling the material, in view of the many stylistic similarities between the texts and Caradog's known hagiographical works.[24] In what follows, I shall refer to the 'compilers' of *LL*, a deliberately vague expression intended to embrace the work of Scribes A and B and the work of the lost drafts which they presumably copied out. That there must have been various drafts behind the clean copy that is *LL* stands to reason and is confirmed by British Library, Cotton Vespasian A.xiv, written at Monmouth, in the last third of the twelfth century. Although this manuscript is much later than *LL*, it is clear that some material in it is based on drafts of *LL* (including some charters) which were probably transmitted from Llandaf to St Peter's Gloucester.[25] Vespasian A.xiv also included a *Life* of St Teilo, ascribed to Urban's brother Geoffrey Stephen, which is more primitive than the *Life* included in *LL*.[26]

The present study is chiefly concerned with *LL*'s 159 charters which purport to date from the fifth or sixth centuries to the eleventh.[27] These are mainly in the form, current in Wales down to the twelfth century,[28] which Wendy Davies called the '"Celtic" charter-tradition' on account of parallels in the other Celtic-speaking countries: Ireland, Scotland, Cornwall, and Brittany.[29] The parallels most relevant to *LL* are the roughly ninth-century charters and memoranda in Latin and Welsh in the Lichfield Gospels (or 'Book of St Chad'), which belonged to a church of St Teilo (Llandeilo Fawr) before reaching Lichfield in the tenth century.[30] Evans included plates and transcripts of these on pp. xliii–xlviii of his edition of *LL*, wrongly

---

[23] J. R. Davies, '*Liber Landavensis*: its date and the identity of its editor'; Huws, *Medieval Welsh Manuscripts*, 156; cf. J. R. Davies, *The Book of Llandaf*, 142 n. 63; Charles-Edwards, *Wales and the Britons*, 246 and n. 4 and 249.

[24] J. R. Davies, *The Book of Llandaf*, 108 and 142; Brooke, Review.

[25] Hughes, *Celtic Britain*, 61–4; J. R. Davies, *The Book of Llandaf*, 1 n. 1, 108, 118–19, 124, 129, and 133; Smith, *Walter Map*, 110–15. Evans collated the Vespasian passages (*LL* pp. 358–62), but wrongly regarded them as imperfect transcripts of *LL* (*LL* xxxiii–xxxiv, already corrected by E. Phillimore in *DP* IV 367 n. 1). On Vespasian A.xiv see Lewis, 'A possible provenance', and on its date see Guy, 'The *Life* of St Dyfrig', 6, quoting Teresa Webber.

[26] Hughes, *Celtic Britain*, 61–3; J. R. Davies, *The Book of Llandaf*, 86, 118–19, and 129.

[27] On the way charters are referenced see above, Introduction, 5 n. 27.

[28] Pryce, 'The church of Trefeglwys'.

[29] *WHEMA* XI–XII. In addition there are less formal statements of land grants (Brett, 'Hagiography as charter'); several of the 'charters' to St Teilo in *LL* are such 'hagiographical charters'. For debate, which need not be discussed here, over how consistent the non-Welsh material is see Broun, *The Charters of Gaelic Scotland*, with Wendy Davies, Review, also Hodge, 'When is a charter not a charter?'.

[30] 'Chad 1' reads: 'Ostenditur hic quod emit Gelhi filius Arihtiud hoc euangelium de Cingal, et dedit illi pro illo equm optimum, et dedit pro anima sua istum euangelium Deo et sancti Teliaui super altare. + Gelhi filius Arihtiud, et + Cincenn filius Gripiud'. The origin of the book is unknown, but England is a strong possibility: Brown, 'The Lichfield/Llandeilo Gospels reinterpreted'.

1. The Book of Llandaf and the early Welsh charter

assuming that Llandaf was the Teilo church in question. It is clear, however, from the topography of the 'Chad' charters, that the book is from Llandeilo Fawr, the ancient church of St Teilo in Carmarthenshire.[31] Although Evans's inclusion of the 'Chad' charters was a mistake, it was a happy one, not only because Urban laid claim to many of the charters, traditions, and lands of Llandeilo Fawr, but also because the laconic 'Chad' charters, which are under no suspicion of forgery, provide a welcome point of comparison for the more inflated *LL* charters, which *are* under suspicion. They provide a good introduction to the structure of the early Welsh charters that may underlie the more elaborate charters in *LL*. 'Chad 3' is an example:[32]

> [*Notification*:] Ostendit ista scriptio quod [*Disposition*:] dederunt Ris et luith Grethi Treb Guidauc – imalitiduch cimarguitheit, hic est census eius: douceint torth ha maharuin in ir ham, ha douceint torth in ir gaem, ha huch ha [do]uceint mannuclenn – Deo et sancto Eliudo. [*Witness list*:] Deus testis, Saturnnguid testis, Nobis testis, Guurci testis, Cutulf testis; de laicis: Cinguernn testis, Collbiu testis, Cohorget testis, Ermin testis, Hourod testis. [*Sanction*:] Quicunque custodierit benedictus erit, et qui franxerit maledictus erit a Deo.

> [*Notification*:] This writing shows that [*Disposition*:] Rhys and the kindred of Grethi gave Trefwyddog – according to the experts, this is its render: forty loaves and a ram in summer, and forty loaves in the winter, and a pig and forty *mannuclenn* – to God and St Eiludd (Teilo). [*Witness list*:] God witness, Sadyrnwydd witness, Nobis witness, Gwrgi witness, Cuthwulf witness; of laymen: Cynwern witness, Collfyw witness, *Cohorget* witness, Erfyn witness, *Hourod* witness. [*Sanction*:] Whoever keeps this will be blessed, and whoever breaks it will be cursed by God.

How much older than the ninth-century 'Chad' charters is the Welsh charter tradition? Wendy Davies would push it back to mid-fifth-century sub-Roman Britain.[33] She takes her stand on two main considerations. The first, to which we shall return in detail, is the antiquity of the *LL* charters: she at first dated the earliest credible *LL* charters to the second quarter of the sixth century, later revising this to the second half.[34] We shall see, however, that the evidence does not require us to date the charters in question earlier than the seventh century, which leaves an awkward hiatus. Her other consideration is that the Welsh charters' formal similarity to charters in Brittany and Ireland, which were colonised and evangelised from late (or sub-) Roman Britain, could be due the dissemination of the 'Celtic charter' by the earliest western British emigrants and evangelists 'when their respective churches were still in contact'.[35] A problem here is that the 'Celtic' churches remained in close contact well beyond the fifth century, with influences moving in various directions:

---

[31] Jones, '"Tir Telych"'. Most of the 'Chad' charters are printed and translated by Howlett, *Sealed from Within*, 60–9. On their dates see Jenkins, 'From Wales to Weltenburg?', 78.

[32] Cf. *WHEMA* XI 263; Davies, *The Llandaff Charters*, 26; Jenkins and Owen, 'The Welsh marginalia', 52–4. Further see Jones, 'Post-Roman Wales', 308–16, and '"Tir Telych"', 93–4.

[33] *WHEMA* VII 162–3; XI 279. Cf., on the structure of Roman private deeds and Anglo-Saxon charters, Snook, 'Who introduced charters into England?'.

[34] *WHEMA* II 351; *The Llandaff Charters*, vii and 92.

[35] *WHEMA* VII 162–3 and XI 279–80. Cf. Charles-Edwards, *Wales and the Britons*, 318.

Gildasian influences running from Britain to Ireland, for example, and Irish canon law influencing Brittany.[36] It is admittedly tantalising that the largest extant collections of early Welsh charters, those from Llandaf and Llancarfan, happen to come from the most highly Romanised part of Wales, the south-east. To judge, however, by the evidence for lost charters at Clynnog in the north-west and St Davids in the south-west (see below), the survival of more charters from the Romanised south-east may be due to the fact that the Normans, like the Romans before them, settled the most fertile and accessible part of Wales first, thereby provoking the clerics of Llandaf and Llancarfan to fight back with the best weapons they could muster – new cartularies.[37]

For present purposes we do not need to discover the origin of the 'Celtic' charter or to define the extent of its Celticity. It is sufficient to note that it must have been current in Wales by the time of the ninth-century 'Chad' charters and that it lingered on down to the time of the twelfth-century Trefeglwys charters.[38] While there is absolutely no reason to presume that it only began in the ninth century – quite the reverse, given the catastrophic loss of all early manuscripts in Wales[39] – the putatively pre-ninth-century evidence of the Llandaf and Llancarfan charters has to be considered on its own merits.

How were charters transmitted in Wales? One possibility is in the margins of sacred books, like the Lichfield Gospels, and another is on single sheets. The Lichfield Gospels is the only surviving Gospel Book from early Wales (from Llandeilo Fawr), with the possible exception of the eighth-century Hereford Gospels (Hereford, Cathedral Library, P.i.2), so we are free to imagine either that its inclusion of marginal charters was exceptional or that it was typical of many other such Welsh Gospel Books which have perished, along with almost every other pre-Conquest Welsh manuscript.[40] These included some books which may have been comparable to the Lichfield Gospels. In 1594 we hear of a book (*llyfr*) of St Beuno at Clynnog, Caernarfonshire, known as *Diboeth* ('unburnt'), perhaps because it had escaped the destruction of Clynnog by Vikings in 978, and believed to have been written in St Beuno's own (seventh-century) lifetime by St Twrog. A polished black stone, associated with the book or its case, is already referred to by the fourteenth-century poet Iolo Goch. Almost certainly it was identical with the *Liber sancti Bongnobi* [i.e. *Bougnobi*], cited in Clynnog's privilege from Edward IV, and the *Graphus sancti Bewnoi* to which witnesses appealed in a case at Caernarfon in 1537. Edward's privilege includes obvious quotations from its lost charters, including one recording the seventh-century founder's grant of Clynnog to St Beuno 'so that his name should be written in St Beuno's book' (*propter scribere nomen eius in libro sancti Bongnobi*).[41] From the quotations it is clear that the affinities of the Clynnog charters

---

[36] Sharpe, 'Gildas as a Father of the Church'; Dumville, 'Ireland, Brittany, and England'. For the importance of documentation *more Romanorum* in the seventh century see *The Irish Penitentials*, ed. Bieler, 10, 196–9, and 255 (*Synodus II S. Patricii*, §30). Note also the evidence for emulation across the Irish Sea in the erection of memorial stones: Sims-Williams, *Studies*, 182.

[37] *Idem*, 'The uses of writing', 25–6.

[38] Pryce, 'The church of Trefeglwys'.

[39] Cf. Sims-Williams, 'The uses of writing'.

[40] *Ibid.*, 25; J. R. Davies, 'Cathedrals', 112–14. On the possible Welsh origin of the Hereford Gospels see Gameson, 'The insular gospel book', 72–3.

[41] *The Record of Caernarvon*, ed. Ellis, 257–8. See Sims-Williams, 'The uses of writing', 22 and 26, and 'Edward IV's confirmation charter' (not Edward I as in Seebohm, *The Tribal*

1. The Book of Llandaf and the early Welsh charter

– genuine or not – were with the early Welsh diplomatic of the Lichfield Gospels and, to a lesser extent, of *LL*. Thus *et omnis populus fiat fiat* (cf. Psalm 105:48) at the end of an anathema recalls 'Chad 5': *sit maledictus a Deo et a Teiliav in cuius euangelio scriptum est et [dica]t* (or *[dice]t*) *omnis populus fiat fiat* ('may he be cursed by God and by Teilo in whose Gospel it has been written, and let all the people say "So be it, So be it"'), and *sicut insula in medio maris* ('like an island in the midst of the sea') reminds one of a liberty formula in *LL*,[42] while *quamdiu fuerit lapis in terra* ('while stone be on earth') recalls *quandiu lapis fuerit super lapidem* ('while stone be upon stone') in *LL* 198a. It is unclear whether the Book of St Beuno was a Gospel Book; it could be a Liber Vitae, for example. The same applies to another lost book, geographically closer to Llandaf, which is mentioned in one of the charters appended to the *Vita Cadoci* in Vespasian A.xiv: *pro anima sua et ut nomen eius in libro Catoci apud Nantcarban scriberetur* ('for his soul's sake and so that his name may be written in the Book of Cadog at Llancarfan').[43] This book was conceivably identical with the ancient Llancarfan Gospel described by Lifris of Llancarfan and Caradog of Llancarfan, who assert that it was written by Gildas himself.[44] There is now no way of knowing how old the Books of Beuno and Cadog really were, nor at what date the donors' names, with or without charters, were entered in them.

Outside Wales we have many examples of the insertion of charters and charter-like material in Gospel Books between the ninth century and the twelfth: in Ireland (the Book of Kells), in Scotland (the Book of Deer), in Cornwall (the Bodmin Manumissions), and, above all, in England, and there are also examples on the Continent, for instance from tenth-century Weltenburg.[45] Wherever the custom began – Dafydd Jenkins argued for Wales – the various Insular nations must have known that their neighbours practised it, and it could therefore have been borrowed in various directions. The Lichfield Gospels came from Llandeilo Fawr to their present home in Lichfield complete with Welsh charters, as we have seen, and in the eleventh century an Anglo-Saxon document was added in a spare margin.[46] An Old English account of a lawsuit in Cnut's reign (1016–35) over lands north of Hereford between a Welsh aristocrat, Edwin ab Einion (*Edwine Enneawnes sunu*), and his mother, who was based near Dilwyn, to the north-west, ends with the statement: 'And Thurkil then rode to St Æthelberht's minster, with all the people's consent and knowledge, and had it recorded in a Gospel Book' – and that is where the record survives, on the penultimate folio of the eighth-century Hereford Gospels mentioned above.[47] (Was Edwin's nationality a motive here?) Sometimes older documents were recopied into

---

System, 173 and 178, and Davies, *The Llandaff Charters*, 29 n. 21); *Gwaith Iolo Goch*, ed. Johnston, 323.

[42] See the *LL* formulae cited by Davies, *The Llandaff Charters*, 139. Cf. Doble, *Lives*, 227. The equation of *insulae* and *ecclesiae* was common in the exegesis of Psalm 96:1. See *Corpus Corporum* (Universität Zürich) <mlat.uzh.ch> under 'laetentur insulae multae' and 'insula' + 'ecclesia'.

[43] *VC* 56.

[44] *VC* 33–34; *Vita Gildae*, ed. Williams, *Gildas*, II, 406–7; *EA* II, 509; Sims-Williams, 'The uses of writing', 21 and 25.

[45] *WHEMA* XI; Jenkins, 'From Wales to Weltenburg'.

[46] Ker, *Catalogue of Manuscripts Containing Anglo-Saxon*, 158, no. 123.

[47] Ibid., 156, no. 119; *Anglo-Saxon Charters*, ed. Robertson, 152; Sawyer 1462 (cf. 1469); Gameson, 'The insular gospel book', 69–72. See Johansson, 'The place-names'; Coplestone-Crow, *Herefordshire Place-Names*, 80. *Eadwine* is an English name that was

sacred books. In the tenth century, for example, a mid-ninth-century Old English charter (now lost) was copied into the sixth-century St Augustine's Gospels.[48] Up to a point the Book of Llandaf, being prefaced by St Matthew's Gospel, belongs in this tradition,[49] as well as resembling more recent cartularies such as the Cartulary of Landevennec (prefaced with hagiography), Hemming's Cartulary at Worcester (appended to the great Offa Bible), and the Sherborne Cartulary (which combined charters with liturgy).[50]

It is possible, therefore, that some *LL* charters may have been transmitted in sacred books similar to the Lichfield Gospels and Hereford Gospels. It is doubtful, however, whether any charters were recorded in sacred books before the ninth century. At least, Dafydd Jenkins was unable to find examples anywhere in Europe,[51] even though a great number of pre-800 sacred books survive.[52] It is more likely therefore that earlier charters were written on single sheets; that would easily explain their disappearance.[53] There is, in fact, some evidence that some single-sheet Welsh charters survived the Reformation. In his preface to Salesbury's Welsh New Testament of 1567 Bishop Davies of St Davids, speaking of the former currency of biblical names, says:

> A' mi ved[r]wn ddangos ichwi mewn carp o Siarter hen ddyhenydd, y sydd yn perthyn im Escopawt i yma Uenew, vot vn ai enw Noe, yn Urenhin Dyvet.[54]

> And I could show you in a fragment of a very ancient charter which belongs to my see of St Davids here, that someone named *Noe* [Nowy] was king of Dyfed.

Salesbury himself speaks more fully in a letter to Archbishop Parker: 'my Lorde hath certain outworne fragments of auncient Recordes of Donations, wch differ mvch in the forme of some lettres from those that men vse in our dayes'. Salesbury quotes part of a charter in facsimile (beginning *tenuit Iudnerth grafum eternum ...*), and part of its witness list (including the name *Jesus*), and goes on to cite other proper names,

---

popular in Old Welsh as *Edwin*. On this and the family concerned see Thornton, 'Some Welshmen', 149 and 158.

[48] Ker, *Catalogue of Manuscripts Containing Anglo-Saxon*, 95, no. 55; Sawyer 1198.

[49] It is intriguing to note that Jones, 'The Book of Llandaff', 127, found 'some faint suggestion' that the scribe of the Gospel 'had a half uncial exemplar in front of him'.

[50] J. R. Davies, *The Book of Llandaf*, 143–7.

[51] Jenkins, 'From Wales to Weltenburg?'. In England the entering of charters and legal records in sacred books begins in the tenth century: Francis Wormald, 'The Sherborne "Chartulary"', 106; Patrick Wormald, 'Celtic and Anglo-Saxon kingship', 177 n. 29; Keynes, 'Athelstan's books', 189 n. 216. Although Chaplais speculated that the custom of writing charters in Gospel Books may have been prevalent as early as the late sixth century ('The origin and authenticity', 33, and 'Who introduced charters into England?', 105–6), he could cite no evidence. Cf. Snook, 'Who introduced charters into England?'.

[52] McGurk, *Latin Gospel Books from A.D. 400 to A.D. 800*, 11, listed 138 of these, more than half of them Insular.

[53] Cf. Wormald, 'Celtic and Anglo-Saxon kingship', 157: 'If we depended on texts written into Biblical manuscripts for all our Anglo-Saxon charters, we should have a pathetic fraction of the extant total'.

[54] Salesbury, *Testament Newydd*, towards end of preface. Cf. *DP* I 246 n. 1 and III 201 n. 2; *EA* I 13. On Nowy see below, 143.

presumably from charters, since one of them is the above *Noe Rex Demetiae*.[55] According to Caroline Brett, the script of Salesbury's facsimile 'looks very much like the script of the earliest ninth-century charters written into the Gospels of St. Chad'.[56] If the charter mentioning Nowy was contemporary with Nowy it must have belonged to the early seventh century, but it could, of course, have been either a forgery (like the charter of *Noe* [Nowy] *filius Arthur* in *LL*, no. 77) or a later confirmation of a grant by him. It was perhaps from a ninth-century confirmation of a seventh-century grant[57] that Leland copied (without comment) the following names, which include that of Arthur ap Pedr, father of the above Nowy:

> *Abbas* Cairmardin/ *Laurod abbas* Pennalun/ *Cuhelin abbas* LLan isan/ *Abbas* LLan Sanfrigt/ *Arturius Petri filius sed recentior veteri* Arturio/ *Saturnlius episcopus* Menevensis.[58]

Saturnbius (sic leg.), bishop of St Davids, died in 831 (*Annales Cambriae*). He could be the same person as the *Saturnbiu* who attests 'Chad 5', while *Cuhelin*, a bishop's son who attests 'Chad 5', may be the same person as Leland's *Cuhelin*, abbot of Llanisan (St Ishmael's in Pembrokeshire).[59] Possibly Leland took his witness list (or lists) from charter(s) in the 'Book *De Dotatione Ecclesiae S. Davidis*' to which he refers elsewhere as containing a reference to 'the Abbay of Llanfride'.[60]

Salesbury's charter beginning *tenuit Iudnerth grafum eternum* would at least seem to reflect a single sheet rather than a charter in a codex. In view of it we may, surely, give some credit to phrases referring to single-sheet charters, ostensibly of the eighth century, in the Llancarfan charters attached to the *Vita Cadoci*: for instance, *Rodri tenuit cartam siue graphium super manum Conigc, abbatis Nantcarbanan, in confirmationem huius donationis* ('Rhodri held a *carta* or *graphium* on the hand of Cynyng, abbot of Llancarfan, in confirmation of this grant').[61] Seebohm commented on 'the formality of placing the writing upon the hand (*super manum*) of the recipient in the presence of witnesses':

---

[55] Flower, 'William Salesbury, Richard Davies and Archbishop Parker', 11 and plate IV, from Cambridge, Corpus Christi College, MS 114. Cf. Strype, *The Life and Acts of Matthew Parker*, I, 417–19; *WHEMA* XI 261 n. 19.

[56] Brett, 'John Leland, Wales, and early British history', 180.

[57] Alternatively, as Brett says (*ibid.*, 180), Leland may be quoting from two separate charters of different dates.

[58] *The Itinerary of John Leland*, ed. Hearne, 2nd edn, Vol. VII, 140 (= Vol. VII, 150 of the third edition and Vol. IV, 168 of the L. T. Smith edition). Cf. *DP* IV, 428 and 459–60.

[59] Note also the Ramsey Island *Saturnbiu* inscription: Edwards, *A Corpus*, II, 448, no. P99. According to one recension of Gerald of Wales's *Itinerary through Wales*, II.1, there were *two* bishops of St Davids of this name (Pryce, 'Gerald of Wales and the Welsh past', 36; Thorpe, *Gerald of Wales*, 161 n. 263). For the translation of *filii episcopis* in 'Chad 5' see Howlett, *Sealed from Within*, 68. Cf. Charles-Edwards, *Wales and the Britons*, 248. Throughout this book I refer to 'St Davids' for convenience, without implying that I am siding against the opinion that the see was originally at Henfynyw (Ceredigion), on which see J. R. Davies, 'Cathedrals', 100–2.

[60] *The Itinerary in Wales of John Leland*, ed. Smith, 123; Brett, 'John Leland, Wales, and early British history', 179.

[61] *VC* 55. On its date, see below, 39–41, and 57.

There is an out-of-doors air about this form which seems to show that the transactions did not always take place in a church. Where the transaction took place in a church, the writings, as on the Continent, were laid upon the altar, or upon the copy of the Gospels which lay upon the altar. These Gospels naturally became, as in the case of the copy which Gelhi purchased ... and placed on the altar of St. Teilo, the recipients of memoranda of similar donations, but there is no mention in the Cadoc records of this practice having yet commenced.[62]

In the light of this indirect evidence and, in particular, the tangible evidence of the 'Chad' charters, one may reasonably admit the possibility, as a working hypothesis, that the *LL* charters may be based in part on earlier Welsh charters in the margins of Gospel Books or ones on single sheets.[63] We shall see in Chapter 10 that the *LL* charters in favour of the eighth-century Bishop Berthwyn point strongly towards the availability of single-sheet charters.

---

[62] Seebohm, *The Tribal System*, 226–7. He notes (p. 201) that the only example of *super manum* in *LL* is charter 72a. Gelhi's purchase is mentioned in 'Chad 1'. Seebohm's 'out-of-doors air' goes beyond the evidence, but compare ninth-century Brittany where transactions took place in the open air as well as inside churches: Davies, *Small Worlds*, 109–10, 134–5, 137–8, and 140.

[63] On whether early cartularies existed see below, 79. In a few centres, some Anglo-Saxon charters survived on single sheets without being copied into cartularies (having been either overlooked or deemed useless) (see Tinti, 'The reuse of charters at Worcester', 138), but the vast majority of single sheets must have perished. See Keynes, 'Anglo-Saxon charters: lost and found' (57–9 on Worcester).

2

THE ORIGIN OF THE LLANDAF CLAIMS

When we turn from the pure 'Celtic' diplomatic of the 'Chad' charters to the Book of Llandaf, we enter a more modern world. Not a page goes by without us being reminded of one or more of Urban's aspirations for his see, as we know them from his papal correspondence and elsewhere. Urban, we learn, stands at the end of an illustrious line of bishops of Llandaf whose rights suffered little infringement until the time of his predecessor, Herewald. Since the time of St Augustine these bishops had been the loyal subjects of Canterbury. – It was probably as evidence of the English connection that a list of Welsh bishops consecrated by English archbishops since Alfredian times was drawn up.[1] – Before Augustine's arrival the bishops of Llandaf had been directly subject to the Pope, ever since their church had been founded in honour of St Peter in the time of St Germanus of Auxerre. The see's other patrons, St Dyfrig (*Dubric*), St Teilo (*Teiliau*), and St Euddogwy (*Oudoce*), had been the first bishops of Llandaf, and hence – naturally – Urban was entitled to all lands granted or confirmed to the saintly triad, all churches founded by them, and even many of the churches merely dedicated to them. Since the twelfth-century cults of Dyfrig and Teilo were centred in south-west Herefordshire and south-west Wales respectively, the area of Llandaf's interest was vast, and some of Urban's territorial claims even lay outside the diocese that he claimed. That diocese stretched from the Wye to the Tywi and extended through Gower into Carmarthenshire to the west and through Breconshire and Herefordshire to the north and east. Urban maintained that its bounds followed the (alleged) extent of a primitive Welsh kingdom of Morgannwg, evidently not sharing the opinion of most modern scholars that Morgannwg takes its name from a tenth-century Morgan, king of Glywysing.[2] *LL* (pp. 69 and 133) even claims that until the time of St Euddogwy the diocese extended beyond the Tywi through Dyfed to *insula Teithi*.[3] This justified claims to properties in the west granted to Euddogwy's alleged predecessor, St Teilo.[4]

Urban seems to have convinced the knowledgeable among his contemporaries no more than he convinces us, and his successors inherited a small diocese similar to the diocese of Llandaf as it existed until 1920. South-west Herefordshire (Ergyng or Archenfield) was lost to the bishop of Hereford, while Breconshire, Carmarthenshire, and Gower to the north and west were lost to St Davids, the final boundary reflecting

---

[1] *WHEMA* IV; and below, ch. 3. See also Brooke, *The Church*, 19 n. 15; Richter, *Canterbury Professions*, xciii; J. R. Davies, *The Book of Llandaf*, 27.
[2] See below, 117 n. 4.
[3] Cf. '"Ynys Teithi Hen" . . . between St David's and Ireland' (*TYP*[4] lxxv; Bartrum, *A Welsh Classical Dictionary*, 608).
[4] Cf. Guy, 'The *Life* of St Dyfrig', 9–11.

the Lordship of Glamorgan rather than the alleged ancient kingdom of Morgannwg; only one place outside the diocese, Bishopston in Gower, was retained.[5]

Almost every charter in *LL* has been forged or interpolated in support of Urban's two central tenets: the antiquity of the bishopric and the vast size of the diocese. Yet the charters give little support to these tenets on closer inspection, presenting us with a series of bishops who sometimes appear contemporaneous with each other, who receive grants from rather restricted areas, and whose activities, as indicated by their grants and other references, are often far distant from Llandaf for centuries on end.[6] The chief interest of this curious anomaly is the support it gives to Wendy Davies's contention that most *LL* charters were not forged from scratch but are interpolated versions of early charters in favour of various non-Llandaf bishoprics.

How can one explain the size of the diocese which Urban claimed? The standard explanations can be divided into the ecclesiastical hypothesis and the secular hypothesis.[7] The ecclesiastical hypothesis is that Urban inherited a see whose patrons were Dyfrig, Teilo, and Euddogwy, and therefore claimed the areas in which those saints were culted. The great difficulty with this hypothesis is that we cannot prove that Urban (or one of his immediate predecessors) did not adopt the patrons in question in order to lay claim to the lands in question.[8] The secular hypothesis is that the kingdom of Morgannwg *may possibly* at some stage in the tenth or eleventh centuries have stretched temporarily from the Wye to the Tywi and have thus given a hypothetical prototype of Urban's dream diocese temporary reality. The difficulty with this hypothesis is that even Urban seems not to have been able to produce evidence in support. After the alleged charters of the founding saints of Llandaf, none of the *LL* bishops, with two exceptions, is assigned grants from Breconshire, Carmarthenshire, Gower, or even – significantly – from Glamorgan west of Merthyr Mawr on the Ogmore, where a Bishop Ffili, who does not appear in *LL*, seems to have been active in the eleventh century.[9] The two exceptions are Bishop Gwrfan (mid-eighth century) and Bishop Llibio (*ob*. 929), who both receive grants in Llanfihangel Tal-y-llyn (Breconshire), while Llibio also receives grants in Gower. Yet it is debatable – on the basis of information supplied by Llandaf itself – whether these two bishops were bishops of Llandaf.[10] Were they based nearer Breconshire or Gower, or somewhere between the two?

I have suggested elsewhere that Urban's (non-hagiographical) basis for his ideal diocese is to be found in a tract on the activities of his predecessor, Bishop Herewald,

---

[5] J. R. Davies, *The Book of Llandaf*, 66–7, 70, and 73 n. 73.

[6] Cf. Hughes, 'The Celtic Church'; J. R. Davies, *The Book of Llandaf*, 75.

[7] The same point is made by *EA* I 182–3. Cf. Lewis, 'Agweddau', 62 and 127; Cowley, 'The Church', 92–3. *EA* I 45 has the diocese already starting to take form under Herewald.

[8] A case can be made for a cult of Teilo at Llandaf in the time of Bishop Joseph. See above, 7 n. 7; Davies, *An Early Welsh Microcosm*, 155; Edwards, 'St. Teilo at Llandaff'; Lewis, 'The *Liber Landavensis* and the diocese of Llandaf', 60.

[9] *A Corpus* I, ed. Redknap and Lewis, 496 no. G117 (this depends on the reading *EPI*, which is plausible but uncertain).

[10] See Hughes, 'The Celtic Church', 8 n. 28. On the possibility that Gwrfan was based at Glasbury see below, 67 n. 51, and 167. On Llibio's dates see below, 172. The name *Libiau* is to be modernised as *Llibio*, not *Llifio*; see Sims-Williams, *The Celtic Inscriptions of Britain*, 123 n. 684. In favour of Llanfihangel Tal-y-llyn rather than Llanfihangel Cwm Du see Coe, 'The place-names', 443–4.

2. The origin of the Llandaf claims

copied in *LL* pp. 275–80.[11] Herewald, who is described as Bishop of Llandaf even in a St Davids source, died in 1104 at a great age ('aged a hundred years', *Annales de Margam*, etc.), in the forty-eighth year of his consecration by Archbishop Cynesige of York, presumably in 1056.[12] The tract in *LL* is highly circumstantial and convincing,[13] and is probably a summary of the evidence of the witnesses whom Urban produced in Rome in 1129 to swear that they and their fathers had seen Herewald hold the whole *parochia* from the Wye to the Tywi for forty years or more (cf. *LL* pp. 40–1 and 46). The tract is largely made up of lists of churches consecrated by Herewald before *ca* 1081 (*a*) in Ergyng and (*b*) in the disputed areas in Gower and the west, and in Ystrad Yw (in Brycheiniog), with details of the priests (often hereditary) whom he ordained to them. His activities in Ystrad Yw could explain how the above mentioned charters of Gwrfan and Llibio relating to Llanfihangel Tal-y-llyn (just north of Ystrad Yw) reached Llandaf. From remarks interspersed in list (*b*) it is clear that Herewald's activities in the west were only made possible by the conquests of Cadwgon ap Meurig of Morgannwg and of his successor Caradog ap Gruffudd, whose territorial ambitions in the west (Deheubarth) led not only to his own death in 1081 but also, one may suppose, to the eclipse of Herewald's ecclesiastical ambitions there:[14]

> In his [Herewald's] time Cadwgon, son of King Meurig, reigned in Glamorgan as far as the Ford of *Trunci* on the Tywi, while Caradog reigned in Ystrad Yw, Gwent Uwch Coed, Gwynllŵg, and Rhydderch in Ewias and Gwent Is Coed ... Herewald held the aforesaid lands, with the *parochia* of Ergyng, in episcopal subjection ... King Cadwgon was master in Gower and Cydweli and Cantref Bychan for many years until his death, and from thence took hostages. ... (*LL* pp. 278–9).

If, as I have suggested, the activities of Herewald in the west were historical but only made possible by right of conquest, it is unlikely that the bishops whom Herewald ousted regarded them as legitimate. In fact Bishop Bernard of St Davids, arriving in Rome soon after Urban in 1129, was able to produce more witnesses to testify that in the time of his predecessor Wilfred (1085–1115) twenty-four witnesses from St Davids and twenty-four from Urban's diocese had already settled the boundary disputes, presumably in favour of St Davids, a circumstance that Urban had suppressed (*LL* pp. 53–4).

---

[11] Sims-Williams, 'The provenance of the Llywarch Hen poems', 61–2. This section of *LL* is assigned to Hand B by Huws, *Medieval Welsh Manuscripts*, 129 and 142, and not to Evans's later twelfth-century hand Fa (*pace* J. R. Davies, *The Book of Llandaf*, 67 n. 30). For discussion see Charles-Edwards, *Wales and the Britons*, 310–12, 557, 602, and 608.

[12] See *EA* I 262 and II 607–13; Brooke, *The Church*, 92–3; *WHEMA* IV, 65–6.

[13] Brooke, *The Church*, 93 n. 191; J. R. Davies, *The Book of Llandaf*, 67.

[14] *LL* p. 279. On the evidence of the Herewald tract cf. Sims-Williams, 'The provenance of the Llywarch Hen poems', 61–2; J. R. Davies, *The Book of Llandaf*, 67; Thornton, 'Some Welshmen', 161–3. On Ystrad Yw see Coe, 'The place-names', 904–6. Cadwgon appears as benefactor of Joseph and Herewald (*LL* 261 and 267). *Caratocus rex Morcannuc* made a grant to Herewald in recompense for his retinue having consumed the bishop's food-render at St Maughan's, Monmouthshire (*LL* 272). Cf. Maund, *Ireland, Wales, and England*, 204. For the possibility that Llandaf's claims in the west went back to the episcopate of Joseph see J. R. Davies, *The Book of Llandaf*, 17.

The origin of Urban's claim to Ergyng would seem to be rather different. Despite a hint in the tract that Bishop Joseph had been active there before Herewald ('In the time of King William, he consecrated Llangarron, where Bishop Joseph of Llandaf had ordained Idfab as priest'),[15] it is difficult to doubt the tract's picture of an explosion of activity in Ergyng in Herewald's day. Its immediate context must have been Gruffudd ap Llywelyn's devastation of Archenfield; this culminated in the sacking of Hereford in 1055 and the death of the newly appointed Bishop Leofgar of Hereford in 1056, but its effects were still keenly felt at the time of the Domesday survey of Herefordshire.[16] The devastation of Ergyng and the death of Bishop Leofgar must have created a temporal and spiritual vacuum into which Herewald could step after his consecration in 1056, perhaps with the assistance of Gruffudd ap Llywelyn, to which 'undefeated king' *LL* attributes Herewald's election and a charter of privilege.[17]

There was a further coincidence at the time of Herewald's consecration. The *Anglo-Saxon Chronicle* records the death, after the destruction of Hereford in 1055 and perhaps in consequence of it, of *Tremerig* or *Tremerin*, 'the Welsh bishop', who had assisted Bishop Athelstan of Hereford (1012–56) 'after he became infirm'.[18] We do not know what arrangement Bishop Athelstan had reached with this Welsh bishop, nor what his policy was on his diocese's Welsh borders, but it is perhaps significant that the diocesan bounds drawn up by Bishop Athelstan and inserted in a Hereford Gospel Book only concerned its *eastern* boundary with Worcester diocese.[19] His eighth-century predecessor, Bishop Walhstod – whose name meant 'interpreter' – had claimed to be 'bishop of the people who dwell over the river Severn to the west'.[20] The presence of important Welsh people within Bishop Athelstan's diocese is confirmed by the reference to Edwin ab Einion in Hereford's earlier Gospel Book.[21] An episcopal list in a fourteenth-century manuscript at Douai shows that *Tremerin* was the last of a long line of Welsh bishops of the *clas* of St Cynidr (*Clas Chenedre*), – probably Glasbury (*Clas-ar-Wy*) in Radnorshire, judging by the *clas*-element, rather than Kenderchurch (*Lanncinitir*) in Herefordshire – before the bishop 'left for Hereford'.[22] There was thus a precedent for Welsh bishops participating in

---

[15] *LL* p. 277. On the name *Llangarron/Llangarren* see *DP* IV 474 and Charles, 'The Welsh, their language and place-names in Archenfield and Oswestry', 92. J. R. Davies, *The Book of Llandaf*, 29, argues that the diocese of Glamorgan may already have included Ergyng in Joseph's time.

[16] Darby and Terrett, *The Domesday Geography of Midland England*, 94–8. On Gruffudd see J. R. Davies, *The Book of Llandaf*, 18; Charles-Edwards, *Wales and the Britons*, 561–9.

[17] *LL* p. 266 and charter 269. Cf. Maund, *Ireland, Wales, and England*, 202–3.

[18] References in J. R. Davies, *The Book of Llandaf*, 12 and 26, and 'The archbishopric', 300–2.

[19] Finberg, *The Early Charters of the West Midlands*, 225–7; Sims-Williams, *Religion and Literature*, 43, 47 n. 160, and 392–5.

[20] *Ibid.*, 39–40.

[21] See above, 13.

[22] Fleuriot, 'Les évêques'; J. R. Davies, 'The archbishopric', 300 n. 44. Tremerin's predecessors are *Brecchert, Keneder, Gueman, Gurbrit, Meilic, Morgennic, Rederch, Dauit, Wilfret, Hithail, Heruuit*, and *Albri*. J. R. Davies, *The Book of Llandaf*, 12, suggests that *Gueman* is *Gurman* (*Guruan*, Gwrfan), the bishop of 'Llandaf' who is granted Llanfihangel Tal-y-llyn in *LL* 167. For Glasbury see *EWGT*, 21; Hughes, *Celtic Britain*, 59; Charles-Edwards, *Wales and the Britons*, 593. Wendy Davies, *Wales in the Early Middle Ages*, 158–9, considers Kenderchurch a possibility. In addition to Glasbury, it seems that there

2. The origin of the Llandaf claims

the work of the Hereford diocese, and Herewald probably took full advantage of it, even if he was not Tremerin's official successor, which is not impossible. If he also had a foothold in Glasbury, he may have been dislodged in 1088 when Bernard of Neufmarché granted Glasbury to St Peter's, Gloucester.[23]

Herewald's activities evidently did not commend themselves to later bishops of Hereford, for the tract states that after the time of Caradog ap Gruffudd (*ob.* 1081) and Rhydderch ap Caradog (*ob.* 1076), Herewald's control of Ergyng faced continual opposition from Hereford (*LL* p. 278).

We may have here a hint of the context in which Archbishop Anselm placed his interdict upon 'quodam episcopo . . . de Walis qui uocatur Herewardus'.[24]

Herewald had also got off to a bad start by being consecrated by an archbishop *of York*. Urban started better, being consecrated by Anselm himself, but if, as I have argued, the only solid basis for his claims to the diocese of a greater Morgannwg centred on Llandaf was Herewald's activities, it is no wonder that ultimately his case failed.[25]

---

were defunct bishoprics at either Ledbury, Herefordshire, or Lydbury North, Shropshire, at Welsh Bicknor, Herefordshire, and possibly at Dewstow, Monmouthshire (but see below, 61): Sims-Williams, *Religion and Literature*, 91; Barrow, *Hereford*, xxvii–xxviii; J. R. Davies, *The Book of Llandaf*, 12–13; Smith, 'Gerald of Wales, Walter Map and the Anglo-Saxon history of Lydbury North', 93 and n. 4.

[23] See Lloyd, *A History*, II, 397; Brooke, *The Church*, 53, 55, and 65.

[24] J. R. Davies, *The Book of Llandaf*, 26. On Hereford opposition from 1127 see Barrow, *Hereford*, xxxvi–xxxix.

[25] A much more detailed examination of the context of *LL* has been made by J. R. Davies, *The Book of Llandaf*. The above sketch was drafted earlier and should be compared with his work.

3

THE CHARTERS IN THE BOOK OF LLANDAF: FORGERIES OR RECENSIONS?

It is not surprising that the Book of Llandaf has usually been approached with some scepticism. It is a twelfth-century record of a dubious twelfth-century claim to a diocese and bishopric of doubtful antiquity. Furthermore, its allegedly early charters are couched in much the same stereotyped formulae, year in, year out. The following charter (73b), one of those appended to the *Life* of St Dyfrig, is a fairly restrained example of their format, but even here comparison with a second copy of the same charter (163a)[1] suggests that the italicised words – and perhaps others – are additions:

> *Sciant omnes quod* duo filii Pepiav, Cinuin *uidelicet* & Guidci, dederunt tres uncias agri Cum Barruc sancto Dubricio *& omnibus sibi succedentibus in æcclesia Landauiæ in perpetuo, cum omni libertate sine ullo censu homini terreno nisi sancto Dubricio & suæ familie & suis sequacibus & cum omni communione data circumcirca in campo & in aquis, in silua & in pascuis. Finis huius agri est a ualle usque ad lech longitudo, latitudo de lech usque ad petram Crita.* Testes *super hoc pactum* de clericis: Arguistil, Iunabui, Cinguarui, Elheiarun, Cimmareia; de laicis testes: Guoidci & Cinuin, Collbiu & Arcon. *Qui in sacrato isto peccauerint execrentur.*

A further reason for scepticism is the compilers' evident failure to arrange all the charters in a logical sequence of bishops of Llandaf from St Dyfrig to Herewald. Yet while this casts doubt on the assertion that all the recipients were bishops of Llandaf, it does suggest that the charters were not wholly invented by the compilers; they could surely have done a better job if they had relied on imagination alone.

The order of material copied by Hand A is shown in the following list. (Some parts of the material, in earlier drafts, are also preserved in Cotton Vespasian A.xiv.)[2] Some bishops are named but are assigned no charters. The number of charters assigned to each is indicated by the suprascript figures. To clarify the ensuing discussion I have indicated the dates of the charters suggested by Wendy Davies and the 'groups' A to J into which she divides them. It should be noted that C to J are continuous in the manuscript, with no indication of breaks between them:[3]

---

[1] See ch. 11 on the doublets.
[2] See above, 10.
[3] The dates are based on those given by Davies, *The Llandaff Charters*, 92–129, rather than *ibid.*, 12–13. I follow her in not counting 247 (a thirteenth-century addition) as a charter. There are thus 158 charters, or rather 159 since 199b falls into two parts, 199bi to Tyrchan and 199bii, the probable endorsement, to Cerennyr; in the list, however, 199b is counted as a single charter and assigned to Tyrchan. No. 183b (to Berthwyn) includes confirmations to Greciel and Cerennyr not numbered separately. In the list I have counted as Berthwyn

De Primo Statu Landauensis Æcclesiæ (pp. 68–71).

A[9] (72a–77) St Dyfrig[9] (late sixth to mid-ninth century).
Vita Archiepiscopi Dubricii (pp. 78–86).

Vita Sancti Teiliavi Landauensis Æcclesiæ Archiepiscopi (pp. 97–118).
Privilege of St Teilo [*Braint Teilo*] (pp. 118–21).
B[7] (121–127b) St Teilo[7] (early sixth to late eighth century).

Vita Beati Oudocei Landauensis Archiepiscopi (pp. 130–9).
C[21] (140–159b) St Euddogwy/*Oudoce*[21] (early seventh to early eighth century).

D[9] (160–166) Ufelfyw[3], Aeddan[1], *Elgist(us)*[1], Inabwy[2], Cyfwyre[1], Arwystl[1] (late sixth to early seventh century).

E[9] (167–174a) Gwrfan[1], Gwyddloyw[1], Eddylfyw[1], Greciel[6] (mid-eighth to mid-ninth century).

F[53] (174b–216b) Berthwyn[27], Tyrchan[13], *Eluogus*[0], Cadwared[9] (eighth century) and Cerennyr[4] (mid- to late ninth century).

G[6] (217–224) Nobis[0], Pater[3], Wulffrith (*Gulbrit*)[3] (mid-tenth century).

H[20] (225–239) Nudd[9], Cyfeilliog[9], Llibio[2] (late ninth to early tenth century).

J[24] (240–274) Gwgon[5], Marchlwydd[0], Bleddri[3], Joseph[12], Herewald[4] (late tenth to late eleventh century).

The arrangement of the bishops and their charters is easiest to understand (*a*) at the beginning and (*b*) at the end of the alleged sequence.

(*a*) St Teilo follows St Dyfrig in accordance with his *Vita*, and St Euddogwy follows St Teilo in accordance with *his* one. The bishops of charters 160–166 were then inserted at the earliest possible opportunity because the *Vita Dubricii* claimed them as Dyfrig's disciples.

Berthwyn, Tyrchan, and Cadwared form an obvious sequence in the light of the internal evidence of the charters themselves; the other bishops of 167–230b seem to have been fitted in around these three in a random fashion. Charter 183b makes it clear that Greciel lived later than Berthwyn, but the final compilers probably put him and the other 'Group E' bishops in their present position because of their Ergyng orientation, which favoured associating them with Dyfrig's 'disciples' in 'Group D'.[4]

(*b*) From Cyfeilliog (231–237a) to Herewald, the compilers adopted the order of bishops in an extant list of Welsh bishops supposedly consecrated by English archbishops,[5] despite the inconsistencies that arose from the consequent earlier misplacing of the bishops who were omitted from that tract: thus the charters of Cyfeilliog, who flourished in 914 (*Anglo-Saxon Chronicle*) and died in 927 according

---

charters three charters (179a, 193, 196) in which he is not specifically named. It will be seen that some bishops are named in *LL* without having any charters. Marchlwydd (p. 246) is said to have lived in the time of the sons of Morgan, who probably died in 974 (*Annales Cambriae*). (I take the second element of *Marchluid* to be *llwydd*, not *llwyd*.)

[4] Cf. Jones, 'The Book of Llandaff', 136–7 (who needlessly hypothesises an 'Ergyng cartulary'). On Dyfrig's 'disciples' see below, ch. 4.

[5] Davies, *The Llandaff Charters*, 20–1 and 24. On the consecration list see *EA* I 54–66; Brooke, *The Church*, 19 n. 15; *WHEMA* IV; and Keynes, 'Welsh kings', 112–13.

to the copy of the list in *LL* itself (p. 237), appear later in *LL* than those of Pater, even though the latter has a charter (218) specifically dated to 955!

The nature of the confusion can be seen from the following simplified list, in which I have adopted the most plausible readings from the Canterbury and Llandaf texts of the consecration list and have inserted the omitted *LL* bishops in square brackets at the appropriate places. Bishops of St Davids are indented. The dates of consecration are those implied in the lists and the obits are from *LL* or (if in square brackets) from sources such as *Annales Cambriae*.

870×89 – 927 Cyfeilliog [*fl.* 914].
870×89 – 929 Llibio.[6]
   870×89 [874] – [944] Llunferth of St Davids.[7]
[Wulffrith (*Gulbrit*) (*fl.* before 942).[8]]
[Pater (*fl.* 955).]
963×72 – 982 Gwgon.[9]
[Marchlwydd (*fl.* after 974).][10]
995×1005 – 1022 Bleddri.[11]
   995×1005 – 995×1005 Tramerin of St Davids.
   995×1005 – [?] Elnodd of St Davids, successor and *nepos* of Tramerin.[12]
1022 (or 1026) – [1045] Joseph.[13]
   1020×1038 – [*ca* 1073] Bleiddudd of St Davids.[14]

---

[6] On Llibio see below, ch. 7 and ch. 14. He was possibly at a different see from Cyfeilliog, but so as to make him clearly the latter's successor he is said to have an episcopate of only three years.

[7] Even an episcopate of 889–944 stretches credulity. Cf. *WHEMA* IV 63. The explanation may be that the Llunferth consecrated in 874 (*Annales Cambriae*) was different from the one who died in 944. Cf. J. R. Davies, 'The archbishopric', 299. The consecrations of Llibio and Llunferth by Æthelred (*ob.* 889) may be mechanically repeated from that of Cyfeilliog.

[8] King Cadell ab Arthfael of charters 222 and 223 died in 942: Davies, *The Llandaff Charters*, 77 and 88 n. 50

[9] Keynes, 'Welsh Kings', 112, notes that the witnesses to the consecration belong in the 960s.

[10] See n. 3 above. *LL* p. 246 states: 'Marchluid episcopus landauiæ. tempore filiorum morcant. ouein. idguallaun. catell. cinmin.' The following six blank lines of the column (292) were left blank, as if to receive data. What follows (cols 293–6) is by Hand B on an inserted folio (Huws, *Medieval Welsh Manuscripts*, 133 and 142).

[11] The date 983 (inspired by Gwgon's obit?) is given for his consecration. Cf. *WHEMA* IV 67; Maund, *Ireland, Wales, and England*, 184; Keynes, 'Welsh kings', 112–13. I give 995×1005 as being the archiepiscopate of Ælfric.

[12] There is no Bishop *Elnod* of St Davids in Gerald, *Itinerarium*, II.1 (Pryce, 'Gerald of Wales and the Welsh past'; Thorpe, *Gerald of Wales*, 163). Is there some confusion with Archbishop Ælnoth (i.e. Æthelnoth 1020–38) who supposedly consecrated Bleiddudd, and Joseph? Note also the reference to Archbishop Ælnoth at *LL* p. 254.

[13] Obit in *Annales Cambriae*, s.a. 1045. The A.D. date 1022 should possibly be 1026, following the indiction; see E. D. Jones, 'The Book of Llandaff', 139; Davies, *The Llandaff Charters*, 29 n. 32. Cf. Maund, *Ireland, Wales, and England*, 188.

[14] The consecration of Bleiddudd of St Davids by Æthelnoth (1020–38) is impossible if he was the successor of the Joseph who died in 1063 (*Annales Cambriae*). Cf. *WHEMA* IV 63. But some versions of Gerald of Wales, *Itinerarium*, II.1 have two bishops *Blethuth*. See

3. The charters in the Book of Llandaf

1056 – 1104 Herewald, bishop of Glamorgan.[15]
1107 – [1134] Urban, bishop of Glamorgan.

The circumstances in which the consecration list was produced were surely polemical (to show Llandaf's respect towards, and St Davids' subservience to, Canterbury). Nevertheless, some of its information is quite credible in the context of Anglo-Welsh relations from Alfred's time onwards, and it may have a more genuine basis than is sometimes supposed. It is even possible, judging by the location of their grants, that all the non-St Davids bishops listed above, with the arguable exception of Llibio, were Urban's predecessors in a real sense, though hardly all based at Llandaf itself. The *Anglo-Saxon Chronicle* says that the Danes captured *Cameleac biscop on Ircinga felda* in 914 and took him to their ships, whence he was ransomed by King Edward. Even if this means that he was 'bishop of Archenfield', rather than that Archenfield was where he was captured (as John of Worcester understood it), it is possible that the *Chronicle* specifies Archenfield (Ergyng) only because that was his area of activity that lay within the Anglo-Saxon sphere of influence; Cyfeilliog may have performed episcopal functions in Ergyng, like Tremerin of Glasbury and Herewald after him. That would be consonant with King Edward's kindly intervention and, indeed, with Cyfeilliog's alleged consecration by Archbishop Æthelred (870–89).[16] His grants in *LL* are centred in southern Gwent, like those of Pater, Gwgon, Bleddri, and some of Joseph's.[17]

For present purposes, it is sufficient to note that the arrangement of the latter part of *LL* was dictated by the incomplete list of consecrations – genuine or false – and that this led to the obvious misplacing of bishops who had been omitted from the list.

Wendy Davies takes a more complex view of the arrangement of the charters in *LL*, arguing that the present order reflects the prior existence, over several centuries in some cases, of nine collections of charters, A to J, which were placed end to end by the compilers of *LL*.[18] This hypothesis is hardly necessary, and itself raises two obvious problems.

The first problem is that if the charters towards the end of *LL* have been arranged in accordance with the incomplete consecration list – as she accepts – one does not need the theory of separate Groups G, H, J, to explain why the present order is the muddled GHJ rather than the correct chronological order HGJ.

The second problem concerns the charters in favour of St Dyfrig and St Teilo that form Groups A and B. Wendy Davies makes the telling point that it was normal practice for grants to a saint's church to be made 'to' the saint himself, long after his earthly life.[19] We have good early examples of this in the Lichfield Gospels from Llandeilo Fawr. The inclusion of St Teilo himself in the witness list of 'Chad 2' is

---

Pryce, 'Gerald of Wales and the Welsh past', 25 and 36–7; Thorpe, *Gerald of Wales*, 163 n. 269.

[15] Cf. Brooke, *The Church*, 92; *WHEMA* IV 63; Maund, *Ireland, Wales, and England*, 200–1.
[16] See discussion by J. R. Davies, *The Book of Llandaf*, 12, and Charles-Edwards, *Wales and the Britons*, 506 and 594 and n. 66.
[17] Cf. Hughes, 'The Celtic Church', 9 n. 30, and 19–20 (maps 6–8), and ch. 14 below.
[18] Davies, *The Llandaff Charters*, 12–16. She attempts to discover the place of origin of each Group and to reconstruct how they were gradually assembled in a single archive. This depends on unconvincing diplomatic arguments; see below, ch. 9.
[19] Davies, *An Early Welsh Microcosm*, 140. Cf. *WHEMA* I 466–7; Brooke, *The Church*, 32 n. 68.

a manifestation of the same mentality, and can be paralleled by the appearance of God as a witness to 'Chad 3' and, no doubt, that of Jesus in the St Davids charter described by William Salesbury to Matthew Parker.[20] Many of the charters in A and B 'to' St Dyfrig and St Teilo have witness lists closely related to those of later bishops' charters (especially those of her Group D) and the name of one or other of these later bishops often appears in the A and B witness lists immediately after the saint.[21] Thus, if the A and B charters are genuine at all, they are likely to belong to the time of the cleric mentioned immediately after the saint as the mortal recipient of the grant, not to the timeless world of the saints. Again it is difficult to see where this interpretation leaves the theory of the Groups, which entails supposing that A and B represent discrete earlier collections. The natural conclusion is surely that the compilers of *LL* simply picked out from batches of later charters those whose phrasing allowed them to be misinterpreted, mistakenly or wilfully, as charters in favour of the saint *in his own lifetime* and duly placed them in their 'correct' position in *LL*, near the appropriate *Vita*.[22] 73b and 74 can serve as examples. They are both placed before the *Vita Dubricii* as grants during the saint's earthly lifetime. However, 73b recurs later on in *LL* as 163a, presumably because the compiler of the later section rightly recognised it as a charter to St Dyfrig *and* Bishop Arwystl, his earthly representative.[23] 74 is a grant 'to' God, St Peter, and St Dyfrig by two people called *Britcon* and *Iliuc*, with the consent of a mysterious King Meurig.[24] The same grant recurs as 171b, together with other grants by *Britcon* in the time of King Meurig, who was probably the ninth-century dynast mentioned by Asser in his *Life of King Alfred*, §80, and this time the Disposition is 'Deo & sanctis Dubricio et Teliauo et Grecieli episcopo' and *Greciel episcopus* heads the witness list. Either the first compiler has suppressed Greciel's name, in order to add to his quota of Dyfrig grants for section A, or else the second compiler has added it in the light of other grants to Bishop Greciel (such as 169b–170). There is no reason to suppose that doublets of 73b/163a and 74/171b, assigned to earlier Groups A, D, and E, were in existence before *LL* itself was compiled. It is much simpler to suppose that the Groups A and B result from late misinterpretations of the dispositive formulae of charters later than the saints' own times, plus an admixture of forged charters which from the first were intended to look like real grants to the saints during their earthly lives.

The position with the charters of St Euddogwy (Old Welsh *Oudoce* or *Eudoce*) in Group C is completely different. As Doble recognised,[25] this saint – or, he thought, a saint of the same name – enjoyed a cult which was restricted, as far as we know, to Llandogo in Gwent before Llandaf took him up. The charters in *LL* in his favour are

---

[20] Quoted above, 14.
[21] See, for example, Davies, *The Llandaff Charters*, 14.
[22] This argument would need rephrasing if Dyfrig's cult was first brought to Ergyng by Herewald, as suggested by J. R. Davies (see above, 8, and below, 161). The insertion of Dyfrig's name would then be due to an eleventh-century recension of the Ergyng charters.
[23] See the parallel texts in ch. 11 below. With E/gistus/A/rguistil cf. 'inte/luallum' for 'inte*r*uallum' in charter 143, also the variation Uebrese/Guebrgu*r* (Davies, *The Llandaff Charters*, 104).
[24] Is this the source for King Meurig in *De Primo Statu*, *LL* p. 69? Guy, 'The *Life* of St Dyfrig', 9 n. 27, suggests that *De Primo Statu*'s Meurig is the son of Enynny and Caradog Freichfras, founder of Glywysing. If the compilers thought so, it might justify the placing of 74 early in *LL*.
[25] Doble, *Lives*, 207–29. He was possibly wrong to separate saint and bishop.

not charters 'to' a saint – insofar as some are not late forgeries – but straightforward grants to a Bishop Euddogwy, who also appears in the Llancarfan charters. It is evident from the witness lists of both the *LL* charters and the Llancarfan charters that Euddogwy was succeeded in his bishopric, wherever it was, by Bishop Berthwyn: *LL* 180b even states this explicitly, incompatible though it was with the final doctrine of *LL*, as represented by the present order and by the *Vita Oudocei*, that St Euddogwy succeeded St Teilo. If we may trust charter 192, Berthwyn was a contemporary (perhaps a younger contemporary) of Æthelbald of Mercia (reigned 716–57), so it would seem that Euddogwy's charters are also eighth century. Their separation from those of Berthwyn in 'Group F' is surely due merely to the fact that Euddogwy was brought to the head of the collection as one of Llandaf's three patrons, not to any distinction in source between the two's charters such as Davies's theory of Groups C and F implies. She does mention the possibility that C and F stood together at one time,[26] but does not carry the argument to the logical conclusion that Groups C and F have no reality as discrete collections outside the present arrangement of *LL*. In view of their internal coherence it is very likely that the charters of Euddogwy, Berthwyn, Tyrchan, and Cadwared come from a single, cumulative episcopal archive which was only split up when Llandaf decided to transform the charters' Euddogwy into a sixth-century saint.

The arrangement of *LL*, while not lending support to Davies's theory of an earlier set of archives A–J, does nevertheless point, as indicated above, to *LL*'s being a compilation of earlier material as much as a sheer forgery *tout simple*. This view is not new. Even the most sceptical critics of *LL* have found it hard to believe that so much highly circumstantial information about early Welsh persons and places is entirely due to the imagination of the twelfth-century Llandaf forgers, who can have stood to gain nothing from inventing a good part of the material in the charters.

C. N. L. Brooke argued that the witness lists of the pre-twelfth-century charters, the names of the donors, and so on, were inspired by associations suggested by earlier Welsh charters available to the compilers of *LL*, such as the Llancarfan charters, and by chronological indications from early Welsh genealogies, not all extant, plus a large measure of Geoffrey-of-Monmouth-like imagination.[27] Wendy Davies came to a more optimistic conclusion, arguing that about 85% of the charters can be shown to have some original basis.[28] Her considered opinion was that the charters with an original basis are expansions of shorter charters, similar to those in the Lichfield Gospels, which had been gathered together at Llandaf from various earlier episcopal centres. The expansions, she argued, were mainly verbal, but also affected the substance of the originals in two important ways: the recipients were all made bishops of Llandaf in succession to the alleged triad of founding saints; and many charters had long, quasi-historical or hagiographical Narrations added on the basis of unreliable oral tradition or sheer imagination, in order to explain how the estate came to be granted to Llandaf and so on.

The keys to Davies's interpretation are her analysis of the witness lists, which she regards as substantially original, and her diplomatic analysis, in which she attempts to distinguish early formulae in the charters from the verbiage in which later redactors

---

[26] Davies, *The Llandaff Charters*, 13–15; *An Early Welsh Microcosm*, 11–12. Cf. Brooke, *The Church*, 47.

[27] *Ibid.*, 33–4 and 46–7. On the genealogies see further Sims-Williams, 'The kings', and ch. 13 below.

[28] *An Early Welsh Microcosm*, 21.

chose to clothe them. Together with useful indices to the names in the charters and a calendar of charters, these analyses form the core of her *The Llandaff Charters*. By contrast – and unfortunately in view of Brooke's argument, cited above – she devotes hardly more than a few footnotes to a discussion of the relationship between *LL* and the Llancarfan charters and the genealogies, especially since it is here, if anywhere, that Conway Davies's dictum breaks down that

> it was the strength of the *Book of Llan Dav*, and it is now its weakness, that there probably were not then and there certainly are not now, any documents contemporary with its alleged grants by which its authority or accuracy could be tested.[29]

My own impression is that the compilers of *LL*, if they knew the Llancarfan charters and the genealogies, did *not* use them as a source. I therefore turn to these two sources.

The Llancarfan Charters

The manuscript of the Llancarfan charters is late twelfth century – BL Cotton Vespasian A.xiv, in which they are appended to the earliest extant copy of Lifris of Llancarfan's *Vita sancti Cadoci* – yet it is possible that they had already been redacted in more or less their present form before *LL* was compiled and could have been known to its compilers.[30] But if so, and if the compilers of *LL* really were making bricks with very little straw, one would have expected them to have lifted witness lists wholesale from the Llancarfan cartulary. In fact, however, there is only a *slight* overlap between *some* of the charters in each collection, little more than is consistent with them each including genuine witness lists from roughly the same historical period (see Chapter 4 below). This point has been lost sight of in most discussions of *LL* and the *Vita Cadoci* charters. These discussions have been dominated by the two grants that appear in both sources, in favour of Llandaf in one and Llancarfan in the other,[31] and by the assumption that Llancarfan must have been the original recipient of both.[32] Yet in both cases a comparison of the texts shows that both *LL* and *VC* were probably modifying a common source, which cannot be assumed to have been wholly in favour of either Llandaf or Llancarfan.[33]

The grant of Llangadwaladr (*LL* 180b/*VC* 67)[34] was made to Bishop Berthwyn (of 'Llandaf') according to *LL*; according to *VC* it was made to Llancarfan but the donor, Gwyddnerth, 'tandem redditus dedit Docgwinno' (that is, to St Dogwyn's,

---

[29] *EA* I 25.
[30] See Brooke, *The Church*, 92, who suggests a date *ca* 1100 or soon after for the Llancarfan charters. (James, 'The Book of *Llan Dav* and Canon G. H. Doble', 19, is not convincing.) For some comments on the Cadog charters see *WHEMA* IX 6 (cf. *WHEMA* XIV on the *Vita Cadoci* in general) and J. R. Davies, *The Book of Llandaf*, 91–4.
[31] See Brooke, *Church*, 32–3.
[32] Exceptions are Newell, Review, 335, Morris, Review, 231, and, greatly overstated, James, 'The Book of *Llan Dav* and Canon G. H. Doble', 19–24.
[33] See now the nuanced treatment by Charles-Edwards, *Wales and the Britons*, 256–61.
[34] Printed in parallel by Brooke, *The Church*, 32–3, and (abbreviated) by J. R. Davies, *The Book of Llandaf*, 93; translated in Charles-Edwards, *Wales and the Britons*, 258–9. See also below, ch. 11. In view of the other charters it is difficult to accept Brooke's interpretation

Llandough) and the *VC* clerical witness list is headed by *Berthgwinus episcopus, Conmil, Terchan, et congregatio eius* and ends with *Saturn, princeps altaris Docgwinni*. Wendy Davies makes the attractive suggestions that Llandough may have been an episcopal seat and that that is how the charter got into the episcopal archive and the property into the hands of Llandaf (whence Llangadwaladr's later name Bish(ops)ton or *Trefesgob*).[35] Another possibility is suggested by the fact that while Sadwrn usually appears in the *LL* witness lists as abbot of Llandough, he earlier appears (assuming it is the same man) as abbot of ?Llandaf (*princeps Taui urbis*, charter 149). If this is correct, an original copy of the Llangadwaladr charter may already have formed part of the archive of a church at Llandaf.[36]

The other shared charter (*LL* 210b/*VC* 66) may have a similar explanation, as a charter in favour of both the church of St Cadog and the church of Bishop Cadwared, from which Llancarfan and Llandaf preserved the elements deemed relevant to themselves.[37] It may be significant that the two shared charters stand together in the Llancarfan cartulary as *VC* 66–67.[38]

These are unprovable possibilities, of course, but it does seem that the tendency to use the Llancarfan charters to attack the veracity of the Llandaf charters has been unjustified. The former, which are almost as standardised in language as the latter, are probably also the product of controversy, as Llancarfan tried to escape the clutches of Gloucester abbey, so neither set can be trusted without question. In the Llancarfan charters, as Brooke remarked, we seem to have 'the first lesson in revising old charters, which was to end in *Liber Landauensis*'.[39] The connection between Llandaf and Llancarfan was close,[40] so that the compilers of both collections of charters may have been able to draw extensively on each other's archives. That they refrained from doing so may be not so much a tribute to their scruples as an indication that they each had plenty of relevant material to draw on, without needing to plagiarise.

The genealogies

The relationship between *LL* and the genealogies is also rather oblique. The earliest and most important extant collection, in BL Harley MS 3859 (*ca* 1100), has two genealogies relevant to the main area covered by *LL*: a short pedigree of *[B]rocmail*

('St Peter of Gloucester', 314 [omitted in *The Church*, 91]) of *illi* in *VC* 67 as referring to Gwyddnerth rather than to St Cadog (as in Charles-Edwards, *Wales and the Britons*, 258).

[35] Davies, *The Llandaff Charters*, 110; *An Early Welsh Microcosm*, 142 n. 2. For *VC* grants in favour of other houses see *VC* 57 (Llantwit). Charles-Edwards, *Wales and the Britons*, 258–9 suggests emending *tandem* to *totidem*, hence 'And he gave as many renders to Dogunni'.

[36] *EA* I 184, suggesting that it was a daughter-house of Llandough. *Taui urbs* could also refer to Cardiff, 'the *caer* on the Taf'. Cf. below, ch. 13, 143 n. 137.

[37] Translated in parallel columns by Charles-Edwards, *Wales and the Britons*, 257, and discussed *ibid.*, 257–8 and 260–1.

[38] See below, 92. *LL* 209b is a grant to Cadwared by the same donor; other members of the same family seem to occur elsewhere in *LL* (see Davies, *The Llandaff Charters*, 58).

[39] Brooke, *The Church*, 32 n. 68.

[40] *Ibid.*, 91–2. The reference to *Cetnig*, abbot of Llandough, in the *Vita Oudocei* (*LL* p. 131), suggests knowledge of charters such as *VC* 65 and 68, but no use is made of such charters in *LL*. Cf. below, 40 and n. 39.

map Mouric, who was king of Gwent in the 880s (Asser, *Life of King Alfred*, §80), and a pedigree of a certain *[I]udhail map Atroys* back to *Teudubric* (Tewdrig), the ancestor of the kings of Glywysing (the forerunner of Morgannwg). These are shown in **bold** type in Table 3.1, Fig. 1. Much later collections provide us with a further genealogy, of uncertain authority in its middle generations, tracing Morgan, the tenth-century king of Morgannwg, back to Tewdrig. The manuscripts are inconsistent; the version given in Fig. 1, in ordinary type, is from the earliest manuscript, Oxford, Jesus College, MS 20 (s. xiv/xv).[41]

While Wendy Davies does not give any tables of genealogies, it is clear from her passing references to them that she accepts a number of usual, but unnecessary, emendations to the texts which produce a single early line in Glywysing, with a ninth-century cadet branch in Gwent (as in Table 3.1, Fig. 2, which reflects these emendations). This view results in her conclusion that before the emergence of the 'intrusive' dynasties of the tenth and eleventh centuries south-east Wales was fairly stable under a single dynasty, a conclusion that adds fuel to a questionable hypothesis about a breakdown in society in the later period.[42]

Whichever view one takes on the textual question (discussed fully in Chapter 13 below), it is clear that several generations in the genealogies are not mentioned in *LL* at all. (I have marked those who *are* mentioned with a star.[43]) This is more significant in the case of the Harley genealogies, which were certainly in existence when *LL* was compiled. The *Iudhail* son of *Atroys* of the Harley genealogy 28 is definitely *not* the earlier king of this name in *LL* 157 and 259. Conversely many members of major and minor dynasties appear in the charters, but not in the extant genealogies. One would have expected the writers of *LL*, if working from scratch, to have worked through the royal genealogies systematically, fabricating grants by each dynast in turn, rather as Geoffrey of Monmouth used some version of the Harley genealogies when compiling his *Historia Regum Britanniae*.[44] There are, it is true, various genealogical

---

[41] Texts in *EWGT*, 12 (HG 28–29) and 45 (JC 9). *Nud hael* in JC 9, which Bartrum emends to *Iudhael*, should possibly read *Nud* or *Einud* (without epithet); see Sims-Williams, 'The kings', 77, and below, 124–6. Bartrum, 'Corrections', 171, doubted whether he should have accepted Gwriad ap Brochfael in JC 9. Cf. Davies, *The Llandaff Charters*, 87 n. 42, and *An Early Welsh Microcosm*, 102 n. 2.

[42] See tables in Davies, *An Early Welsh Microcosm*, 66–73, and her references to a 'single dynasty' (*ibid.*, 17, 94, and 102; *eadem*, *The Llandaff Charters*, 74, and *WHEMA* IX 8) and to its 'two branches' in the ninth century (*The Llandaff Charters*, 76, and *An Early Welsh Microcosm*, 65).

[43] *Ris in Fig. 2 is starred to reflect the view that he is the *Ris filius Iudhail* of *LL* (references in Davies, *The Llandaff Charters*, 183). I do not think that the latter *Ris* occurs in the genealogies, however.

[44] Piggott, 'The sources of Geoffrey of Monmouth', 276–86. That the 'forger' of *LL* worked from Morgannwg genealogies corresponding to HG 28–29 and JC 9 was suggested by Brooke, *The Church*, 33–4. The opposite, that the Harley genealogies were influenced by the charters underlying *LL*, was suggested by Guy, 'Did the Harleian genealogies draw on archival sources?', arguing that Brochfael and his son Gwriad (JC 9) do not appear in the Harley genealogies because they were absent from the charters (cf. above n. 41), and that the compiler of the Harley genealogy made a 'leap of faith in assuming that Arthfael was the son of Rhys' (p. 130), and that his *Iudhail* son of *Atroys* (see above) is a 'ghost' due to misunderstanding the date of *LL* 157 and 159a. This seems unlikely to me. Cf. Sims-Williams, 'The kings', passim. Cf. ch. 13 below.

3. The charters in the Book of Llandaf

notes scattered through *LL*;[45] but these look more like valiant attempts to find order in a pre-existing chaos of charters than anything else. *LL* resembles a genuine archive that has suffered the arbitrary ravages of time rather than the product of a forger with genealogies as his guide, especially if the available genealogies resembled those attested in the Harley and Jesus College manuscripts rather than the 'improved' texts produced by modern scholars.

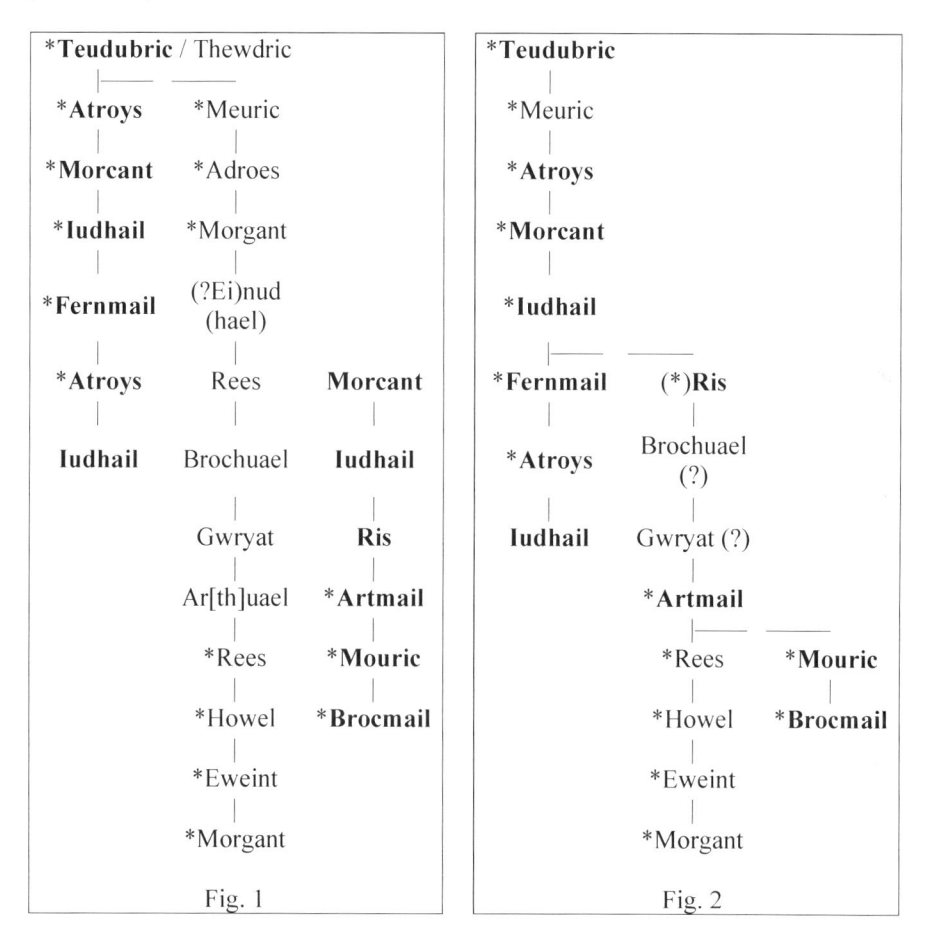

```
Fig. 1 (Unemended)

*Teudubric / Thewdric
    ├─────────┐
  *Atroys   *Meuric
    │         │
  *Morcant  *Adroes
    │         │
  *Iudhail  *Morgant
    │         │
  *Fernmail (?Ei)nud
    │        (hael)
    │         │
  *Atroys   Rees      Morcant
    │         │         │
  Iudhail   Brochuael Iudhail
              │         │
            Gwryat     Ris
              │         │
            Ar[th]uael *Artmail
              │         │
            *Rees     *Mouric
              │         │
            *Howel    *Brocmail
              │
            *Eweint
              │
            *Morgant
```

```
Fig. 2 (Emended)

*Teudubric
    │
  *Meuric
    │
  *Atroys
    │
  *Morcant
    │
  *Iudhail
    ├─────────┐
  *Fernmail (*)Ris
    │         │
  *Atroys   Brochuael
    │         (?)
    │         │
  Iudhail   Gwryat (?)
              │
            *Artmail
              ├─────────┐
            *Rees     *Mouric
              │         │
            *Howel    *Brocmail
              │
            *Eweint
              │
            *Morgant
```

Table 3.1 Unemended (Fig. 1) and emended (Fig. 2) genealogies

---

[45] See e.g. 24 n. 10 above, and below, 142–3.

4

THE AUTHENTICITY OF THE WITNESS LISTS

The foundation of Wendy Davies's rehabilitation of the *LL* charters is her analysis of the witness lists. The great majority of the charters in *LL* have witness lists – one of the main justifications for calling them 'charters' rather than 'memoranda'. In nearly all of them the clergy and the laity are listed separately, as in the Llandeilo Fawr charters in the Lichfield Gospels and the Llancarfan charters attached to the *Vita Cadoci*.[1] On the basis of recurrent names and patronymics Davies arranged most of the witness lists in three approximately chronological sequences on pp. 35–7, 41–53, and 59–69 of *The Llandaff Charters*. Sequence i contains lists from charters 72a to 122 (not 74) and 160–166, Sequence ii contains lists from charters 140 to 159b and 174b–211b (not 199bii), and Sequence iii contains lists from charters 168 to 174a and 212–274, plus 74 and 199bii. The probable *chronological* order within these broad limits differs considerably from the *paginal* order in *LL*, as one would expect from the compilers' chronological uncertainties, discussed in Chapter 3 above. Each of the three Sequences is self-contained, with no persons being securely identifiable in more than one Sequence. (Davies's tentative identification of *Athruis rex Guenti regionis* in charter 165 of Sequence i with the Athrwys ap Meurig of Sequence ii is uncertain.[2]) For ease of reference I shall number the charters in Davies's proposed Sequences as i.1–19, ii.1–64, and iii.1–61; for a concordance see Appendix I at the end of this book.

The tables in *The Llandaff Charters* are fuller, more logical, and more consistent than those offered by earlier scholars, which they supersede in nearly all respects. Users may regret, however, that Davies did not follow Anscombe's practice of indicating the order of attestations in each witness list,[3] since this can indicate probable equations of persons with the same name, order of precedence or kinship of witnesses, and close or suspicious relationships between particular charters.[4]

An ideal arrangement of charters should show a changing order of precedence between witnesses A, B, C, etc. over a chronological sequence a, b, c, etc.:

---

[1] Cf. *WHEMA* I 471–2.
[2] See below, 55 n. 34. Cf. Davies, *The Llandaff Charters*, 37–8, 40, 75, and 105–6. On the lack of overlap between ii and iii see *ibid.*, 58.
[3] Anscombe, 'Landavensium ordo chartarum'.
[4] Compare the work on Anglo-Saxon witness lists by Keynes, *The Diplomas*, and *An Atlas of Attestations*.

4. The authenticity of the witness lists

	a	b	c	d	e	f	g
A	1						
B	2	1					
C	3	2	1				
D	4	3	2	1			
E		4	3	2	1		
F			4	3	2	1	
G						2	1

Needless to say, so ideal a progression is not to be found even in reliable Anglo-Saxon cartularies. Bearing this in mind, there are only three places in Sequences ii–iii where there is room for serious disagreement with Davies's order.[5]

One is her placing of two charters of Bishop Tyrchan (204b and 205) as ii.27 and ii.24, among the charters of Bishop Berthwyn (ii.19–44), on the basis of the appearance in 204b–205 of three abbots who were Berthwyn's contemporaries. In view of the other witnesses to these two charters, it seems more reasonable to follow Anscombe in placing both charters among those of Tyrchan himself (ii.45–55), and to regard the three abbots as a misguided interpolation.[6] The second place is early in Sequence iii, where I suggest moving the charters of Gwyddloyw and Eddylfyw (168 and 169a) back from iii.14–15 to just before iii.1, and rearranging the charters of Nudd and Cerennyr between three bishops: Nudd I (currently iii.8 and 11–13), Cerennyr (currently iii.9–10 and 16–18), and Nudd II (currently iii.19–23).[7]

Her table for Sequence i is more troubling. It is confusing to have the attestations of St Dyfrig and St Teilo included, since saints are irrelevant chronologically, as we have seen,[8] and more serious confusion results from the inclusion of the list of 77, the grant by Nowy, king of Dyfed, of Penally, Llandeilo Fawr, and Llanddowror, which is a clear forgery in support of one of Llandaf's most preposterous claims against St Davids. As Davies is aware, its long clerical witness list – there is no lay list[9] – is a crude conflation of some version of 72a (or 76a) and 75. There is thus nothing to be gained by including 77 in the tables of witnesses, where it distorts the proper progression of clerical witnesses, casting unnecessary doubt on their plausibility. She regards the clerical witness lists of Sequence i as in any case suspicious because they share many names with the list of St Dyfrig's disciples in the *Vita Dubricii* (*LL* p. 80).[10] An examination of the *Vita* list will show, however, that the relevant part of the list of 'disciples' was lifted from the witness lists (principally from that of 77), not vice versa, and therefore has no bearing on the authenticity or plausibility of the clerical lists.[11]

---

[5] Some further adjustments to the order of the putatively eleventh-century charters are suggested by Maund, *Ireland, Wales, and England*, 187, 199, and 205–6.

[6] Anscombe, 'Landavensium ordo chartarum', 292–3, nos lxxi and lxviii. Cf. Davies, *The Llandaff Charters*, 45, 56, 84 nn. 17 and 19, and 117. The abbots in 214 (iii.10) are also interpolated according to Charles-Edwards, *Wales and the Britons*, 596 n. 82.

[7] See below, 168–71.

[8] See above, 25–6.

[9] 'De laicis Noe solus testis est cum innumerabili copia hominum'. On 77 see Guy, 'The *Life* of St Dyfrig', 10–12.

[10] Davies, *The Llandaff Charters*, 12, 38, 83 n. 5, and 95.

[11] See Appendix below, 41. On the list of disciples see J. R. Davies, *The Book of Llandaf*, 81–4 and 87.

If we ignore 77 as a forgery and the list of disciples as a red herring, the clerical witness lists of Davies's Sequence i can be rearranged in a logical order, as in Table 4.1: 166, 121, 122, 72a, 76a, 72b, 73a, 73b/163a (Bishop Arwystl), 162b (Bishop Aeddan), 76b, 160, 161, 162a (Bishop Ufelfyw), 163b and 164 (Bishop Inabwy), 165 (Bishop Cyfwyre), and 75 ([Bishop?] Elhaearn).[12] Note that 73b and 163a are doublets, with minor variation in the content and order of the witnesses.[13] The conflated charter 77 list and the list of disciples are included at the right side of Table 4.1 (below) for comparison.

In Table 4.1 I have omitted witnesses who occur in only one charter,[14] with the exceptions of one of the 'disciples' of Dyfrig (*Merchguin*) and the five king-grantors who are marked with an asterisk; to have included all the unique witnesses would have confused the table without shedding light on the progression of witnesses from charter to charter. There are more unique witnesses in the lay lists than the clerical lists, presumably because the clergy formed a more coherent body whereas the kings (marked in **bold**) had their own personal entourages of laymen. For this reason, the progression of witnesses is best worked out from the clerical lists (at the top half of the Table). Ignoring appearances of the patron saints (marked with a tick), there seems to be a clear development from bishop to bishop (marked in bold, from Arwystl to Elhaearn).[15] All Arwystl's successors apart from Aeddan have appeared lower down the hierarchy before becoming bishop (for instance, Ufelfyw starts as second in command to Arwystl), and there are various other links between their episcopates. *Iudon* attests under Arwystl and Cyfwyre, as does *Guordocui* who further attests under Inabwy and Elhaearn. *Iudnou* attests under Arwystl and Inabwy, and *Bithen* and *Guernabui* attest under Inabwy and Cyfwyre, with *Guernabui* continuing under Elhaearn (and perhaps already appearing under Aeddan).[16] *Gurguarui*'s attestations span the episcopates of Aeddan, Inabwy, and Cyfwyre. A further clerical link between the episcopates of Aeddan and Elhaearn is probably provided by *Iudnerth* in 162b and *Iudner* in 75, despite the variation in spelling.

The lay links between the episcopates are fewer. *Erbic* in 121 may well be distinct from the *Eruic* son of King Gwrfoddw of 161–162a.[17] *Peipiau* (son of *Erb*) and *Condiuill* reappear in the dubious charter of King Erb to Elhaearn (75), but this charter cannot be authentic as it stands; perhaps Erb and his son have been inserted – as well-known dynasts – into a charter of a later generation.[18] On the other hand *Condiuill* in 75 could be an error for *Conuc* son of *Condiuil*, and conversely

---

[12] As in Sims-Williams, Review, 126, but putting 162b in the position advocated by Guy, 'The *Life* of St Dyfrig', 22. On the identification of bishops in Group A see ch. 3 above. Some possible links are not shown in the Table. The incomplete abbot's name *Cu* in 160 may correspond to the *Cuelino* of 76b, and 160's *Iohannesque cum clericis suis* may be the *Iouan* of 72a and 72b (*Johann* in the Vespasian A.xiv version of charter 77: *LL* p. 359).

[13] See below, 93.

[14] The lay witness *Biuan* in 166 is conceivably the *Biuan* in the main text of 122 (cf. *DP* IV 376). He and his co-witnesses may have perished together. See below, 162 n. 36.

[15] Elhaearn's episcopal status is inferred from his position after Archbishop Dyfrig in 75 but is not explicit.

[16] The MS reading in 162b is *guenopoui*.

[17] A problem with these names is that it is not clear whether *Erb, Erb-* is distinct from *Eru-* (*Erf-* in modern spelling). In this book I retain the spelling *Erb, Erb-*, but cf. Sims-Williams, *The Celtic Inscriptions of Britain*, 190 and 232.

[18] On the inclusion of donors in witness lists see below, 44.

its witnesses 'Gurtauan . mabon' should perhaps be emended so as to refer to the *Guruthon* son of *Mabon* of the preceding episcopate.[19]

On the positive side, note that *Cinuin* and perhaps *Congual* span the episcopates of Arwystl and Ufelfyw. *Guorbur/Guebregur* son of *Eifest* (161–162a) may attest the charters of both Ufelfyw and Inabwy (164 *Uebresel filius Eifest*), as may *Gurdauau*, whom I have put at the foot of the Table, owing to his uncertain clerical or lay status. *Guorguol* links the episcopates of Inabwy and Cyfwyre, as may *Morcant/Morgon*.

In short, the progression of Sequence i witnesses as rearranged in Table 4.1 is quite plausible if we ignore 77 as a forgery and regard the lay witnesses of 75 as doctored or corrupt.

Some of the *LL* charters have no witness lists, apparently either because they are mere summaries or *notitiae* (e.g. 179a, cf. 188b) or because they are forgeries or, if one prefers, hagiographies (for example, several of the charters appended to the *Vita Teiliaui*). There are also three witness lists which cannot be included in the Sequences because they show no overlapping persons. This lack of overlap is understandable since they belong to charters which purport to come from the outlying kingdoms of Dyfed and Brycheiniog (125b, 127a, 167), and is indeed a point in their favour. Nevertheless, in the case of two of them (125b and 127a), two verbose charters to St Teilo in the time of King Aergol (*ca* 500!), one feels that the short lists may be pure invention.[20] If so the invention was not necessarily during the compilation of *LL*. The occurrence of a *Fidelis* in both charters (125b and 127a, and thence in the list of Teilo's 'disciples' in the *Vita Teiliaui*, *LL* p. 115) looks like a misinterpretation of the epithet *fidelis*, as commonly found in Anglo-Saxon charters. It seems possible, on geographical grounds, that both charters may be based on texts taken over from the great centre of Teilo's cult at Penally, Pembrokeshire. In this connection one may suggest, on similar grounds, that the list of churches and estates sandwiched between 123 and 125 is a list of Penally's possessions.[21] This list clearly formed the basis for a much longer list of properties appended to the alleged privilege of Bishop Joseph (253), in which it may have been conflated with a similar list of the properties of Llandeilo Fawr, the other great western centre of Teilo's cult and a possible source for two more Teilo charters (125a and 127b). Both lists may have figured in the chirograph described in Gruffudd ap Llywelyn's privilege for Bishop Herewald (269).[22]

The fact that once the witness lists are disentangled from their present order they form a logical sequence does not in itself prove that they are authentic and contemporary records; it all depends on the degree of cunning that one is prepared to attribute to the Llandaf forgers or their predecessors.[23] Thus, on the one hand, C. N. L. Brooke was not convinced by Anscombe's work on the early witness lists,

---

[19] See nn. ii–iii to Table 4.1. Cf. *Gurcinnif. Gurci* (*sic*) in 251 = *Gurcinnif filius Gurci* in 262, cited below, 175 n. 133.

[20] On 127a see Charles-Edwards, *Wales and the Britons*, 308.

[21] On this list see J. R. Davies, *The Book of Llandaf*, 88. On Penally (Penalun) see Charles-Edwards, *Wales and the Britons*, 660–1. Doble, *Lives*, 164, suggested that the list is from Llandeilo Fawr.

[22] See above, 20. For doubts about 253 and 269 see Maund, *Ireland, Wales, and England*, 188 and 202, and Charles-Edwards, *Wales and the Britons*, 283.

[23] Clearly the lists are not due to whoever arranged the *LL* charters in their present order, but there are indications that some other redactors had a better idea of the charters' chronology. See charters 180b and 183b.

	166	121	122	72a	76a	72b	73a	73b 163a	162b	76b	160	161	162a	163b	164	165	75	77	Disc.
TEILO																			1
DYFRIG		√	√	√	√					√						√	√	√	
Arguistil	1	1	1	1	1	1	1	1										1	10
Elguoret	3	2	2																5
Conguarui		3	3			3	3	3											12
Conbran	5	4		5	5													5	
Iudon			5													2			
Guordocui		6												5	4	4	3	9	16
Aidan									1										19
Ubelbiu				2	2					1		1	1					2	3
Iouan				3	3						1	1						3	18
Iunabui				4	4	2	2	2						1	1			4	11
Guoruan				6	6													6	13
Cimmareia							4	[5]											
Iudnou							5							3	3			8	15
Merchguin										2									4
Meilic												2	3						
Deui												3	2						
Comereg														2	2	1			
Elhearn							6	4						4		3	1	7	14
Bithen														6	6	7			
Guernabui									2?					7	7	5	4	10	17
Gurguarui									4					8	8	6			
Iudner(th)									7								2		
[Cinuarch][1]																√			20
LAY	166	121	122	72a	76a	72b	73a	73b 163a	162b	76b	160	161	162a	163b	164	165	75	77	
Idon	1	1	1																
Morguid		2	2																
Merchion		3	3																

Guinabui	6	4										
Eruic	5								2	2		
*Erb											1	
Peipiau			1	1	1						2	
Guorbrir			3		5							
Condiuill			5								5	
Cinuin				2?		2			2?			
Guidci				3								
Congual				5					8?			
Collbiu					2	3?						
Cintiuit					3	7	[5]					
Aircol						4	4					
*Merchguin								1				
*Mouric												
Guruodu									1	1		
Guorbur									3	3	2	
Circan									6	5		
Gurcant											1	
*Athruis											1	1
Morcant											2	6?
Guruthon[ii]											5	3?	3?
Guidcon											7	5?
Conuc[iii]											8	6
Guorguol											9		3
*Noe												
Gurdauau[iv]									5		6	4	1

Table 4.1 Sequence i (re-ordered)

[i] Cinuarch is mentioned in 165 but is not a witness. [ii] Guruthon/Guordoi is son of Mabon, which suggests that he is identical with 'Gurtauan . mabon', lay witness(es) 3 and 4 in charter 75. [iii] Conoc is son of Condiuil, for whom see 72a. In 75 perhaps restore [Conuc fil.] Condiuil. [iv] He is the last cleric in 161, but a layman in 163b-164.

remarking that it made clear 'the element of hazard and the freaks of planning'; John Morris and Ian Jack, on the other hand, found the number of names 'so large and cohesive' and 'so consistently inter-related' that they could not be the work of any known forger.[24] The medievalist is always haunted by the bugbear of the hypothetical perfect forgery, but for practical purposes I think most scholars would agree that the progression of witnesses in Wendy Davies's tables (in particular the progression of abbots in Sequence ii)[25] is so complex and the detectable freaks so few and so blatant (for instance, the three abbots in the Tyrchan charters mentioned above) that the witness lists must, on the whole, come from authentic documents, or at least from near contemporary forgeries.

In *The Llandaff Charters* Davies's tables of witness lists are left to speak for themselves, and they do so eloquently. Yet several subsidiary points can be made in their favour. As Morris remarked and others have shown in detail, there is orthographical evidence.[26] The compilers of *LL* modernised spellings rather haphazardly, so they are unlikely to have deliberately archaised Sequence i charters or deliberately modernised Sequence iii charters in order to add credibility to the witness lists. It is therefore significant that initial *Uu-* for later *Gu-* appears only in Sequence i, that *e* for *ui* does not occur after about ii.59 (211a), that *au* replaces *o* about iii.10, and that *Cun-* is gradually replaced by *Con-* and then *Cin-*, and so on. All these orthographical developments, detectable despite much sporadic modernisation throughout, reflect well-attested phonological developments in Welsh and are paralleled in the Llancarfan charters. It is significant, too, that the proportion of names of English origin increases markedly from Sequence to Sequence,[27] so much so, in fact, that the occasional occurrence of an Anglo-Saxon name in an early context is a cause for suspicion: for example, the eponymous Gower abbot *Mergualdus* in the text (but not the witness list!) of ii.17 (charter 145 granting *Lann Merguall*) is Anglo-Saxon *Merewald* or *Merewalh* (curiously a name meaning 'famous Welshman').[28] It is also striking that clerics rarely occur with patronymics in Sequences i and ii, and that the title *princeps* seems to give way to *sacerdos* and finally to *presbiter*.[29] All these matters would repay some statistical analysis.[30]

Further confirmation for some combinations of names and progressions of witnesses can be found in the Llancarfan cartulary attached to the *Vita Cadoci* (*VC*) in Cotton Vespasian A.xiv. This contains ten charters that overlap in their witness

---

[24] Brooke, *The Church*, 47; Morris, Review, 232; Jack, *Medieval Wales*, 146.

[25] Cf. Anscombe, 'Landavensium ordo chartarum', 124–5. It might be argued that Davies's argument is circular, in that if a name occurs twice close together in a Sequence she takes it to refer to a single personage, and the reverse with names occurring at a distance. Yet in fact her procedure is logical since the latter names never recur in combination with groups of names from the other place in the Sequence.

[26] Morris, Review, 231 ('orthography varies from Iudhail to Ithel, etc.'). For more detail and references to work by Phillimore, Loth, Wendy Davies, and Koch see Sims-Williams, 'The emergence', from which the following examples are taken. Brooke seems to have come round to accepting the philological evidence: Review, 77.

[27] Davies, *The Llandaff Charters*, 145. On genuine trends in personal names in *LL* see Cane, 'Personal names'.

[28] On the name see Sims-Williams, *Religion and Literature*, 26 and 48 n. 163. His name may be included as the eponym of the *llan.* See differently Davies, *The Llandaff Charters*, 98.

[29] *An Early Welsh Microcosm*, 125–7 and 129. On *sacerdos* cf. below, 60 n. 7.

[30] On the method for distinguishing early historical from late stylistic change see below, ch. 8.

4. The authenticity of the witness lists

lists with *LL* to a limited extent.[31] It is probable that the Vespasian scribe omitted some names, as he does in copying the Dyfrig charters also known from *LL*,[32] and that his source had savagely abbreviated witness lists, as was the habit of some cartulary compilers.[33] The witness lists of the two charters shared between *LL* and *VC* seem to have been abbreviated by both sources. *LL* retains only four witnesses of *LL* 210b/*VC* 66, who all occur in charters around Sequence ii.57, while *VC* retains only Cynyng (abbot of Llancarfan). Cynyng does not appear in *LL* at all, but we have two more of his charters in *VC*: *VC* 55 and 56, which share four witnesses with each other. Now five other names in *VC* 55–56 (*Guornemet*, *Colbiu*, *Samson* abbot of Llantwit, *Iouan*, and *Meuc*) recur in *LL*, in each case around ii.59, and the Rhodri mentioned in the text and witness list of *VC* 55 may be the King *Rotri filius Iudhail* who appears in 210b (ii.57),[34] for a stone cross at Llantwit bears an inscription recording its erection by Abbot Samson for the soul of King Ithel.[35] Thus although *LL* and *VC* share no witnesses in *LL* 210b/*VC* 66 they are quite consistent and have probably independently abbreviated a common original. The same applies to *LL* 180b (ii.25) and its doublet *VC* 67. Although their witness lists share only a few names (Bishop Berthwyn, Tyrchan, [King] Morgan, Gwyddnerth) there is reason to think the other names were not mere invention. *LL* 180b's other names agree with the other witness lists for the *beginning* of Berthwyn's episcopate and this fits in well with the statement in the text that it was one of the first items of his episcopate, after he succeeded Euddogwy.[36] It is difficult to believe that the compilers of *LL* were capable of compiling such an appropriate list. Similarly one of the names peculiar to the *VC* version (Abbot Sulien of Llancarfan) appears in *LL* witness lists only at the *end* of Euddogwy's episcopate.[37] Thus the names peculiar to the *VC* doublet do not seem to be invention either. This is confirmed by *VC* 62, which must be of similar date to *LL* 180b/*VC* 67 since Morgan *rex* and (Abbot) Sulien both appear in it; for *VC* 62 mentions Danog who has become abbot of Llancarfan in *LL* ii.29, *Guengarth alumpnus regis* who appears in *LL* ii.4–18 *passim* as well as in 180b itself (ii.25), *Cuncuan* who may appear in ii.22, and Iacob, who may be the *Iacob filius Mabsu*

---

[31] See below. Cf. *EA* I 171; Bartrum, 'Some studies', 291–6; Davies, *An Early Welsh Microcosm*, 118–19; Charles-Edwards, *Wales and the Britons*, 272–3 and 309. Four *VC* charters (57, 58, 60, 63) do not overlap with *LL*, *pace* (in respect of *VC* 60) Davies, *An Early Welsh Microcosm*, 119, and Koch, 'When was Welsh literature first written down?', 65 n. 5.

[32] Three witnesses of 77 are omitted in Vespasian A.xiv (see *LL*, p. 359, note on *LL* p. 77, line 25). These are clerics 7, 8, and 9 of my Table 4.1 above, and recur in the same order in the list of Dyfrig's disciples (both in *LL*, p. 80, and in Vespasian A.xiv). Evidently it is the Vespasian scribe who has omitted them, not the *LL* scribe who has added them, since the list of disciples seems to depend on charter 77.

[33] Cf. Keynes, *The Diplomas*, 4, 43, 45, 62, 89, 154, and 234. Thus the witness list of *VC* 56 includes only one of the three sons named in the body of the charter.

[34] In 210b he consents. I suggest in ch. 5 that many of the names in consent formulae in *LL* may be taken from the witness lists of their originals.

[35] Sims-Williams, *The Celtic Inscriptions of Britain*, 278. Cf. Redknap and Lewis, *A Corpus*, I, 381–2 (no. G65).

[36] That Berthwyn succeeded Euddogwy was an old feature, against standard *LL* doctrine; see Doble, *Lives*, 215; Brooke, *The Church*, 47–8. The reference to fratricide in both *VC* 67 and *LL* 180b suggests that an element of the Narration was original.

[37] ii.24 and 27 (205 and 204b) have to be ignored here (see above, 33).

who appears in ii.25 only. Hence *VC* 62 and *VC* 67/*LL* 180b have appropriate witness lists for around ii.25. They are rather earlier than the charters of Abbot Cynyng's time (*VC* 66/*LL* 210b = ii.57), with which they have some links. (*Cuncuan* of *VC* 62 may be the *Concuu*n of *VC* 66,[38] *Boduan* of *VC* 62 may be the *Beduan* of *VC* 56, and *Gurhitr* of *VC* 62 was probably the father of the *Spois filius Gurhitr* of *VC* 55.) They are rather later, however, than the group *VC* 64, 65, 68 (discussed in the following paragraph), with which they also have some links. Abbot Sulien of Llancarfan of *VC* 62 and 67 was probably the mere cleric of this name in *VC* 68, *Conmogoi*, the *presbyter* of Llantwit in *VC* 64, 65, 68, is higher up the hierarchy of witnesses in *VC* 62; and among the laity *Morcant* occurs both in *VC* 64 and in *VC* 62 and *VC* 67/*LL* 180b, *Guengarth* occurs both in *VC* 64 and 65 and in *VC* 62 and *LL* 180b, while *Guallunir* of *VC* 64, 65, 68, was probably the father of the *Guidnerth* [*filius Guallonir*] in *VC* 67/*LL* 180b and various *LL* charters from ii.8 to ii.25.

VC 64, 65, and 68, are charters in favour of Abbot Iacob of Llancarfan and have closely related witness lists. Abbot Iacob appears in *LL* ii.1–3, but the *charters* in *LL* have no trace of Abbot *Catthig* (or *Cethig*) of Llandough (*VC* 65 and 68) or of Abbot *Rumceneu* (presumably) of Llantwit (*VC* 68). Since there is no room for these last two in the succession of abbots in Sequence ii, it is probable that they were abbots before Sequence ii began, and this is confirmed by a reference in the *Vita Oudocei* to *Cetnig* [*sic*] *abbas Docguinni* among the clerics present at the start of Euddogwy's episcopate.[39] A placing of all three charters immediately before Sequence ii fits in with the later *VC* witness lists (as discussed above) and with *LL*. All three charters include Bywonwy and Cadien among the *familia* of Llantwit, whereas in Sequence ii they become successive abbots of that community (ii.1; 2–4).[40] Similarly Eudeyrn (*Outegurn*) of *VC* 68 is probably the person who has become abbot of Llandough in ii.1–3,[41] and its Sulien may be the cleric of ii.5–6 and later abbot of Llancarfan (ii.17–23), while its *Guorgeneu* recurs in ii.5, 7, 8, 15, and its lay witness *Morceneu* recurs in ii.1 only. Most important of all, the only bishop in the three charters, *Eudoce* in *VC* 65, is Bishop *Oudoce* of ii.1–19 (*Eudoce* is a less archaic spelling of *Euddogwy* than *Oudoce*). There are also important links with the laity of the beginning of Sequence ii. King Meurig and his sons (*VC* 65 and 68) appear in ii.1–4, *Morcant* or *Marcant*

---

[38] The former is a layman and the latter possibly a scribe (but cf. *VC* 55, 56, 62, 65, where laymen hold a charter on the hand of a cleric).

[39] *LL* p. 131. On *Cethig* = *Cetnig* see Sims-Williams, 'IE **peug'- /*peuk'-* "to pierce" in Celtic', 121 n. 28. For the abbot sequence see Anscombe, 'Landavensium ordo chartarum', 123–5; Bartrum, 'Some studies', 291–6; James, 'The "Concen charters"' (unconvincing); Davies, *The Llandaff Charters*, 41–8 and 54–5; and below, 92 n. 24, and 151 n. 191. If *Rumceneu* in *VC* 68 is *not* abbot of Llantwit, *VC* 64, 65, and 68 could perhaps be fitted in between the third and fourth charters of Sequence ii (charters 143 and 147), where there is a change of abbot both at Llancarfan and at Llandough. But see the point about *Biuone* and *Catgen* below and the following note.

[40] That is, in charters 144 and 140, 143, 147 respectively. But note that in the witness list of 144 (*Oudoceus episcopus. catgen. biuan. cum sua familia. Iacob abbas altaris sancti Cadoci . . .*) it is not impossible that it is *Catgen* who is intended as abbot and *Biuan* is merely the first person in the original list of his *familia*, despite the statement in the body of the charter. On the other hand, *Biuone* always attests immediately before *Catgen* in *VC* 64, 65, and 68, suggesting precedence.

[41] Charters 144, 140, and 143. The *Eutegyrn lector* of the dubious witness list of *VC* 57 may be distinct.

4. The authenticity of the witness lists

(*VC* 64) may be the king from ii.5 onwards, *Guengarth procurator regis* (*VC* 64–65) recurs in ii.4–25 *passim*, *Guedgen filius Brocmail* and *Guallunir* (*VC* 64, 65, 68) reappear respectively in ii.1–17 *passim* and ii.1, and several more laymen in *VC* 65 can probably be identified in *LL*: *Bramail* (ii.3–17),[42] *Iudnerth filius Mourici* (ii.2), *Geintoc* (ii.1–14 *passim*), and perhaps *Eliud* (ii.16).

In view of this converging evidence we can fit the majority of the *VC* charters into the sequence of *LL* charters as follows, naming the abbots of Llancarfan as a guide:

Iacob: *VC* 64, 65, 68; then *LL* ii.1–3.
Cyngen: *LL* ii.4–14.
Sulien: *LL* ii.17–23 with *VC* 62 and *VC* 67/*LL* 180b (ii.25).
Paul: *VC* 59, 61 (see below).
Gnouan: *LL* ii.28.
Danog: *LL* ii.29.
Daan (*Dagan*): *LL* ii.30–41.
Cynyng (*Conigc*): *VC* 55, 56, and *VC* 66/*LL* 210b (ii.57).

There may have been one or two further abbots of Llancarfan between Daan and Cynyng, for *LL* gives up giving the titles of the abbots after Daan. Apart from Cynyng the only abbot in the above list not mentioned in *LL* is Paul. The above placing of him depends heavily on identifying the *Gnouan*[43] who heads the clerical list of *VC* 61 with the person of this name who is abbot by *LL* ii.28 and on trying to reconcile this identification with various links between Paul's charters and the *later* charters of the above list: *Guallunir* of *VC* 59 may be the person in ii.28, 30, and 45 (not the earlier person of this name discussed above) and *Concu*n and *Tanet* seem to recur in ii.45 and 55 and *VC* 66, while *Brenic* and *Elionoe* of *VC* 61 recur in *VC* 55–56, and so possibly does *Matganoi*.[44]

Not all the above identifications can be regarded as certain, but their evidence is cumulative, for nowhere else in *LL* do the same names recur in the same significant combinations. The relationship between the *VC* and *LL* witness lists is so oblique that it is impossible to believe that it is the result of late forgery. Rather, the Llancarfan and Llandaf cartularies appear to have drawn on earlier documents (in two cases the *same* document) of the same early date. Thus the Llancarfan witness lists give strong support to those who accept the authenticity of the Llandaf witness lists.

Appendix

St Dyfrig's disciples in his Vita *(LL p. 80) who witness Sequence i charters*

Fifteen of Dyfrig's alleged twenty disciples (*LL* p. 80) appear in the witness lists of the Sequence i charters, as shown in Table 4.2, which is a rearranged version of Table 4.1 above. The relevant names are in the first column, starting with *Teiliaus*; the italicised names are not disciples. Ten of these disciple names may be taken from the forged charter 77 (although Teilo does not appear in its witness list, 77 refers

---

[42] Wade-Evans emends *VC* 65 to 'Guedgen [filius] Bramail', but *DP* IV 711 thinks that the latter is the *Briauael filius Luuarch* of *LL*.
[43] Cf. *VC* 11 and 53 — cf. *DP* II 290 n. 3 and Charles, *The Place-Names of Pembrokeshire*, I 266–7, according to whom *Gnouan* and *Gnawan* are identical.
[44] Cf. *Minnocioi*, *Manacoi* in *VC* 55–56 (this is presumably scribal corruption).

Disc	166	121	122	72a	76a	72b	73a	73b = 163a	76b	162b	160	161	162a	163b	164	165	75	77
	Dubricius			√	√				√								√	√
-	*Conguarui*		3	3		3	3	3										
-	*Iudon*			5												2		
-	*Cimmareia*						4	[5]										
-	*Meilic*											2	3					
-	*Deui*											3	2					
-	**Comereg**													2	2	1		
-	*Bithen*													6	6	7		
-	*Gurguarui*										4			8	8	6		
-	*Iudner(th)*										7						2	
1	Teiliaus	√[i]		√[ii]														
3	**Vbeluius**				2[iii]	2[iv]				1[v]	1[vi]	1[vii]	1[viii]					2[ix]
4	Merchguinus									2[x]								
5	Elguoredus	3[xi]	2[xii]	2[xiii]														
10	**Arguistil**	1	1	1	1	1	1[xiv]	1	1[xv]									1
11	**Iunabui**				4[xvi]	4[xvii]	2	2	2						1[xviii]	1[xix]			4
12	Conbran	5[xx]	4		5[xxi]	5[xxii]													5
13	Guoruan				6[xxiii]	6[xxiv]													6
14	**Elheharn**							6[xxv]	4[xxvi]						4[xxvii]		3[xxviii]	1[xxix]	7[xxx]
15	Iudnou							5							3	3			8
16	Guordocui		6												5[xxxi]	4	4[xxxii]	3	9[xxxiii]
17	Guernabui										2?[xxxiv]				7[xxxv]	7	5[xxxvi]	4	10
18	Louan[xxxvii]				3[xxxviii]	3[xxxix]													3[xl]
19	**Aidan**										1								
20	Cinuarch																√[xli]		

Table 4.2 St Dyfrig's disciples in the Sequence i charters

4. The authenticity of the witness lists

[i] Teliaus. [ii] Teliaus. [iii] Vbeluiu. [iv] Uuelbiu. [v] Vbeluiuo (dative). [vi] Vueluiu. [vii] Vuelbiu. [viii] Vueluiu. [ix] Ubelbiu. [x] Merchguino (dative). [xi] Elguaret. [xii] Elguoret. [xiii] Elguoret. [xiv] Elgistil. [xv] Elgistus 163a. [xvi] Iunapius. [xvii] Iunapius. [xviii] Iunapeius. [xix] Iunapeius. [xx] Conuran. [xxi] Conuran. [xxii] Conuran. [xxiii] Goruan. [xxiv] Guruan. [xxv] Elharnn. [xxvi] Elheiarun 73b; Elhearn 163a. [xxvii] Helhearn. [xxviii] Elhearn. [xxix] Elhearn. [xxx] Elhearn. [xxxi] Guordoce. [xxxii] Gurdocoe. [xxxiii] Gurdocui. [xxxiv] Guenopoui. [xxxv] Guenuor. [xxxvi] Guernapui. [xxxvii] Evans prints *Louan*, but cf. pp. xli, n., 348 and 359. Cf. *VC* 55. [xxxviii] Iouann. [xxxix] Iouan. [xl] Iouann. [xli] *Cinuarch* is mentioned in 165 but is not a witness.

to *Teiliaus* as *alumnus sancti Dubricii & discipulus*). Disciples 4 (*Merchguinus*), 19 (*Aidan*), and 20 (*Cinuarch*) may come from 76b (note the shared latinate form *Merchguino*), 162b, and 165. The remaining two names, *Elguoredus* and *Conbran*, may be from 166 or 121, perhaps specifically the latter which has spellings closer to those of the list.

It is not wholly clear why some of the clerics named in the charters were selected as disciples and others were omitted (e.g. Cynwarwy in 121, 122, 72b, 73a, and 73b/163a). In many cases, however, the ones who were included were regarded as important persons in connection with Llandaf's claims.[45] This would include the names in bold in Tables 4.1 and 4.2 who were bishops: Bishop Arwystl, Bishop Aeddan, Bishop Ufelfyw, Bishop Inabwy, and [Bishop?] Elhaearn.[46] Bishop Cyfwyre (*Comereg*) is not among the disciples, perhaps because his only charter (165) gives the impression that he lived at a later period; it grants him the church of Cynfarch, who is listed as Dyfrig's twentieth disciple (*Cinuarch*).

---

[45] See J. R. Davies, *The Book of Llandaf*, 81–4.
[46] Abbot of Garway according to 163b and 165, but he could have become bishop afterwards. I assume that the Gwrfan witnessing 72a, 76a, and 77 was not the later bishop of charter 167, but they may have been imagined to be identical.

5

THE INTEGRITY OF THE CHARTERS

In *The Llandaff Charters* Wendy Davies proceeds directly from establishing the relative chronology of the witness lists to a discussion of the vexed question of the absolute chronology of the charters, only one of which bears an A.D. date (charter 218: A.D. 955).[1] Some readers may be unprepared to make this leap until it is demonstrated that the witness lists originally belonged to the transactions to which they are attached in *LL*, since it is often the persons named in the transaction that enable us to suggest an absolute date for the list. It is easy to imagine how an originally independent witness list might wrongly be attached to a statement to the effect that 'X gave Y to Z', in which case one could not use any chronological indication of the date of X or Z to settle the date of the witness list and, hence, of other related lists. It could be countered that in *LL* the names of X and Z often reappear at the head of the lay and clerical witness lists, were it not that the inclusion of the names of X and Z in the witness lists is inconsistent.[2] For instance, *Greciel episcopus* (the recipient) heads the clerical list in 171b and *Mouricus rex* (who consents to the grant) heads the lay list, but both names are absent from the lists in the doublet 74.[3] Again *Berthguinus episcopus* (the recipient) heads the list of 186b but is absent from the list in its doublet 175. More seriously, in 158 the Disposition gives the recipients merely as 'Deo & sanctis Dubricio et Teliauo & Oudoceo et omnibus suis successoribus ecclesiæ Landauiæ' but the witness list is headed by *Episcopus Oudoceus*, almost certainly an interpolation, since the otherwise convincing list resembles those attributed elsewhere to Bishop Berthwyn.[4] Because the occurrence of the name of X or Z in the witness list cannot be taken as proof that a Disposition and a witness list were originally connected, it will be worth assembling some evidence to show that generally the two's relationship was not fluid.

In a collection of 159 charters it is almost inevitable that some will have appropriated witness lists, and indeed we have already seen that the list of charter 77 is under that suspicion.[5] Yet there is no evidence that the compilers of *LL* took a large number of floating lists and attached them to irrelevant transactions. If they had, we

---

[1] Davies, *The Llandaff Charters*, 73–82.
[2] For an extraordinary case of tidy-mindedness cf. Keynes, *The Diplomas*, 234–5, on *Codex Wintoniensis*.
[3] For comparison of 171b and 74 see below, 94, and 171. Charter 74 may have suppressed the names. On names in consent phrases taken from witness lists see below, 109.
[4] Davies, *The Llandaff Charters*, 47 and 102.
[5] See above, 33–5. For an eleventh-century Worcester forgery which replaces the place-name in its exemplar with another see Finberg, *The Early Charters of the West Midlands*, 93, and Tinti, 'The reuse of charters at Worcester', on Birch, *Cartularium Saxonicum*, no. 204 (Sawyer 60). For cartulary scribes abbreviating or changing witness lists see Keynes, *The Diplomas*, 234–5, and for Worcester in particular see Atkins, 'The church of Worcester', 4.

5. The integrity of the charters

would surely detect them in error, reusing the same list for transactions of widely different periods.[6] Moreover, when the same transaction occurs in two doublets in *LL* we find that the same list recurs (apart from minor variations, like those noted in the previous paragraph, and occasional shortening). Even the *LL* lists which are attached to the two charters with doublets in *VC* seem to derive from the same original lists, as we have seen,[7] although they share few names. The Llancarfan charters have the further value that they tell us what sort of witness lists charters of the time of Bishops Euddogwy and Berthwyn ought to have, and what they tell us is consistent with the lists attached to the charters of these bishops in *LL*. The fact that the name of *Episcopus Oudoceus* in the 158 list is so immediately suspicious is testimony to the normal consistency of the lists.

There are some further reasons for thinking that most of the lists rightly belong with the grantors, estates and recipients named in the attached Dispositions.

(1) The relative sequence of charters implied by the witness lists agrees, wherever it can be tested, with the relative chronology of the donors suggested by their patronymics and, in some cases, by references in annals and genealogies preserved in non-Llandaf sources such as Harley MS 3859 (*ca* 1100).[8] We do not often find grandfathers having the same witnesses as their grandsons. Erb of Ergyng in charter 75 is a rare exception that proves the rule.[9]

(2) As John Morris pointed out, certain non-royal witnesses only appear in grants relating to particular areas.[10] This suggests that the association of the grants of the estates in question and their attached witness lists is not factitious, unless one presumes some extraordinarily foresighted forgery.

(3) There is a marked tendency for the size of land grants to diminish between the 'early' and the 'late' charters, as Wendy Davies has noted.[11] This tendency, whatever its precise historical explanation, cannot entirely be attributed to the presence of forged claims to large tracts of land early in *LL* or to any preoccupation with the effects of partible inheritance in the minds of its compilers. Charters are defined as 'early' or 'late' on the basis of their attached witness lists. Since the relationship between the relative chronology of the witness lists and the size of the grants to which they are attached is not random, it seems to follow that the witness lists properly belong, in the main, to transactions concerning the estates specified. There are some more patterns of this sort: estates tend to be described by measures alone in the 'early' grants, in particular by the measure *uncia* which drops out of use in the 'later' charters;[12] the term *ager* seems

---

[6] There are examples of apparently contemporary transactions with similar or identical lists – e.g. 72a and 76a – but this is not in itself a reason for suspicion, being paralleled in 'Chad' 3–4 as well as in Anglo-Saxon charters that are contemporary but preserved in widely separated archives. See Keynes, *The Diplomas*, 37 and 41–2.
[7] Above, 39, and below, 99–103.
[8] See above, 29, and below, ch. 13.
[9] Above, 34.
[10] Morris, Review, 232; Davies, *An Early Welsh Microcosm*, 108–20.
[11] *WHEMA* VIII and IX 11–12; Davies, *The Llandaff Charters*, map facing 97; cf. Charles-Edwards, *Wales and the Britons*, 274–92, and Seaman, 'Landscape'.
[12] Davies, *An Early Welsh Microcosm*, 37 and 57; *WHEMA* VIII; Charles-Edwards, *Wales and the Britons*, 275, 279, 283, and 288. That measures of size are original is supported by the doublets 73b/163a and 175/186a. The *uncia* was typically eastern, and many of the earliest grants are eastern, but not enough to explain away the chronological inference.

'early' while *villa* is 'late';[13] and the term *maenawr* seems to be typical of 'later' charters.[14] Again, the granting of churches and monasteries is a characteristically 'early' phenomenon.[15] Davies notes, too, that the term *podum* is 'early' but the apparently synonymous *monasterium* is typical of 'later' usage.[16]

(4) Although only a few of the recipients of grants are attested outside *LL*, the relative chronology of those who are (namely Euddogwy, Berthwyn, and Tyrchan in the Llancarfan charters, Cyfeilliog in the *Anglo-Saxon Chronicle* s.a. 914, and Herewald in many sources) agrees with the relative chronology of the sequences of witness lists, and the same is true for the chronology of recipients suggested by the list of consecrations and other memoranda in *LL* itself.

(5) Further arguments for the relative chronology of the lists matching that of the recipients can be drawn from the lists themselves. In every Sequence one can trace *future* clerical recipients (bishops) working their way up the clerical hierarchy in 'earlier' lists. In the first Sequence we have no external check that this is not the result of ingenious forgery, hard though that is to credit.[17] For Sequence ii we have evidence from Llancarfan charter *VC* 67 in which the future bishop Tyrchan appears among the *congregatio* of Bishop Berthwyn.[18] Some of the members of the hierarchy in the Sequence iii lists can be identified outside *LL*, such as Herewald (in Joseph's charters) and his son Lifris of Llancarfan (in Herewald's own charters).[19]

To these arguments in favour of accepting *in general* the association of the witness lists with their respective donors, estates, and recipients we may add, as a further check on the substantial integrity of the charters (excepting their interpolated Llandaf connection) some evidence that indicates that the associations of donor, estate, and recipient is original for the most part.

It is hardly surprising that kings of Brycheiniog tend to grant lands in Brycheiniog, kings of Gwent in Gwent, and so on; any forger might have contrived that.[20] What is more significant is the realistic way in which certain non-royal donors, or families of them, make grants in restricted areas.[21] It is also very significant that many of the recipients receive grants from very restricted areas. The bishops of Sequence i, for instance, receive almost entirely from Herefordshire south of the Wye (Anergyng and Ergyng) and northern Gwent, which was no doubt their real sphere of influence before the compilers of *LL* turned them into bishops of Llandaf. As one of the main tenets of *LL* was that all bishops of Llandaf had been bishops of the great diocese claimed by

---

[13] *Ibid.*, 284–6 and 288. This is partly because *ager* is eastern and 'early' charters tend to be eastern.

[14] *Ibid.*, 282–4 and 288–9 (noting some instances in 'early' charters as suspicious). Here again there is a geographical aspect, the *maenawr* being typically western.

[15] Davies, *An Early Welsh Microcosm*, 59; cf. 132 and 134–8.

[16] *Ibid.*, 36–8 and 122. On *podi* glossed 'lo[ci]' see now Falileyev and Russell, 'The dry-point glosses in *Oxoniensis Posterior*', 96 and 99.

[17] For the order of Sequence i charters see ch. 4 above.

[18] This is misunderstood by James, '*The Book of Llandav*: the church and see of Llandav', 16–17. See below, 100 n. 23.

[19] *EA* II 507–8; Pearson, *Fasti*, IX, 17.

[20] But the ninth-century Glywysing kings grant more in Gwent than Glywysing, perhaps because they were overlords there, and perhaps because the bishoprics were based in Gwent.

[21] Davies, *An Early Welsh Microcosm*, 115.

5. The integrity of the charters

Urban, one would have expected any forger left to his own devices to have assigned them all grants from all over the diocese, instead of providing ammunition for sceptics.

It is curious, too, that the compilers of *LL*, if they were forging from scratch, provide no charters for many of the estates claimed by Llandaf and confirmed in Urban's papal bulls,[22] especially those in Glamorgan, which is poorly represented in *LL*, whereas they do give charters for St Dyfrig's native Anergyng (the Herefordshire hundred of Webtree, formerly the northern part of the early kingdom of Ergyng according to *LL*), which was not claimed by Llandaf in the twelfth century and which had been Anglicised by the time of the Domesday survey.[23] Another indication that many of the *LL* charters were 'out of date' is that 'even the large churches [of *LL*] did not all survive to become post-Conquest parish churches'.[24] Furthermore, the relative sizes of the Herefordshire estates cannot be correlated with their hidation in Domesday,[25] and their bounds, when given and traceable, do not correspond to those of the later English parishes.[26] The apparent anachronism of their bounds in the twelfth century seems to put the Herefordshire charters themselves still further back in time than those bounds if, as is generally thought, the bounds appended to the 'early' charters are somewhat later additions.[27] Davies argues that some of the Herefordshire bounds must be as old as the ninth century, 'before the Anglicisation of Ergyng'.[28] This argument applies best to a few Anergyng charters with short and linguistically early bounds, notably Dorstone(?) (*Lann Cerniu*, 72b)[29] and Madley/Eaton Bishop (*Tir Conloc*, 76a),[30] rather than those in Ergyng proper (Archenfield) which was still thoroughly Welsh when *LL* was compiled, and was claimed by Llandaf, having been worked in by Bishop Herewald;[31] indeed it is quite possible that Herewald himself collected some of the Herefordshire bounds in the later eleventh century. Even in Dorstone there were still Welshmen at the time of Domesday Book,[32] and one might argue that the very short description of *Tir Conloc* in 76a

---

[22] See *ibid.*, 25; J. R. Davies, *The Book of Llandaf*, 63 and 73–5; cf. *EA* I 165–6.
[23] Cf. Davies, *An Early Welsh Microcosm*, 26 and n. 1 (the passage cited from *Vita Oudocei* should be compared with charter 192, mapped in Hughes, 'The Celtic Church', 18, map 3, and cf. Coe, 'The place-names', 41); Richards, *Welsh Administrative and Territorial Units*, 6 and 269; Rees, *South Wales and the Border* (map); Charles-Edwards, *Wales and the Britons*, 613 (map). Contrast Glamorgan in the map in Davies, *Wales in the Early Middle Ages*, 144.
[24] *Eadem, An Early Welsh Microcosm*, 25.
[25] *WHEMA* VIII 114.
[26] Information from Dr Lynda Rollason.
[27] It is not impossible, however, in view of the 'Chad' charters and other parallels, that some of the early bounds are contemporary with their charters, as Davies suggests (*An Early Welsh Microcosm*, 29 n. 2, and *The Llandaff Charters*, 143–4). The linguistic evidence is discussed by Coe, 'Dating the boundary clauses'. He establishes a relative chronology for the bounds; the absolute chronology remains obscure, depending chiefly on imponderables over when areas became too Anglicised for Welsh bounds to be collected. On Ergyng and Anergyng bounds see *ibid.*, 40–3.
[28] *The Llandaff Charters*, 144; cf. *An Early Welsh Microcosm*, 29 n. 2.
[29] If not Dorstone, at least nearby; see below, 162 n. 38.
[30] On whether *Tir Conloc* was Madley or the adjacent Eaton Bishop, see below, 93 n. 2.
[31] *DP* III 265; Charles, 'The Welsh, their language and place-names in Archenfield and Oswestry', 87–96; Darby and Terrett, *The Domesday Geography of Midland England*, 75; Charles-Edwards, *Wales and the Britons*, 613.
[32] Darby and Terrett, *The Domesday Geography of Midland England*, 74.

could be indebted to the same late(?) knowledge of the topography of the Madley area as is shown in the *Vita Dubricii*.³³ The best case can be built on the short bounds of *Ystrat Hafren* in 174b and 229b (charters with eighth- and ninth-century witness lists), for this estate (Tidenham in Gloucestershire) was probably lost when King Athelstan (*ob.* 939) fixed the Anglo-Welsh border at the Wye; Tidenham was granted to Bath Abbey in 956 by King Eadwig.³⁴ Even here, however, there may have been an intermittent Welsh presence: Lancaut had been exempted from the line of Offa's Dyke; another part (in Sedbury?) of the Anglo-Saxon manor of Tidenham was rented out to Welsh sailors (*scipwealan*); and in 1049 King Gruffudd [ap Rhydderch] and his allies crossed the Wye, burnt Tidenham, 'and slew all whom they found there'.³⁵ At various periods, therefore, the Welsh were in a position to know the quite basic bounds of Tidenham as given in the *LL* charters. Nevertheless, in such a case it is hard to imagine the circumstances in which the bounds would have been committed to writing in the eleventh or twelfth centuries.

The force of the above arguments is hardly affected by the possibility that in some individual cases the object of the original grants may have been altered in *LL*, deliberately or inadvertently. The doublets 176a and 190b, for example, both concern the *uilla in qua sepulchrum est Gurai*, but whereas 176a rubricates this *Villa Conuc* and gives bounds which show that it was in Glamorgan, 190b rubricates it *Maerun* (Marshfield, Monmouthshire) and adds the latter's bounds (in Hand B).³⁶ Again 175 reads 'dedit Ilias podum quattuor modiorum agri circa se . . . Facta est ista elemosina in aper Mynuy', whereas its doublet 186b reads 'Ilias . . . dedit podium [*space*] in medio aper Myngui cum agro quattuor modiorum circa se', as if confused whether or not Aber Mynwy (Monmouth) were the object of the grant.³⁷ If such confusion was at all common the patterns noted above would not be detectable.

---

³³ *LL* p. 79. Note, however, that Guy, 'The *Life* of St Dyfrig', argues that this material is much older.

³⁴ Sawyer 610, also 1426 and 1555. Cf. *DP* III 188 n. 3 and 267 n. 1. Wormald, *The Making of English Law*, I, 233, 321, and 388, speculated that the *Dunsæte* tract on Anglo-Welsh relations was preserved by an abbot of Bath, *ca* 990. For early features in the Tidenham bounds see Coe, 'Dating the boundary clauses', 41, and note also the use of the word *podum*. Intermittently friendly cross-border relations are indicated in 1005 by Æthelred the Unready's grant of Over in Almondsbury, Gloucestershire (near the Beachley-Aust crossing of the Severn) *ad episcopalem sedem que dicitur Deowiesstow*; see below, ch. 7, 60.

³⁵ Smith, *The Place-Names of Gloucestershire*, III xiv and 265 and IV 32 n. 1; Noble, *Offa's Dyke Reviewed*, 1–4; Sawyer 1555; Robertson, *Anglo-Saxon Charters*, no. CIX; Grundy, *Saxon Charters and Field Names of Gloucestershire*, Part II, 244–5; *The Chronicle of John of Worcester*, II, ed. Darlington and McGurk, 550–3. Cf. Maund, *Ireland, Wales, and England*, 197. On fisheries see Darby and Terrett, *The Domesday Geography of Midland England*, 36–7.

³⁶ See also below, 97 n. 13. This case, incidentally, supports Davies's contention that the bounds attached to pre-tenth-century charters are likely to be additions (*An Early Welsh Microcosm*, 29; cf. Geary, 'Language and memory', 183), and her hint that bounds which are placed before the witness list are likely to be part of the original charter (*The Llandaff Charters*, 144), for while the (Welsh) bounds of 190b follow the witness list, the (Latin) bounds of 176a precede. There is a correlation between the placing of bounds before the witness list (which predominates at the beginning of *LL*) and the use of Latin for the bounds, in particular short bounds. See Coe, 'Dating the boundary clauses', 16–21 and 35–40.

³⁷ See Charles-Edwards, *Wales and the Britons*, 262, Davies, *The Llandaff Charters*, 108, and below, 96.

5. The integrity of the charters

More serious examples of error are provided by the two Breconshire grants by Awst, king of Brycheiniog, to Bishop Euddogwy (146 and 154). It is almost incredible that Euddogwy, a south-eastern bishop, really received these grants in the independent kingdom of Brycheiniog, especially as one of them concerns Llangors which apparently was a Brycheiniog royal centre (see *Anglo-Saxon Chronicle* s.a. 916) and because the witness list common to both charters seems to have been appropriated from some version of 157, another Euddogwy charter.[38] In this case, at least, the association between donor/estate on the one hand and recipient/witness list on the other was fabricated. One derives comfort, nevertheless, from the fact that the forgery is so blatant, in that these Euddogwy grants are placed far away from his normal area and in that the witness lists were clearly appropriated. Apart from a few such exceptions, which are commonest among the Euddogwy charters,[39] there are good reasons, as indicated above, for thinking that *most* of the grants properly belong to their donors and, in particular, to their recipients.[40]

Finally, it may be added that the contemporaneity of donors and recipients seems plausible in most cases, in that the progression of donors from father to son matches the progression of recipients in an acceptably steady way.[41]

For all these reasons we may come round to accepting the conclusion that *LL* is a basically credible collection of grants of named estates by named donors to named recipients, with contemporary witness lists, even though, like most early medieval cartularies, it contains some distortions (notably that all the recipients are made bishops of Llandaf) and some crude forgeries that can be easily detected – as well, possibly, as some very ingenious forgeries that never will be found out.

With some confidence that most witness lists and the transactions in the charters belong together, we may return to the question of their absolute chronology, drawing on the data from both.

---

[38] Davies, *The Llandaff Charters*, 43, 83–4, 98, and 102. The bounds are eleventh-century according to Coe, 'Dating the boundary clauses', 38–40. Did they get to Llandaf via Tremerin of Glasbury (cf. J. R. Davies, *The Book of Llandaff*, 12) and Herewald?

[39] (I except the charters without witness lists here.) For the location of Euddogwy's grants see Hughes, 'The Celtic Church', 9–10 and 17 (map 2).

[40] As further exceptions note the arguments of Maund, *Ireland, Wales, and England*, 196–7 and 205, that King Meurig is interpolated as approving the grant of 263 (he is not in the witness list) and that Bishops Joseph and Herewald are interpolated as the recipients of 264a and 274.

[41] Cf. E. D. Jones, 'The Book of Llandaff', 142. He makes an exception for Euddogwy, 'a colossus taking eight generations in his stride'. In his case, however, a distinction must be made between his charters and his hagiography. See Hughes, 'The Celtic Church', 10 n. 34. The correlation noted by E. D. Jones is not surprising, of course, if one takes the view that the compilers of *LL* merely followed the guidelines of genealogies (but see above, 29–31); thus, for instance, the correlation of Euddogwy and King Awst in the forgeries discussed above is *chronologically* credible (see below, 57). Jones argues that it is suspicious that three of the bishops of Sequence iii (Cerennyr, Nudd, and Cyfeilliog) are shown as contemporaries of the same successive kings, and hence as contemporaries of each other, contrary to the Llandaf doctrine of a single line of bishops. His argument could be turned around to suggest that the correlation of donors and recipients cannot be the result of forgery by the Llandaf compilers, against their own interests. For a different view of these bishops, however, see below, 168–9.

6

THE CHRONOLOGY OF THE CHARTERS

Approximate dates for the charters are most easily given for Sequence iii. Wendy Davies's Sequence iii begins with the charters of Hywel ap Rhys, who flourished in the 880s according to Asser's *Life of King Alfred*, §80, and those of Meurig, the father of Hywel's contemporaries Brochfael and Ffernfael, who are also mentioned by Asser. It ends with the charters of Herewald (*ob.* 1104), which include people mentioned in Domesday Book in their witness lists.[1] Many checks on the chronology on the way have been noted by Davies,[2] and it is not necessary to discuss the chronology of Sequence iii further here.[3]

The absolute chronology of the other two Sequences is much more obscure and the approximate dates for the charters (all ±fifteen years)[4] which Davies uses throughout *The Llandaff Charters* and *An Early Welsh Microcosm* have to be treated with reserve.

She suggests dates for the Sequence i charters ranging between the mid-sixth century and the mid-seventh, working on the basis on an average of thirty years for each male generation.[5] Really, though, we have no firm and unequivocal evidence for *any* date in Sequence i. For reasons which we have already discussed, the appearance of St Dyfrig in the witness lists cannot be used as evidence for a sixth-century date for any of the charters.[6] Some of the donors are said in the charters to have fought against the English, which Davies thinks unlikely before the battle of Dyrham in 577 (cf. *Anglo-Saxon Chronicle* s.a.);[7] yet this argument depends on accepting the value of the Narrations attached to the charters,[8] and in any case provides only a *terminus post quem*.

In seeking an absolute date for the Sequence i charters, then, we are forced to fall back on some inherently unreliable hagiographical evidence which Davies understandably passed over.

---

[1] Sims-Williams, 'The kings'; Davies, *An Early Welsh Microcosm*, 117–18.
[2] Davies, *The Llandaff Charters*, 76–9 and nn. See Sims-Williams, 'The kings', and ch. 13 below.
[3] On dating the eleventh-century charters see also Maund, *Ireland, Wales, and England*, 183–206.
[4] Davies, *The Llandaff Charters*, 74–9 and 146.
[5] *Eadem*, *An Early Welsh Microcosm*, 15, and *The Llandaff Charters*, 75. On this method cf. the remarks of F. Jones (brief) and of M. Miller (elaborate but inconclusive) cited below, 140 n. 125.
[6] See above, 25.
[7] *An Early Welsh Microcosm*, 17.
[8] Cf. below, 112: 'Narrations with some authentic basis perhaps start in the episcopate of Euddogwy ... or that of Berthwyn'.

6. The chronology of the charters

For instance, Rhygyfarch, in his late-eleventh-century *Life of St David*, says that St David cured *Pepiau regem Ercig* of his blindness.[9] This gives a vague late-sixth-century *floruit* for the king Peibio of Ergyng who appears in the earlier Sequence i charters, since the St Davids view, as represented by the (St Davids) *Annales Cambriae*, was that David died in 601 (*recte* 604?).[10] It is difficult to believe, however, that Rhygyfarch had more authority than, at best, oral tradition from some house in Ergyng (perhaps Dewchurch, *Lann Dewi*)[11] or, at worst, and assuming that some version of the *Life* of Dyfrig was already in existence, his own desire to make David rival Dyfrig, who is said to have cured his grandfather King Peibio of the drivelling that gave him his epithet *clauorauc* 'spumosus'.[12] The common factor between Peibio's two afflictions may have been supposed to be leprosy, blindness being a common symptom of it, noted in medieval Insular texts,[13] and *clafhorec*, the Old Cornish cognate of *clauorauc* 'drivelling', being equated with *leprosus* in the Old Cornish Vocabulary in Vespasian A.xiv, a manuscript which also includes a copy of the *Life* of Dyfrig;[14] moreover, a stream called *nant y clauorion* near Tenby in the bounds of charter 125b invites comparison with a *vallis leprosorum* in charter 227a (Splott in Cardiff?) as well as a *finnaun i cleuion* ('spring of the sick people/?lepers') in charter 227b (Dingestow).[15]

---

[9] 'Rhygyfarch's *Life* of St David', ed. and transl. Sharpe and Davies, 120–1, §13.

[10] Charles-Edwards, *Wales and the Britons*, 619–20. Cf. Jacobs, '*Non, Nonna, Nonnita*', 31–2.

[11] Cf. Dickins, '"Dewi Sant" (St David) in early English kalendars and place-names', 207.

[12] *LL* pp. 78–9. A later example, again as an epithet, occurs in the name of Hettwn *Clauyr(y)awc* in *Culhwch and Olwen*, ed. Bromwich and Evans, lines 708–9. I have suggested (apud Sayers, 'Bisclavret', 81 n. 15) that a Breton cognate of *clauorauc* may underlie Old French *bisclavret* (with *-et* for *-ec*), if this means 'salivating (i.e. rabid) wolf' (differently Boyd, 'The ancients' savage obscurity').

[13] Jacobs, 'Drysni geirfaol', 68–70. As its vowel shows, Middle Welsh *clafwr* 'leper' is a distinct formation (< *claf* + *gŵr*), though liable to be confused with the singular of *clauorion*, and also with *clawr* 'board' in the expression *wynepglawr* 'leper' (lit. 'board-face'), as shown by Jacobs, 'Clefyd Abercuog', and 'Drysni geirfaol', eventually giving rise to forms like *clafr/clawr* and *clafri* 'scurf, leprosy'. The form of Peibio's name in JC 10 (*EWGT* 45), *Pibiawn glawrawc*, may show the influence of *clafr* or *clawr*.

[14] *clauorauc* and *clafhorec* are identical compounds of *claf* 'sick' + an obscure element *-or-* + the adjectival suffix Welsh *-awg*/Old Cornish and Breton *-ec*. As Williams, 'claforawg', showed, *clauorauc* must be compared with words in sixteenth-century Welsh dictionaries such as *glovor* 'slavr, slabber' and its plural/collective(?) *gloforion* 'slaferyng', and the related verb *gloforio, goloforio, glouoerio* 'slaver'. These are now *glafoerion* 'saliva', etc. Presumably Old Welsh *clauor-* developed on the one hand to *glofor-* by assimilation and on the other to *glafoer-* by hypercorrection, perhaps under the influence of *poer* 'spittle' and/or *oer* 'cold'. The obscure element *-or-* may, as Williams suggested, be seen in *llinor* 'pustule', *llinorog* 'pustulous', presumably compounds of *llin* 'liquid discharge' and *gôr* 'pus, rheum'. He also mentions *gwlyborawg* 'moist', but this seems secondary to *gwlybyrog* < *gwlybwr* 'liquid' with *-wr* rather than *-or*.

[15] They are compared by Williams, 'claforawg', and Coe, 'The place-names', 861, though of course we cannot be sure that the *clauorion* were lepers like the people in the *Vallis leprosorum*. Possibly *clauorion* is the plural of a different word, **clauawr* 'group of sick people', with the rare collective ending discussed by Nurmio, 'Middle Welsh *-awr*'. Welsh *claf* 'sick' often referred to leprosy, though not to the same extent as Irish *clamh*.

A better chronological indication is provided by the 612 obit for St Dyfrig found in both *LL* and *Annales Cambriae*.[16] The earliest manuscript of the latter, BL Harley 3859, dates from *ca* 1100, earlier than the compilation of *LL*. Needless to say, the date 612 is incompatible with the mid-sixth-century obit surmised by modern scholars on the basis of hagiographies.[17] In particular, the much earlier *Vita Samsonis* associates Dyfrig with Samson, who is believed to be the person of that name who attended a council of Paris *ca* 561.[18] Yet while the 612 obit is unlikely to be historical, it may be that the charter compilers and hagiographers who originally brought Dyfrig into contact with the dynasty of Erb were working on the assumption that he died about 612 after a life-span of not inordinate length. This *floruit* conflicts, of course, with Llandaf's *final* view of Dyfrig's date, as found in *De Primo Statu Landauensis Æcclesiæ*, one of the latest and most factitious strands in *LL*: *De Primo Statu* has Dyfrig being consecrated by Germanus and Lupus, that is in 429![19] While a 429 consecration and a death in 612 might be allowable in hagiography, it is obvious that such a consecration pushes the period of Dyfrig's grandfather Peibio ab Erb so far back into the mists of time as to wreck the chronology of the *LL* charters.[20] No doubt the Germanus connection was a late invention in the course of compiling *LL* by a person who failed to heed considerations of chronology. There may have been three historiographical stages:

(1) the real Dyfrig in the mid-sixth century, if one may trust the *Vita Samsonis* and date Samson himself by the Paris council;
(2) a rather later date for Dyfrig running into the seventh century (*ob*. 612), assumed in 'his' charters and those of his supposed disciples;
(3) a very early *floruit* for him in the fifth century, possibly invented by the final compilers of the material in *LL* in order to prove Dyfrig's churches' priority over the other Welsh churches, including St Davids – a very evident aim in the *De Primo Statu*.[21]

---

[16] *LL* p. 84. See 137. The obit is under suspicion of being an addition to an earlier obit for St Kentigern alone.
[17] See *DP* I, 226 n. 5; Doble, *Lives*, 59 n. 8.
[18] *La vie ancienne de saint Samson*, ed. Flobert; *St Samson of Dol*, ed. Olson, passim; Charles-Edwards, *Wales and the Britons*, 250 n. 29 (medieval writers, including Hand B who included a version of *Vita Samsonis* in *LL*, pp. 6–24, would not have had the Paris council as a point of reference). Cf. Davies, *The Llandaff Charters*, 86 n. 31. Note also that Samson meets Childebert (*ob*. 558) and was ordained priest by Illtud, who was believed to have been ordained priest by St Germanus. Even if this was during Germanus's second mission (*ca* 447?), Iltud would have to have lived to a great age to overlap with Samson.
[19] *LL* p. 69; cf. Jones, 'The Book of Llandaff', 128–31, who while favouring an early date for Dyfrig says that 'it is difficult to reconcile many of the references to him in other saints' lives with such an early dating as is required by the Garmon [Germanus] link' (p. 131).
[20] And that of the Jesus College genealogies (*EWGT* 45).
[21] The Chapter of St Davids' alleged letter to Honorius II (1124–30), quoted by Gerald of Wales, *De Invectionibus* (ed. W. S. Davies, 'The Book of Invectives', 18 and 143; *EA* I 249), accepts that Dyfrig was David's predecessor as archbishop, but of course says nothing about Llandaf. The letter may be a post-Geoffrey of Monmouth fiction: Barrow, *St Davids Episcopal Acta*, 4; cf. J. R. Davies, *The Book of Llandaf*, 65, 110, and 117; Pryce, 'Gerald of Wales and the Welsh past', 29–30 and 42 n. 81.

6. The chronology of the charters

The best deduction from this conflicting material is that the Sequence i charters granted to Dyfrig's alleged disciples were supposed to postdate his death in 612.

Possibly the inventor of the 612 obit was led to bring Dyfrig into the seventh century by consideration of the charters 'to' him by persons such as Peibio of Ergyng *whom he may have known to be seventh-century figures*. Similar considerations may have inspired the choice of Nowy of Dyfed as the donor for the forged charter 77 granting estates in Dyfed to Dyfrig. According to the Harley genealogies Nowy was the great-great-great-great-grandfather of Maredudd of Dyfed, who died in 796 (*Annales Cambriae*), so Nowy's obit may have been imagined to be *ca* 616 (using the thirty-year rule of thumb), which would indeed make him a contemporary of a saint who died in 612.[22] Here again, then, we have an indication that the Sequence i charters to Dyfrig's 'disciples' may start in the early seventh century.

The earliest credible charters of Sequence i, as argued in Chapter 4 above, are grants by Iddon ab Ynyr Gwent, some of them ostensibly in favour of St Teilo. There is no clear indication when Teilo was supposed to have flourished. The view in the *LL Vitae* of Dyfrig, Teilo, and Euddogwy is that the three saints belonged to three successive but overlapping generations, with Teilo being a contemporary of St David and St Samson, and Teilo and Euddogwy both living at the time of the Yellow Plague in which Maelgwn Gwynedd died.[23] This is inconsistent with *Annales Cambriae*, where David's death is in 601 and Maelgwn's is in 547.[24] The chronological incompetence of the final compilers of *LL* is further illustrated by the list of contemporaries of Teilo on p. 118: they include *both* Aergol Lawhir, great-great-great-grandfather of Nowy of Dyfed in the genealogies,[25] *and* Cadwgon *Tredicil* who is Nowy's great-grandson in the genealogies.[26] Teilo is also associated with Aergol in charters 125b–127b, and if versions of these charters were in existence earlier than the compilation of *LL*, as is generally agreed, they may have been one reason why Dyfrig, Teilo's teacher, had to be antedated to the fifth century. In the *LL Vita Oudocei* (*LL* pp. 130 and 133) the saint's father is a contemporary of Aergol while the saint himself is a contemporary of Cadwgon, who restored him lands given to Llandaf in the time of Nowy! At least this confusion makes it is clear that the comparatively consistent chronology of the majority of the charters cannot be attributed to the final compilers of *LL*. Guy suggests that the royal donors of the Teilo charters were lifted randomly from the Dyfed royal pedigrees, and notes that Llandaf wanted to show that the diocese of St Davids was under Llandaf until the time of St Euddogwy.[27]

While Teilo's chronology is quite obscure, a better clue to the date of the Sequence i charters 'to' the saint may be found by considering the date of the grantor, Iddon ab Ynyr Gwent. The Middle Welsh *Life of St Beuno*, which is probably a translation of an early-twelfth-century Latin *Vita* written at Clynnog by someone who had access

---

[22] *EWGT* 9–10 (HG 2).
[23] *LL* pp. 107 and 131.
[24] 'The *Annales Cambriae* and Old-Welsh genealogies', ed. Phillimore, 155–6. Note also the reference to this plague in *LL* charter 144. The Chapter of St Davids also associated Samson with it in their alleged letters to Honorius II and Eugenius III quoted by Gerald of Wales in his *De Invectionibus* (*EA* 1 249 and 262) — on the former letter see above, n. 21.
[25] *EWGT* 10 (HG 2).
[26] Assuming that he is the same as as Cadwgon *Trydelig* of *EWGT* 106 and 228 (ABT 18a [G, H₂]). See Guy, 'The *Life* of St Dyfrig', 10 n. 31.
[27] *Ibid.*, 9–12.

to the early charters of that house,[28] makes Cadwallon ap Cadfan of Gwynedd, who was killed in 634 (Bede), a contemporary of Iddon ab Ynyr Gwent.[29]

If Iddon's charters (121, 122, 123, and 166) are the earliest charters of Sequence i and the earliest credible charters of *LL*,[30] it is likely that Sequence i begins in the seventh century, perhaps *ca* 625. To judge by the progression of witnesses it spreads over about three generations.

The best evidence we have, then, suggests that the Sequence i charters should all be placed in the seventh century, about fifty years or more after the dates suggested by Wendy Davies.[31] References to the 'seventh-century Church' (as in Chapter 14 below) make this assumption.

The links which have been suggested between Sequence i and Sequence ii are all uncertain and if they were certain they would not be very helpful in dating Sequence i, since Sequence ii itself cannot be dated securely, as we shall see. The statement in the genealogies attached to the *Vita Cadoci* in Cotton Vespasian A.xiv and in later sources that Erb of Ergyng (who appears in Sequence i) was the great-grandfather

---

[28] *Buchedd Beuno*, ed. Sims-Williams.

[29] Bartrum, *EWGT*, 143, supposes that the Iddon ab Ynyr Gwent who was a contemporary of Teilo was a different and earlier Iddon ab Ynyr Gwent from Beuno's contemporary; this harmonises with his early dating of the Dyfrig and Teilo charters in *LL*. (See also Bartrum, *Welsh Genealogies*, I, charts [13] and [18], and *A Welsh Classical Dictionary*, 379 and 643). Yet the evidence for an earlier Ynyr Gwent is tenuous: (a) in the *Vita S. Tathei*, §6 (*VSB* 274), there is a Caradog ab Ynyr as king of Gwent in the time of St Tatheus (date nebulous) and Bartrum equates him with the *Caradawc vreichvras* of JC 9, who, on one interpretation of the pedigree, may be the father of the Meurig ab Enynny of Gwynllŵg who in *VC* 25 and JC 5 marries Dyfwn, daughter of Glywys and aunt of Cadog, Glywys's grandson (*EWGT* 138–9 and *Welsh Genealogies*, I, chart [18]). This gives us an early-fifth-century Ynyr Gwent if we accept the statement in *VC* 45 and JC 4 that Glywys was the great-great-grandson of the emperor Maximus (*ob*. 388). Yet, according to *VC* 46 and JC 5 Meurig ab Enynny was the grandson of Cynfarch, father of Urien Rheged who flourished in the later sixth century. Thus Meurig had one grandfather (Ynyr) in the early fifth century and the other (Cynfarch) in the mid-sixth! It seems that the genealogists were at sea. If we trust the Urien point of reference rather than the Maximus one we arrive at a mid-sixth-century Ynyr whose son Iddon could easily be contemporary with Cadwallon of Gwynedd (*ob*. 634). It must be emphasised, though, that all the above depends on a shaky identification of Caradog ab Ynyr Gwent with JC 9's *Caradawc vreichvras*. See also *DP* III 285, *TYP*[4] 404, Bartrum, *A Welsh Classical Dictionary*, 100, and Haycock, *Legendary Poems from the Book of Taliesin*, 379–81. (b) In a late-fifteenth-century manuscript of *Bonedd y Saint* §§44–45 Ynyr Gwent marries Madrun daughter of Gwrthefyr Fendigaid (Vortimer). As the latter was the son of Gwrtheyrn (Vortigern), who was associated with the *Adventus Saxonum*, and Severa daughter of Maximus, we again get a fifth-century Ynyr (see also Anscombe, 'Some Old-Welsh pedigrees', 81). Yet Bartrum himself shows how the marriage of Ynyr and Madrun grew out of a mistaken fusion of §§44 and 45 and also that the compiler himself made no distinction between an early and a late Ynyr (*EWGT* 143–4). James, 'The *Book of Llan Dav* and Bishop Oudoceus', 27, associates Ynyr Gwent with the plague of 547, but I can find no evidence for this idea, which seems to come from *LBS* IV, 364 (cf. James, 'Chronology', 126).

[30] See above, ch. 4. These charters are dated *ca* 600 and *ca* 595 by Davies, *The Llandaff Charters*, 95 and 106.

[31] She dates her earliest arguably authentic charters (72a and 76a) *ca* 572: *ibid.*, 35, 92, and 94.

6. The chronology of the charters

of Tewdrig[32] (the progenitor of the principal kings of Glywysing in Sequence ii) is hardly reliable, for the earlier text of the relevant genealogy in Harley 3859 ventures back no further than Tewdrig. Nor is it certain that the *Gurcant* son of *Cinuin* son of *Peipiau* son of *Erb* of Sequence i (163b–164) is the same person as the *Gurcantus magnus*, described in an early Sequence ii charter (140) as the father-in-law of Meurig ap Tewdrig.[33] Neither do we know if *Athruis rex Guenti regionis* in a late charter of Sequence i (165), one granting Ergyng estates *pro anima patris sui Mourici*, is really the same as the (apparently Glywysing) *Athruis filius Mourici, Gurcanti magni nepos* (144), who appears in the early charters of Sequence ii in his father's lifetime.[34] This is not to assert that there was no chronological overlap between Sequence i and Sequence ii – in view of the differing geographical areas covered by the charters of the two Sequences it would be possible for them to overlap in time without sharing many or any of the same personal names – but we do not know for certain one way or the other.

The Sequence ii charters comprise those of the apparently successive[35] bishops Euddogwy, Berthwyn, Tyrchan, and Cadwared. These bishops may have had long episcopates, to judge by the occurrence of four generations of two families in the whole span of lists,[36] by the turnover of abbots of Llancarfan, Llantwit, and Llandough in the charters of Euddogwy and Berthwyn, and, on my reading of the genealogies (Chapter 3, Table 3.1, Fig. 1 above), by the passage of five generations of the main line of the Glywysing dynasty (or six, according to the conventional reading, *ibid.*, Fig. 2).[37] One may suppose that Sequence ii may cover up to a century. Davies suggests that it may cover as much as 135 years, but there seems to be a fallacy in her argument. She states that the four generations of one family – Gwyddien (ii.1–17 cf. *VC* 68), Elffin (ii.25–41), *Erbic* (ii.[27]–48), and Cors (ii.62) – 'may be assumed to cover about a hundred and twenty years between them'.[38] Leaving aside the question of the reliability of the thirty-year generation average, this statement seems to take it for granted that the *charters* of Gwyddien and Cors at either end extend over their full allotment of thirty years. In reality charters containing the names of a man and his great-grandfather can span as little as fifty years or more than two hundred. The very rough figure of a century for Sequence ii preferred above is inspired by the consideration that while we have only four episcopates (the first and fourth not necessarily completely covered by the archive) we have three examples

---

[32] *VC* 46; JC 9. Cf. HG 28 and Bartrum, *A Welsh Classical Dictionary*, 610–11.

[33] Cf. *LL* p. 132. See below, 149 n. 170.

[34] Davies, *The Llandaff Charters*, 38, 40, 75 and 105–6; cf. above 32 n. 2, and below, 146 and n. 157. It seems to have been possible to make a grant for somebody else's soul during their lifetime; cf. *VC* 62, and in general see Davies, *Acts of Giving*, 116, and 'When gift is sale', 231.

[35] Judging by the witness lists.

[36] Davies, *The Llandaff Charters*, 58, and *An Early Welsh Microcosm*, 43, 115, and 118–19.

[37] In both cases I do not count Tewdrig in charter 141 as part of Sequence ii since he is only named in this suspicious charter.

[38] Davies, *The Llandaff Charters*, 58. Another four-generation family cited there is *Gurceniu* (ii.5–15 cf. *VC* 68), *Conuil* (ii.22–(27)), *Conuc* (ii.41–45), and *Conuelin* (ii.52–58 cf. *VC* 66); cf. *eadem*, *An Early Welsh Microcosm*, 43. Note that charter 204b may be misplaced as ii.27 (see above, 33), in which case *Erbic*'s charters begin at ii.46, and *Conuil* may have flourished later than ii.27.

of four or five non-episcopal generations witnessing, which are not likely all to have been compressed into a mere sixty or seventy years.

Wendy Davies assigns the Sequence ii charters approximate absolute dates ranging from *ca* 650 (144) to *ca* 785 (208), at either end of the Sequence. The fixed point from which these dates are worked out, by counting back generations using the thirty-year rule and assuming that we have charters from at least thirty years of every king's reign on average, is the 775 obit in the *Annales Cambriae* for Ffernfael ab Ithel, whom she identifies with the person of this name and patronymic who appears in the Harley 3859 genealogies and in *LL* charters dating from those of Berthwyn to the early ones of Cadwared (ii.28–56). There are two problems, however. First, although Ffernfael is in the fourth generation after Meurig (the first king of Sequence ii) according to her reading of the genealogies, yet according to the unemended evidence of the manuscripts he is only in the third generation (cf. above Chapter 3, Table 3.1, Fig. 1). Secondly, although the identification of the dynast in *LL* and the genealogies with the person mentioned in the *Annales* is probable and generally accepted without question,[39] it is hardly certain, for both name and patronymic were common ones and may have been 'leading names' in Glywysing. Moreover, the *Annales* entry gives no hint of Ffernfael's status or origin: *Fernmail filius Iudhail moritur*. It is worth repeating what Bartrum has said about the difficulty of equating people mentioned in later Welsh genealogies with persons mentioned in the late medieval extents and surveys: 'identification of persons cannot always be certain unless the survey gives *at least two generations of ancestors*, and even then there is danger of mis-identification'.[40]

Wendy Davies's other guide to the date of Sequence ii is *LL* 192, a memorandum (without witness list) mentioning Æthelbald [of Mercia] (716[*sic. leg.*]–757).[41] From this circumstantial and plausible document we learn of battles between English and Welsh, especially on the Wye near Hereford, *in tempore [e]telpaldi & ithaili regum britanniæ*, and, *post tempus*, the restoration to Bishop Berthwyn of the churches which he had lost in the area, by the same King Ithel, who is clearly the Ithel ap Morgan whose reign (ii.26–45) corresponds closely to Berthwyn's episcopate in *LL*. (He was the father of its Ffernfael ab Ithel, discussed above.) The synchronism of Æthelbald and Ithel is valuable, but not very useful for close dating, since Æthelbald reigned for forty years. Wendy Davies refers to his campaign against the Britons mentioned in the *Anglo-Saxon Chronicle* s.a. 743,[42] but there may have been others. Bartrum preferred to associate Ithel's restoration of land with the British victories mentioned in the *Annales Cambriae* s.a. 722, and another possibility is their Battle of Hereford s.a. 760, which may have been a British victory for all we know.[43] As we cannot tell whether Ithel's reign overlapped with the beginning, middle, or end of Æthelbald's, all we can say is that the Sequence ii charters were probably centred somewhere in the eighth century. A *floruit* for Ithel ap Morgan in the first half or middle of the eighth century would, of course, fit in well with the identification of his son Ffernfael with the person whose obit is given by the *Annales* s.a. 775.

---

[39] See below, 137 n. 115.
[40] Bartrum, 'Notes', 69 (my italics). Elsewhere, in fact, Bartrum rejected the equation of the *Annales*' Ffernfael with the one mentioned in the genealogies, in pursuit of a different, but erroneous, chronology. See below, 137 n. 115.
[41] Davies, *The Llandaff Charters*, 76. See below, 153.
[42] Davies, *The Llandaff Charters*, 80, 86 n. 37, and 113.
[43] Bartrum, 'Some studies', 279; *DP* III 271–2; Lloyd, *A History*, I, 197.

6. The chronology of the charters

There are two other points to be considered in dating Sequence ii. The first is the inclusion of charters of Awst of Brycheiniog among the grants received by the Sequence's first bishop, Euddogwy (146 and 154). Although these charters are forged, as we have seen,[44] they may indicate when Euddogwy was believed to have flourished, before the Llandaf writers transformed him into a sixth-century saint.[45] According to charter 167, Awst's son, Elwystl, was slain by his contemporary Tewdwr ap Rhain (joint ruler of Brycheiniog).[46] The genealogies in Oxford, Jesus College MS 20, make Tewdwr's father the same person as the Rhain ap Cadwgon who appears in the Dyfed royal pedigree in the Harley 3859 and later collections.[47] If this is true – and there is no reason why it should not be – Awst must have been a contemporary of Rhain of Dyfed. Rhain's *floruit* can be placed in *about* the first half of the eighth century, for Maredudd of Dyfed who died in 796 (*Annales Cambriae*) was Rhain ap Cadwgon's grandson.[48] The forger of 146 and 154 may, therefore, have regarded Euddogwy as an early-eighth-century bishop. Indeed he may even have had some authority for making Euddogwy and Awst contemporaries.

The second point to be considered concerns the cross at Llantwit mentioned already[49] as possibly containing the names of Ithel (Iudhael) ap Morgan, who disappears from Sequence ii after ii.45, and Abbot Samson of Llantwit, who appears towards the end of Sequence ii (ii.58–59), and in the Llancarfan charter *VC* 55:

IN NOMINE Dei SUMMI INCIPIT CRUX SALUATORIS QUAE PREPARAUIT SAMSONI APATI PRO ANIMA SUA ET PRO ANIMA IUTHAHELO REX ET ARTMALI ET TECANI.[50]

---

[44] See above, 49.

[45] On the origin of St Euddogwy see Doble, *Lives*, 207–29; Brooke, *The Church*, 47–8; and 26–7 above. Note that Geoffrey of Monmouth knows nothing of him, unlike Dyfrig and Teilo.

[46] Bartrum, *A Welsh Classical Dictionary*, 34, unnecessarily distinguished between Awst the contemporary of Euddogwy and Awst father of Elwystl.

[47] JC 8 and HG 2 in *EWGT*. See ch. 13, Table 13.5. Lloyd, *A History*, I, 271 n. 239 thought that the Dyfed connection in JC 8 was due to confusion, but Bartrum, 'Noë, king of Powys', shows that it is possibly correct and is followed in this by Dumville, 'Late-seventh- or eighth-century evidence', 48–51.

[48] HG 2. Cf. Davies, *The Llandaff Charters*, 76, 79, and 87 n. 41, who assigns Awst and Tewdwr dates *ca* 720 and *ca* 750, and Bartrum, *Welsh Genealogies*, I, chart [20]. (There is no early evidence that Rhain and Awst were brothers, as shown with a query on Bartrum's chart and, without a query, in his 'Noë, king of Powys', 57; the idea starts with Hugh Thomas (1673–1720) according to Bartrum, *A Welsh Classical Dictionary*, 34.) Lloyd, *A History*, I, 271, notes that charter 167 has Tewdwr ap Rhain while Asser gives us Elisedd ap Tewdwr *ca* 880; but it is impossible connect them (and perhaps Lloyd does not mean us to), for the identity of the two Tewdwr's is quite uncertain — JC 8 gives *Elisse m. Thewdwr m. Gruffud* (see Bartrum, *Welsh Genealogies*, I, chart [23]). Anscombe, 'Some Old-Welsh pedigrees', 82, supposes that the Tewdwr ap Rhain of charter 167 was a son of Rhain ap Brychan, but there is no evidence for such a son.

[49] See above, 39.

[50] Redknap and Lewis, *A Corpus*, I, 377–82, no. G65. 'In the name of God the Most High begins the Cross of the Saviour that Abbot Samson prepared for his soul, and the soul of King Iuthahel [Ithel], and of Artma(i)l [Arthfael] and Tecan [Irish Tecán?].' See below, 152 and 154.

Although this stone has been dated between the ninth and eleventh centuries, the current dating is 'probably late eighth century'.[51] This dating is in favour of bringing the date of the last charters of Sequence ii down to the end of the eighth century or into the ninth.

It must be concluded that the absolute chronology of the *LL* charters cannot be fixed at all closely. In criticising Wendy Davies's dates for the charters, it is only fair to point out that they are a great advance on earlier attempts to date the charters, which could be out by a century or more.[52] Her approximate dates for the Sequence iii charters (±fifteen years), from the mid-ninth century to the second half of the eleventh, are fairly secure, and it is only in Sequence i and ii that her dates seem unnecessarily early. As we have seen, Sequence i seems to cover about three generations, and Sequence ii seems to cover four or five. For convenience the Sequence i charters may be described as 'seventh-century' and the Sequence ii charters as 'eighth-century'; but these dates are approximations only. If the absence of exact dates makes it impossible to write certain kinds of history using *LL*, so it must be.

---

[51] Redknap and Lewis, *A Corpus*, I, 381–2.
[52] Bartrum, 'Some studies'; James, 'Chronology'; Finberg, *Early Charters of the West Midlands*, passim.

7

THE STATUS OF THE DONORS AND RECIPIENTS OF THE CHARTERS

If it is accepted that *LL* contains at least some records of authentic transactions with authentic witness lists, stretching from the seventh to the eleventh century, its historical value needs no underlining. Yet historians will want to know whether they can trust the main details of the charters in the admittedly doctored form in which they see them. In particular, were the donors and recipients really of the royal/non-royal and episcopal statuses assigned to them?

Wherever *LL* can be tested, it seems to be reliable on the status of the persons mentioned. Several of the *LL* donors who are styled *reges* are so styled outside *LL*, for instance Peibio (*Peipiau*) of Sequence i in Rhygyfarch's *Life of St David*, §13, and two of the kings in Sequence iii in Asser's *Life of King Alfred*, §80 ('Houel filius Ris, rex Gleguising' and 'Brochmail fili[us] Mouric, re[x] Guent').[1] The compilers may sometimes have added the title *rex* out of their own knowledge, of course; but they have not been detected in any errors. 73b is a grant by *duo filii Pepiav Cinuin uidelicet & Guidci*, witnessed by *Guoidci & Cinuin*, while its doublet 163a calls them *Cinvin rex & Guidci frater suus*, possibly having added the title *rex*. But the title *rex* is supported by charter 162b (which possibly influenced the copyist of 163a) and the royal status is inherently plausible (*Gurcant rex Ercicg* in 163b is *filius Cinuin*). Strikingly there are no other examples of doublets in which a donor is royal in one version but not explicitly so in the other; thus the compilers seem to have been careful on this point.

A further point in favour of the compilers is the pattern that emerges by which the arguably authentic early grants are grants by kings.[2] It is unlikely that this pattern, which must surely have some historical basis, was invented by the compilers, who wrongly placed a non-royal Sequence iii grant (74/171b = iii.5–6) in the Sequence i period,[3] and further obscured the pattern by dividing up the Sequence i charters in *LL*; thus the royal grants 160–166 (Sequence i) were placed after the Sequence ii charters of Bishop Euddogwy, which include two apparently non-royal grants (151a and 159b).[4]

---

[1] 'Rhygyfarch's *Life*', ed. Sharpe and Davies, 120; Dumville, 'The "six" sons of Rhodri Mawr', 5 and n. 6.

[2] See below, 105. Exceptions are 76b, by which a layman *Guorduc* grants *Porth Tulon* along with his daughter, the eponymous *Dulon*, and two hagiographical charters by which laymen make grants to St Teilo (127a and 127b); these three are regarded as 'very dubious charters' by Davies, *An Early Welsh Microcosm*, 50 n. 2.

[3] For the witnesses see *eadem*, *The Llandaff Charters*, 59.

[4] If 76b is excluded (see n. 2 above) and the doublet 73b/163a is counted as a single grant, there are 17 royal grants in Sequence i, but this total should be reduced to 16 if King

The problem of whether the recipients of the *LL* grants were really abbots who have been transformed into bishops by Llandaf is to some extent a peculiarly modern problem, arising from modern preoccupation with the allegedly monastic (*sciat* non-episcopal) character of the 'Celtic Church'.[5] Wendy Davies has shown that there is plenty of evidence outside *LL* for the existence of bishops in southeast Wales from Dyfrig's day onwards.[6] There are three items to add. The first is the ninth-century inscription at Llanddeti (near Llangynidr), mentioning GUADAN SACERDOS, *if* this title means 'bishop', as Nash-Williams speculated, rather than 'priest'.[7] Secondly, there is the list of bishops of Glasbury on the Wye (Radnorshire), which extends through thirteen names, ending with Tremerin, who died in 1055 (*Anglo-Saxon Chronicle*).[8] Lastly, and more relevant to the area covered by *LL*, there is a grant by Æthelred the Unready in 1005 of Over in Almondsbury, Gloucestershire – conveniently placed for the Beachley-Aust crossing of the Severn – *ad episcopalem sedem que dicitur Deowiesstow*.[9] *Deowiesstow* had been assumed to be St Davids, until Dorothy Whitelock argued that the reference in Æthelred's charter is more likely to be to the less distant Dewstow in Caldicot, Monmouthshire (*Dewystowe* in 1219–75).[10] Dewstow lies in the midst of a large number of estates which were confirmed to Llandaf by the twelfth-century papal Bulls.[11] To judge solely by the distribution

---

Nowy's charter (77) is dismissed as a forgery. Davies places the start of non-royal grants in the episcopate of Berthwyn (*An Early Welsh Microcosm*, 50 and n. 2, 65, and 161), regarding the donors of 151a and 159b in the previous episcopate as royal (cf. *ibid.*, 119, and *The Llandaff Charters*, 100). In the case of 151a (ii.9) this depends on taking *Rex solus. Guidgen cum suis* in the witness list to mean that the donor, *Guidgen* son of *Brochmail*, is the *rex*, which is possible (*pace* Doble, *Lives*, 76) – *rex solus* would mean 'sole king/monarch' or 'the king himself', referring to *Guidgen*, not 'the [unnamed] king, witnessing alone [without named retinue]'; cf. charter 77: 'De laicis Noe solus testis est cum innumerabili copia hominum'. For *solus* 'himself' as in *ipse solus*, see Charles-Edwards, *Wales and the Britons*, 625 (cf. *solus rex* 'the king himself' in charter 165 and *super ipsum solum* in *VC* 68). Cf. below, 150 n. 175. In the case of the other grant, 159b (ii.10), Davies's view involves identifying its donor *Brochmail filius Guidgentiuai* with the *Brocuail rex* of 205, which belongs in the episcopate of Tyrchan (ii.45–55), much later in Sequence ii than ii.24, where Davies places it (see above, 33, and cf. *WHEMA* IX 14). Be this as it may, note that we already have non-royal grants in *VC* 64 and 65, which belong to the period immediately before Sequence ii (see above, 41). Non-royal grants are the norm in the 'Chad' charters.

[5] Cf. Hughes, 'The Celtic Church'.
[6] *An Early Welsh Microcosm*, 146–9.
[7] Nash-Williams, *The Early Christian Monuments of Wales*, no. 46 and p. 14. Redknap and Lewis, *A Corpus*, I, 175, no. B10, translate 'priest'. On *sacerdos* cf. Davies, *An Early Welsh Microcosm*, 126 n. 3 (on the passage in the *Vita Samsonis* which she mentions at 127 n. 2 see Chadwick, 'The evidence of dedications', 173–5); *eadem*, *Wales in the Early Middle Ages*, 158; Pryce, *Native Law and the Church*, 190; J. R. Davies, 'The archbishopric', 297; Charles-Edwards, *Wales and the Britons*, 587–91 and 594; and Woolf, Review, 161–2. *Episcopus*, *summus sacerdos*, and *sacerdos* contrast in *LL* 162a.
[8] See above, 20.
[9] Sawyer 913; Ker, 'Hemming's Cartulary', 73; Finberg, *Early Charters of the West Midlands*, 66.
[10] Whitelock, *English Historical Documents*, 352; Dickins, '"Dewi Sant" (St David) in early English kalendars and place-names', 209 n. 1. For translation and discussion see Charles-Edwards, *Wales and the Britons*, 254–5 and 591–2.
[11] Rees, *South Wales and the Border in the Fourteenth Century*, SE Sheet. Dewstow was

7. Donors and recipients of the charters

of their grants, some of the bishops in *LL* could have had it as an *episcopalis sedes*; naturally any reference to St Dewi in their charters would get removed by the compilers of *LL*, who were working in the context of a struggle against St Davids. Tempting though Whitelock's suggestion is, however, one cannot rule out that the charter does refer to St Davids, whose bishops might have welcomed a stopping place on the route to Canterbury. Tramerin, the contemporary bishop of St Davids, had been consecrated by Ælfric, archbishop of Canterbury (*ob.* 16 November 1005).[12]

There is evidence outside *LL* and the consecration lists that some of the Sequence iii recipients were bishops (Cyfeilliog and Herewald), and Euddogwy and Berthwyn of Sequence ii are styled *episcopus* in the Llancarfan charters' witness lists (*VC* 65 and 67). The only indication that any of the *LL* bishops may really have been abbots is in a tract dated 'July 19, 1729' on 'The Antiquities of Lantwit Major, Com. Glamorgan', ascribed to its vicar, the Revd David Nichols, and printed by David Williams in his *History of Monmouthshire* (1796) from an alleged transcript received from Edward Williams (the forger 'Iolo Morganwg'). I correct some obvious misprints within square brackets:

> There is a loose parchment at Landaff very decayed and rent; some parts of it rotten, and others worm eaten, very little of it can be read; but in it appear these names of the Abbots of Lantwit, Iltutus, Piro, Ifanus [= *Isanus*],[13] Cennit,[14] Samson,[15] Guorthauer, Congers [= *Congen*],[16] Elbod, Tomre,[17] Gwrhaval, Nudh, Elifet [= *Elised*],[18] Segin, Camelauc, Bletri, and many more that cannot be read

---

granted to Llanthony Priory after 1165: Crouch, *Llandaff Episcopal Acta*, 20

[12] See above, 24. Unless the dates are wildly wrong, this bishop cannot be the identically named Tremerin who died in 1055 (see above, 20), *pace* Finberg, *Early Charters of the West Midlands*, 66, and Grosjean, 'Saints anglo-saxons', 166.

[13] In two of Iolo's three manuscripts that contain the list the reading is ambiguous (NLW 13153A p. 167 and 13116B p. 164), but 13114B p. 122 definitely reads *Isanus*. The latter and *Piro* appear in the Continental *Lives* of St Samson (e.g. *La vie ancienne de saint Samson*, ed. Flobert). *Piro* is retained in the abridged *Vita Samsonis* in *LL* pp. 12 and 15, but not *Isanus* (see Doble, *Lives*, 89, 92, and 123). He could have been known in the eighteenth century through Mabillon, *Acta Ordinis Sancti Benedicti*, I, 168 (cited *DP* II 307 n. 1), but this has *Isannus*. The spelling *Isanus* is found in the abridgement (cf. Flobert, *La vie ancienne de saint Samson*, 43) in Vincent of Beauvais's *Speculum Historiale* (1624), 851, Book XXI, cap. 105. The existence of this edition is mentioned in two works known to Iolo: Ussher, *Britannicarum Ecclesiarum Antiquitates*, 277, and Stillingfleet, *Origines Britannicae*, 204. *Isanus* is not mentioned in the notes on Samson and Illtud which Iolo copied from Robert Vaughan in NLW 13116B (Llanover C.29), pp. 254–5. Leland mentioned him in his *Commentarii* (ed. Hall, I, 69), but the name was misprinted *Isamus*.

[14] St Cenydd figured prominently in Iolo's pseudo-history. See *DP* I 233 n. 2; *LBS* II 111–12; *The Correspondence of Iolo Morganwg*, ed. Jenkins et al., II, 123 n. 3; Bartrum, *A Welsh Classical Dictionary*, 121. He does not appear in *LL*, although *Lann Cinith* in Gower is mentioned there (p. 279), with *langynydd* in the margin (p. 343).

[15] St Samson becomes abbot of Llantwit in *LL* pp. 15–16. See further Bartrum, *A Welsh Classical Dictionary*, 575–9.

[16] Cf. *Congen* in Iolo's three manuscripts that contain the list (n. 13 above).

[17] Cf. *Fomre* in *LL*. In Iolo's hand *F* and *T* are often indistinguishable, but he definitely has *T*- in NLW MS 13158A (Llanover C.71), p. 250.

[18] *Elised* in Iolo's three manuscripts that contain the list. In two of these Iolo inserts *Elifled*, which looks like a misreading of *Elised*, as an extra name before Gurhavel (13153A p. 167

now. So old and decayed is this parchment which I take to be some decree of a Pope; or it may be some charter of a King to the Abbot and church of Lantwit ...[19]

As noted in the tract, many of these names appear in the *LL* charters as abbots of Llantwit,[20] and 'some of these names, or what are much alike, are among the Bishops of Landaff in those days' – the latter names are *Nudh*, *Camelauc*, and *Bletri*, who appear in the same (chronological) order in *LL* (Sequence iii.8–23, 24–32, 44–46). The reasonable explanation suggested in the tract is that they were abbots of Llantwit who were raised to episcopal rank. One may compare the case of Bishop Cyfwyre in Sequence i, who witnesses charters of Bishop Inabwy (163b–164) as abbot of Moccas, but becomes bishop himself in charter 165, from which the name of Inabwy is absent, no doubt through death or retirement.[21] In the case of *Camelauc* we have evidence in the *Anglo-Saxon Chronicle* s.a. 914 that 'Cameleac' was a *biscop*; but it must also be noted that his grants in *LL* are (like those of *Nudh* and *Bletri*) centred on Gwent, not on Llantwit.[22]

---

and 13114B p. 122). He also inserts this name, along with *Camelauc*, *Nudh*, and *Bledri/ Bletri* (at a point corresponding to page 50 of Williams, *The History of Monmouthshire*, Appendix XIX) in NLW MS 13116B p. 159 and MS 13114B (Llanover C.27), p. 118. See *The Correspondence of Iolo Morganwg*, ed. Jenkins et al., II, 127, where a different explanation of *Elifled* is suggested in n. 3. *Elised* appears before *Gurhavel* (and not between *Nudd* and *Sigin*) on p. 615 of Dublin, Royal Irish Academy, MS 12.N.4 (on which see below).

[19] Williams, *The History of Monmouthshire*, separately paginated Appendix XIX, p. 52. The date is given at p. 45; '1792' on p. 53 must be a misprint.

[20] *Gurhaual* (145, 176a, 176b, 183b, 204b, 205), *Congen* (152, 155), *Gurthauar/Guorhauarn* (156, 190b), *Eluod* (179c), *Fomre* (180a), *Elised* (212, 214, 228, 229b, 230a). The occurrence of the spelling *Elbod*, where *LL* has *u*, may suggest that *LL* was not the direct source (see below). *Elvod* also appears (at a point corresponding to page 50 of Williams, *The History of Monmouthshire*, Appendix XIX) in NLW 13089E p. 92, 13158A p. 250, and 13153A p. 162, and in Dublin, Royal Irish Academy, MS 12.N.4, p. 613. But at the same point 13116B p. 159 and 13114B p. 119 offer *Elbod* as an alternative (presumably drawing on the abbot list) and say: 'in some places written Elbod' (for the latter manuscript see *The Correspondence of Iolo Morganwg*, ed. Jenkins et al., II, 127). The names do not all appear in Spelman's extracts from *LL* in *Concilia*, I, 381–6, nor in the *Monasticon* of Dugdale (1655–73) and the *Concilia* of Wilkins (1737), so they cannot be the source. If the tract was composed in 1719 or 1729, its author could have not have seen *LL* at Llandaf, whence it had disappeared into Selden's library in 1619×27 (Huws, *Medieval Welsh Manuscripts*, 153), but there were various copies in circulation (see *The Correspondence of Iolo Morganwg*, ed. Jenkins et al., II, 117 n. 4). Iolo himself had access to some material from *LL* (*Braint Teilo*) and to the transcript in Oxford, Jesus College, MS 112. See his extracts in NLW MSS 13098B (Llanover C.11), pp. 13–15, 13100B (Llanover C.13), pp. 25–7, and 13116B (Llanover C.29), pp. 324–6. In 1797 he wrongly supposed that *LL* was in the British Museum (*The Correspondence of Iolo Morganwg*, ed. Jenkins et al., II, 33). He transcribed part of the Jesus College copy in 1792 (*ibid.*, III, 375). He told his son that he had seen the original 'at Llandaff': see Rees, *The Liber Landavensis*, xxix–xxxi, who supposes this 'original' to have been a facsimile by Robert Vaughan (cf. *LL* xvi and Huws, *Medieval Welsh Manuscripts*, 154) – the latter would already have been available at Llandaf to Nichols in 1719.

[21] Cf. Guy, 'The *Life* of St Dyfrig', 19–21.

[22] See above, 25, and maps 6 and 8 in Hughes, 'The Celtic Church', 19–20.

7. Donors and recipients of the charters

Medievalists have generally accepted the genuineness of the 'loose parchment'.[23] Modernists, however, have objected that Nichols could not have written a tract in 1729 since he died in 1720, and have argued that it was forged, at least in part, by Iolo Morganwg himself.[24] The objection about the date is not conclusive, because the date is given as 1719 in various manuscripts in Dublin and Cardiff which derive from Iolo's papers;[25] possibly '1729' was just a copying error.

The evident signs of Iolo's tampering are more disturbing. It is instructive to compare the various versions of 'The Antiquities of Lantwit Major' in Iolo's manuscripts. The shortest and simplest (NLW MS 13089E [Llanover C.21], pp. 90–3), dated 12 June 1729, is not attributed to Nichols, lacks the passage quoted above, and could be a copy of genuine work, composed in 1729 (or 1719) by someone with access to the Book of Llandaf (or a copy of it) and to Spelman's *Concilia*.[26] Iolo has another similar short version, also dated 12 June 1729, but to this he has added 'David Nicholls 1729' at the end (NLW MS 13158A [Llanover C.71], pp. 243–55). This version is slightly closer than 13089E is to the text in Williams's *History of Monmouthshire*.[27] Closer still is NLW 13153A (Llanover C.66), pp. 149–70. This bears the date 19 July 1729 (p. 149) and concludes 'written by me David Nicholls 1729' (p. 170), after which Iolo adds some remarks, which conclude:

> I have another transcript from a first, or rather another copy, dated June 12. 1729. not differing with regard to facts from the foregoing more amply expressed account. E. Williams.

In fact the 19 July version, which is very similar to that printed by David Williams, contains much additional material reflecting Iolo's own reading[28] and personal obsessions, such as *Caerurgorn* as the old name of Llantwit[29] and *Kennit* as an abbot

---

[23] *DP* III 286; *LBS* II 112 n. 2; *EA* I 184 n. 269; Bartrum, *A Welsh Classical Dictionary*, 549; J. R. Davies, *The Book of Llandaf*, 14.

[24] Knight, 'The Welsh monasteries and their claims for doing the education of later medieval Wales', 270–1; Williams, *Iolo Morganwg*, 316 n. 120; *The Correspondence of Iolo Morganwg*, ed. Jenkins et al., II, 117 n. 2 and 118 n. 1. Iolo seems to have forged various lists of bishops: Rees, *The Liber Landavensis*, 623 n. 2 and 625 n. 3.

[25] On these see below. These '1719' versions are not mentioned in *The Correspondence of Iolo Morganwg*, ed. Jenkins et al., but Royal Irish Academy, MS 12.N.4, pp. 595–632, is cited by Suggett, 'Iolo Morganwg: stonecutter, builder, and antiquary', 221 n. 97, and Cardiff, Central Library, MS 1.185, pp. 62–73, is cited by B. Davies, 'Archaeology and ideology', 50 n. 1.

[26] The writer cites Spelman's *Concilia* (1639).

[27] Note that both share a lacuna corresponding to the last line of p. 49 and the first four lines of p. 50. This results in an incomplete sentence. It is complete in 13153A, p. 161.

[28] 'Dr. Stillingfleet' is cited by name. See Stillingfleet, *Origines Britannicae* (1685), pp. 202–5. Silent use is also made of Carte, *A General History of England*, I, 185–6, which could not have been available in 1729 of course, and reference is made to writings allegedly shown to the writer by Sir Edward Stradling (*ob.* 1735). On the latter and his library see references in *The Correspondence of Iolo Morganwg*, ed. Jenkins et al., II, 120 n. 1. Significantly, Iolo includes extracts from Carte after his copies of the 'Antiquities of Lantwit' tract in NLW 13089E pp. 94ff. and 13158A pp. 256ff. In 1797 he listed Camden, Stillingfleet, Carte, Robert Henry, and Jeremy Collier as authorities on Llantwit: *The Correspondence of Iolo Morganwg*, ed. Jenkins et al., II, 34. Cf. *ibid.*, I, 597.

[29] See Williams, *Iolo Morganwg*, 314–16; *The Correspondence of Iolo Morganwg*, ed.

of Llantwit.[30] These additions include the abbot list, which is introduced: 'There is a loose parchment at Landaff, very decayed and rent, some parts of it rotten and others worm eaten ...'. Iolo then struck through 'a loose parchment' and replaced it with 'another old book' (p. 167), the same wording as appears in a longer version of the tract appended to Iolo's letter of 20 October 1798 to David Thomas in NLW MS 13114B (Llanover C.27): 'There is another old book at Landaff, worm eaten and rotten ...'.[31] Quite similar is the long version in NLW MS 13116B (Llanover C.29), pp. 149–65, which also has 'There is another old book <at Landaff> worm eaten and rotten ...' (p. 164 –'at Landaff' is inserted above the line). The same 'another old book' wording recurs in 'The Antiquities of Llantwit Major and Boverton in the county of Glamorgan Collected from various authors and manuscripts by Henry Tucker. Lantwit 1820', preserved in the Petrie Papers (Dublin, Royal Irish Academy, MS 12.N.4, p. 615).[32] Other versions of Tucker's compilation, which obviously draws on Iolo Morganwg, appear in Cardiff, Central Library, MSS 1.185 (copied in 1911), 3.704 (*ca* 1835), and 4.409 (dated 1852). In Cardiff 4.409 Nichols's tract is simply dated 1719, while RIA 12.N.4 has June 1719, Cardiff 3.704 has 12 June 1719, and 1.185 has 17 June 1719. Perhaps Tucker, who was Llantwit parish clerk, 'corrected' Iolo's impossible 1729 to 1719 after consulting the parish registers for David Nichols's obit.

It seems, then, that Iolo may have used a genuine short tract on 'The Antiquities of Lantwit Major', dated June 1729 or 1719, and based on the Book of Llandaf (or a copy of it) and on Spelman's *Concilia* of 1639. In view of the tract's reference to the Nichols family and their supposed descent from St Illtud, it may be by some member of that family.[33] In his copy in NLW MS 13089E it is anonymous, but in that in MS 13158A Iolo has ascribed it, rightly or wrongly, to David Nichols. Iolo then created a 'more amply expressed account' dated 19 July 1729, as in NLW 13153A and Thomas's *History of Monmouthshire*. This 'amply expressed' version includes additional material from Stillingfleet (1685) and other authorities, the abbot list, and some of Iolo's own inventions. The abbot list itself also reflects Iolo's inventions by including both *Cennit* and *Segin*, the latter being the supposed eponym of Sigginston/Tresigin in Llantwit parish.[34] In his most extensive versions of the tract in NLW MSS 13114B (20 October 1798) and 13116B, Iolo adds the name *Elifled* to the abbot list and inserts references to 'Segin or Sigin' and 'Elifled' in the body of the tract.[35]

Jenkins et al., I, 349–50.

[30] See above, 61 n. 14.

[31] Printed in *The Correspondence of Iolo Morganwg*, ed. Jenkins et al., II, 131, from NLW MS 13114B, p. 122.

[32] Internal evidence (p. 621) shows that this was written after 1815. On p. 629 mention is made of Tucker's role in moving the *Houelt* Cross 'into the old church' in 1812 (cf. Redknap and Lewis, *A Corpus*, I, 370); this is an addition to the passage printed in *The Correspondence of Iolo Morganwg*, ed. Jenkins et al., II, 135. Iolo distributed material on Llantwit in manuscript to, among others, Carlisle, *A Topographical Dictionary*, s.n. *Llan Illtyd, Fawr*, and *The Cambrian Visitor*, 1 (1813), 509–21. Cf. *The Correspondence of Iolo Morganwg*, ed. Jenkins et al., III, 220 n. 1.

[33] On Iolo's connection with the Nichol(l)s family see Williams, *Iolo Morganwg*, 120.

[34] See *ibid.*, 318.

[35] See *The Correspondence of Iolo Morganwg*, ed. Jenkins et al., II, 126–7, for the NLW MS 13114B text, where the tract is again dated 12 June 1729. In MS 13116B it is 19 June (*sic*) 1729!

7. Donors and recipients of the charters

The question arises: is the abbot list entirely Iolo's invention or did he tinker with an existing list and only partially harmonise it with the tract? In favour of the latter hypothesis is the fact that the order of names in the abbot list differs from that in the tract. In the '12 June 1729' version of the tract, the abbots in the *LL* charters appear in the following order: *Ildutus*; *Samson*; *Congen*; *Gurthaver*; *Catgen*; *Colbrit*; *Guorhaval*; *Elvaid/Elvaed/Elvod*; *Elguoid/Elgoid*; *Tomre*; *Guorhavarn*; *Gurhaval*; *Elised* (NLW MS 13089E, pp. 90–2). In the abbot list, however, *Catgen*, *Colbrit*, and *Gourhavarn* are entirely absent, and a number of new names appear: *Piro*, *Isanus*, *Cennit*, *Nudh*, *Elised*, *Segin*, *Camelauc*, and *Bledri*. Leaving aside *Isanus*, who derives from the Continental Lives of St Samson, and the dubious *Cennit* and *Segin*, all of these appear in *LL* where they occur in the following order: *Piro* (abbot pp. 12 and 15); *Nud* (cleric pp. 200–17, bishop pp. 225–31); *Elised* (abbot pp. 212–30); *Cime(i)lliauc/ Ciue(i)lliauc* (bishop pp. 231–7); and *Bledri* (bishop pp. 247–52). It seems evident that Iolo or whoever created the abbot list, did not rely on the preceding tract, but drew on *LL* (or a copy of it) or a lost source, at least for the five additional names. That *LL* was not the source is suggested not only by the omission of *LL*'s abbots *Catgen*, *Colbrit*, and *Guorhavarn* and the treatment of *Nudh*, *Camelauc*, and *Bletri* as abbots, but also by three points of orthography. One is the spelling *Elbod*, which suggests a source in a medieval hand (not that of *LL*) in which *v* resembled *b*.[36] The second is the (intermittent) spelling *Bletri* which does not occur in *LL* (unlike *Bledri*). The third is the spelling *Camelauc* where *LL* has *Cime(i)lliauc/Ciue(i)lliauc*. This very peculiar spelling[37] recalls *Cameleac ... biscop on Ircinga felda* ('bishop of/in Archenfield/ Ergyng') in the Parker manuscript of the *Anglo-Saxon Chronicle*, s.a. 918 (*recte* 914), quite likely the same bishop.[38] It is likely that Iolo knew of this annal and that it was the basis of the fictitious statement in his *Gwentian Brut* s.a. 754, recording a battle of Hereford in which *Cyfelach*, bishop of Morgannwg, was slain.[39] If so, his spelling *Camelauc*, rather than *Cime(i)lliauc/Ciue(i)lliauc*, in the abbot list may be influenced by the *Anglo-Saxon Chronicle*. The spelling *Elbod* is harder to explain away, however.

This still leaves the problem of how the bishops of *LL* became abbots in the list. Possibly Iolo, in his zeal to enhance the prestige of Llantwit, was solely responsible, yet we cannot rule out the possibility that he used, and tinkered with, an existing list of Llantwit abbots, of uncertain date and reliability. Perhaps the 12/17 June 1729 (1719?) tract really had spawned a later enlarged version, dated 19 June/July 1729 (1719?), which included the abbot list from a genuine 'loose parchment at Llandaff'. If the abbot list ever existed, it may have been a medieval invention.[40]

---

[36] Cf. 62 n. 20 above. It is clear that the *LL* spellings *Eluoid*, *Elguoid*, *Elgoid*, *Eluod* all refer to the same abbot (Davies, *The Llandaff Charters*, 163). In this name *u* in *Eluoid* (179c) represents /w/ (cf. Sims-Williams, 'The emergence', 52–6), so there is no question of an Old Welsh *Elbod* with *b* for /v/.

[37] In *LL a* occasionally occurs before *n*, but not before *m*. See Sims-Williams, 'The emergence', 44–5.

[38] A text already available in 1692 in *Chronicon Saxonicum*, ed. Gibson, 105, who translates: 'Cameleacum Episcopum in Ircingafeld'.

[39] *Myvyrian Archaiology*, ed. Jones et al., 686; *DP* III 259–60 and 286; *LBS* II 215–16. On the name cf. McKee, *Juvencus: Text and commentary*, 27–8, and Charles-Edwards, *Wales and the Britons*, 594. The spelling *Cyfelach* is due to the eponym of Llangyfelach. Cf. Rees, *The Liber Landavensis*, 625 n. 3 and 627 n. 1.

[40] Compare the lists of St Davids bishops discussed by Pryce, 'Gerald of Wales and the Welsh past'.

Iolo's first opinion, in 1793, seems to have been that Llantwit itself was the seat of bishops:

> Samson is in many old Welsh manuscripts termed bishop of Lantwit and, it is probable that Lantwit had a considerable number of bishops in a pretty long succession.[41]

The opinion in the Nichols tract, that some abbots of Llantwit became diocesan bishops at Llandaf, is more plausible, but it depends on the reliability – and indeed the existence – of the 'loose parchment at Landaff'. There is no indication in *LL* that *Nudh*, *Camelauc*, and *Bletri* had been abbots before their consecration as bishops. Nudd is styled *lector* in charters 170 and 169b (iii.1–2).[42]

Confronted with an abbot as a recipient in a charter, the compilers of *LL* would probably have discarded it, for we have no other evidence that any abbots were turned into Llandaf bishops; and it is a measure of the compilers' limited good faith that they did not turn any of the abbots who received the Llancarfan grants into bishops of Llandaf. This is not to say that *LL* may not contain forgeries designed to appropriate monastic lands.[43] One of the charters of Bishop Euddogwy (144) alludes to disputes with an Abbot Bywon of Llantwit (*abbas Ilduti*) about estates in Gower, and since Gower is well outside the normal area of Euddogwy's grants, whereas Illtud's cult there is widespread and at least as old as the ninth century,[44] one suspects that the three charters granting Euddogwy estates in Gower (140, 144, and 145) are anti-Llantwit forgeries. Yet there is no attempt to adapt charters that were in favour of Llantwit by making (say) Abbot Bywon a bishop of Llandaf. Instead the forgers seem to have been able to draw on authentic witness lists of Bishop Euddogwy himself, as in the case of the forged charters of Awst of Brycheiniog discussed earlier.[45] By and large, then, the *LL* charters can be accepted as records of genuine episcopal communities and the estates which supported them from the seventh century to the eleventh.

We may finish by considering a partial exception to the rule that confronted with an alien bishop as a recipient in a charter, the practice of the compilers of *LL* appears to have been to transform him into a 'bishop of Llandaf'. This is provided by the material relating to the church of Clodock in Ewias, Herefordshire, on pp. 193–7 of *LL* (and also, in a different order, *ibid.*, p. 362, in Cotton Vespasian A.xiv as a *Vita sancti Clitauci regis et martyris*). It is clear that this material, though adapted

---

[41] *The Correspondence of Iolo Morganwg*, ed. Jenkins et al., I, 596. There is no evidence for such a bishop of Llantwit. Iolo may have misunderstood the association between Samson and Llantwit in the *Vita Samsonis* (see below, 158).

[42] See below, 169, on 'Nudd I'; the career of 'Nudd II' also seems to have been within the episcopal *familia*.

[43] In the case of the charters with doublets in the *Vita Cadoci* (180b/*VC* 67 and 210b/*VC* 66) it seems, at the least, that *LL* and *VC* selected and emphasised the elements that suited the interests of Llandaf and Llancarfan respectively (see Charles-Edwards, *Wales and the Britons*, 256–61, and below, 102). Guy, 'The *Life* of St Dyfrig', 25–7, raises the unprovable possibility that some of the Sequence i grants in *LL* were really to monasteries.

[44] *HB* §71. For the cave mentioned there cf. Emery, 'Edward Lhuyd', 97. For Euddogwy's estates, see Hughes, 'The Celtic Church', 17, map 2.

[45] Cf. above, 57 on the Awst charters. The list of electors in the *Vita Oudocei* (*LL* pp. 131–2) shows the availability of lists of apparently genuine names.

7. Donors and recipients of the charters

in the interests of Llandaf, is based on traditions redacted at Clodock and related to that church's endowments.[46] Thus we are given an account of the martyrdom of the eponymous Clydog – a grandson of Brychan according to the genealogies – and of various miracles that led to gifts to his shrine at Clodock. On the advice of an unnamed bishop of Llandaf, the site of Clydog's martyrdom is first settled by three hermits from the cantref of Penychen (which included Llandaf) – Llibio and Gwrfan (two brothers), and their sister's son (*sororius*) Cynwr – and its territory is granted to them by an otherwise unknown king of Morgannwg; subsequently the territory is re-granted to Berthwyn, bishop of Llandaf, by Ithel ap Morgan, eighth-century king of Glywysing. It is more than curious that the names of the hermits Gwrfan and Llibio appear elsewhere in *LL* as *bishops*, both associated with Llanfihangel Tal-y-llyn, Brycheiniog (*LL* 167 and 237b) and both associated with kings of Brycheiniog called Tewdwr – two different Tewdwrs in fact, but the coincidence may have helped to suggest that the eighth-century Gwrfan and tenth-century Llibio were contemporary, indeed brothers. Bishop Llibio also receives a grant in Gower (239). Have hermits been elevated into bishops in the charters or have bishops been reduced to hermits in the hagiography? On balance, the latter seems more likely. Confronted by seemingly alien bishops in the Clodock documentation, the Llandaf apologists who wrote up the Clydog material, apparently at one of the early stages in the compilation of *LL*,[47] have turned them into hermits from Penychen, acting under the jurisdiction of Llandaf. It is much harder to explain why two hermits should have been turned into two bishops, both of whose charters sit somewhat uneasily in the *LL* collection, as we shall see.

Llanfihangel Tal-y-llyn (in charters 167 and 237b) and all the places named in Gower (239) were claimed for Llandaf by Urban. The relevant charters may have passed into his archive in the time of Herewald, who had consecrated churches in Ystrad Yw (just to the south of Llanfihangel Tal-y-llyn) and in Gower and appointed priests to them.[48] At the same period, Herewald may have obtained the earlier charter of Bishop Gwrfan (167), which also concerns Llanfihangel Tal-y-llyn and is diplomatically linked to Llibio's Llanfihangel charter (237b) by the dispositive verb *offere* (rare in *LL*).[49] The grantor of 167 is Tewdwr ap Rhain of Brycheiniog, atoning for the murder of his co-ruler Elwystl ab Awst, who probably flourished in the early eighth century.[50] This Gwrfan may have been an eighth-century predecessor of Llibio. John Reuben Davies has plausibly suggested that he is the bishop 'Gueman' in the list of the bishops of Glasbury.[51] Llibio does not appear in that list, so he was presumably based elsewhere.

The charter of Tewdwr ap Rhain granting Llanfihangel Tal-y-llyn to Bishop Gwrfan (167) has a witness list of nine names which do not re-appear elsewhere in *LL*, a clear sign that the entourages of both grantor and recipient were distinct from those which appear in the other *LL* charters. We are dealing with a distinct area, with its own personnel, and this must be why the charter cannot be fitted into Sequence ii; Llanfihangel Tal-y-llyn is well north-west of the main area of the other charters in

---

[46] Davies, *The Llandaff Charters*, 114–15; J. R. Davies, *The Book of Llandaf*, 72, 94–6, and 122–4; Charles-Edwards, *Wales and the Britons*, 305–6. Cf. Guy, 'The *Life* of St Dyfrig', 5 n. 15.

[47] J. R. Davies, *The Book of Llandaf*, 124.

[48] *LL* p. 279 etc.

[49] Davies, *The Llandaff Charters*, 135–6, notes only 167, 211b, 237b, and 263. Cf. *ibid.*, 106.

[50] See above, 57, and below, 167.

[51] J. R. Davies, *The Book of Llandaf*, 12, and 'The archbishopric', 302 and n. 52.

LL, with the obvious exceptions of the blatantly forged charters granting Llan-gors (146) and Llandeilo'r-fân (154) in Brycheiniog to Euddogwy.[52] The witness lists of Llibio's charters show some contact with other *LL* charters,[53] but they are still fairly isolated, presumably for geographical reasons.

A further eccentric feature of Bishop Llibio is that according to the Canterbury version of the Welsh consecration list he and Bishop Cyfeilliog (*fl.* 914) were both consecrated bishop by Archbishop Æthelred (870–89); if so Bishop Llibio would really have been contemporary with *LL*'s Bishop Cyfeilliog 'of Llandaf',[54] rather than being his successor as claimed in *LL*. The Llibio of the consecration list cannot be explained away by making him a bishop of St Davids since Bishop Llunferth of St Davids (*ob.* 944, *Annales Cambriae*) appears together with Bishop Llibio in charter 237b, and was thus his contemporary. According to the Canterbury consecration list, Llunferth was also consecrated by Æthelred, which is just about possible; unless there were two bishops of the same name (which is plausible), his episcopate would have spanned at the least 889–944,[55] and he would have been over eighty when he died. (Consecrations by Æthelred are understandable in the context of King Alfred's relations with the Welsh kingdoms in the 880s, as described by Asser.)[56] There thus seemed to be three bishops – Cyfeilliog, Llibio, and Llunferth – at a period when there were only two dioceses (St Davids and Llandaf) according to Urban's propaganda. The Canterbury text of the tract on consecrations, probably close to the original as it came from Llandaf, has Cyfeilliog being consecrated by Æthelred and dying in 927 and Llibio also being consecrated by Æthelred and dying in 929 'ordinationis suae anno tertio' – the last phrase making him Cyfeilliog's successor at Llandaf, rather than his contemporary somewhere else. The final compilers of *LL* may have realised the chronological impossibility of Æthelred (*ob.* 889) consecrating Llibio in 927, for they omitted the references to the consecrations in both obits (*LL* pp. 237 and 240), while of course keeping the 'ordinationis suae anno tertio' phrase.[57] This may be interpreted as a device to integrate Llibio into the Llandaf tradition, as Cyfeilliog's successor, bringing with him the disputed lands in Brycheiniog and Gower that had once belonged to Llibio's church, according to his two charters. Alternatively – and more simply – we can suppose that Llibio really was Cyfeilliog's successor and that the consecration by Æthelred was wishful thinking or a mistake.[58]

---

[52] See Davies, *The Llandaff Charters*, 98 and 101, on these, and map 2 in Hughes, 'The Celtic Church', 17. A further distant estate is *Lanncoit*, granted to Bishop Arguistl (charter 166, just before the Llanfihangel Tal-y-llyn charter 167), assuming that this is Llangoed in Cantref Selyf, as stated in *LL*, p. 255 (see Coe, 'The place-names', 131 and 518–19). This was four miles west of Glasbury.

[53] See below, 173.

[54] For the consecration list see above, 24, and *WHEMA* IV 70.

[55] No obit of a bishop of St Davids is recorded during this period (Asser being bishop of Sherborne, although cf. J. R. Davies, 'The archbishopric', 299); cf. Hughes, *Celtic Britain*, 68 n. 13. Is the inclusion of a St Davids bishop in 237b a sign of authenticity, or was it intended to stave off St Davids objections to the grant? On the likelihood of two bishops Llunferth see above, 24 n. 7.

[56] Asser's *Life of King Alfred*, §80.

[57] It seems unlikely that either consecration was due to 'a post-*LL* phase of embellishment', as suggested in *WHEMA* IV 59–60. Davies, *The Llandaff Charters*, 78, views the 'ordinationis suae anno tertio' phrase as historically accurate.

[58] See below, 173.

7. Donors and recipients of the charters

Llibio's charter concerning Llanfihangel Tal-y-llyn, Breconshire (237b), was granted by Tewdwr ab Elisedd, king of Brycheiniog, in recompense for taking the bishop's food-render at, apparently, Llan-gors monastery close by (a known royal centre in Brycheiniog).[59] This Tewdwr was probably the son of the Elisedd ap Tewdwr mentioned by Asser and the same monarch as the *Teowdor subregulus* in an original Athelstan charter of 934.[60] The other grant to Bishop Llibio is of Paviland in Rhosili, Gower, granted by a King Gruffudd in recompense for crimes against three churches in Gower (239).[61] On the basis of his two grants, one is tempted to place Llibio's early-tenth-century episcopal seat somewhere between Llanfihangel Tal-y-llyn and Gower, perhaps at Llan-gors, Brycheiniog.[62] Another possibility is that it was at Clodock, only twelve miles east of Llanfihangel Tal-y-llyn as the crow flies, albeit across high ground.[63] If Herewald or his successor obtained charters from Llan-gors or Clodock in favour of Gwrfan and Llibio, those same charters could have given rise to the hermits of the Clydog hagiography, the slightly doctored Gwrfan and Llibio charters of *LL*, and the Llibio of the consecration list.

Enticing though this scenario may be, it is possible that Llibio really was Cyfeilliog's successor and that it was through him that Gwrfan's charter reached the 'Llandaf' archive,[64] eventually giving rise to Gwrfan the hermit.

At this point we may return to the third hermit in the Clydog hagiography, Cynwr (*Cinuur*). While his uncles remained chaste, Cynwr had five sons, whence the territory (Clodock) was divided into five portions in perpetuity.[65] Despite this suggestion that he remained at Clodock in a lesser role, it is curious that Gruffudd's grant of Paviland in west Gower to Llibio (239) was partly in atonement for sacrilege *in monasterio sancti Cinuuri. id est Lannberugall* (i.e. in Bishopston in central Gower). While the recurrence of the name Cynwr could be mere coincidence,[66] it seems quite likely that

---

[59] See *Anglo-Saxon Chronicle*, s.a. 916.

[60] Sawyer 425. See Keynes, 'Welsh kings', 90–1.

[61] There are two possible Gruffudds: (1) On the one hand, the Disposition of 239 calls him *Grifud rex filius Yugein*, which probably makes him the son of the Owain who is styled king of Gwent in the *Anglo-Saxon Chronicle* s.a. 927, the son of the Hywel ap Rhys of Glywysing mentioned by Asser. It is quite possible that Gruffudd ab Owain ruled in Gower, for *Brut y Tywysogion* and *Brenhinedd y Saeson* say that his death in 935 (*Annales Cambriae*) was at the hands of the men of Ceredigion; this suggests an expansionist policy on Gruffudd's part. Cf. Lloyd, *A History*, I, 338 n. 66, and Charles-Edwards, *Wales and the Britons*, 517 and 537–8; *Brut y Tywysogyon: Peniarth MS. 20 Version*, translated by Jones, 141. (2) On the other hand, the witness list of Llibio's charter reads *Grifud filius Higueid*, which could make Gruffudd an otherwise unattested son of the Hyfaidd of Dyfed (*ob. ca* 893) mentioned by Asser. (*Higueid* is a possible Old Welsh form of *Hyfaidd*, on which see Jones, *Brut y Tywysogyon: Peniarth MS. 20 Version*, 141.) It seems preferable, however, to accept that the charter was from Gruffudd ab Owain (*ob.* 935) of Gwent/Glywysing.

[62] Sims-Williams, 'The provenance', 61–2, and J. R. Davies, 'The archbishopric', 302 n. 53.

[63] J. R. Davies suggests *(The Book of Llandaf*, 12 n. 23) that charters 167 and 237b 'probably emanate from a Llan-gors archive'; also that Llibio may have been interpolated in 237b, the grant originally having been made to, or under the auspices of, Bishop Llunferth of St Davids. On the latter's inclusion cf. above, n. 55.

[64] See below, 173.

[65] *LL* p. 195. For parallels see Sims-Williams, *Irish Influence*, 203.

[66] On the name see Davies, *The Llandaff Charters*, 97–8 and 124; *DP* IV 398–400. He appears in the lists of the disciples of Dyfrig and Teilo (see J. R. Davies, *The Book of Llandaf*, 82 and 87).

some speculation on the relationship between Llibio, Clodock, and this church in Gower gave rise to the third mythical hermit. According to other *LL* charters, *Lann Conuur / cella Conguri* in Bishopston also formed part of a Dyfrig estate restored by Athrwys ap Meurig to Bishop Euddogwy in his dispute with the abbot of Llantwit (144) and of a Teilo estate restored to him by King Morgan (145). Bishopston was the one Gower estate that Llandaf succeeded in retaining in perpetuity.[67] While it may have come to Llandaf through the Euddogwy connection, the Clodock material in *LL* hints that Llandaf may have obtained a swathe of estates from Ewias to Gower through the Gwrfan-Llibio connection.

The strategy of turning bishops into hermits that we see in the Clydog material is isolated, and of course it conflicts with the retention of Gwrfan and Llibio as bishops (sanitised as 'bishops of Llandaf') elsewhere in *LL*. Retaining bishops as bishops seems to have been the normal policy of the compilers. Their bishops *were* real bishops, if rarely bishops *of Llandaf*.

---

[67] *EA* I, 180–81; J. R. Davies, *The Book of Llandaf*, 87, 172, and 174–5.

8

THE FAKE DIPLOMATIC OF THE BOOK OF LLANDAF

Many questions about the validity of the wording of the charters must lead historians into a study of their diplomatic, and that study must in turn lead them back to the question of how *LL* was compiled, for it is clear that many of the charters' formulae were added during compilation, as seen by E. D. Jones, noting 'the uniformity displayed over what we are asked to believe was a period of five centuries'.[1] Similarly Brooke saw 'a unity about these documents of a very exceptional kind, even for large collections of forgeries' and concluded that:

> The charters are a classic statement of the principles of fake diplomatic. Centuries pass; dynasties come and go. But the charters of the bishops of Llandaff vary little in their form, which is a curious amalgam of local custom and the practice of the chanceries of Europe in the late eleventh or early twelfth century. ... The words vary, but only like the variations on a musical theme. ... A single ingenious mind presides over the whole enterprise.[2]

Wendy Davies, in her paper 'St Mary's, Worcester and the *Liber Landavensis*', demonstrated that some of the characteristic *LL* verbiage is parallelled in Hemming's Cartulary, which was compiled at Worcester *ca* 1095,[3] and, without explicitly supporting Brooke's idea of a single presiding mind, noted the significant circumstance that Bishop Urban is said to have been a priest of Worcester.[4] John Reuben Davies, however, has since shown that the relevant formulae are found widely among Anglo-Saxon cartularies. Without rejecting Urban and Worcester as a possibility, he is 'inclined to suggest that the Anglo-Saxon features of the Llandaf charters are likely to have been formed by the "artistic" mind of, perhaps, a Caradog of Llancarfan, working from a general knowledge of Anglo-Saxon diplomatic'.[5]

An invaluable tool for investigating the diplomatic of *LL* is Appendix I of Wendy Davies's *The Llandaff Charters* in which she lists the occurrences of all the major formulae in the charters.[6] There are two drawbacks in the arrangement, however, which could not have been eliminated without the expense of a lot of space. One is that her Appendix I only shows one how the formulae are distributed through *LL* paginally (i.e. in the order of the manuscript), not how they are distributed

---

[1] Jones, 'The Book of Llandaff', 143.
[2] Brooke, *The Church*, 45 and 31 respectively.
[3] *WHEMA* I. See Ker, 'Hemming's Cartulary'; Wareham, 'The redaction of cartularies'.
[4] *WHEMA* I 478.
[5] J. R. Davies, *The Book of Llandaf*, 108. See further Charles-Edwards, *Wales and the Britons*, 256.
[6] *The Llandaff Charters*, 131–44. In using the data for statistical purposes 199bi and 199bii must be distinguished, making a total of 159 charters.

chronologically (i.e. in the order of the Sequences), which is equally important in deciding whether they are editorial or original. The other drawback is that the presentation of the formulae in separate lists, rather than tables, makes it difficult to tell what formulae occur in conjunction; and all sense of the charters' internal organisation is lost. To give a trivial example, one would not easily tell from the lists that *largitus est* and *in elemosina* tend to occur together (doubtless because of a liking for the phrase *largitus est in elemosina*), for the two formulae are listed separately;[7] and the same applies to *dedit* and *successoribus* (discussed below). Nor can one tell that Dispositions expressing some kind of religious motive (*pro anima sua*, etc.) tend *not* to occur in charters with Narrations,[8] perhaps because the writers felt that the latter, which usually explain the reason for the grant, rendered a clause about religious motivation superfluous.[9] It is also difficult, without much labour, to confirm Wendy Davies's statement that 'it is rare to find charters with the same Notification that also have the same Disposition or Sanction'.[10] This observation is quite damaging for the diplomatic authenticity of *LL*.

In *The Llandaff Charters* Davies attempts to distinguish the original formulae of the charters from those added at various stages of editing, supposedly stretching over several centuries before the compilation of *LL*.[11] On the one hand, some features are too rare to be significant: for instance the fact that there are no Preambles in charters recording grants in Glamorgan and that all the references to inhabitants of *dextralis Britanniae* occur between 151b and 237b means little since the sample is so small – these features occur in only fourteen and eight of the 159 charters respectively.[12] Other features are so abundant, on the other hand, that they merit detailed statistical investigation – for example, the alternative dispositive verbs *largitus est*, *dedit*, and *immolauit*. On these she comments that the first 'hardly occurs before 188a, and preponderantly from the mid-eighth century; *dedit* rarely occurs after 190a; and *immolauit* hardly before 176b, and predominantly from the mid-eighth century'.[13] One is left wondering if the variation is really due to diplomatic developments in the

---

[7] Davies, *The Llandaff Charters*, 135 and 139. She thinks that *in elemosina* reflects 'genuine practice' (*ibid.*, 9 and 143); this interpretation is doubtful in view of the association with *largitus est*, which is editorial (see below). In *WHEMA* I 466 she describes *in perpetuam elemosinam* as 'a very typical post-conquest formula', giving an example at p. 475 from Hemming's Cartulary (the spurious Sawyer 205).

[8] Other than Narrations of sales.

[9] 47 charters out of 159 have Narrations (excluding sales), 71 have have Dispositions expressing religious motives, and only 12 have both (Davies, *The Llandaff Charters*, 134–5), whereas on a random basis one would expect 21 to have both. The pattern varies, however: six out of the nine charters in Sequence iii.28–36 have Narrations and six out of the nine have Dispositions expressing religious motives, and four of the nine have both. On statistical grounds I am sceptical of the argument of Davies, *The Llandaff Charters*, 8, 135, and 142, that the formulae *pro scriptione nominis sui in libro uitae* (four examples) and *pro commertio regni caelestis* (eight examples) are conceivably original because they do not occur after the early tenth century. 262 in the eleventh century (cf. Maund, *Ireland, Wales, and England*, 195) has *pro redemptione regni celestis*.

[10] Davies, *The Llandaff Charters*, 10.

[11] *Ibid.*, 6–30. Cf. ch. 9 below.

[12] *Ibid.*, 8 and 132–4.

[13] *Ibid.*, 8. On *immolare* see *WHEMA* I 466, XI 270, 273, 277, and XII 104. Cf. Sims-Williams, *Britain and Early Christian Europe*, XIII 84 n. 38. *Immolauit* in charter 195 is glossed '.i. obtulit' in the Vespasian copy (*LL* p. 362).

8. The fake diplomatic of the Book of Llandaf

eighth century, as she suggests,[14] or merely to the changing whim of the compilers of *LL*, introducing some elegant variation in the charters as they prepared them for a twelfth-century audience.

In such a case there are two tests which can be applied.[15] The first is made possible by the fact that the paginal order of the charters in *LL* does not correspond to their chronological order, as revealed by the Sequences.[16] It follows that when the charters are considered 'chronologically' (i.e. in the order of the Sequences) any *original* formulae are likely to show a pattern of distribution, reflecting historical developments in diplomatic fashion, that is less arbitrary than the pattern of distribution that is visible when the charters are considered 'paginally' (i.e. in their present order in *LL*); conversely, any pattern of distribution of formulae introduced according to the changing whims of the compilers should show up paginally but appear more arbitrary when the charters are rearranged in their chronological order. As an example, the Table 8.1 graphs show the pattern of distribution of the three main dispositive verbs from the paginal and the chronological standpoints. *Dedit* is the continuous line, *largitus est* the broken line, and *immolauit* the dotted line. The paginal graph (Table 8.1, Fig. 1) is based on all the charters in the order in which they occur in *LL*, including the ones not arranged in the Sequences because they lack witness lists (if these were omitted the general conclusion would not be affected). The charters have been taken in groups of nine (72a–77, 121–141, 143–150b, etc.) and the odd six left over at the end (264b–274) have been evened up by multiplying by 3/2. For the chronological graph (Table 8.1, Fig. 2) I have divided up the charters in each Sequence into groups of nine, and have evened up the odd groups of ten, ten, and seven, at the beginning of i and the end of ii and iii respectively.[17] The height of each 'curve' shows the number of charters out of nine in which the formula appears. It is immediately apparent from the graphs that the distribution of the three dispositive verbs makes little sense as the result of historical change in diplomatic practice over the centuries (Table 8.1, Fig. 2), but makes good sense, especially in the case of *dedit*, as the result of a gradual change in fashion among the compilers of *LL* itself (Table 8.1, Fig. 1). This is not to say that (for example) there *may* not indeed have been some historical decline in the use of *dedit*, which *may* have influenced the compilers of *LL* to some extent. Clearly, however, the distribution of the verb owes much to the whim of the compilers and one cannot agree that 'we may assume that *dedit* tended to give way to the more elaborate *largitus est* and *immolauit* in the course of the eighth century'.[18] Paginal 'curves' less consistent than that of *dedit* may be just as conclusive insofar as they draw attention to paginal bunching of formulae that can only be editorial. The early peak of *immolauit* in Table 8.1, Fig. 1, for instance, is due to the paginal cluster 171b, 173, 176b, 178, 179b, 179c. As these six charters belong to various periods (respectively Sequences iii. 5, 7; ii. 19, 44, 33, 29)

---

[14] Davies, *The Llandaff Charters*, 26–7 and 143.
[15] See Sims-Williams, 'The emergence', 32–6.
[16] See chart in Appendix I below, 182.
[17] The order of charters in the Sequences follows that suggested by Wendy Davies, for the sake of argument, rather than the minor corrections suggested above in ch. 4, but this does not affect the general conclusion. There are fewer charters in Fig. 2 than in Fig. 1 since a few charters are not in the Sequences, notably ones without witness lists.
[18] Davies, *The Llandaff Charters*, 27.

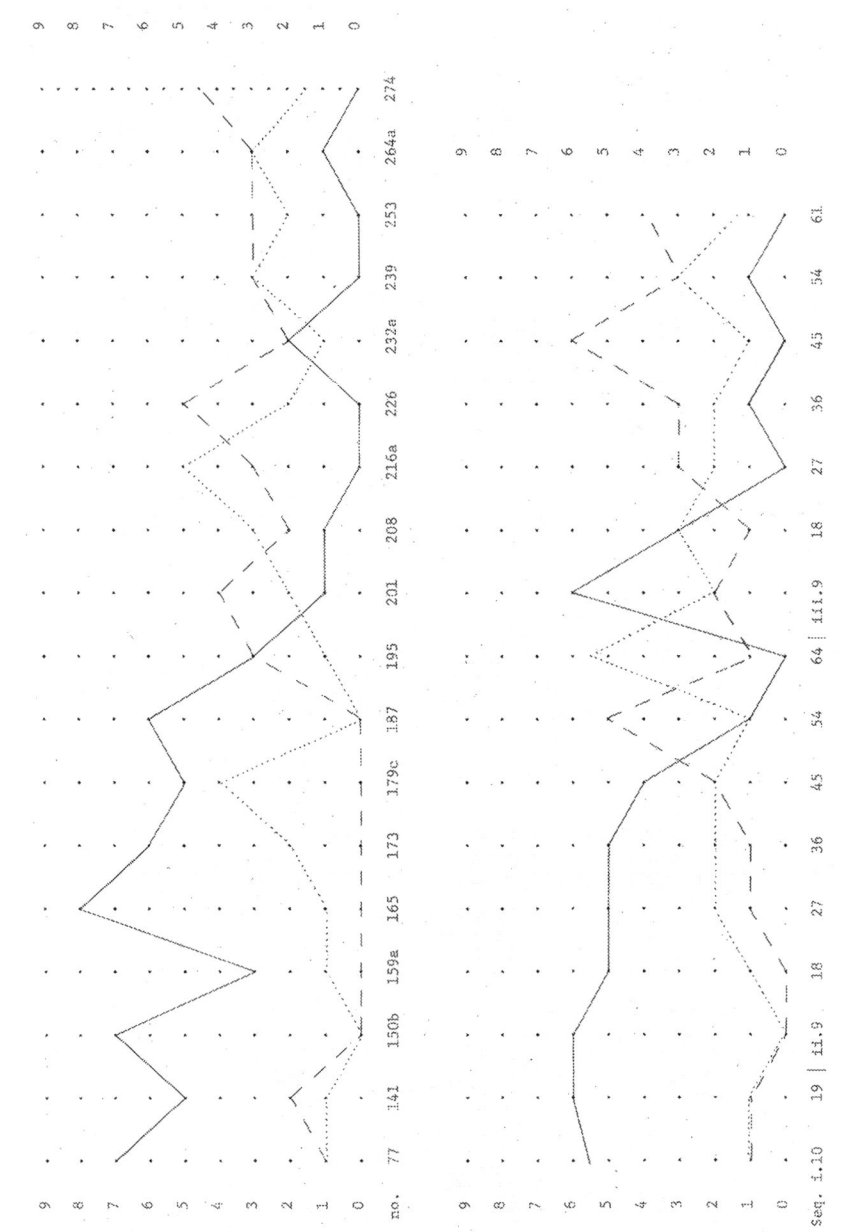

Table 8.1 *Dedit, largitus est*, and *immolauit* paginally (Fig. 1, above) and chronologically (Fig. 2, below)

8. The fake diplomatic of the Book of Llandaf

it is clear that the sudden introduction of *immolauit* here must be a paginal (editorial) feature. I shall argue later that it is probably due to a Llandaf compiler dubbed 'P'.[19]

The second test confirms these conclusions. It is based on the occurrence of eight charters in *LL* which have doublets elsewhere either in *LL* or among the Llancarfan charters (*VC*) and on the assumption that these doublets reflect one and the same archetype in each case, not independent originals made at the time of the original grants (for which there is no evidence). It follows that where the wording of the pair is in mutual conflict one or other, or both, must have modified the wording of the original. Hence the doublets are an excellent guide to what later editors regarded as the immutable essence of a charter (such as the names of the persons and places mentioned) and to what they regarded as fair game for elegant variation. If one looks at the doublets (73b/163a; 74/171b; 175/186b; 176a/190b; 179a/188b; 179b/191; 180b/*VC* 67; 210b/*VC* 66) one finds the following variations in the dispositive verbs: *dederunt/reddiderunt*; *dederunt/dederunt*; *dedit/dedit*; *dedit/largitus est*; *dedit/dedit*; *immolauerunt/largitus est*; *donauit/dedit*; *immolauit/dedit* (respectively). Some of the agreements on the use of the 'obvious' verb *dare* may be due to coincidence or to the chance that both members of the pairs in question fall into sections of *LL* in which that verb is in favour with the compilers. It is more significant that in five cases out of eight the texts diverge.

These tests can be applied to any of the common formulae of *LL*. For another example let us consider the standard dispositive clauses such as 'largitus est ... Deo et sanctis Dubricio, Teliauo, et Oudoceo, et Nud episcopo & *omnibus episcopis* Landauiæ in perpetuo' (229a). Wendy Davies comments that the changes in *LL* from *successoribus* to *omnibus episcopis* to *presulibus* 'presumably represent stylistic variation *or conceivably changes in the exemplars*', while John Morris seems to have taken the latter view.[20] In Table 8.2 *successoribus* is the continuous line, *omnibus episcopis* the broken line, and *presulibus* the dotted line. A comparison of the paginal graph (Fig. 1) for 'stylistic variation' with the chronological graph (Fig. 2) for 'changes in the exemplars' enables one to decide firmly in favour of stylistic variation.[21] Examination of the doublets confirms our conclusion. Only three, 74/171b, 175/186b, and 179b/191, agree on the phrasing, and this is probably coincidence, for *successoribus*, the word in question in the three, is the dominant word between 171b and 191 (in twenty out of twenty-five charters). It is more than likely that the insertion of all these phrases including future bishops (of Llandaf) in the grants are insertions made during editing at Llandaf. It is interesting to note, by comparing Tables 8.1 and 8.2, that *dedit* and *successoribus* were simultaneously popular with the writers of the *verba dispositiva*, though one cannot prove that the correlation of the two fashions is not coincidental.[22]

---

[19] See below, 87.
[20] Davies, *The Llandaff Charters*, 15 (my italics); Morris, Review, 231 ('early bishops are styled *episcopus*, later ones *pontifex* or *praesul*'). Cf. Sims-Williams, 'The emergence', 35–6.
[21] Although it is not unknown in diplomatic for formulae to go out of use and be revived later (cf. Keynes, *The Diplomas*, 86–7 and 117), no-one would argue that Table 8.2, Fig. 2, reflects a retro-fashion that, by an amazing coincidence, managed to foreshadow the *later* paginal dislocation of the chronological order of charters in *LL*.
[22] *Dedit* occurs in fifty-five of the 159 charters, *successoribus* in forty-six, but they both occur in twenty-nine charters, which is higher than the sixteen that one would expect at random.

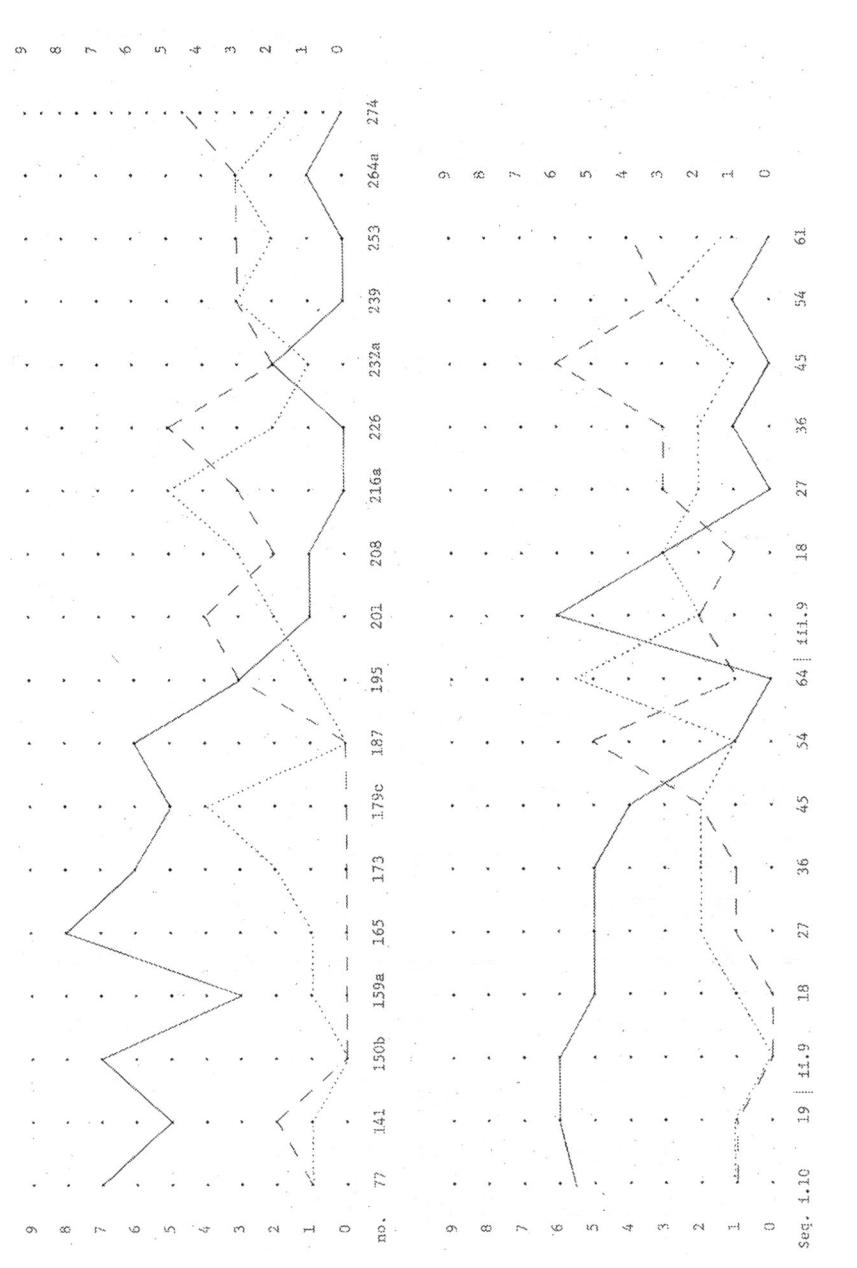

Table 8.2 *Successoribus*, *omnibus episcopis*, and *presulibus* paginally (Fig. 1, above) and chronologically (Fig. 2, below)

8. The fake diplomatic of the Book of Llandaf

These tests are not a panacea. There are many problems which they cannot solve, especially in the 'later' charters ('later' both paginally *and* chronologically), because there are no doublets paginally after 210b or chronologically after iii. 5/6 (171b/74) and because the paginal order is not always wildly wrong, especially towards the end of *LL*, so that there may be little to choose between the graphs (see *presulibus* in Table 8.2, Figs 1–2, for example). Nevertheless a systematic examination of all the common features of the charters in the ways described above helps to confirm Davies's conclusion that most of the formulae are editorial and reveals that some which she regards as original or possibly original are unlikely to be so.[23]

By contrast, the orthography of the names in the witness lists develops chronologically across the Sequences.[24]

---

[23] See above, 72 n. 7 and n. 9, and below, 78–116.

[24] See above, 38. Exceptions in the early charters seem to be due especially to re-editing the charters attached to the *vitae* (Sims-Williams, 'The emergence'). Compare the 'circular' diplomatic features discussed below, 83–4, 86, 106 and 111.

9

THE BOOK OF LLANDAF: FIRST EDITION OR SEVENTH ENLARGED REVISION?

Examining the diplomatic of *LL* not only puts us on our guard against accepting the authenticity of the charters' formulae; it also offers valuable clues about the compilation of *LL*.

The paginal variations in the frequency to which certain formulae are employed was used by Wendy Davies to support her theory that *LL* is made up of nine independent archives, A to J, which had been gradually gathered together over the centuries in various centres before finally being copied end to end in *LL*, as in Table 9.1, interspersed with *Vitae* and other items.[1] I have already noted that this hypothesis is not necessary to explain the arrangement of charters in *LL*,[2] and now turn to the diplomatic arguments. Her hypothesis is that the charters went through at least seven stages of collection, at least four of them involving rewriting or expansion, before appearing in *LL*.

Stage 1 is the existence of the nine archives A to J, at various dates. The main basis for positing these separate archives is the chronological or geographical discontinuity between adjacent groups of charters in *LL*,[3] which can be equally well explained in terms of the compilers' uncertainties over the correct order of bishops; the *diplomatic* evidence for distinguishing the nine Groups is very slight.[4]

Stage 2 is the assimilation of C to F and of D to E. Both assimilations are dubious, but for different reasons. The charters of Euddogwy in C and of his three successors at the beginning of F probably came from a single, cumulative archive that did not get divided (as far as one can tell) before the charters of Euddogwy (C) were moved earlier to join those of the other saints at the head of the collection;[5] thus there is no case for any assimilation of C and F. The charters of D and E, on the other hand, need not have stood together before *LL* was compiled. The peculiarity which appears to mark out DE from the other charters is the occurrence of *Dubricio* alone among the saints in the Disposition, sometimes with *et Teliauo* as well (often a clear interpolation) but never with *Oudoceo*; but this is due to the compilers' evident

---

[1] Davies, *The Llandaff Charters*, 12–16, and *An Early Welsh Microcosm*, 10–14. Table 9.1 is from the latter (p. 12).

[2] See above, 23, where the charters in the proposed Groups are enumerated.

[3] See above, 23–7.

[4] Thus Preambles are said to be a feature of A (73a, 75, 76a, cf. *The Llandaff Charters*, 8, 132, and 142), but that could be a paginal feature, due to the final compilers once they had separated the grants 'to' Dyfrig from the other early ones. Consent is hardly a distinctive feature of F (*An Early Welsh Microcosm*, 104 n. 2; cf. *The Llandaff Charters*, 136).

[5] See above, 27.

9. First edition or seventh enlarged revision?

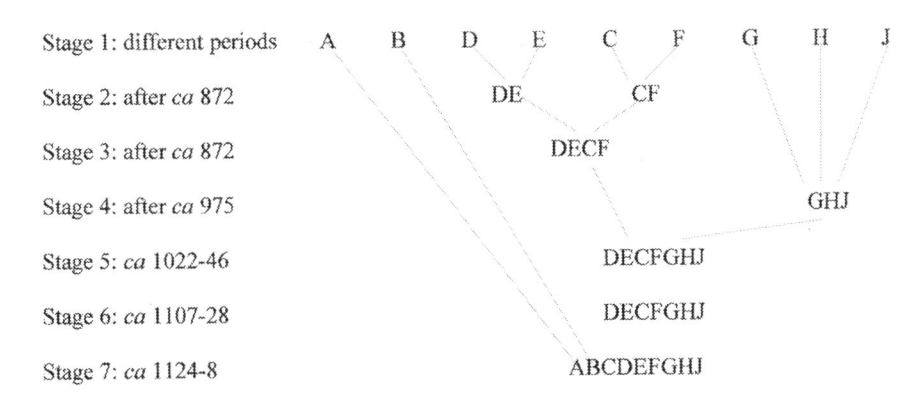

Stage 1: different periods	A	B	D	E	C	F	G	H	J
Stage 2: after *ca* 872			DE		CF				
Stage 3: after *ca* 872				DECF					
Stage 4: after *ca* 975							GHJ		
Stage 5: *ca* 1022-46				DECFGHJ					
Stage 6: *ca* 1107-28				DECFGHJ					
Stage 7: *ca* 1124-8				ABCDEFGHJ					

Table 9.1   Wendy Davies's archives A–J

vacillation over whether these charters' bishops came before or after Euddogwy.[6] Since D and E stand together in *LL* any other similarities between them may be due to passing paginal fashions on the part of the compilers of *LL*, rather than to earlier re-editing of DE as a discrete archive.[7] A general objection to the latter hypothesis is the rarity of cartularies in the early Middle Ages; the earliest Worcester one, *Liber Wigorniensis* (*ca* 996–*ca* 1016), is said to be the earliest extant cartulary in Europe.[8]

Stage 3 is the rewriting of C, D, E, F, as a single archive in a south Glamorgan house, possibly Llancarfan, after *ca* 872 (her suggested date for the latest charter in F). She has two diplomatic arguments for this rewriting. One is that the editor of CDEF had a 'particular concern' with perjury.[9] The figures are too slight to support the weight placed upon them: three Narrations mentioning perjury are included in F, two in C, and one in E, but none in D and there is only one in J. (There are none in ABGH). Her second argument depends on the distribution of Notifications containing gerundives (especially *Sciendum est quod* ...), which are supposed to have been added at Stage 3.[10] The evidence for regarding these Notifications as an early Glamorgan speciality is very weak: the Ogmore inscription and the Llancarfan charters attached to the *Vita Cadoci*. It must be emphasised that Ifor Williams's ingenious reconstruction of the Ogmore inscription ([SCIENDUM] EST [OMNIBus] QUOD DED[IT]....) was inspired by the Llandaf and Llancarfan charters and that the inscription is as late as the eleventh century.[11] The Llancarfan charters can hardly be used as evidence for *early* Llancarfan usage either, since the manuscript is late twelfth century and the charters have been edited, like those in *LL*.[12] While the

---

[6] See above, 23.
[7] In fact Davies says that stage 2 need not have involved rewriting, only collecting (*The Llandaff Charters*, 27).
[8] Wareham, 'The redaction of cartularies', 190.
[9] *The Llandaff Charters*, 22–3 and list at 21.
[10] Ibid., 13, 25, 27, and 133–4; *An Early Welsh Microcosm*, 9.
[11] Williams, 'The Ogmore Castle inscription', 233; Redknap and Lewis, *A Corpus*, I, 496, no. G117.
[12] See above, 28–9, and Brooke, *The Church*, 90–1.

Llancarfan charters and *LL* may well share a common background, it may be an eleventh- or early-twelfth-century background.[13] It is interesting to note that *VC* 66 has a Notification (*Sciendum est quod*) but its doublet *LL* 210b lacks one, and that the Notification in *VC* 67 (*Notificandum est posteris quod*) is independent of that in its doublet *LL* 180b (*Scitote karissimi fratres quod*). The doublets in *LL* itself support the view that the presence and wording of Notifications was a matter of editing, but there is no evidence that the editing occurred at a stage earlier than the compilation of *LL* itself. The rise and fall of Notifications in general, and of those containing gerundives in particular, can easily be explained as a paginal fashion rather than as a relic of an earlier revision of CDEF. Table 9.2 sets out, under the letter for each alleged Group, (a) the number of charters in it, (b) the number and percentage of charters in it with Notifications, (c) the number of charters with Notifications containing a gerundive, (d) the number of (c) in which the gerundive is *sciendum*, (e) the number of (c) in which the gerundive is not *sciendum*, (f) the number and percentage of charters in the Group with a Narration, and (g) the number with a Preamble. It will be seen that the *proportion* of Notifications (b) in A is higher than in C or F and that the *proportion* in H is not much less than in C. Thus Notifications hardly differentiate CDEF from the rest of the alleged Groups. Insofar as there is any pattern, there are traces of an inverse relationship between Notifications (b) and Narrations (f);[14] doubtless a charter starting with a lengthy Narration was felt to be less in need of the padding of a high-sounding Notification (or Preamble) than one without. Note, for instance, that B has the highest proportion of Narrations and no Notifications (nor Preambles) whereas D and E have the highest proportion of Notifications but only two Narrations between them. The distribution of Notifications should probably be understood in relation to the distribution of Narrations, not *vice versa*, since Narrations are an important feature and Notifications merely decorative. The decline in the number of Notifications in the latest charters (in J) may be attributed partly to the increase in the number of Narrations in the later charters,[15] and partly to a purely paginal change in fashion, not to a hypothetical eclipse of the Notification in eleventh-century diplomatic.[16] The proportion of gerundive Notifications in each Group (c : a) merely reflects the distribution of Notifications in general. The proportion of gerundive Notifications to the total number of Notifications in each Group (c : b) is indeed high in CDEF; but the figures are too small in the other Groups to provide a fair comparison (0% in G, 100% in J!). The data for the individual gerundives is still slighter, but consistent with their being mere elegant variation.[17] One must conclude that the popularity of Notifications and gerundives around the middle of *LL* does not require us to postulate a Stage 3 at which these features were added, some centuries before *LL* was compiled; it can be regarded as a mere fashion on the part of the compilers of *LL*, partly dictated by the relative absence of Narrations.

---

[13] Cf. *WHEMA* I 463–4, also Keynes, *The Diplomas*, 111–14.

[14] Forty-nine Notifications occur out of 158 charters in Table 9.2 and fifty-six Narrations, so we expect both in (49/158 × 56/158) = 17.36 cases; actually there are only fourteen cases with both (144, 152, 161, 180b, 185, 186a, 192, 204b, 212, 223, 233, 237b, 239, 257), which may therefore be significant.

[15] See below, 112.

[16] Note that the account of Herewald's consecration in 1059 on p. 265 begins 'Notum sit . . .'.

[17] Cf. Jones, 'The Book of Llandaff', 144.

9. First edition or seventh enlarged revision?

	A	B	C	D	E	F	G	H	J
a	9	7	21	9	9	53[18]	6	20	24
b	4 (44%)	0 (0%)	7 (33%)	5 (56%)	5 (56%)	20 (38%)	1 (17%)	5 (25%)	2 (8%)
c	2	0	4	4	3	15	0	3	2
d	2	0	2	3	1	9	0	3	2
e	0	0	2	1	2	6	0	0	0
f	0 (0%)	5 (71%)	5 (24%)	1 (11%)	1 (11%)	21 (40%)[19]	4 (67%)	6 (30%)	13 (54%)
g	3	0	0	1	0	3	1	2	4

Table 9.2   Notifications, Narrations, and Preambles

Wendy Davies's Stage 4 is the collection together of the originally separate H, G, and J, as GHJ, and Stage 5 is the collecting and rewriting of CDEFGHJ as a single archive, probably under the aegis of Bishop Joseph at Llandaf, *ca* 1022–46. Of these two stages, Stage 4 presents two obvious problems. First, as she observes, the charters in J range from *ca* 975 to *ca* 1075, so they cannot all have been joined to GH in the time of Joseph so that GH(J) has to be regarded as an archive 'in progress'. A second, more serious problem is that we have no evidence that GHJ *is* a single archive – the fact that it comprises all the late charters in *LL* is not evidence – nor that G, H, and J, represent discrete earlier collections. The present arrangement GHJ, instead of the chronologically correct order HGJ, can easily be explained as the result of the compilers of *LL* assembling the late charters from various sources and rearranging them in their present order on the basis of their imperfect list of episcopal consecrations, which included H and J's bishops, but not those of G.[20]

The evidence for Stage 5, being simply the features which differentiate CDEFGH(J) from A and B, is also weak, since the peculiarities of A and B may be due entirely to their separate position in *LL* (a paginal feature) and to their association with the *Vitae* (an editorial factor). There are three such differentiating features in CDEFGH(J):

(1) The three Llandaf saints are included as recipients in CFGHJ (apart from 174b–175, the first two charters of F)[21] and *Dubricio* and *Teliauo* are often both included in DE. The reason for the absence of these additions from the charters 'to' St Dyfrig (in A) is obvious, however, and little significance can be attached to the lack of reference to St Dyfrig in the Dispositions of the B charters, since these are so closely connected to hagiographical Narrations about St Teilo.

(2) Similarly, a second difference between AB and C–J may also be attributed to the final compilation of *LL*: this is the formula *in manu episcopi N*, which only occurs in C–J (except for *in manu archiepiscopi Dubricii* in charter 77, Group A), for the obvious reason that its chief use is to differentiate ordinary non-saintly receiving bishops, who do not occur in the Dispositions of A and

---

[18] Not 54 (in view of the irrelevance of 199bii here).
[19] 12 (23%) if sales are excluded; these are an exceptional type of Narration (see below, 112).
[20] See above, 25.
[21] These two have Dyfrig and Teilo only; 186b, 175's doublet, adds Euddogwy. It took two charters before the compilers got into their stride.

B of course, from saintly recipients.[22] See Table 9.3, where (b) is occurrences of examples of *in manu episcopi N*.

(3) Thirdly, Wendy Davies suggests that the addition of the Sanction *Quicunque custodierit benedicetur, qui autem uiolauerit maledicetur* occurred at Stage 5, before CDEFGH(J) was complete, because it is predominant from about charter 175 and less common after charter 234.[23] Yet, since the elements in this Sanction are found throughout *LL* to some extent, their smooth rise and fall can more easily be explained as a purely paginal fashion during the final editing of *LL*. Table 9.3 indicates, Group by Group, (c) the number of charters including a Sanction clause, the number with (d) *Quicunque custodierit benedicetur / benedictus sit*, (e) *Qui autem uiolauerit*, (f) *Qui ... maledicetur / maledictus sit*, and, for comparison (see below), (g) *Quicunque custodierit custodiat illum Deus*, (h) *Qui autem ab ecclesia Landauiæ separauerit*, and (i) *Qui ... anathema sit*.

	A	B	C	D	E	F	G	H	J
a	9	7	21	9	9	53[24]	6	20	24
b	1 (11%)	0 (0%)	5 (24%)	5 (56%)	5 (56%)	32 (59%)[25]	3 (50%)	7 (35%)	3 (12%)
c	9	6	20	9	9	45	6	20	19
d	0 (0%)	0 (0%)	1 (5%)	1 (11%)	2 (22%)	20 (44%)	2 (33%)	6 (30%)	5 (26%)
e	1 (11%)	0 (0%)	0 (0%)	0 (0%)	1 (11%)	17 (38%)	2 (33%)	6 (30%)	4 (21%)
f	1 (11%)	0 (0%)	0 (0%)	0 (0%)	0 (0%)	14 (31%)	2 (33%)	6 (30%)	4 (21%)
g	1 (11%)	0 (0%)	14 (70%)	8 (89%)	7 (77%)	25 (56%)	4 (67%)	10 (50%)	8 (42%)
h	2 (22%)	2 (33%)	13 (65%)	9 (100%)	8 (88%)	26 (58%)	4 (67%)	12 (60%)	10 (53%)
i	0 (0%)	0 (0%)	11 (55%)	7 (78%)	7 (78%)	26 (58%)	4 (67%)	12 (60%)	10 (53%)

Table 9.3 *In manu episcopi N* and Sanction formulae

Davies's Stage 6 merely involved the appending of the Sanction *Quicunque custodierit custodiat illum Deus, Qui autem ab ecclesia Landauiæ separauerit anathema sit* to some charters in CDEFGHJ in the early twelfth century.[26] The late date is suggested because of a similarity with the diplomatic of the eleventh-century Worcester cartularies (*si quis custodierit omnipotens Deus illum custodire dignetur*)[27] and because the Sanction in question occurs in the latest charters of J, which could not have existed at an earlier stage, if Stage 5 was early-eleventh-century. Here again an objection is that elements of this Sanction can be found to some extent throughout the Groups, including AB (see (g)–(i) in Table 9.3) and that their rise and fall can be explained paginally, like those ascribed to Stage 5. Indeed it seems most likely that both sets of Sanctions, which are complementary, were composed at the same

---

[22] On *in manu episcopi* see further below, 84, and 87.
[23] *The Llandaff Charters*, 15; cf. 140–1 and 143 on Sanctions.
[24] Not 54 here since 199bi is irrelevant to sanctions, the topic of (c)–(i).
[25] However, this percentage is given out of fifty-four, since both 199bi and 199bii could potentially have included *in manu episcopi N*.
[26] *The Llandaff Charters*, 15, 20, and 25.
[27] See *WHEMA* 1 473, 475, and 476 n. 157 (on Sawyer 215 and 216), criticised by J. R. Davies, *The Book of Llandaf*, 102 and 104–5.

9. First edition or seventh enlarged revision?

time, doubtless during the final compilation of *LL*. Davies's view that the addition of the Sanctions took place over three stages lasting a century (Stages 5–7) seems inherently unlikely. It is more probable that all the Sanctions were added during compilation, either to replace hypothetical earlier Sanctions in the originals (for which we have no strong evidence in the doublets)[28] or to make up for the originals' hypothetical lack of Sanctions.

The final Stage 7 is the supposed twelfth-century discovery of archives A and B and the transcription of *LL* itself, with the addition of more stock formulae throughout (e.g. *in campo et in aquis, in siluis et in pascuis*), partly under Worcester influence,[29] including the addition of certain eccentric Sanctions at the beginning and end of the collection.[30] These Sanctions *are* significant. They are marked by combinations of the following formulae: *seruaturis*; *uiolaturis*; *separaturis*; *benedictione facta/data*; *maledictione facta/data*; *excommunicatione facta/data*; *facta anathemate*; *facta absolutione*; *perpetuo anathemate*.[31] The number of Sanctions in each Group containing one or more of those formulae is in Table 9.4. The charters in question are 72b, 73a, 74, 76b, 77; 121, 122, 123, 125a, 125b, 127b; 143, 144, 150b, 152, 154, 159a; 225, 237a; 246, 267, 271, 272. Of these, 246 is by Hand B, the 'editor' of *LL*.[32]

A	B	C	D	E	F	G	H	J
5 (56%)	6 (100%)	6 (30%)	0 (0%)[33]	0 (0%)	0 (0%)	0 (0%)	2 (10%)	4 (21%)

Table 9.4 Further Sanction formulae

These figures do not prove that A and B were not joined to the rest of the charters until Stage 7. Rather they suggest that the compilers, after producing one draft of the charters in much their present order,[34] then went back and reworked the charters attached to the *Vitae* (ABC) using some of the phrases that had occurred to them as they had approached the end of the collection (HJ). The connection of the ABC charters with the *Vitae* would justify giving them special attention (and perhaps their Sanctions had been neglected the first time round). This interpretation is supported by the appearance of some of the relevant formulae in the passage towards the end of the *De Primo Statu Landauensis Æcclesiæ* which forms a transition to the A group of charters (*LL* p. 71),[35] and helps to explain the fact noted by Brooke that 'phrases from the charters creep into the Lives of the saints, and vice versa'.[36] There are a number of other features which are predominant towards the end and near the beginning of

---

[28] See below, ch. 11.
[29] See, however, J. R. Davies, *The Book of Llandaf*, 101.
[30] Davies, *The Llandaff Charters*, 15–16 and 91, and *An Early Welsh Microcosm*, 10.
[31] Cf. *eadem*, *The Llandaff Charters*, 9 and 141. But on *perpetuo anathemate* see J. R. Davies, *The Book of Llandaf*, 99–100.
[32] Idem, '*Liber Landavensis*: its date and the identity of its editor', 4.
[33] Not counting 165 as its *data benedictione* and *absolutione facta* are not in a Sanction.
[34] As most paginal trends imply.
[35] '... *data benedictione* omnibus con*seruaturis* elemosinam cum omni predicta dignitate priuilegii & refugii. *maledictione* autem [+ *incussa* Vesp. A.xiv] *uiolaturis* in magno aut in modico ut predictum est'. See Davies, *The Llandaff Charters*, 17.
[36] Brooke, *The Church*, 31; cf. Davies, *The Llandaff Charters*, 16–17.

the *LL* charters, suggesting 'circular' composition of the sort indicated above. The formulae *pro anima(bus)* + gen. sg. or pl. (*amicorum, parentum, aui*, etc.)[37] and *incolis* (in the liberty formula *et/cum (omni/tota) communione incolis*)[38] are both commonest in the charters attached to the *Vitae* of Teilo and Euddogwy and in the last charters of *LL*. There is also a noticeable tendency in the charters attached to the *Vitae* and in H and J to place bounds *before* the attestations, which may indicate influence from foreign models;[39] and the wording of the Preambles, which are a feature of the charters attached to the *Vita Dubricii*, show close resemblances to the wording of those towards the end of *LL*.[40] A similar 'circular' distribution may be seen in various orthographical features.[41]

It has been necessary to criticise Wendy Davies's reconstruction of the gradual compilation of *LL* because much hinges upon it. If she were right, the cult of the three patron saints of Llandaf, for instance, would have to go back at least to Stage 5 in the early eleventh century, and it would be proved that CDEFGH(J) is an episcopal archive, if it were at Stage 5 that *in manu episcopi* was added. Indeed she even suggests that *in manu episcopi* may already have been a feature of CDEF at Stage 3 and could be original.[42] Above all, if she were right, we would have to assume a great deal of literary activity over the centuries which, while of great interest in itself, would inevitably cast still more doubt on the validity of the charters that have finally come down to us.

There can be no doubt that she is right to maintain that *LL* is composed of charters from a number of episcopal archives at various places in south Wales. The identification of these archives is best approached, however, not by looking at the present arrangement of *LL* and stylistic variations in the charters, but by examining

---

[37] English and Continental parallels from the eleventh century onwards in *WHEMA* I 464–5. I am here excluding *pro anima sua/animabus suis* (Davies, *The Llandaff Charters*, 135), which is old, appearing for instance on eighth- and tenth-century crosses at Llantwit and Margam (Redknap and Lewis, *A Corpus*, I, nos G65, G66, and G81) and in 'Chad 1'. By contrast, despite modern Continental scholars' use of terms like 'gifts *pro anima*', *pro anima mea* was rare outside 'Celtic' contexts before the eleventh century according to Davies, *Acts of Giving*, 117 n. 13. (But *pro remedio animae meae* is ancient: Snook, 'Who introduced charters into England?', 266 and 276.)

[38] Davies, *The Llandaff Charters*, 16–17, 138, and 143. Note *Vita S. Oudocei, LL* p. 133. See below, 106.

[39] Cf. Davies, *The Llandaff Charters*, 144; Coe, 'Dating the boundary clauses', 35–9. But see above, 48 n. 36.

[40] See Davies, *The Llandaff Charters*, 132–3.

[41] See above, 77 n. 24.

[42] Davies, *The Llandaff Charters*, 28 n. 14, 137, and 143, noting *in manu abbatis* in the Redon Cartulary (but cf. *WHEMA* I 467–8 and n. 84 and 473: 'can hardly be of pre-twelfth-century origin' – in this connection, Dr Martin Brett drew my attention to the increasing emphasis after 1100 in the English Church on the need for churches to pass through the hands of bishops; see Brett, *The English Church*, 142–8). On *in manu episcopi* see above, 81–2, and below, 87–8. Examination of the doublets does not support it being an original formula (cf. 175/186b and 210b/*VC* 66) and the distribution through *LL* is consonant with its being an editorial addition at the final stage. It is not particularly characteristic of CDEF, for a lower proportion of charters in C have it than charters in G or H; and it is striking that the doublets 175 and 186b, which disagree over the inclusion of the formula, both lie within the alleged entity CDEF.

9. First edition or seventh enlarged revision?

the areas from which the various bishops receive grants,[43] the places designated as episcopal seats in the charters themselves[44] or in external sources such as the 1005 Æthelred charter,[45] the evidence for the cults of the saints mentioned in the Dispositions, and the evidence in *LL* and elsewhere for episcopal succession, discontinuity, and contemporaneity.[46] Quite how and when the charters reached Llandaf may always remain uncertain, since more than one plausible route can often be hypothesised.[47]

---

[43] See ch. 14 below, and maps in Hughes, 'The Celtic Church'. A complication, as Anglo-Saxon parallels remind us, is that bishops could receive grants outside their own dioceses and at a distance from their sees.

[44] Cf. Davies, *An Early Welsh Microcosm*, 134 n. 1.

[45] See above, 60; J. R. Davies, *The Book of Llandaf*, 10–13. The reference to 'bishop-houses' in the Welsh laws is possibly relevant (Charles-Edwards, *Wales and the Britons*, 596–8; Petts, *The Early Medieval Church in Wales*, 162–3).

[46] See ch. 14 below. A start in these directions was made by Davies, but her discussion is closely bound up with and dependent on her theory of the nine original groups of charters: *The Llandaff Charters*, 91, and *An Early Welsh Microcosm*, 149–59.

[47] For example, see 164 and 177, on the Ergyng charters.

10

A NEW APPROACH TO THE COMPILATION OF THE BOOK OF LLANDAF

The charters in *LL* that were not forged from scratch at the time of compilation must have been based on earlier charters, of varying authenticity, gathered together in the twelfth century or before from Gospel Books, single sheets, cartularies, and so on. Although it is inherently unlikely that *none* of the charters used were copies of copies, I have not been able to find any evidence for a 'long history of interference'[1] with the material before Urban chose to make it the basis of his claims. The indications of more than one stage of editing, such as the 'circular' features discussed above,[2] need indicate no more than that *LL* went through several drafts in the Llandaf scriptorium, as one would expect with so large a project. As we have seen, no diplomatic features have been detected that prove or even indicate the existence of pre-Llandaf, *intermediate* collections of charters, and the present arrangement of *LL* can be explained solely in terms of the Llandaf compilers' inconsistent attempt at arranging all the bishops in a single chronological sequence, with the aid of their notions about the three patron saints, the internal evidence of the charters themselves, and the incomplete list of ninth- to eleventh-century consecrations. It is difficult to imagine any circumstance before the advent of the Normans and the new ideas about 'proper' diplomatic form that Urban or his collaborators may have acquired at Worcester or elsewhere that would have led early Welsh clerics to attempt any purely diplomatic revision of their ancient charters. Given their evident reverence for ancient books,[3] it would be strange for them to have attempted to rewrite their ancient documents merely in order to have crisp new copies. One of the proofs of ownership in the early Irish Laws was a *senscríbend deodae*, 'an *ancient* ecclesiastical writing',[4] and it is reasonable to suppose that a similar attitude would have prevailed in Wales. Manipulation in favour of a different recipient was another matter, of course; but there is little evidence that the *LL* charters had suffered any such alteration before Urban associated all their bishops with Llandaf in support of his great cause, a cause which had its roots not much further back, so far as we know, than the episcopate of his predecessor Bishop Herewald.[5]

A fuller understanding of the compilation of *LL* can come from a close scrutiny of the 'paginal bunching of formulae'[6] and from an examination of the doublets in *LL*. As an example of 'bunching' let us examine the charters assigned to the episcopate of

---

[1] Davies, *An Early Welsh Microcosm*, 22.
[2] See above, 77 n. 24.
[3] See above, 13, on the *Vita S. Cadoci* reference to the Gospels of Gildas.
[4] Kelly, *A Guide to Early Irish Law*, 204.
[5] See above, ch. 4.
[6] Above, 73.

10. A new approach to the compilation

Berthwyn, 174b–195.[7] We notice the curious fact that the formula *in manu episcopi* occurs in all eight of charters 180b–187, but only once elsewhere (174b). These eight charters have no geographical or chronological common denominator to account for this peculiarity, so it cannot be maintained that they come from a separate archive relating to a special area or a particular period in Berthwyn's episcopate. The obvious conclusion is that we have a merely passing fashion on the part of the compiler of the Berthwyn section of *LL*, perhaps working on separate occasions, or else the work of one of several compilers in the Llandaf scriptorium, preparing material for transcription into *LL*. I shall adopt the second hypothesis, and label our compiler 'Q', but the hypothesis of the single compiler working in several stints is equally possible and what I shall argue will apply equally well to it, *mutatis mutandis*.

Table 10.1 shows the charters of the Berthwyn group in the order they appear in *LL* on the left and their approximate chronological order (as defined by the kings, donors and witnesses) on the right.[8] The occurrences of *in manu episcopi* are indicated by ¶; it will be seen at once that there is no chronological rhyme or reason to them. I have also indicated some other features that tend to differentiate Q from the compilers of the sections before and after him ('P' and 'R'). Q seems to have had a particular liking for the formula *sine ullo censu* (*), which is shared by R but eschewed by P.[9] Q and R have also preserved some references to sales from their originals (which can have had no relevance to Llandaf's case[10]), whereas P omits them, though they were probably among some of his originals (176a is a doublet of 190b, and 179b is a doublet of 191); these sales are denoted by Σ. However, Q has avoided *immolauit* (ι) and *largitus est* (λ), which are favoured by P and R respectively. If he includes gerundive Notifications, P always has *sciendum* (s), whereas Q and R also have other gerundives (x): 183a *notandum*; 186a *videndum*; 187 *previdendum*; 190a *demonstrandum*.

There are several reasons for thinking that the sections written by P, Q, and R, were written in that order and in the context of their present position in *LL* (which is in itself a reason for suspecting that P, Q, and R were really one and the same compiler working on successive occasions): the one stray ¶ at the beginning of P's stint is the tail end of an earlier paginal trend; the noting of sales (Σ), which only begins at 185, is common after 195 (until 209b); the revival of *sine ullo censu* (*) in Q and R

---

[7] 179a, 192, and 193 lack lists and therefore are omitted from the Sequences. 179a does not mention Berthwyn specifically but its doublet 188b does. 193 has no real connection with Berthwyn (other than its placing between 192 and 195); it refers to an unnamed bishop of Llandaf. Charters 193, 195, and 196 concern the cult of St Clydog and are tacked on to the final charters of Berthwyn, before those of Tyrchan which start with 197.

[8] Davies, *The Llandaff Charters*, 45, lists charters 205 and 204b as ii.24 and 27, but these are charters of Bishop Tyrchan and probably belong later (see above, 33). Charter 158 probably belongs in Berthwyn's episcopate, judging by its witness list (ii.30), but is misplaced in *LL* among Euddogwy's charters (see Davies, *The Llandaff Charters*, 47 and 102).

[9] While the existence of royal and other *census* is likely to have been ancient (Davies, *An Early Welsh Microcosm*, 48–9; *WHEMA* I 470 and n. 114, also XI 271 on Clynnog) the distribution of references to it through *LL* (Davies, *The Llandaff Charters*, 138) seems to be purely paginal. However, the formula *cum omni censu*, rare in *LL* (Davies, *The Llandaff Charters*, 139, cites only 175/186b, 198a, and 218), may be original since it occurs in both 175 and 186b (doublets). See Davies, *An Early Welsh Microcosm*, 49 n. 3. Cf. J. R. Davies, *The Book of Llandaff*, 99. An estate's *census* is mentioned in 'Chad' 3.

[10] On sales (Σ) see below, 106–11.

			PAGINAL		CHRONOLOGICAL			
¶	ð	s	P 174b		19		ι	
	ð	s	175		20	¶ *	ð	
	ð	s	176a		21	¶	ð	s
	ι		176b		22}		ð	s
	ι		178		23}		Σ λ	
	ð	s	179a					
	ι		179b		25	¶ *		
	ι		179c		26		ð	
			180a		28			
¶ *			Q 180b		29		ι	
¶ *	ð	x	183a		31	¶ *	ð	x
¶ *	ð		183b		32	*	ð	x
¶			184		33}		ι	
¶ * Σ	ð	s	185		34}		Σ λ	
¶	ð	x	186a		35}		ð	s
¶	ð		186b		36}	¶	ð	
¶ *	ð	x	187		37	¶ *	ð	x
	λ		R 188a		38		ð	
	ð		188b		39	¶		
	ð		189		40		λ	
*	ð	x	190a		41		ι	
Σ	λ		190b		42	¶ * Σ	ð	s
Σ	λ		191		43	¶	ð	x
		s	192					
*			193					
*			195		44		ι	

Table 10.1 Charters of Bishop Berthwyn

is continued into the charters after 195; the *immolauit* (ι) phase in P had begun in 171b–173 and picks up again from 195–196; and *largitus est* (λ) does not occur for fifty-nine charters before 188a, but is dominant after 196.[11] There are further signs of continuity with the adjacent sections of *LL* in the Dispositions. Dispositions in favour of St Dyfrig and St Teilo (omitting St Euddogwy) continue from 160 into the first two charters of P; a spate of *dedit* (ð) connects P and Q with the preceding charters, while its decline connects R with the following charters; a mixture of *successoribus* and *pastoribus* runs into P, is replaced by a solid block of *successoribus* from 179b to 191, which is in turn followed by a block of *omnibus episcopis* at 192 rarely broken before 240; and *in elemosina* appears for the first time since 161 about twice every nine charters from R until 206.[12] All this strongly suggests that all these formulae

---

[11] Apart from an interesting relapse into *immolauit* between 204a and 210b, visible in the graph in Table 8.1, Fig. 1. For data on all these trends see Davies, *The Llandaff Charters*, 134–9.

[12] Cf. above, Table 8.1, Fig. 1, and for data on Dispositions see Davies, *The Llandaff Charters*, 135–7 and 139.

10. A new approach to the compilation

were given their present distribution during the final compilation of *LL*, not at any earlier stage. Since they are all major *LL* formulae very little room is left for any hypothetical earlier editing of the originals before the production of *LL*.

The occurrence of doublets in the Berthwyn charters is noted in Table 10.1 by **bold** figures in the Paginal column and by curly brackets in addition in the Chronological column. It will be seen that their distribution between the sections P, Q, and R reinforces the suggestion that P, Q, and R, represent three separate stints in editing the charters: 175 in P is repeated in Q; 176a and 179b in P are both repeated in R; and 179a in P (which has no witness list and is therefore not included in the chronological sequence) is a doublet of 188b in R. The reason for the greater amount of overlap between P and R than between Q and P or R may well be that by the time the compiler(s) came to work on R they had begun to forget what had already been included in P. Something of the immense difference between each member of the doublets in formulae can be seen from the symbols adjacent to the bracketed items in Table 10.1.

This line of enquiry raises again the question of the origin of the doublets in *LL*. For Wendy Davies the fact that doublets occur shows that *LL* is made up of partly overlapping independent collections which have duplicated each other's material.[13] The doublets do not require this explanation, however. The very fact that the compilers allowed the doublets to stand in *LL* testifies to their incompetence (or, just possibly, their desire to increase its bulk); it is equally possible, then, that the creation of the doublets is also due to their carelessness in editing the same texts twice. Doublets could most easily arise when using charters on single sheets, which could get shuffled and be reused in error. None of the very considerable differences between each member of each pair of charters is inconsistent with the view that each represents an independent working-up of a short shared original, or copy of such, during the compilation of *LL* itself over a period of years or even months or weeks. (There will, of course, have been more than one draft of *LL* before the extant fair copy was made by Scribe A; we have evidence for the existence of part of such a draft in Cotton Vespasian A.xiv.)[14] If this view is correct – and it has the merit of simplicity – a comparison of the texts of the doublets is telling evidence both for the essence of the originals and for the degree to which the compilers were willing to go in their diplomatic and orthographical modification and manipulation. Such a comparison indicates that nothing was sacrosanct, save the substance of the transaction and the attached witness lists. Thus any feature present in only one charter of a pair can only be attributed to the shared original after careful consideration, and some features in both (such as Llandaf as recipient and many of the stock *LL* formulae) may have to be rejected as due to coincidence or consistent re-editing. This is discussed further in Chapter 11.

There is a further dimension to the doublets. A curious fact which has never been pointed out is that one member of every pair stands next to one member of another pair, either in *LL* or in *VC*. See the brackets in Table 10.2.

---

[13] For instance that 73b in her Group A archive recurs as 163a in her Group D archive. Since her Group F itself contains doublets, she regards it as a composite of still further earlier, smaller archives. See Davies, *The Llandaff Charters*, 12 and 28 n. 10.

[14] See above, 10.

I {
   α 73b = 163a

   β 74 = 171b

II {
   γ 175 = 186b

   δ 176a = 190b
              } II/III
   ε 179b = 191

III {
   ζ 179a = 188b

   η 180b = *VC* 67
             } IV
   θ 210b = *VC* 66

Table 10.2 Doublets and hypothetical single sheets

How is this to be explained? The only explanation I can see supposes first that all these charters were on single sheets (not necessarily 'originals' rather than copies), and secondly that some of the sheets carried more than one charter,[15] with the result that their contents got copied out continuously in *LL* or *VC*. We can posit four such sheets (or three if II and III were all one sheet II/III). Sheet I would have contained α and β, both charters (seventh- and ninth-century) relating to Ergyng. II and III would have contained γ, δ, ε, and ζ, all eighth-century charters from the archive of Bishop Berthwyn further south. IV would have contained η and θ; its origin is more obscure – possibly Llancarfan, Llandough, the old church at Llandaf, or wherever the archive of the Berthwyn–Tyrchan–Cadwared episcopates was held.[16] Mechanical copying of the contents of the sheets explains how α stands next to β in *LL* 73b–74, θ next to η in *VC* 66–67, and so on. The compilers' sporadic attempts at grouping contemporary and related charters together will explain why α and β are separated elsewhere, as 163a and 171b, and so on.

The two charters of our hypothetical sheet I were grants to St Dyfrig and his successors. The compiler of the Dyfrig hagiography of *LL*, on the one hand, took them as grants to St Dyfrig himself and so copied out α and β as 73b–74. The compiler of a later section, on the other hand, realised that α was in favour of Bishop 'Elgistus'[17]

---

[15] Compare multiple seventh-century charters on now lost single sheets at Worcester: Sims-Williams, *Britain and Early Christian Europe*, VII 6–10 and the Addendum referring to Keynes, *The Councils of Clofesho*, 36 n. 154. The Worcester single sheet discussed by Keynes was, as he says, probably not an 'original', but a document 'produced for the purposes of a dispute in the later ninth century (or thereafter)'; it contained copies of three transactions with three different dates (Sawyer 1260, 1430, and 1432). For single sheets in ninth-century script surviving at St Davids see above, 14 (referring to Caroline Brett's dating).

[16] See below, 100, and 166. For locations, see Hughes, 'The Celtic Church', 18, map 3.

[17] Probably the same name as *Arguistil*, the first witness of 73a, although *Arwystl* and *Elwystl* are different names (cf. Davies, *The Llandaff Charters*, 162, and above, 26 n. 23).

10. A new approach to the compilation

and copied it out as 163a and saw that β was in favour of Bishop Greciel and therefore left it aside for later use, when Greciel's episcopate was reached (171b).[18]

The first compiler of the Berthwyn section (P = 174b–180a) picked up II and copied out γ and δ as 175–176a. After copying two more Berthwyn charters from elsewhere (176b–178), he picked up III and copied out ζ and ε, as 179a–179b.

The second compiler of the Berthwyn section (Q = 180b–187) picked up IV and copied out η (180b) because it referred to Berthwyn (it does in *LL and* in *VC*), but left θ (210b) for later because it did not. He then copied out five more Berthwyn charters from other sources (183a–186a), the last of which was a grant by a certain Ilias (186a). As γ was also a grant by Ilias he took II and copied out γ from it as 186b, perhaps not realising that it had already been copied by P as 175. He did not, however, follow γ with δ, possibly because he noticed that he had begun to duplicate the work of P, and his work broke off after one more Berthwyn charter (187).

The third compiler of the Berthwyn section (R = 188a–195) began by copying a grant by a certain Elffin (188a). He then took III and copied out ζ as 188b because it, too, was a grant by Elffin. He may not have realised that ζ had already been included by P as 179a or he may have noticed that that earlier copy was defective, lacking both witness list and bounds. R did not proceed to copy ε at once, but put III down, probably because he had to hand another charter (189) which also referred to Elffin: by this charter Gwrgan gave an estate to Berthwyn and took back his *uxorem propriam, filiam Elfin*.[19] Thus distracted from III, R copied out a further charter from some other source (190a) and then took II and copied out δ from it as 190b, before returning to III for ε, which he copied out as 191. (He may have refrained from copying γ from II, when he had it before him, in the knowledge that it had already been copied by Q, not to mention P as well.) One may wonder if it is merely a coincidence that δ from II and ε from III stand together in R's work as 190b–191; as noted above, a possible explanation is that II and III were really a single document or page (II/III), containing four charters (γ, δ, ε, and ζ).

After he had copied ε as 191, R rounded off the series of Berthwyn charters with the memorandum recording churches restored to Berthwyn that had been lost during wars with Æthelbald of Mercia (192). This was followed by charters relating to Clodock in Herefordshire (193, 195, and 196), only the second of which is explicitly connected with Berthwyn. A late-twelfth-century copy of a draft of these three charters may also be found in Cotton Vespasian A.xiv under the heading *Incipit Vita sancti Clitauci regis et martyris*, in the order 196, 193, 195; the compiler may have used discarded early drafts of *LL*.[20]

After the Clodock material, the charters of Bishop Tyrchan (197–205), and a brief note of his successor *Eluogus*, the compilers of *LL* give the charters of Bishop Cadwared (206–211). Here they turned back to IV for the charter previously omitted (for chronological reasons) in the Berthwyn section, and copied out θ as 210b. The compiler of the Llancarfan cartulary attached to the *Vita Cadoci* in Vespasian A.xiv,

---

[18] On these doublets see above, 22, and below, 93.
[19] This argument suggests that 189 already had the germ of its Narration when it was reworked by R.
[20] See *LL* p. 362 and above, 66. According to Evans (*LL*, p. 362) the passage corresponding to *LL* p. 195, which ends the '*Vita*', is in a hand similar to the early-thirteenth-century hand of *LL* pp. 247–9 (cols 294–5); this is Hand Fc in Huws, *Medieval Welsh Manuscripts*, 138 and 143.

who had no chronological scruples, simply copied out IV *en bloc* as *VC* 66–67, though 66 is undoubtedly a much later charter than 67.[21]

It is always assumed that the charters attached to the *Vita Cadoci* were simply transcribed from a much earlier Llancarfan cartulary that was available to the Monmouth scribe, and this is very likely in the case of the majority of them. Yet it is not impossible that IV was taken directly from the Llandaf archive (perhaps because of some perceived connection with Llancarfan or St Cadog) by the Vespasian compiler and was adapted by him to swell his existing quota of Llancarfan charters. It is noteworthy that *VC* 67 is not really in favour of Llancarfan as it stands,[22] that *VC* 66–67 stand near the end of the Llancarfan cartulary (only *VC* 68 follows), and that there is a long blank in the Vespasian manuscript 'as though more charters were to be inserted' after *VC* 68 before the final text (*VC* 69), De obcecatione Mailguni regis (which concerns St Cadog and the *refugium* of Llancarfan).[23] While it is possible that the Monmouth scribe got tired of copying his exemplar and intended to go back later and fill in the space he had left, it is also possible that he had begun to *compile* the cartulary from near the place where he breaks off and that *VC* 66–67 were among the documents which he added on his own initiative.

The processes behind the compilation of *LL* would repay further study.[24] For, unless this brief visit to the Llandaf scriptorium has been wholly imaginary, it is evident that a sound judgement on the reliability of the charters must depend not on speculations about hypothetical earlier compilers of pre-*LL* cartularies, but on close examination of the vagaries and methods of the compilers of *LL* and comparison of the texts of the doublets which they so helpfully left to posterity.

---

[21] See above, 41. On the two charters shared between *LL* and *VC* see Charles-Edwards, *Wales and the Britons*, 256–61, and below, 99–103; it seems possible that different elements were preserved in *LL* and *VC* according to whether they suited the interests of Llandaf and Llancarfan respectively.

[22] See above, 28.

[23] *VSB* 136 n. 1; Charles-Edwards, *Wales and the Britons*, 294–5.

[24] Anscombe, 'Landavensium ordo chartarum', 124–5, argued that the *LL* compiler used the names of the Llancarfan abbots as aid to ordering Euddogwy's charters. This seems unlikely, as the order in *LL* is: *Iacob* (× 3), *Sulgen, Concen* (× 7), *Sulgen, Concen* [*sic*], *Dagan, Concen*! See also Bartrum, 'Some studies'; James, 'The "Concen charters"'; Davies, *The Llandaff Charters*, 41–7 and 54–5; and above, 38–41.

11

THE EVIDENCE OF THE DOUBLETS

The doublets within *LL* (73b/163a, 74/171b, 175/186b, 176a/190b, 179a/188b, and 179b/191) and between *LL* and *VC* (180b/*VC* 67 and 210b/*VC* 66) shed important light on the extent – and the limits – to which the charters' editors were prepared to go.[1] In this chapter I examine them in turn, in rather more detail than was required in Chapter 10 above. The text of *VC* is that of Wade-Evans (checked against fo. 40r of BL Cotton Vespasian A.xiv). The *LL* texts have been lightly edited in respect of capitalisation, word separation, punctuation, and the use of *æ*.

73b/163a

This charter concerns an estate, apparently a monastery, in the Dore valley.[2] The formulae rarely agree, and where they do agree, in the liberty-formula, the phraseology is so hackneyed[3] that the agreement may be coincidental. Clearly, one cannot rely on the diplomatic of either version. The boundary appears in 73b only and, although of the earliest type, may be an addition,[4] as may the interesting antiquarian details about the dynasty of Ergyng. By contrast, the names of donors, estate, and witnesses correspond closely, and may well derive from a brief original similar to the 'Chad' charters in the Lichfield Gospels.[5] The title *episcopus* given to *Elgistus* (i.e. Arwystl)[6] in 163a, may have been deliberately omitted in 73b, so as to make it a grant to St Dyfrig in person. The duplication is further justified by making 163a a *restoration* of land earlier granted to St Dyfrig.

73b De **Cvm Barrvc**.
Sciant omnes quod duo filii Pepiav **Cinuin** uidelicet & **Guidci** dederunt **tres uncias agri Cum Barruc** sancto Dubricio & omnibus sibi succedentibus in æcclesia Landauiæ in perpetuo **cum**

163a **Cvm Barrvc**.
Cinvin rex & **Guidci** frater suus reddiderunt Deo et Elgisto episcopo **tres uncias agri Cumbarruc, cum** sua tota **libertate & omni communione in** campo et **in silu**is, **in aqua & in pascuis**,

---

[1] See Sims-Williams, 'Review', 127, and 'The emergence'; Charles-Edwards, *Wales and the Britons*, 256–67; and ch. 10 above.
[2] It is identified with *Lann Calcuch/Colcuch* in charter 192 (cf. 165), and reached as far as *Tir Conloc*, which is not Madley but Eaton Bishop according to Coe, 'The place-names', 200–1, 405–6, and 809–10. 73b is translated by Birch, *Memorials*, 36 (cf. 121–2).
[3] See Davies, *The Llandaff Charters*, 137–8.
[4] On these bounds, see Coe, 'The place-names', 960, and 'Dating the boundary clauses', 42–3.
[5] As noted in Sims-Williams, 'The emergence', 33.
[6] On *Elgistus/Arwystl* see above, 26 n. 23, and 90 n. 17.

omni **libertate** sine ullo censu homini terreno nisi sancto Dubricio & suæ familiæ & suis sequacibus **& cum omni communione** data circumcirca, **in campo** & **in aqu**is, **in silu**a & **in pascuis**. Finis huius agri est a ualle usque ad lech longitudo, latitudo de lech usque ad Petram Crita. **Testes** super hoc pactum **de clericis Arguistil. Iunabui. Cinguarui Elheiarun**. Cimmareia. **De laicis** testes **Guoidci & Cinuin. Collbiu**. **& Arcon. Qui** in sacrato isto peccauerint execrentur.	quas in priori tempore accepit sanctus Dubricius archiepiscopus dextralis Britanniæ & sedis Landauiæ a Peibiau rege Ercicg cum sua tota **libertate**. **De clericis testes** sunt **Elgistus** episcopus. **Iunabui. Cinguariu. Elhearn. De laicis Cinuin & Guidci** frater eius. **Colluiu. Aircol**. Cintiuit. Quicunque custodierit custodiat illum Deus. **Qui** autem ab ecclesia Landauiæ et a pastoribus eius separauerit, anathema sit.

The witness lists are similar, but each version has one unique name. There is some variation in spelling: 73b/163a: Arguistil/Elgistus Iunabui/Iunabui Cinguarui/Cinguariu Elheiarun/Elhearn Guoidci/Guidci Cinuin/Cinuin Collbiu/Colluiu Arcon/Aircol.

74/171b

Lann Bocha/*Mocha* – St Maughan's[7] – is the third church in 171b, which combines a version of 74 with several other grants, allegedly all involving the same grantor *Britcon*. The reference to 'filiorum Guoleiduc, Caratauc & Cincu' in 74 may be original, accidentally omitted in 171b. It is probably a coincidence that both versions have a Notification in *Sciendum/Sciant quod*, the dispositive formula *omnibus successoribus in perpetuo*, and an anathema with *Qui ... ab ecclesia Landauiæ separauerit*.[8]

74 De **Lann Bocha**. Sciendum est nobis **quod dederunt Britcon & Iliuc Lann Mocha** pro animabus suis cum omni sua **libertate** in campo & in silua, in pascuis & in aquis **Deo** & sancto Petro apostolo & archiepiscopo **Dubricio** archimonasterii[9] Landauie. **& suis omnibus**	171b .VI. æcclesiæ . I. Lann Budgualan in hostio Crican super Guy. II. Merthir Cynfall. III. **Lannmocha**. IIII. Lann Typallai. V. Lanndiniul. VI. Mafurn. VII. Mable. **Sciant** omnes Christiani **quod Britcon** Hail filius Deuon immolauit .VI. æcclesias in una die **Deo** et sancto **Dubricio** pro salute animæ suæ et in manu Grecielis episcopi **et omnibus successoribus suis** in ecclesia sanctorum Dubricii et Teliaui, & cum sua tota libertate et omni communione in campo et in siluis, in aqua et in pascuis, & cum suis territoriis

---

[7] See Coe, 'The place-names', s.n. *Llanfocha*. For the boundary shared by 74/171b see *ibid*., 513–14 and 961–2; for the other bounds see 986–8 and (*Mafwrn*) 984. Coe, 'Dating the boundary clauses', 37, puts 74 in his earliest period. The *Mafwrn* boundary is also attached to 162b, with the same lacuna before *Dour* (the river Dore). 74 and 171b are partly translated by Birch, *Memorials*, 36–7 and 132–3. On the fate of St Maughan's see J. R. Davies, *The Book of Llandaf*, 48 n. 19, and 171–2.

[8] All commonplace in *LL*; see Davies, *The Llandaff Charters*, 133, 137–8, and 141.

[9] *archi-* is not in Vespasian A.xiv (*LL* p. 358). Cf. Guy, 'The *Life* of St Dyfrig', 8 n. 23.

11. The evidence of the doublets

successoribus in perpetuo uerbo & consensu **Mourici regis** simul cum dono filiorum Guoleiduc, Caratauc uidelicet & Cincu, sine principatu & potestate alicuius super eam, nisi episcoporum Landauiæ. Quicunque ab **ecclesia Landauiæ** & a pastoribus eius eam **separauerit**, perpetuo anathemate feriatur. **Finis** istius podi **est** de **fossa ad Castell Merych. ex hinc tendit ad Uallem Lembi usque ad Uallem Cilcirch, recte** tendit in **longitudinem uallis usque** ad **Baudur. deinde in longitudine** uallis **Eclin usque ad caput siluæ. deinde medium siluæ usque ad caput Nan Pedecon.** & inhit **dir Tnou Guinn usque ad Uadem Rufum, Sata Tinnuhuc dir auallen Hendreb Iouoniu, deinde** exit **ad rubum salic**ulum & **destendit in primam fossam ubi inceptus est. Finis** agri istius podij. Testes sunt **de clericis. Num. Simon. Sciblon. Araun. Blainrit. Iudon. Ioubiu. Guor**en. **Cinguan.** & multi alij testes qui hic non nominantur. **De laicis. Britton & Iluic. Gloiu. Biuonui. Lilli. Cimuireg.** Coram illis omnibus posuerunt hanc dotem super quattuor euangelia in perpetuo sine herede nisi ecclesia Landauiæ & benedicentes omnes uno ore omnibus seruaturis hanc elemosinam, maledicentes autem communiter his **qui** istud podum cum sua tellure omnibus. In primis æcclesia, id est æcclesia Lannbudgualan, in hostio Circan quæ dudum fuerat sancti Dubricii & Methirchinfall cum omni tellure sua, id est tribus modiis terræ, & agrum quem dedit Iudhail et augmentum preterea quam Biuon dederat huic æcclesiæ. & **Lann Bocha dederunt** simul **Britcon et Iliuc Deo** & sanctis **Dubricio** et Teliauo et Grecieli episcopo Landauiæ **et omnibus** pastoribus illius **in perpetuo** cum toto agro suo et tota **libertate** et finibus istis subscriptis, & **uerbo Mourici regis** liberam ab omni seruitio. **De clericis** testes sunt. Greciel episcopus. **Nu**d. **Simon. Isciplan. Araun. Blainrit. Iudon. Ioubiu. Gur**ou. **Cincuan. De laicis.** Mouricus rex. **Britcon. et Iliuc. Gloiu. Biuonui . Lilli. Cimuireg. Finis** illius **est**. Incipit a **fossa** usque **ad Castell Meirch. Ex hinc tendit ad Uallem Lembi usque ad Uallem Cilcirch. recte in longitudine uallis usque Baudur. deinde in longitvdine Eilin usque ad caput siluæ, deinde per medium siluæ** tendit **usque ad caput Nant Pedecou, deinde dir Tnou Guinn usque ad Rufum Uadum.** [*blank*] **Sata Tinnuhuc dir aballenn Henntre Iguonui, deinde ad rubum**, de salicibus descendit in primam fossam ubi inceptus finis est. Quicunque custodierit, benedicetur. **Qui** autem **ab ecclesia Landauiæ separauerit**, excomunicetur. Ecclesiam Tipallai, et ecclesiam Diniul atque Mafurn, et ecclesiam Mable habens vi. modios cum silua et campo. Finis illius est. Or Glasguern dir Dubnnant Du. de hinc per transuersum inter flumen Iacob et Brinn Cornou, iterum per siluam, de hinc descendit in Manach riuulo, recte dir Halannauc, recte per siluam dir Oncir, bet ir finnaun eithaf, fraxina custodiente, tendit recte inter duo castella ad Longam Insulam, istius donec descendit in riuulo Trodi. Finis Lanntipallai. Licat Arganhell ar traus ir coit, ar hit i claud di Luch ir Eilin, hit ir pant, nihit di Cestill Meirch, in iaun di Cil Fotul, traus i mais ar hit i claud bet Duuir in Dair, ar hit i pant trui i coit bet licat Argannel, ubi incepit. Finis Lann Cinfall. Cirn Cinfall i tal ir foss ar hit ir foss, di licat Finnaun Efrdil, i guuer nihit bet Mingui. Mingui nihit bet Pull Rud, di uinid bet tal ir brinn, di guairet di Lech Forch, di aper Gefiat. Gefiat nihit di tal ir aithnauc, ad dexteram ir all, mal i duc i claud bet Cirn Cinfall ubi incepit. Finis Lann Diniul. Mouric di genou Pant Pull Penhic, per medium mal i duc ir pant di uinid bet i ford maur, di Pull i Ceth iuxta uiam magnam, or Pull dir guairet mal i duc ir pant, Tref Guid ad dexteram, dir carn, dir ford. ar hit ir ford.

& finibus istis **ab ecclesia Landauia separauerint,** donec ad emendationem uenerint. Amen.	Cilliuen nihit trui i coit. Ar hit i ford bet Mouric in hi Sichpull, mal i duc Mouric di uinid, ar i hit bet genou Pant Pull Pennic ubi incepit. Finis Mafurn Di guarr Alt Rudlan [*space*] Dour.

The witness lists are similar, except that *Greciel episcopus* has probably been suppressed in 74 so as to make it a grant to St Dyfrig in person. The allusion to 'multi alij testes' in 74 may be to cover the omission of Greciel! The other names are: 74/171b: Num/Nud Simon/Simon Sciblon/Isciplan Araun/Araun Blainrit/Blainrit Iudon/Iudon Ioubiu/Ioubiu Guoren/Gurou Cinguan/Cincuan Britton/Britcon Iluic/Iliuc Gloiu/Gloiu Biuonui/Biuonui Lilli/Lilli Cimuireg/Cimuireg.

175/186b

It is unclear whether the church (*pod[i]um*) granted was at Monmouth ('the confluence of the river Monnow') or whether that was the place where the transaction was performed – perhaps it was both.[10] The recurrence of the rare phrase *cum omni censu* may go back to the common exemplar, and perhaps the original eighth-century charter.[11] The same may be true of *magno uel modico* and *uerbo*, although these are more common in *LL* generally.[12] The other shared verbiage is probably coincidental.

175 Sciendum est nobis quod **dedit Ilias podum quattuor modiorum agri circa se cum omni censu suo magno** uel **modico** Deo et **Dubricio, & Teliauo, & Berthguino episcopo, & omnibus suis successoribus æcclesiæ Landauiæ** in perpetuo. Facta est ista elemosina **in aper Mynuy uerbo** et consensu **Ithail** patris et **filiorum Fernuail & Mouric & cum omni sua libertate et** omni **communione in campo et in siluis, in aqua et in pascuis,** & tribus abbatibus attestantibus. **Dagan abbate Carbani uallis. Saturn abbate Docunni. Eluoed abbate Ilduti. Trican** lectore. **De laicis** testes sunt. **Iudhael rex** cum filiis **Fernuail et Mouric. Ilias. Elcun. Mabsu. Iudnerth. filius Iudgualon. Dounerth filius Iudic. Ceriau. Iudnoe. Quicunque custodierit** benedicetur. **Qui autem** uiolauerit, maledicetur.	186b **Ilias** pro anima sua et pro scriptione nominis sui in libro uitæ **dedit podium** [*blank*] **in** medio **aper Myngui cum agro quattuor modiorum circa se uerbo Iudhaili** regis **filiorum**que eius **Fernuail et Mouric & cum omni censu** a **magno** usque ad **modicum** sanctis **Dubricio, Teliauo** et **Oudoceo.** et in manu **Berthguini episcopi & omnibus successoribus suis** in **ecclesia Landauiæ & cum omni sua libertate** et tota **communione in campo et in siluis, in aqua & in pascuis.** De clericis testes sunt. Berthguinus episcopus. **Turchan. Dagan abbas Caruani uallis. Elguoid abbas Ilduti. Saturn abbas Docunni. De laicis. Iudhail rex. Fernuail & Mouric** filii eius. **Ilias. Elfin. Mabsu. Iudnerth. filius Iudguallaun. Duinerth filius Iudic. Ceriau.** Guoruodu. Conhae. **Iudnoe. Quicunque custodierit** custodiat illum Deus. **Qui autem** ab ecclesia Landauiæ separauerit, anathema sit. Amen.

---

[10] See Coe, 'The place-names', s.n. *Aper Myngui*, and Charles-Edwards, *Wales and the Britons*, 261–4, who translates both versions.

[11] On *cum omni censu* (Davies, *The Llandaff Charters*, 139), see above, 87 n. 9.

[12] Davies, *The Llandaff Charters*, 136, 138, and 143. See below, 111.

11. The evidence of the doublets

186b has three extra witnesses (*Berthguinus episcopus*, *Guoruodu*, and *Conhae*), but otherwise the lists are similar: 175/186b: Dagan/Dagan Saturn/Saturn Eluoed/Elguoid Trican/Turchan Iudhael/Iudhail Fernuail/Fernuail Mouric/Mouric Ilias/Ilias Elcun/Elfin Mabsu/Mabsu Iudnerth/Iudnerth Iudgualon/Iudguallaun Dounerth/Duinerth Iudic/Iudic Ceriau/Ceriau Iudnoe/Iudnoe. It is remarkable that a superfluous full stop occurs after *Iudnerth* in both versions; they are close to a common exemplar.

176a / 190b

Villa Conuc seems to be Ogmore, but in 190b the wrong rubric – *Maerun* (Marshfield) – has been supplied, and the 190b bounds, added at the end by Hand B, presumably refer to Marshfield. This may be due to a genuine error after the location of *Gurai*'s tomb was forgotten.[13] The commonplace shared formulae may be coincidental. By contrast, the purchase of the estate, and the queen's name, both in 190b alone, may be original, omitted as superfluous details in 176a.[14]

176a Villa Convc.
Sciendum est quod **Conuilius filius Gurceniu uerbo Morcanti** & **filii eius Ithail** dedit **uillam in qua sepulcrum est Gurai**, id est uillam Conuc Deo et tribus **sanctis Dubricio, Teliauo et Oudoceo cum sua tota libertate** et tota communione in campo et **in aquis, in silua et in pascuis. Et Berthguino episcopo** et episcopis **omnibus Landauiæ in perpetuo**, & cum data elemosina. Precepit Cormil filio suo Conuc et filiis suis a generatione in generatione ut semper seruirent altari Landauiæ de predicto agro. Finis illius A uertice Montis Gurai usque ad amnem Euenhi. Latitudo autem a fossa magna usque ad fossam contra mare. **De clericis testes sunt. Berthguinus episcopus. Sulgen abbas Carbani uallis. Saturn abbas Docguinni. Gurhaual abbas Ilduti. De laicis. Morcant rex** et **filius eius Ithail. Conuil. Iunet. Condiuit. Cuncuman. Mabsu. Gurhitir. Samuel.**

190b Maervn.
Conuilius Gurceniu filius emit agrum id est **uillam in qua sepulchrum est Gurai** a **Morcanto** rege **et** a **filio eius Iudhail**. & ab uxore eius. Ricceneth. et empta uilla illa **uerbo** regis et consensu largitus est illam in elemosina **Deo & sanctis Dubricio, Teliauo et Oudoceo & Berthguino episcopo** et omnibus successoribus suis in æcclesia **Landauiæ in perpetuo, cum tota sua libertate**, & cum silua et maritimis, et cum omni **communione in aqua** et **in siluis, in campo et in pascuis. De clericis testes sunt. Berthguinus episcopus. Sulgen abbas Carbani uallis. Saturn abbas Docunni. Guorhaua**rn **abbas Ilduti. De laicis Morcant rex. Iudhail filius eius. Conuilius. Iunet. Conteuit. Mabsu. Gurhitir. Sauuil. Iudic.** Cenguri filius Gabran. **Gaidnerth** filius **Morcanti frater. Quicunque custodierit** benedicetur. **Qui autem** uiolauerit, maledicetur. Fin[15] i Main

---

[13] See Coe, 'The place-names', s.nn. For the bounds see *ibid.*, 990–1 and 994–5, and above, 48. Charles-Edwards, *Wales and the Britons*, 264–6, translates both versions, except for the 190b bounds, which are in Hand B (cf. J. R. Davies, '*Liber Landavensis*: its date and the identity of its editor', 4). *Gurai*, son of Glywys, was the eponym of the cantref of Gwrinydd. See Charles-Edwards, *Wales and the Britons*, 295; Jenkins, 'Regions and cantrefs', 43; Petts, *The Early Medieval Church*, 151.

[14] Cf. Charles-Edwards, *Wales and the Britons*, 306. On sales, see above, 87, and below, 103.

[15] The words which follow *Fin* are in Hand B. See above, n. 13.

Iudic. Guednerth frater Morcanti. Quicunque custodierit custodiat illum Deus. **Qui autem** ab ecclesia Landauiæ separauerit, anathema sit. Amen.

Brith dir claud. bet i Pillou Bichein. di Dibleis. dir Drausguern. ar i hit bet y penn i Guern Du di Luch Edilbiv, ar hit i claud bet i mor.

Both witness lists preserve a unique name (*Cuncuman* in 176a and *Cenguri filius Gabran* in 190b), but are otherwise similar: 176a/190b: Berthguinus/Berthguinus Sulgen/Sulgen Saturn/Saturn Gurhaual/Guorhauarn Morcant/Morcant Ithail/Iudhail Conuil/Conuilius Iunet/Iunet Condiuit/Conteuit Mabsu/Mabsu Gurhitir/Gurhitir Samuel/Sauuil Iudic/Iudic Guednerth/Gaidnerth Morcanti/Morcanti (gen.). In 190b *filius* after *Gaidnerth* looks like a slip for *frater*, but more probably it is 176a that is at fault, so that *Guednerth/Gaidnerth* is Morgan's nephew.[16] One may wonder whether *Cuncuman* in 176a may be the same person as the scribe 'Concuu*n*' of *VC* 66 (discussed below). Perhaps the scribe's name appeared at the end of the charter and was mistaken for a lay witness when 176a was copied.

179a / 188b

Tull Coit is Fairwater (just west of Llandaf) and 'Ystrad Ancr' was presumably an alternative name for it.[17] 179a is more a memorandum or summary (basically 'Elfin dedit uillam Strat Hancr') than a charter since it lacks a witness list. Possibly the scribe failed to copy the entire text. The formulae are commonplace in *LL* and need not derive from a shared exemplar.

179a Villa Strat.
Sciendum est **quod Elfin dedit** uillam **Strat Hancr pro anima sua Deo et sanctis Dubricio, Teliauo et Oudoceo & omnibus** pastoribus **æcclesiæ Landauiæ cum tota sua libertate in perpetuo.**

188b Tvll Coit.
Sciatis **quod Elfin dedit** agrum **Estrat Agcr**, id est Tollcoit **pro anima sua** cum sex modiis terræ **Deo & sanctis Dubricio, Teliauo et Oudoceo** & Berthguino episcopo **& omnibus** successoribus suis in **ecclesia Landauiæ in perpetuo, cum tota sua libertate** & omni communione uerbo Iudhali regis et consensu. De clericis testes sunt. Berthguinus episcopus. Gunnuiu lector. Confur. Conguaret. De laicis. Concar. Guorhoidil. Aironbrit. Consicc. Guorbuth. Hinbiu. Finis ab oculo Fontis Tollcoit usque ad Fossam Paludis in capite, et ab occidente per transuersum usque ad Petram Iacinthinum, uallo ducente usque ad Petram Onnbrit. Quicunque custodierit custodiat illum Deus. Qui autem uiolauerit, anathema sit. Amen.

---

[16] Charles-Edwards, *Wales and the Britons*, 307. See below, 151.
[17] Coe, 'The place-names', s.nn. *Estrat Agcr* and *Tyllgoed.* On the bounds of 188b see *ibid.*, 994. The two charters are summarised/translated by Birch, *Memorials*, 139 and 147–8.

11. The evidence of the doublets

179b / 191

The land granted was probably in Matharn.[18] As in 190b above, the purchase of the estate and the particulars of the royal family may be original, omitted as superfluous details in 179b. Conversely 179b may have retained the title *hereditarius*, omitted in 191.[19] Most of the similarities in formulae between 179b and 191, such as *cum sua tota libertate/cum tota libertate sua*,[20] could be coincidental.

179b Villa **Gvinnonvi.**	191 Gvenno * noe.[21]
Ithail rex et **Iudon** hereditarius **filius Ceriau** immolauerunt **uillam Guinnoui iuxta paludem Mourici Deo et sanctis Dubricio, Teliauo et Oudoceo et Berthguino episcopo et omnibus successoribus suis** in ecclesia **Landauiæ cum sua tota libertate** in campo et in siluis, in aqua et in pascuis, **in perpetuo. De clericis testes sunt Berthguinus episcopus. Guruodu. Tutnerth. Etelic. Candau. Iudon**ai **De laicis Iuthail rex. Iudon** & ceteri. **Quicunque custodierit,** benedictus sit. **Qui autem ab ecclesia Landauiæ separauerit,** maledictus **sit.** Amen.	**Iudon filius Ceriau** emit **uillam Guennonoe iuxta paludem Mourici** a **Iudhailo rege** Gleuissicg & a filiis eius Fernuail et Mourico et Rotri in eterna emptione pro .xx. ii^{bus}. equis indomitis. Et empta uilla illa quæ prius fuerat sancti Dubricii a primo tempore largitus est eam liberam ab omni tributo sine aliquo seruitio magno uel modico, & **cum tota libertate sua** et omni communione Deo et sanctis Dubricio, Teliauo et Oudoceo et Berthguino episcopo, & omnibus successoribus suis Landauiæ in perpetuo. De clericis testes sunt. Berthguinus episcopus. Guoruodu. Tutnerth. Etelic. Condiuiu. Iudne. De laicis Iudhail rex & filii eius. Arthuail. Mouric. Rotri. Ris. **Iudon. Quicunque custodierit,** custodiat illum Deus. **Qui autem ab ecclesia Landauiæ separauerit,** anathema sit.

The witness list in 179b is abbreviated, having *& ceteri* instead of *& filii eius. Arthuail. Mouric. Rotri. Ris.* Apart from this the two versions are similar: 179b/191: Berthguinus/Berthguinus Guruodu/Guoruodu Tutnerth/Tutnerth Etelic/Etelic Candau/Condiuiu Iudonai/Iudne Iuthail/Iudhail Iudon/Iudon.

180b / VC 67

Lann Catgualatyr, the subject of this grant, is probably *Trefesgob* (Bishton), a Llandaf estate.[22] The greatly elaborated version in *LL* is exclusively in favour of Llandaf. The

---

[18] Coe, 'The place-names', s.n. For a summary translation see Birch, *Memorials*, 140 and 150.
[19] Cf. Charles-Edwards, *Wales and the Britons*, 313.
[20] Davies, *The Llandaff Charters*, 137. Davies, *An Early Welsh Microcosm*, 49 n. 3, suggests that *liberam ab omni tributo sine aliquo seruitio magno uel modico* in 191 is original, like *cum omni censu suo magno uel modico* in 175/186b (discussed above), but these phrases in 191 are commonplace in *LL*: Davies, *The Llandaff Charters*, 138.
[21] Evans's * denotes an erased letter.
[22] Richards, *Welsh Administrative and Territorial Units*, 125, and Coe, 'The place-names',

VC version, by contrast, refers to renders to Docgwinnus (i.e. to Llandough) as well as to St Cadog (i.e. to Llancarfan), and Bishop Berthwyn is its first witness. It may be, as suggested by Charles-Edwards, that the original charter provided food-renders for more than one religious community but has been reworded to prioritise the interests of Llandaf and Llancarfan respectively.[23] Although the long Narration in 180b is suspicious, the fratricide is noted in *VC* as well, and may be original.[24] The detail that Euddogwy was Berthwyn's immediate predecessor, contrary to standard *LL* doctrine, may also be original; certainly it is supported by the *LL* and *VC* witness lists.[25]

180b Lann Catgualatyr
Scitote karissimi fratres **quod** in tempore Oudocei episcopi diabolica admonitione occidit Guidnerth fratrem suum **Merchion** causa contentionis regni, et perpetrato homicidio, **fratricid**a excommunicatus est a beato Oudoceo, et a sinodo simul congregata ab hostio Guy usque ad hostium Tyui Landauiæ, et ita remansit depositis crucibus ad terram simul et cimbalis uersis tribus annis sub eadem excommunicatione, et ex toto sine aliqua Christianorum communione. Finitis tribus annis, requisiuit ueniam apud beatum Oudoceum, et data ci uenia, misit eum in peregrinationem usque ad archiepiscopum Dolensem in Cornugalliam propter ueteranam amicitiam et cognitionem quam sancti patres habuerant antecessores sui inter se, sanctus Teliaus uidelicet et sanctus Samson archiepiscopus primus Dolensis ciuitatis. Et propter aliam causam eo quod ipse Guidnerth et Brittones et archiepiscopus illius terræ essent unius linguæ et unius nationis quamuis diuiderentur spatio terrarum, et tanto melius poterat renuntiare scelus suum, et indulgentiam requirere cognito suo sermone. Post hec data sibi remissione cum sigillatis litteris rediit ante caput anni ad patriam et ad beatum Oudoceum,

VC 67
Notificandum est posteris, **quod** dedit **Guoidnerth Lann Catgualader Deo** et sancto Cadoco, quatinus quot annis uas .iii. modiorum ceruise illi persolueretur cum omnibus debitis propter **fratricid**ium germani sui **Merchiun**, atque tandem redditus dedit Docgwinno. Super hoc testes fuerunt **Berthgwinus episcopus**, Con**mil**, **Terchan**, et congregatio eius; Sulien abbas Nant Carban, Lumbiu presbiter, Biuonoi, Iouab, et congregatio sancti Cadoci; Saturn princeps altaris Docgwinni. **Marcant, Guoidnerth. Quicunque** seruauerit, **benedictus** erit. Et **qui** temerauerit, **maledictus** erit a Deo.

---

s.n. On the bounds of 180b see *ibid.*, 991–2. The two versions are compared and in part translated by Charles-Edwards, *Wales and the Britons*, 258–60. Cf. Birch, *Memorials*, 141–2.

[23] Charles-Edwards, *Wales and the Britons*, 259–60. See also above, 28, and 39. (For earlier views see *EA* I 171, James, 'The *Book of Llandav*: the church and see of Llandav', 15–17, and Brooke, *The Church*, 32–3.) I take it that the clerical witnesses in 180b are all members of Berthwyn's *congregatio*, including *Torchan / VC* Terchan, probably his successor as bishop and clearly in his congregation in Sequence ii.31–44, *lector* in charter 175, while '*Conmil*' could be the priest *Confur* who often attests with Tyrchan in *LL*, as in 180b. *VC*'s 'congregatio eius' refers to *Berthgwinus*, not *Terchan*. Hence there are only three religious establishments specified in *VC* 67: those of Berthwyn (the bishop), Sulien (Llancarfan), and Sadwrn (Llandough).

[24] See below, 112.

[25] See Charles-Edwards, *Wales and the Britons*, 260 n. 47, and above, 27.

11. The evidence of the doublets

et quia nondum fecerat annum quem promiserat in exulatu neque finierat, noluit illum absoluere, sed potius in eadem fieret excommunicatione, non seruato ab eo primo iugo penitentiæ, manente eo in eadem preuaricatione et excommunicatione. Ante finem anni sanctus Oudoceus famosissimæ uitæ episcopus Landauiæ transiuit ad dominum. Cui successit Berthguinus Landauiæ, quem Morcant rex simul et Guednerth requisierunt apud Landauiam cum multis senioribus Morcannuc uno ore deprecantes episcopum, uidentes cruces adhuc depositas ad terram simul et reliquias cum cimbalis super Guednerth ut ueniam daret Guednerth **fratricidæ**, & ut solueret excommunicationem eleuando cruces de terra et reliquias sanctorum. Post hæc Guednerth promittens emendationem uitæ suæ amplius in ieiunio et oratione et elemosina fusis lacrimis cum magna deuotione absolutus est de episcopo, et iuncta sibi penitentia plenaria admodum culpæ. Postmodum **Guidnerth** memor diu[i]ni sermonis, sicut aqua extinguit ignem, ita elemosina peccatum, donauit Deo et sanctis Dubricio, Teliau et Oudoceo, et in manu Berthguini episcopi et omnibus successoribus suis æcclesiæ Landauiæ **Lann Catgualatyr** cum omni sua tellure cum silua et cum maritimis et cum omni sua libertate sine ullo censu homini terreno nisi ecclesiæ Landauiæ et pastoribus eius & cum refugio suo in perpetuo. De clericis testes sunt **Berthguinus episcopus**. Gunuiu lector. **Con**fur. Conguarui. **Torchan**. De laicis **Morcant** rex. **Guednerth**. Iudic filius Nud. Iacob filius Mabsu. Guengarth. Elioc. Gabran. Elfin. Samuel. **Quicunque** custodierit **benedictus** sit. **Qui** autem uiolauerit, **maledictus** sit. Amen. Finis illius est. Aper nant Alun in i cors, mal i duc i nant di uinid bet i blain. Oi blain trus i cecn in iaun statim di blain ir sichnant in alia parte ir cecyn, mal i duc ir sichnant dir guairet bet ir pant in i coit. mal i duc ir sichnant ad dexteram nihit dir guairet bet crib ir alt emil Cestill Dinan. mal i duc cecyn crib ir alt ar i hit di Riu Merchiau. ar hit ir riu dir guairet bet licat i glible. i gulible in i hit di guairet het i cors. trui i cors in iaun di circhu Hentref Merchitir. or hentref dir marulinniou uersus occasum, ar hit Cecyn Ch̦ethin trui ir cors bet Lontre Tunbulch. or Lontre Tunbulch in iaun trui ir cors bet aper Nant Alun ubi incepit.

As noted above, the witness lists differ because *LL* has concentrated on the 'Llandaf' clerics. Nevertheless some names are common to both: 180b/*VC* 67:

Berthguinus/Berthgwinus Confur/Conmil(?) Torchan/Terchan Morcant/Marcant Guednerth/Guoidnerth.

210b / VC 66

The *llys*, or *llystin* 'fortified court', of *Din Birrion/Borrion* is unidentified.[26] While the *LL* version grants three *modii* of land to Bishop Cadwared, the *VC* version grants the same *ager* and a food render of six *modii* from it to Cynyng, who was abbot of Llancarfan (as other charters confirm). On the face of it, one text could have been directly adapted from the other, to promote the interests of one establishment or the other, perhaps with a scribal confusion between Roman *iii* and *ui*.[27] Alternatively, and more plausibly, both may reflect the same original charter, by which different renders from the same estate (rather than the estate itself) were granted to the bishop and to the abbot (compare 180b/*VC* 67 above).[28] As Charles-Edwards says, 'it will always have been a temptation for churches to try to convert the right to a render from an estate into outright ownership of that estate'.[29]

210b Din Birrion.
Cinuelin filius Conuc immolauit **Deo & sanct**is Dubricio, Teliauo et Oudoceo & in manu Catguareti episcopi & omnibus episcopis Landauiæ **Dinbirrion** uerbo et consensu regis Rotri filius Iudhail cum tribus modiis terræ & cum sua tota libertate & omni communione in campo et in siluis, in aqua & in pascuis. De clericis **testes** sunt. Catguaret episcopus. Guodel. Lulic. Guorapui.

VC 66
Sciendum est quod dedit **Conbelin** agrum Lis**din Borrion** uocat*us* (*sic*) pro commercio regni celestis cum corpore suo **Deo et sancto** Cadoco, quod ei annuatim persolueret sex modios ceruise cum pane et carne et melle. **Testis** est Conigc, qui super manum suam [tenuit quod] scripsit Concuu*n*,[30] i[d est], cyrographum.

The reason why only two charters are common to *LL* and *VC* (*LL* 180b/*VC* 67 and 210b/*VC* 66) may be because these were the only two in favour both of Llancarfan and the bishopric represented by Berthwyn and Cadwared. If the compilers of *LL* or *VC* had access to the other's collection and were completely unscrupulous, they would surely have borrowed more charters and changed the beneficiaries.[31]

---

[26] Coe, 'The place-names', s.n. The charter is translated and discussed by Charles-Edwards, *Wales and the Britons*, 257–8 and 260–1.

[27] Ibid., 260. Three *modii* (approximately 125 acres) was a standard estate size: Davies, *An Early Welsh Microcosm*, 33.

[28] Cf. Charles-Edwards, *Wales and the Britons*, 260 (by a slip he names Tyrchan rather than Cadwared as the head of the community that received the 210b grant). He envisages two separate transactions with two separate charters. To fit in with the hypothesis outlined in ch. 10, I envisage a single charter from which different elements were selected in *LL* and *VC*. See also above, 29, and 39.

[29] Charles-Edwards, *Wales and the Britons*, 260.

[30] On his possible identity with *Cuncuman* in 176a see above. *Concuum* is an equally possible expansion. The words in square brackets are Wade-Evans's restoration.

[31] Cf. ch. 7 above.

11. The evidence of the doublets

To sum up, the doublets tend to agree on the details of who gave what to whom, and on the names of the witnesses. Only once does a background detail in a Narration seem to be original (the fratricide in 180b/VC 67). Sometimes only one of the paired charters preserves an element that is arguably original, notably the sales in 176a/190b and 179b/191; these pairs also include details about the royalty involved, which may be original. Material about royalty is also found in one charter of the pair 73b/163a, where it could again be original, although antiquarian elaboration cannot be ruled out. It is very rare to find shared formulae that are likely to be original (see on *cum omni censu* in 175/186b). This is surprising, since Notifications already occurred in the early charters from Llandeilo Fawr (e.g. *Ostenditur ista (con)scriptio quod dederunt ...*), as did Sanctions (e.g. *Quicunque custodierit benedictus erit, quicunque frangerit maledictus erit*).[32] Perhaps in a few cases in the doublets where the wording happens to agree (e.g. the Sanction *Quicunque ... benedictus ..., Qui ... maledictus ...* in LL 180b and VC 67) it is really is original, even though it is so conventional as to appear potentially coincidental. But perhaps the copyists produced their own Notifications and Sanctions without troubling to follow the details of their exemplars. Only once do both doublets include the bounds (74/171b), presumably because these were often archived separately (as in Anglo-Saxon England).[33] Significantly 176a/190b have *different* bounds, those in 190b being added by Hand B.

---

[32] 'Chad' 2–4.

[33] For separate transmission of bounds see Sawyer 1540–602. Cf. Davies, *The Llandaff Charters*, 143; Coe, 'Dating the boundary clauses', 2–4 and 36; Geary, 'Language and memory', 183.

12

THE BOOK OF LLANDAF AS AN INDICATOR OF SOCIAL AND ECONOMIC CHANGE

Is it possible to use the Llandaf charters to reveal significant changes in Welsh society? The most daring attempt to do so has been Wendy Davies's 'intentionally speculative' article in *Past and Present* in 1978.[1] According to her hypothesis, changes in 'the capacity of rulers to control the disposal of property in the late and post-Roman world remain fundamental to any understanding of the wider political and social change'.[2] In the sixth and seventh centuries only kings could make land grants in south-east Wales.[3] Then by the eighth century other members of royal dynasties, and non-royals, began to make grants, but, since 'some royal action was at first essential to lay alienation',[4] two devices assisted them initially: either the king made the grant in association with the non-royal donor, described as the estate's 'heir' (*heres* or *hereditarius*, perhaps a royal tenant), or the king sold the estate to the non-royal so that he could donate it to the Church.[5] There was a surge in such donations and therefore charters around the eighth century,[6] and a subsequent, 'possibly consequent', change was that the estates granted became much smaller, sometimes being fragments of previous large estates, causing 'considerable upheaval'.[7] Lawlessness 'becomes apparent in the material of the later ninth century',[8] raising the question: 'Did the massive donation of lay properties in the eighth and ninth centuries effectively destroy the self-regulating mechanisms of ... society and allow the development of social and political chaos, a chaos which occurred when the landed possessions of the kingship (which had no tradition of government anyway) were too depleted to allow for any alternative system?'[9] – A contrary trend, however, was that a 'general royal capacity to exact taxation ... appears to have developed by the ninth century'.[10]

---

[1] 'Land and power in early medieval Wales', *WHEMA* IX 22. Some points are developed in Davies, *An Early Welsh Microcosm*.
[2] *WHEMA* IX 3; cf. *An Early Welsh Microcosm*, 63 and 162.
[3] *WHEMA* IX 10 and 16 (referring to the period of Sequence i).
[4] *WHEMA* IX 11. Charles-Edwards, *Wales and the Britons*, 611, comments: 'the Llandeilo documents in the Lichfield Gospels do not indicate that royal participation or consent was required. The greater Gwent (including Glywysing), with its stronger Roman inheritance, may have been different'. Those documents are probably post-eighth-century. Cf. Davies, *Small Worlds*, 67 n. 18.
[5] *WHEMA* IX 11–12 and 21 (referring respectively to the period of Sequence ii – *ca* 660–*ca* 770 on her chronology – and *ca* 705–*ca* 765, her dates for 190b and 209b).
[6] *WHEMA* IX 13 ('not merely an effect of chance survival').
[7] *WHEMA* IX 11–13 and 21–2.
[8] *WHEMA* IX 15.
[9] *WHEMA* IX 22.
[10] *WHEMA* IX 18

12. An indicator of social and economic change

If this was a real *development* (but see below), might one not expect it to enhance royal power and authority? In any case, how essential was king-centred government for the maintenance of law and order and the prevention of anarchy?

Although the numbers of relevant charters are small, it does seem that all the earliest plausible grants (some sixteen of them in Sequence i in *LL*, excluding two likely forgeries) are by kings.[11] This does not necessarily indicate that they were the Church's only benefactors,[12] or that only peculiarly royal land could be alienated, or that only kings – having assumed 'quasi-imperial powers' – were able to supervise the alienation of land in general.[13] The real purpose of the ostensibly royal grants of Sequence i could have been simply to confirm the Church in the possession of its estates, free from secular obligations to the king (such as the provision of food renders), irrespective of when and from whom the Church had in fact received the estates in question; the use of the charter form to record the gifts of kings and non-kings alike could be a later extension of its use. One can compare the evolution of the Anglo-Saxon charter.[14]

This suggestion depends, of course, on the assumption that in Wales obligations were normally due to kings from all estates from the earliest times, as in other countries. Davies's warning that 'there are no indications in any early source of a general royal capacity to exact taxation (though this seems to have developed by the ninth century)'[15] is based on negative evidence. In fact there is no indication anywhere that royal taxation *developed* rather than being present all along.[16] *If* royal rights and ecclesiastical exemptions were not mentioned in the original charters – which is uncertain[17] – that could be because they were taken for granted by contemporaries.[18]

---

[11] See above, 59 and nn. 2 and 4.

[12] This contradicted by the *La vie ancienne de saint Samson*, ed. Flobert, I.301. Cf. *WHEMA* IX 14 n. 33 and 16 n. 38, where this is attributed to Breton influence.

[13] *An Early Welsh Microcosm*, 162.

[14] Stenton, *Anglo-Saxon England*, 308; Keynes, *The Diplomas*, 303 and 108.

[15] *WHEMA* IX 18 and n. 46. *An Early Welsh Microcosm*, 101, is more neutral: 'it would appear highly likely that from the reign of Ithel (*ca* 710–45), kings normally expected a render from all land unless specifically exempted. It may or may not have been so before that period; both possibilities are conceivable and the point cannot be resolved on evidence available at present'.

[16] The selection of 'genuine' *LL* immunity clauses for the eighth and ninth centuries in *An Early Welsh Microcosm*, 49 n. 3 seems rather arbitrary (cf. *ibid.*, 101 n. 3). They contain formulae such as *liberam/quietam ab omni (regali/laicali) seruitio, liberam ab omni (fiscali) tributo*, and *cum omni censu* (cf. fuller lists in *The Llandaff Charters*, 138–9). See above, 87 n. 9, and below, 106.

[17] Charter 152 (Sequence ii.5) supposes that Llantwit was previously obliged to render the king a vessel of honey and an iron cauldron (see Davies, *The Llandaff Charters*, 101, and translation in Birch, *Memorials*, 107). Davies explains away these circumstantial details by saying that they 'need not represent distinctively royal dues: Llantwit could have been royal property and does not therefore furnish evidence of early royal fiscal rights' (*An Early Welsh Microcosm*, 101). A later such incidental reference is in charter 218 (dated A.D. 955), by which laymen grant land 'cum omni censu *qui antea dabatur regi*' (cf. paraphrase by Birch, *Memorials*, 184). It is natural that such allusions only occur when royal rights were being lost; as E. D. Jones remarked, 'Whatever he had before him the compiler of *Liber Landavensis* was not interested in any reservations of regalities or of service or of rent' ('The Book of Llandaff', 145).

[18] Cf. Stenton, *The Latin Charters*, 56; Brooks, 'The development of military obligations in

The formulae conferring rights, liberties, and immunities in the extant charters may be twelfth-century additions, as E. D. Jones maintained.[19] Similarly Davies argues that many of these formulae are based on the Latin version of Llandaf's false privilege, *Braint Teilo*, and were inserted during the final editing of *LL*.[20] She makes exceptions for *liberam ab omni tributo*, which 'only occurs in eighth- to ninth-century contexts, and is likely to be original', and for *incolis*, which is 'frequent from 216b, and almost invariable from 244' and is 'likely to reflect genuine practice of the tenth century and later'.[21] The former exception presumably underlies her claim, quoted above, that 'a general royal capacity to exact taxation ... seems to have *developed* by the ninth century' (my italics). Their evidence can hardly be admitted, however. There are so few examples of *liberam ab omni tributo* – seven – that it is impossible to say that it is a chronological rather than a paginal feature, and in view of its rarity the fact that it does not occur later than 228 (iii.21), paginally or chronologically, is insignificant. Note that 191 has it, but not its doublet 179b. It is difficult to agree that the partial correlation between exemptions from royal *tributum* or *seruitium*[22] and sales signifies that the former formulae are original;[23] the compiler(s) who decided to retain the sales may simply have had a fondness for these formulae as opposed to *sine ullo censu* etc. The doublets suggest that *tributum* and *seruitium* are not original (74/171b; 179b/191). *Incolis* appears in the formula *communione incolis*, which is merely a minor variant on *et/cum (omni/tota) communione*, which occurs inexorably throughout *LL* and is agreed to be a standard addition, arguably borrowed from the papal bulls received by Urban,[24] so *incolis* is also not to be regarded as original without strong reason. It predominates in the 'early' charters and in the latest charters, which suggests strongly that its appearance in the former at least is editorial.[25] There are also signs that it is editorial in the late charters. There is a suspicious bunching of *incolis* in the eight charters 216b–225, which contain five examples, whereas there are none in 196–216a and 226–233. The five charters in question have no chronological or other common denominator, except for their placing in *LL* itself. (Chronologically they are iii.12, 17, 35, and 38–39.) It is surely significant that the 'Chad' charters, uninfluenced by Anglo-Saxon and Anglo-Norman diplomatic, contain no royal immunities. While it is inherently likely that royal immunities were a fact of life in the period covered by *LL*,[26] it has yet to be shown that they featured in the diplomatic of that time or that taxation *developed* during the period.

As on the other side of Offa's Dyke and on the Continent,[27] the clergy may have paid their kings for their written 'grants'. In the Welsh *Life of St Beuno*, which is

---

eighth- and ninth-century England', 75.
[19] Jones, 'The Book of Llandaff', 145.
[20] *The Llandaff Charters*, 9–10, 12, 15–19, and 143. On *Braint Teilo* see *WHEMA* III and Russell, '*Priuilegium Sancti Teliaui* and *Breint Teilo*'.
[21] *An Early Welsh Microcosm*, 9; *The Llandaff Charters*, 27, 139, and 143. On *elemosina* (also 'likely to reflect genuine practice of the tenth century and later', *ibid.*, 143), see above, 72 and n. 7.
[22] *The Llandaff Charters*, 138–9.
[23] *An Early Welsh Microcosm*, 49 n. 3 and 53.
[24] *WHEMA* II 344 and 346; *The Llandaff Charters*, 16–17 and 138 (but see 29 n. 19).
[25] It is also in *Vita Oudocei* on p. 133. On circular features see above, 83.
[26] Jones, 'The Book of Llandaff', 146, citing Seebohm, who had referred to the *Collectio Canonum Hibernensis* and the Clynnog material (*The Tribal System in Wales*, 172–8).
[27] Cf. Dyer, *Lord and Peasants*, 12 and 31, and for Continental 'countergifts' to kings and

partly based on Clynnog charters, the saint gives King Cadwallon ap Cadfan (*ob.* 634) a gold or silver pin or brooch for a grant of land that turns out to be someone else's inheritance,[28] and an eighth-century Llancarfan charter records that King Morgan was paid a gilded sword to confirm a donation in writing.[29] How significant is it that payments to kings start to occur in eighth-century charters? There are eight brief Narrations in *LL* which simply record a king's sale of the land concerned to the donor before he granted it, all eight between 190b and 209b, in the episcopates of Berthwyn, Tyrchan, and Cadwared, during the reigns of Ffernfael and Rhodri and their father Ithel and grandfather Morgan (Sequence ii.23, 27, 34, 45, 50, 51, 54, 58). Since the compilers of *LL* had no motive to invent these eight royal sales, they are unlikely to be editorial inventions.[30] For Wendy Davies they reflect a transitional period when kings were losing the sole prerogative of alienating land for ecclesiastical purposes and were being compensated by non-royal donors who had to purchase royal alienable lands or the right of alienation from their king.[31] Three objections may be made to this hypothesis:

(1) There is a ninth sale among Berthwyn's charters in which the initial sale is clearly by one non-royal person to another (185 = ii.42):

Sciendum est quod emit Riataf unciam agri Guruarch a filiis Clodri, Gueidcui [et] Conuin pro xx iiii [*lacuna*] & Saxonica muliere et gladio pretioso & equo ualente uerbo Iudhailo regis et consensu ... Post hæc dedit Riataf ... terram Gurmarch ... in manu Berthguini...[32]

(2) We already have charters recording non-royal donations in the episcopate of Berthwyn, and apparently in that of his predecessor Euddogwy too, in which no royal presence is noted, even in the witness lists (151a,[33] 159b,[34] 178, 179a, 184, 186a, 188a). Moreover the proportion of such wholly non-royal charters among the non-royal grants is at its highest in the same period as the recorded sales. As the compilers of *LL* are most unlikely to have suppressed any references to kings in their exemplars, the distribution of charters not mentioning kings in any capacity, even as witnesses, is surely significant (Sequence ii. 9(?), 10, 39, 40, 43, 44, 46, 48, 49; iii. 3, 4, 14, 15, 47[?], 52, 60). Far from being uncommon, grants by non-royal persons without any apparent

---

others to confirm donations see Campbell, 'The sale of land', 256, and Davies, 'When gift is sale', 233 (cf. *eadem, Acts of Giving*, 135–6).

[28] *Buchedd Beuno*, ed. Sims-Williams, 54 and 67.

[29] *VC* 62. On its date see above, 40.

[30] On sales/purchases see Charles-Edwards, *Wales and the Britons*, 286–8, and Maund, 'Fact and narrative fiction', 177–8 and 185–6.

[31] *WHEMA* IX 11 and 16. See also *An Early Welsh Microcosm*, 52, 101, and 104 n. 1, where further possible interpretations are suggested which do not explain the eighth-century prominence. See also Charles-Edwards, *Wales and the Britons*, 286–8.

[32] 'Be it known that Riadaf bought the *uncia* of the land of Gwrfarch from Clodri's sons, Gwyddgi [and] Cynfyn, for 24 [ ] and an Englishwoman, a precious sword, and a strong horse, with the assent and consent of King Ithel ... Afterwards Rhiadaf gave ... the land of Gwrfarch ... into the hand of Bishop Berthwyn ...'

[33] If the unnamed(?) *Rex solus* of 151a (ii.9) is an interpolation.

[34] On 151a and 159b see above, 59 n. 4, and below, 149–50.

royal involvement seem to have been common at the time of the recorded sales.³⁵

(3) The distribution of the sales can be explained without assuming that they 'only occurred in the period of change'.³⁶ The *recording* of royal sales may have been a fashion in eighth-century diplomatic (possibly reflecting conditions of the sort suggested by Davies, while they were a novelty), in which case such sales may have carried on later than the eighth-century in practice; compare Anglo-Saxon charters where reference to such payments was 'largely a matter of preference'.³⁷ Alternatively it is possible that records of sales were a part of many of the originals, but were suppressed by all the compilers of *LL*, except those of the section from 185 to 209b, on the grounds that information not directly in favour of the see was irrelevant.³⁸ Some evidence favours this last possibility. Two of the charters of Bishop Berthwyn in the section of *LL* mentioning sales (190b and 191) have doublets elsewhere in *LL* in which reference to the sales has been omitted: 176a and 179b. 176a simply leaves out the clause noting the sale, while 179b transforms the charter into a joint grant by king and non-royal donor (perhaps an indication of how the royal sales were understood). None of the other doublets refer to sales but, to judge by these two, the concentration of the sales in the eighth century may be more an aspect of editing than of peculiarly eighth-century conditions. In the case of the Berthwyn charters the elimination of sales may be due to the compiler 'P', responsible for 174b–180a.³⁹ Compare the English situation, where 5% of charters refer to payments, but 'no point or period of Anglo-Saxon England mentioned by charters from the late seventh century onwards was devoid of payments for land or privilege'.⁴⁰

While there are references to *heredes* and *hereditarii* throughout *LL* in various contexts, Davies notes that it is only in a few charters in Sequence ii that such persons are associated with kings in the making of grants, and she suggests that these references reflect the 'major socio-political change' allegedly implied by the appearance of donors other than kings in the charters of the same period.⁴¹

---

[35] Cf. Davies, *An Early Welsh Microcosm*, 50. Note also that all the 'Chad' grants are non-royal.

[36] *WHEMA* IX 16.

[37] Keynes, *The Diplomas*, 33 and n. 55 and 107–8. See further Naismith, 'Payments for land and privilege'. Naismith, 'The land market and Anglo-Saxon society', 22, notes 'examples of payments recorded only as an afterthought, below the main text of a charter or on the dorse of a surviving single-sheet'.

[38] Thus there are no manumissions among the *LL* charters, unlike the 'Chad' charters; the compilers had no motive to include them. To quote Naismith, 'The land market and Anglo-Saxon society', 22, 'Even the act of donation itself could have carried an element of dissimulation and stage-management, treating as a gift what all parties knew was at least in part an economically motivated exchange. A "donation" from a layman to a church could be engineered out of a purchase from the king so that the "donor" could build ties with the house in question'. In these circumstances, churches might wish to gloss over the mercenary aspect.

[39] See above, 87.

[40] Naismith, 'Payments for land and privilege', 277 and 279. Cf. Campbell, 'The sale of land', 23–4.

[41] *An Early Welsh Microcosm*, 51; *WHEMA* IX 10–11. She suggests that '*heredes* were occupying hereditary tenants, often clerical, whose acquiescence in the alienation of the

12. An indicator of social and economic change

The question which arises is whether the association of kings with these persons in the Sequence ii grants is a peculiarity of diplomatic practice – or even life – in approximately the eighth century, or is merely the result of the editors of charters 143–209a having conserved (or inserted) such references, unlike their collaborators in other parts of *LL*. There are certainly problems:

(1) First of all, as Davies remarks, there are few relevant charters (143, 148, 150a, 158, 179b, 195, and 209a, across Sequence ii.3–58). As more than 40% of the *LL* charters refer to the eighth century approximately (Sequence ii), the approximately eighth-century concentration of the grants under consideration may be coincidental.
(2) Some of the relevant charters can be interpreted as meaning that the *heres/hereditarius* was part of the object of the grant, not one of the donors (143, 148, 209a; cf. 207, 239),[42] which hardly denotes a revolution in non-royal land tenure.
(3) A number of charters include persons described as *heres* or *hereditarius* in their witness lists, presumably thereby indicating the latters' consent, and these charters belong to the seventh (76a), ninth (229b), and eleventh century (264b, 264a) as well as the eighth.[43]
(4) There is evidence for some editorial manipulation in the above-mentioned doublet 179b/191. 179b is a grant by 'Ithail rex et Iudon hereditarius', but its doublet 191 records simply that the latter (not styled *hereditarius*) purchased the estate from King Ithel and granted it himself (see above). As the designation *hereditarius* has either been added or left out in one case or the other it is clear that the distribution of the term in *LL* is as unreliable as that of the sales.[44] Thus the occurrence of the references to sales and to *heredes/hereditarii* being associated with grants may be clustered in the eighth century merely because some of the compilers of the relevant section of *LL* were more tolerant of including circumstantial information not directly relevant to Llandaf claims.

Many of the non-royal grants in *LL* – at all the periods when such charters occur – have phrases signifying the consent of a king.[45] If these formulae are genuine, they may signify some particular royal involvement, such as a sale of the right to alienate property. It is possible, however, that many of them are additions by tidy minded compilers who lifted the required royal name from the lay witness list. Significantly charter 262, which has no king in its witness list, reads 'uerbo et consensu [*blank*]', as if the compiler included a consent formula before noticing that there was no name

---

property was sometimes noted', whereas the *hereditarii* were men 'with some hereditary rights to the produce of an estate': *An Early Welsh Microcosm*, 44 and 46. Cf. *EA* I 122; Charles-Edwards, *Wales and the Britons*, 308–13.

[42] Cf. Davies, *The Llandaff Charters*, 117–18 and 124; Flechner, 'Identifying monks', 809.

[43] *An Early Welsh Microcosm*, 44; Charles-Edwards, *Wales and the Britons*, 309; Flechner, 'Identifying monks', 809. See also Davies, *The Llandaff Charters*, 112, on *Eres* in 188a. It is not impossible that such allusions in witness lists may have been the compilers' source for the fuller allusions to the participation of such persons in the eighth-century charters.

[44] A further indication that such concepts were of only spasmodic interest to the compilers is provided by another doublet, 176a/190b. According to 176a the donor 'precepit ... filio suo Conuc et filiis suis a generatione in generatione ut semper seruirent altari Landauiæ de predicto agro', but 190b lacks this clause.

[45] Non-royal consents appear in 143, 195, and 199a.

in the witness list.[46] Fifty-eight of the seventy-six non-royal grants mention kings, and of these fifty-eight there are forty-one in which the king is named in both a consent clause and a witness list, eleven in which he is named in a witness list but not a consent clause, and only eight in which he is named in a consent clause but not in a witness list (74, 127b, 188b, 196, 210b, 211b, 262, 274). In some, at least, of these eight the lack of a king from the witness list may be merely a secondary error in transcription.[47] Clearly, then, most of the consent phrases may be editorial, with the royal names having been taken from the witness list of the charter. If, on the one hand, one looks at the proportion of non-royal grants at different periods that have royal consent the figures show a wild fluctuation that is unlikely to reflect historical reality or historical changes in diplomatic practice. If, on the other hand, one looks at the proportion of non-royal grants that have kings witnessing but not consenting, it becomes clear that there is a paginal fluctuation between sections of *LL* where the compilers inserted a consent clause if they could (i.e. if there was a king in the witness list whose name they could use) and sections where they were less careful. For instance all the sixteen non-royal grants of the twenty-one grants to Bishops Tyrchan, Cadwared and Cerennyr between 200 and 216b have consent clauses, and so do all three of the non-royal grants of the six grants to Bishops Pater and Wulffrith between 217 and 224 (these two groups range between ii.45 and iii.18[48] and between iii.35 and 40 respectively), yet among the charters assigned to Nudd (225–230b = iii.8–23 *passim*), roughly contemporary with Cerennyr, and the charters of Cyfeilliog (231–237a – iii.24–32), out of ten non-royal grants, all with attestations by kings, only five have consent clauses. The simplest explanation is that the compilers of pp. 200–24 took trouble over including consent clauses, whereas the compilers of pp. 225–37 were more careless.[49]

Davies argues that the inclusion of a consent formula was a concern of the collector of her hypothetical earlier archive, Group F, comprising 174b–216b.[50] This is unlikely, for twelve non-royal grants between 174b and 199bii lack royal consent, even though a king's name occurs in the witness lists of five of the twelve; thus the paginal distribution of the formula (pp. 200–24) cuts across the divisions between her hypothetical Groups F and G. She also suggests that the formula *uerbo (regis N)* may be original, whereas the formula *uerbo (regis N) et consensu (regis N)* is an editorial

---

[46] Cf. Davies, *An Early Welsh Microcosm*, 104 n. 2.

[47] I count Roger fitzWilliam fitzOsbern (274) as a 'king' in these statistics. In *An Early Welsh Microcosm*, 104 n. 2, Davies notes that four charters have a consent formula but lack the king's name in the witness list. In one of them (127b) there is no witness list. In 210b the *LL* scribe seems to have omitted the whole lay list while *VC* 66 (its doublet) has no consent phrase or lay list. Another (74) has a doublet in which the king's name heads the list (171b), so he may have been omitted in the copying of the list of 74, though it is also possible that his name was introduced from the consent formula into the 171b witness list. Cf. above 44, for this possibility. Note also 196 and 262 for consents without attestations (both special cases).

[48] The starting point is ii.24 if Davies's placing of 205 and 204b (*The Llandaff Charters*, 45) is accepted, but see above, 33.

[49] The frequent Narrations of pp. 200–24 versus pp. 225–37 give a similar impression. It cannot be argued that the first five bishops' original draftsmen invariably included a consent phrase, for one is lacking in two of Tyrchan's, 197 and 198a; significantly these are his earliest charters *paginally*, not necessarily chronologically.

[50] *An Early Welsh Microcosm*, 104 n. 2.

12. An indicator of social and economic change

addition or an expansion of *uerbo (regis N)*.[51] The present distribution of these alternative formulae is purely paginal and the doublets are quite inconsistent, but that does not disprove her suggestion, since the present distribution could theoretically be the result of editorial insertion of *et consensu* after *uerbo*. There is no evidence for this, however. Quite possibly *both* formulae are mostly additions by the compilers of *LL*. The doublets point to that conclusion.[52] 188b and 210b have consent formulae, but their respective doublets 179a and *VC* 66 do not. 74/171b, 175/186b, and 176a/190b have consent formulae but the wording varies between *uerbo* and *uerbo et consensu* and the formulae tend to be inserted in different places. (179b/191 and 180b/*VC* 67 both lack a consent formula, and 73b/163a is a royal grant.) Thus whereas the sales appear to be part of original charters, of potentially great interest to the economic historian, the formulae of royal consent are probably merely part of the verbiage with which the compilers of *LL* eked out their laconic native charters in order to impress the wider world with the legitimacy of their documents. Significantly, such formulae are completely absent from the 'Chad' and Llancarfan charters.

Table 12.1 sets out, under the letter for each alleged Group, (a) the number of charters in it, (b) the number (and percentage) of non-royal grants in it containing a royal consent formula,[53] (c) the number (and percentage) of (b) in which the consent formula is *uerbo et consensu*, and (d) the number of (and percentage) of (b) in which the consent formula is *uerbo* (alone).[54] It will be seen from the percentages (b) that royal consents are typical of the latter part of *LL* (E–J) and are more prominent in G than in F. The percentages under (c) and (d) show that *uerbo et consensu* overtakes *uerbo* after E and has started to infect the final redaction of the charters attached to the Dyfrig and Teilo *vitae* (AB) at the start of the volume, following the 'circular' pattern noted in Chapter 9 above. The phrase *uerbo et consensu* is used within the *Vita Dubricii* itself (pp. 84–5), referring to the translation of the saint's bones in 1120, *uerbo et consensu Radulfi Cantiarensis ecclesiæ metropolitani*.

	A	B	C	D	E	F	G	H	J
a	9	7	21	9	9	54[55]	6	20	24
b	1 (11%)	2 (29%)	1 (5%)	0 (0%)	3 (33%)	25 (46%)	4 (67%)	5 (25%)	8 (33%)
c	1 (100%)	2 (100%)	0 (0%)	0 (0%)	1 (33%)	17 (68%)	2 (50%)	3 (60%)	4 (50%)
d	0 (0%)	0 (0%)	0 (0%)	0 (0%)	3 (56%)	7 (28%)	0 (0%)	2 (40%)	3 (37%)

Table 12.1 Consent formulae

It is largely because of the charters' Narrations that lawlessness 'becomes apparent in the material of the later ninth century', leading Wendy Davies to ask 'Did the massive donation of lay properties in the eighth and ninth centuries effectively destroy the self-regulating mechanisms of ... society and allow the development of social and political chaos?'.[56] We have to ask whether it is simply the inclusion of

---

[51] *Ibid.*, 104 n. 2; *The Llandaff Charters*, 136 and 143.
[52] See ch. 11.
[53] Non-royal consents (143, 195, 199a) are not included.
[54] The figures under E are due to the fact that charter 170 includes both formulae.
[55] Counting 199bi and 199bii separately.
[56] *WHEMA* IX 15 and 22. Cf. J. R. Davies, 'Church, property, and conflict', 388–90.

The Book of Llandaf as a Historical Source

Narrations in the later charters that creates the impression of greater lawlessness. Here it is interesting to compare the Anglo-Saxon royal charters issued after 993. The 'series is dominated by a type of diploma incorporating in the dispositive section an account of the circumstances leading up to the transaction', and some of them are 'characterized by the incorporation of a narrative section describing the crimes of an individual'.[57] Keynes cautions that 'one should hesitate before interpreting the account of crimes contained in Æthelred's diplomas as a sign that lawlessness prevailed', and emphasises 'that a development in the habits of draftsmen of diplomas has created a misleading impression that wicked deeds were especially or even uniquely characteristic of his reign'.[58]

Narrations are not evenly distributed through *LL*. They predominate in the paginally 'earliest' and 'latest' charters (see the solid line in Table 12.2, Fig. 1), but the 'early' peak is partly due the mostly suspicious Narrations in the charters attached to the *Vitae* of Teilo and Euddogwy, some of which lack witness lists.[59] If the Narrations are considered chronologically (that is, by taking the charters with witness lists in the order of the Sequences), a somewhat steadier rise can be seen (see the solid line in Table 12.2, Fig. 2).[60] This pattern is clearer if we leave aside Narrations recording of sales,[61] which are irrelevant here, and follow the broken line where it departs from the solid line. Narrations with some authentic basis perhaps start in the episcopate of Euddogwy (e.g. 144, 147, 152) or that of Berthwyn (ii.19 = 176b onwards). One of Berthwyn's charters (ii.25 = 180b) has a elaborate Narration about the donor's fratricide, during the episcopate of Euddogwy, his penance, and his donation of *Lann Catgualatyr* (Bishton) to Berthwyn when he succeeded Euddogwy. In view of the close reminiscences of *LL*'s *Vita Teiliaui* it would be easy to dismiss the whole Narration as forgery. However, the phrase *propter fratricidium germani sui Merchiun* in the Llancarfan doublet (*VC* 67), suggests that the *LL* Narration was elaborated from an authentic kernel.[62]

The Narrations are all under suspicion of having been invented or expanded in order to enhance the prestige of Llandaf. The fact that they are repetitive in wording[63] and incident[64] is not necessarily a sign of forgery; the same is true of the crime columns of modern local newspapers! Each Narration has to be assessed on its merits, and in many cases it is impossible to decide whether interesting features are due to statements in an original or to elaboration, or sheer invention, by the compilers of *LL*, who used

---

[57] Keynes, *The Diplomas*, 95 and 97.
[58] *Ibid.*, 201–2.
[59] The following lack witness lists or credible witness lists: 123, 125a, 125b, 127a, 127b, 141, 192, 193, and 196. 167 is not included in the Sequences. The only Sequence i Narration is 161 (i.14). Narrations occur in the following Euddogwy charters: 144, 147, 152, 157.
[60] In Table 12.2, Fig. 2, the charters are grouped in tens, nines, and finally seven, as shown by the heavy line above.
[61] Sales are distinguished in the list of Narrations in Davies, *The Llandaff Charters*, 134, and are rightly regarded as separate by Maund, 'Fact and narrative fiction', 177–8 and 185–6.
[62] See above, 100. Note also the case noted on 91 n. 19. For the reminiscence of the *Vita Teiliaui* see Doble, *Lives*, 228–9.
[63] Davies, *The Llandaff Charters*, 134.
[64] Maund, 'Fact and narrative fiction'; J. R. Davies, 'Church, property, and conflict', 391. Ninth-century Breton disputes in the Cartulary of Redon are 'of a constantly recurring type; exactly the same sorts of case are still evidenced in the abbey's records of the sixteenth and seventeeth centuries' (Davies, *Small Worlds*, 148).

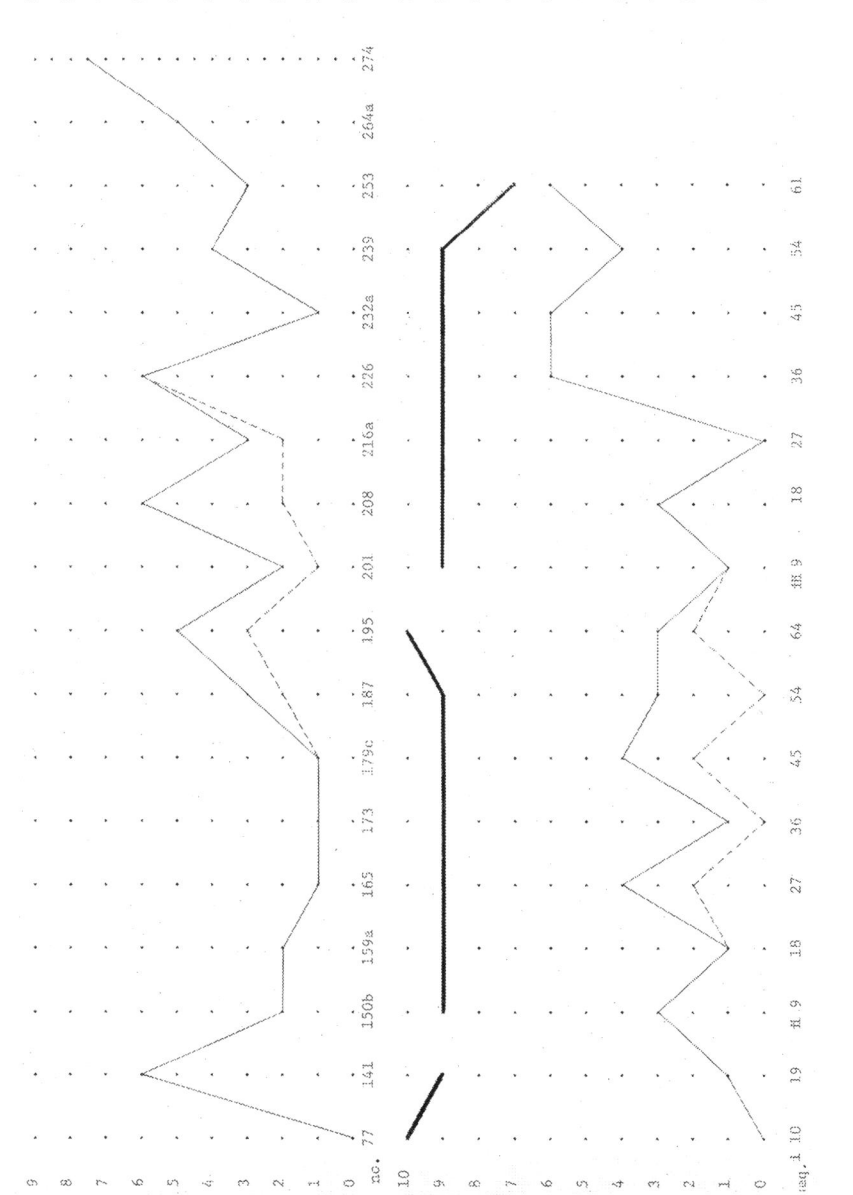

Table 12.2 Narrations paginally (Fig. 1, above) and chronologically (Fig. 2, below)

The Book of Llandaf as a Historical Source

the Narrations as moral exempla for recalcitrant kings and impious laymen in the same way as Lifris used stories of the saint's miracles in his *Vita Cadoci*.[65] Attempts have been made to see historical developments in the Narrations,[66] but the apparent changes may really be mere changes of emphasis on the part of the compilers.[67] For example, Davies notes that 'physical attacks on Llandaff or some other church only occur from no. 216b, from the ninth century onwards; violation of sanctuary is only cited from no. 218 onwards, from the tenth and eleventh centuries'.[68] She uses such distributions as evidence of greater lawlessness and instability in the later period,[69] almost echoing J. W. James's comment that the later Narrations 'reveal a disintegrating society'.[70] Is this certain? Since the latest grants in *LL* chronologically are also the last charters in the collection (212–274 = iii. 8–13, 17–61), the advent of violence against the Church could be the result of a new interest on the part of the compilers as they approached the end, rather than a feature of their originals – or (as seems more likely) it could be a mixture of the two. Even if the Narrations in question are original, it may be that draughtsmen only *began to record* such details in later times. Finally, it must be observed that we would not hear of the acts of violence had they not led to donations to the Church in recompense, so that one might argue that the *increase* in the number of references to them is really an indication of an *increase* in respect for the Church. The picture of lawlessness against the Church in *LL* may be as biased in one direction as Gerald of Wales's picture of Welsh respect for the Church (*Descriptio Kambriae*, I 18) is biased in the other.

Davies's other evidence for an increase in lawlessness is negative or oblique: the lack of evidence for meetings of the elders of the kingdoms in the later charters and the appearance of intrusive royal dynasties in the later period.[71] Intrusive dynasties were not exclusive to the later period, however, and not necessarily even distinctive of it.[72] The references to the elders of named kingdoms (e.g. *seniores Ercycg*)[73] are few in number (152, 180b, 185, 190a, 198b, between ii.5 and ii.52) and cannot therefore be used as evidence that elders did not meet after the eighth century. It is quite possible that the omission of such references from other charters is editorial, or that their insertion, where they occur, is editorial.[74] Moreover, throughout the charters there *are* mentions of elders that do not include references to named kingdoms (e.g. *presentibus pluribus de melioribus regni* in 255),[75] and the insertion of a kingdom

---

[65] *WHEMA* XIV.
[66] James, 'The excommunications'. Cf. Davies, *An Early Welsh Microcosm*, 133–4.
[67] The distribution of the formulae *iuncta penitentia* and *ueniam requisiuit/quaesiuit* (Davies, *The Llandaff Charters*, 134) could be chronological or paginal, for example, and so could the very mention of penance in Narrations. These formulae have an inverse correlation with dispositions with religious motive, listed *ibid.*, 135.
[68] *The Llandaff Charters*, 22.
[69] *WHEMA* IX 15 and n. 37, perhaps modified in *An Early Welsh Microcosm*, 112 ('The selection of material is obviously biased in favour of the church'). See also *ibid.*, 105–6, 116, and 133.
[70] James, 'The excommunications', 8. Cf. J. R. Davies, 'Church, property, and conflict', 390.
[71] *WHEMA* IX 15; *An Early Welsh Microcosm*, 116.
[72] See above, 30, and below, 128.
[73] Davies, *An Early Welsh Microcosm*, 88–9. Cf. Morris, Review, 231: 'Early kings consult *cum senioribus Guent et Ercig*, but later kings have *comites*'.
[74] One may suspect the activity of the compilers Q and R, who are discussed above, ch. 10.
[75] Davies, *An Early Welsh Microcosm*, 108.

12. An indicator of social and economic change

name can hardly be of more than stylistic significance. Finally, though there were surely bodies of elders in early Wales – *degion* ('goodmen, *gwyrda*') as 'Chad 2' calls them – it is quite possible that many or all the *LL* references to them are due to Urban and his fellow compilers' knowledge of English formulae such as *cum consensu principum meorum et omnium seniorum gentis nostre*.[76]

Even apart from questions about their authenticity, the Narrations cannot easily be used as a guide to historical change because they are unevenly distributed chronologically. That there is 'much more evidence of the active social role of the kindred' in the tenth and eleventh centuries, for instance, may be solely due to the increasing number of charters containing Narrations referring to legal disputes.[77] Another case in point is Davies's conclusion, from the fact that 'reference ... to payment in precious metals replaced reference to payment in other objects in the tenth and eleventh centuries', that 'there is some evidence that metals began to replace miscellaneous objects of exchange in the later period'.[78] Really there is a change in the type of Narration here. The references in the early period to payments (often valued with reference to cows) in Saxon women (185), horses (185, 191, 201, 202, 203a, 203b, 204b, 204b, 209b), *scripula*(?) (203b),[79] hawks (201, 203a, 203b), dogs (201, 203a), swords (185, 202, 203a), horns (202, 203b), trumpets (204b), and cloth or clothing (203a, 203b, 204b, 209b) occur in the Narrations describing sales (185–209b), a type of Narration omitted in the later part of *LL*, as we have seen.[80] The references to payment in precious metals in the later charters occur in the Narrations describing the recompense awarded to the Church for crimes against it, and such Narrations are much less common among the early charters. We may have merely a distinction between matter-of-fact sales and legal assessments of compensation, not a chronological development. A Narration concerning Bishop Cyfeilliog (*fl.* 914) says that the Bishop was recompensed with 'the price of his face in length and breadth in pure gold' (*pretium faciei suæ longitudine et latitudine in puro auro*, 233), clearly echoing the legal concept of *wynepwerth* ('honour', literally 'face-worth') and legal ways of assessing it. The concept and the manner of assessment are clearly ancient, being found in all the Celtic-speaking countries and widely elsewhere.[81] No doubt

---

[76] *WHEMA* I 477, citing *The Cartulary of Worcester Cathedral Priory*, ed. Darlington, 19.

[77] Cf. Davies, *An Early Welsh Microcosm*, 111 and 163.

[78] *An Early Welsh Microcosm*, 59–60. Cf. Morris, Review, 231: 'seventh-century prices are expressed as single objects – a chased swordhilt, a "best horse", etc.; in the eighth century they are calculated according to a uniform standard of value, the cow, but from the ninth century onward in gold and silver'. See also *idem*, *The Age of Arthur*, 432 and 463–4.

[79] Breeze, 'Does *scripulum* in the Book of Llandaff mean "piece of gold"?', argues that it does, as opposed to a beast – the *scripulum* is worth twelve cows.

[80] Contrast Anglo-Saxon England which 'stands out for its heavy emphasis on gold and silver in payments for land, beginning in the seventh and eighth centuries. More than 90 per cent of all references to payment explicitly involve gold or silver' (Naismith, 'The land market and Anglo-Saxon society', 37). See *idem*, 'Payments', 312–13. A variety of payments occur in the 'Chad' charters. For parallels elsewhere see Campbell, 'The sale of land', 27 (England), Breatnach, 'Forms of payment' (Ireland), Davies, *Small Worlds*, 56–60 and 98–9 (Brittany), and the colourful sets of payments cited by Hammer, 'Land sales in eighth- and ninth-century Bavaria', 65–70.

[81] See Pryce, *Native Law and the Church*, 158, and Russell, 'From plates and rods', with references to studies by Gaidoz and Loth. Giving a person's weight in gold was a common

assessment in valuable metals was intended to impress[82] and to assuage hurt feelings. Whether honour price was actually paid in the way in which it was assessed is hard to decide. It might be argued, on the one hand, that it is significant that the payment was commuted into land in the above case and most others in *LL*;[83] on the other hand, had that not been the case we would be unlikely to have a record of the transaction. An indication that precious metals could be a *standard* of non-legal assessment in the earlier period as well is provided by 'a horn worth six ounces of silver' (*cornu in pretio .vi. unciarum argenti*) and the like in the eighth-century sales (203b, 204b) and the payment for a manumission in 'Chad 5' in *librae* and *unciae*. Already in the seventh-century *Vita Samsonis* we hear of the saint's father making an offering of three silver rods equal in length to his wife (I.3).[84] All in all, then, the Narrations of *LL*, even if they are authentic, are a poor guide to liquidity.

The compilers of *LL* were concerned to stress the powers of bishops rather than kings. If we conclude that 'insofar as governmental functions *were* exercised between about 900 and 1050, they seem to have been exercised by the church'[85] –'governmental functions' here signifying the administration of justice – we may have become a victim of our source, and in particular the numerous Narrations of Sequence iii which stress the role of the bishop of Llandaf and his court in settling disputes, pursuing, incarcerating, or exiling malefactors, and (inevitably) reaping the reward of further grants. While they say little about them, the existence of secular, royal courts is admitted by the privileges of Dyfrig, Teilo, and Euddogwy in the Book of Llandaf, even as they advance the claims of Llandaf's own ecclesiastical court.[86]

---

literary motif: Kölbing, *The Romance of Beues of Hamtoun*, 294–5 (note on line 1725); Ewert, *The Romance of Tristan by Beroul*, II, 93 (note on line 215).

[82] In Spain 'gold was explicitly associated with high-status people and was the appropriate way to express payment to one who was king' (Davies, 'Sale, price and valuation in Galicia and Castile-León', 161).

[83] See Davies, *An Early Welsh Microcosm*, 60.

[84] *La vie ancienne de saint Samson*, ed. Flobert, 33 n. 51, and 150.

[85] Davies, *An Early Welsh Microcosm*, 163; cf. 110 and 133–4.

[86] Cf. Davies, Holding court', 149–50. For the privileges see *WHEMA* III and Russell, '*Priuilegium Sancti Teliaui* and *Breint Teilo*'. On ecclesiastical synods and courts see Pryce, *Native Law and the Church*, 135–9 and 154–62.

13

THE ROYAL GENEALOGICAL FRAMEWORK

In the seventh century the main division in southern Wales was between Dyfed (derived from the tribal name *Demetai*, recorded by Ptolemy) in the south-west and Gwent (from *Venta Silurum*, Caer-went) in the south-east, while Ergyng (from *Ariconium*), to the north of Gwent, had its own kings. By the ninth century, however, Ergyng was dependent on Gwent, and Dyfed and Gwent were no longer adjacent: the old western part of Gwent (Glamorgan), now known as Glywysing from the legendary ancestor Glywys, and the eastern parts of Dyfed – Ystrad Tywi, Gŵyr (Gower), and Cydweli (Kidwelly) – were sometimes named as separate regions.[1] In the 880s, as we know from Asser, Glywysing and Gwent were independent kingdoms, ruled respectively by Hywel ap Rhys and by Brochfael and Ffernfael, sons of Meurig, but from *ca* 893 Hywel's son Owain may have ruled both kingdoms, being described as 'king of the people of Gwent' in the D-text of the *Anglo-Saxon Chronicle* for 927.[2] Owain's son, Morgan ab Owain (*ob.* 974), later remembered as Morgan Hen or Morgan Mawr, seems to have inherited this role, while allowing his brothers to be sub-kings in Gower and western Glywysing, areas disputed with Dyfed in the second half of the tenth century.[3] His name probably survived in the name of the more restricted kingdom of *Morgannwg* (Glamorgan), the name which had superseded *Glywysing* by *ca* 1000.[4] Gwent, by contrast, fell into the hands of a new dynasty, that of Rhydderch ab Iestyn (*ob.* 1033), and his sons and grandsons are prominent in the south-east in the latest charters in the Book of Llandaf.[5]

While the identity and relationships of the kings mentioned in the later parts of *LL* are mostly straightforward,[6] the earlier kings present many problems, not least because of ambiguities and disagreements in the extant south-eastern genealogies.

---

[1] Charles-Edwards, *Wales and the Britons*, 14–15, 17–20, 285, 315–16, 330–1, and 586 and n. 20.

[2] *Ibid.*, 495, 505–6, and 511. But 'it is unlikely that the English appreciated the niceties of the distinction between Glywysing and Gwent' (*idem*, 'Dynastic succession', 76).

[3] *Idem, Wales and the Britons*, 327, 511–12, 517, 537–8, and 549.

[4] *Ibid.*, 532 and n. 152. Scholars disagree over whether the kingdom of Morgannwg is named from Morgan ab Athrwys or from the tenth-century Morgan ab Owain. For the former view see Lloyd, *A History*, I, 274 and n. 257, Lewis, 'Agweddau', 128–9, and Smith, 'The kingdom of Morgannwg', 2. For the latter (more probable) view see Phillimore in *DP* I, 208 n. 1; Brooke, 'St Peter and St Cadog', 302 n. 3 (a passage not reprinted in *The Church*); *EWGT* 139; Bartrum, 'Rhieinwg and Rheinwg', 24; Davies, *WHEMA* III 132–3 and IV 66 n. 3, and *An Early Welsh Microcosm*, 92; Charles-Edwards, 'Dynastic succession', 76. Cf. *TYP*[4] 453–5.

[5] Charles-Edwards, *Wales and the Britons*, 557–9 and 562–3.

[6] See Davies, *An Early Welsh Microcosm*, 65–98; Maund, *Ireland, Wales, and England*, passim; and the table in Charles-Edwards, *Wales and the Britons*, 253.

These genealogies will be discussed in chronological order of attestation, starting with the Harley genealogies, before turning to *LL* itself in order to see how far the genealogies agree with the charters of Sequences i and ii, and the earlier part of Sequence iii.

The south-eastern male lines in the Harley and Jesus College genealogies

The two main genealogical sources are the Harley genealogies (HG), found in BL, Harley MS 3859 (Canterbury?, *ca* 1100), and the Jesus College genealogies (JC), found in Oxford, Jesus College, MS 20 (Glamorgan, s. xiv/xv).[7]

HG seems to be a careful copy of a lost exemplar from St Davids which had been taken to Canterbury in the later tenth century. The relevant pedigrees (HG 28–29) may originally have been drawn up in Gwynedd towards the end of the reign of Rhodri Mawr (*ob.* 878).[8]

Like HG, JC includes genealogies from various parts of Wales, but unlike HG it gives precedence to the south-eastern material, in particular the genealogies related to St Cadog and his grandfather Brychan Brycheiniog. The section relevant to us, JC 9–16, gives the descent, via male and female lines, of Morgan ab Owain (*ob.* 974), the probable eponym of Morgannwg/Glamorgan.[9] If they go back to Morgan's time, which seems unlikely, considerable corruption must have occurred. As they stand, JC 9–16 look like an attempt to do for Morgannwg what the impressive genealogies of Rhodri Mawr in JC 17–23 do for Gwynedd, and it is likely that Morgan's pedigrees were put together by his descendants long after his death, just as Rhodri's were. Just as JC 17 seems to be a fictitious patrilineage for Rhodri Mawr, suspiciously absent from HG and first found in the twelfth-century *Vita* of Gruffudd ap Cynan, so Morgan's patrilineage (JC 9), suspiciously absent from HG, may be a twelfth-century fabrication.[10] Distinct versions of the patrilineage occur in Early Modern manuscripts, suggesting that it remained controversial.[11]

In 1966, following the example of Egerton Phillimore, Bartrum emended HG 28–31 heavily in his *Early Welsh Genealogical Tracts* (*EWGT*), inserting supposedly missing generations.[12] These emendations are not really necessary, and by 1993 he

---

[7] Both will be cited from *EWGT*. Jesus 20 is dated s. xiv/xv by Huws, *Medieval Welsh Manuscripts*, 60. It is available online at <http://digital.bodleian.ox.ac.uk/inquire/p/d14ae34a-351c-4613-913f-4ea5c9f0dc31> (6 Sept. 2018).

[8] Sims-Williams, 'The kings', 68–70, with references.

[9] Phillimore, *DP* I 208 n. 2, says that Morgan Hen died in 980, but see Bartrum, *A Welsh Classical Dictionary*, 486. On Morgan as eponym of Morgannwg see above, n. 4.

[10] See Sims-Williams, 'The kings', 75–8. On Rhodri's pedigrees and their date see Sims-Williams, 'Historical need', 25–30 (cf. now *Vita Griffini*, ed. Russell, §3), Charles-Edwards, *Wales and the Britons*, 363–4 and 473–5, and Guy, 'Gerald and Welsh genealogical learning', 54–5. For Lloyd's suspicion of Morgan's pedigree see below, 135.

[11] See Sims-Williams, 'The kings', 77–80.

[12] *EWGT* 12. I criticised his emendations to the Powys genealogies in 'Historical need', 36–8, and his emendations to the south-eastern ones *apud* Hughes, 'The Celtic Church', 10 n. 33, and in *Religion and Literature*, 46 n. 154.

himself came round to the view that HG 29 should not be interpolated on the basis of JC 9.[13]

In 1966 Bartrum printed the two south-eastern genealogies, HG 28–29, as follows:

28. [GLYWYSING]. [I]udhail map Atroys map Fernmail map Iudhail map Morcant map Atroys [*map Mouric*] map Teudubric.

29. [GWENT]. [B]rocmail map Mouric map Artmail [*map Guriat map Brocmail*] map Ris map Iudhail map Morcant.

Bartrum and others have equated the *Iudhail map Morcant* of HG 29 with the *Iudhail map Morcant* of HG 28, supposing that the two pedigrees give two branches of a single patrilineage from *Teudubric*. While undeniably possible, the equation is speculative since *Iudhail* and *Morcant* were both common names.[14]

The number of characteristically south-eastern Welsh names in these two lineages points to Glywysing and Gwent, but Bartrum's headings are editorial, as the square brackets indicate. Insofar as the locations do not depend on the emendations to the text, which bring the two pedigrees into line with south-eastern genealogies found elsewhere, they depend both on the reasonable identification of *Teudubric* in HG 28 with Tewdrig,[15] the ancestor of the royal line of Glywysing (known from later genealogies and from the Book of Llandaf), and of its *Atroys*, *Fernmail*, *Iudhail*, and *Morcant* with kings of these names in the Book of Llandaf, together with the identification of the *Brocmail map Mouric* of HG 29 with the king of Gwent who flourished *ca* 880, according to Asser's *Life of King Alfred*, §80:

> Hemeid scilicet, cum omnibus habitatoribus Demeticae regionis, sex filiorum Rotri vi compulsus, regali se subdiderat imperio; Houil quoque filius Ris, rex Gleguising, et Brochmail atque Fernmail filii Mouric, reges Guent, vi et tyrannide Eadred [i.e. Æthelred], comitis, et Merciorum compulsi, suapte eundem expetivere regem, ut dominum et defensionem ab eo pro inimicis suis haberent. Helised quoque filius Teudubr, rex Brecheniauc, eorundem filiorum Rotri vi coactus, dominium regis praefati suapte requisivit ...[16]

---

[13] Bartrum, 'Corrections', 171 (followed by Charles-Edwards, *Wales and the Britons*, 252 n. 32, 253, 468, and n. 9). Dr Bartrum's correction to HG 29 may ultimately be due to a draft of the present chapter, about which we corresponded at length in 1980, when he accepted that 'the solution with the minimum of "corrections" is obviously the most acceptable' (14 June 1980). By 1993, however, when we again corresponded after he had published his 'Corrections', he had forgotten about my draft and asked for another copy (he was by then in his late 80s). It is unclear, therefore, whether or not his silence about HG 28 in the 'Corrections' means that he had reconsidered and stood by his emendation there. In what follows I am indebted to him for some valuable references to late manuscripts, as also to Dr Ben Guy.

[14] As argued in Sims-Williams, 'The kings'. Against this, Dr Ben Guy suggested to me (7.10.2017) that HG 29 does not go beyond *Morcant* because it is assumed that readers will equate him with the *Morcant* of the preceding pedigree, much as readers of the Anglian collection of genealogies are expected to identify each occurrence of *Ida* and *Ecguald* as a reoccurrence of the same person (e.g. Dumville, 'The Anglian collection', 30).

[15] On the name-form see Sims-Williams, 'The kings', 75 n. 32.

[16] Asser's *Life of King Alfred*, ed. Stevenson, 66. On the emendation of *Eadred* ('Æthered' [*sic*] later in the chapter) see *ibid.*, 318, and Charles-Edwards, *Wales and the Britons*, 491 n. 109.

Hyfaidd, with all the inhabitants of the kingdom of Dyfed, driven by the might of the six sons of Rhodri [Mawr], had submitted himself to King Alfred's royal overlordship. Likewise, Hywel ap Rhys (the king of Glywysing) and Brochfael and Ffyrnfael (sons of Meurig and kings of Gwent), driven by the might and tyrannical behaviour of Ealdorman Æthelred and the Mercians, petitioned King Alfred of their own accord, in order to obtain lordship and protection from him in the face of their enemies. Similarly, Elise ap Tewdwr, king of Brycheiniog, being driven by the might of the same sons of Rhodri [Mawr], sought of his own accord the lordship of King Alfred ...[17]

The identification of *Teudubric* in HG 28 with the Glywysing ancestor is fairly secure, since it is an uncommon name,[18] and the identification of the four other names from HG 28 quoted above with the south-eastern kings of the Book of Llandaf also makes good sense.[19] On its own the identification of HG 29's *Brocmail map Mouric* with the one mentioned by Asser might seem speculative, as both are common names; but the identification is strengthened by a Gwent charter in the Book of Llandaf, which speaks of *Mouricus filius Arthuail ... coram filiis suis Brochuail et Fernuail*, thereby confirming the name of the father in HG 29 and the name of the second son in Asser.[20]

While HG 29 is tied to Gwent, HG 28 is more problematic. J. E. Lloyd regarded the *Fernmail* of HG 28 and his son *Atroys* and grandson *[I]udhail* as rulers of Gwent rather than Glywysing.[21] Although there is some support in the Book of Llandaf for locating them there, it must be emphasised that there is no reason to assign the earlier members of the HG 28 line to Gwent, and that Lloyd himself supposed that *Fernmail*'s line was not previously restricted to Gwent. His grandfather *Morcant map*

---

[17] *Alfred the Great*, translated by Keynes and Lapidge, 96. Cf. Charles-Edwards, *Wales and the Britons*, 487 and 489–93.

[18] The only other Tewdrig in *EWGT* is the Brycheiniog ancestor. The two were sometimes equated, as the interchange of their patronymics shows; cf. Sims-Williams, 'The kings', 74–5. The patrilineage above Tewdrig lies outside the scope of this chapter. Tewdrig may have been invented or elaborated to link Brycheiniog to the south-east.

[19] See below, 151. On the question whether these kings should be assigned to Glywysing or Gwent see next paragraph, and Charles-Edwards, 'Dynastic succession', 75–8.

[20] Charter 199bii. In 214 (a Monmouthshire charter not far distant in time from 199bii, to judge by its witness list) there is a reference to *Mourico rege Gleuissicg filio Iudhail*. Bartrum, 'Some studies', 286 and 288, regards him as distinct from Meurig ab Arthfael, but James ('Chronology', 134, and '*The Book of Llandav*: the church and see of Llandav', 22 n. 14) and Davies (*The Llandaff Charters*, 60, 62, 87 n. 44, 119, and 181, and *An Early Welsh Microcosm*, 19 n. 1, 102 n. 2, and 180) suggest that *Iudhail* is an error for *Arthuail*. The reference to Glywysing rather than Gwent may appear surprising, but could be a scribal error or interpolation (cf. 216b where *Mouric (m. Artmail?)* is anachronistically styled *rex Morcannuc*, cf. above, 117 n. 4). E. D. Jones, 'The Book of Llandaff', 137–8 and 141, seems wrongly to allow only for the existence of Meurig son of Ithel and gives him two sons Brochfael and Ffernfael, despite 199bii and HG 29. Cf. Davies, *An Early Welsh Microcosm*, 102 n. 2, Charles-Edwards, *Wales and the Britons*, 253, and below, 128 and n. 66, 140 n. 120, and 155 n. 215.

[21] Lloyd, *A History*, I 274; similarly Lewis, 'Agweddau', 129. Note that Lloyd assumes that '[*map Mouric*]' should be inserted in HG 28. Hughes, 'The Welsh Latin chronicles', 43 n. 3, also regarded HG 28 as the genealogy of the kings of Gwent (the comment is not reproduced in her *Celtic Britain*, 72 n. 40 and 100). See also Davies, *An Early Welsh Microcosm*, 94–5.

13. The royal genealogical framework

Atroys is called *rex Gleuissicg* in the Book of Llandaf,[22] and it and the Llancarfan charters associate him with grants in Glamorgan as well as in Monmouthshire.[23] *Iudhail map Morcant* similarly grants land mostly in Gwent and Ergyng, but also in Glamorgan and is frequently described as *rex Gleuissicg*.[24] *LL* lists his sons as *Mourici, Ris, Fernmail, Rotri, filiorum regis Gleuissicg* (p. 206). Of these sons, *Mouric* and *Ris* appear to grant land in Glamorgan,[25] and the former is associated with his father *Iudhail* and the *seniores Gleuissicg* and the latter is styled *rex Gleuissicg*.[26] *Fernmail* and *Rotri*, on the other hand, and the former's sons *Gurgauarn* and *Athruis*, are associated only with grants in Gwent and Ergyng.[27] *Fernmail*, moreover, holds court at Cemais *coram senioribus Gwent & Ercigc*.[28] *Fernmail*'s grandson *Iudhail* may be the *Iudhail rex Guent* of *Annales Cambriae*, s.a. 848.[29] It is thus possible that with *Fernmail* and his son *Atroys* one branch of the Glywysing line of HG 28 began to restrict its rule to Gwent alone, as Lloyd thought. Yet neither is anywhere described as *rex Guenti* in the Book of Llandaf and the emphasis on their activities in the east in the Book of Llandaf could be due merely to its superior coverage of grants in Monmouthshire and Herefordshire compared to Glamorgan during the period in question. It seems clear that many kings described as kings of Glywysing exercised sway over Gwent as well as Glamorgan, either because their dynasty had established some sort of overlordship in Gwent or because Glywysing was held to encompass Gwent (which may amount to the same thing); thus Hywel ap Rhys, the 'rex Gleguising' mentioned by Asser as contemporary with Brochfael and Ffernfael of Gwent, makes many more grants in Gwent than in Glamorgan in the Book of Llandaf, though the latter agrees with Asser in calling him king of Glywysing.[30] It is reasonable, then, to continue to regard HG 28 as a Glywysing pedigree, while bearing the above complications in mind.

There is no evidence outside the genealogies to show that Brochfael and Ffernfael, the two kings of Gwent mentioned by Asser, and their father Meurig (ab Arthfael) had any connection with the Glywysing dynasty, or any sway outside Gwent. The

---

[22] 229b (see below, 151).

[23] *LL* 174b; 176a/190b; 180b/*VC* 67; *VC* 62. The map of grants by Morgan ab Athrwys given by Davies, *An Early Welsh Microcosm*, 79, covers many more charters in *LL*, but I argue below, 149–51, that many of them do not refer, or do not necessarily refer, to the Morgan ab Athrwys of HG 28. If they were to be included the argument given above would be strengthened rather than weakened.

[24] For the grants see Davies, *An Early Welsh Microcosm*, 80, and for the title see *LL* 191, 195, 204a, and p. 206.

[25] Davies, *An Early Welsh Microcosm*, 81.

[26] See respectively *LL* charters 190a and 209a.

[27] Davies, *An Early Welsh Microcosm*, 81.

[28] *LL* 198b, cf. 199bi. Cf. Davies, *The Llandaff Charters*, 115, and *An Early Welsh Microcosm*, 108.

[29] Sims-Williams, 'The kings', 73–5. Cf. Lloyd, *A History*, I 274; Lewis 'Agweddau', 129; Kirby, 'British dynastic history', 88. See below, 137. Davies, *An Early Welsh Microcosm*, 95, appears to make the same identification ('Ithel is called king of Gwent').

[30] *LL* 212. Cf. Jones, 'The Book of Llandaff', 138, and Davies, *An Early Welsh Microcosm*, 95, and 82 for a map of Hywel's charters. On the later inclusion of Gwent in Morgannwg see *ibid.*, 97–8; *EA*, I, 182; Lewis, 'The *Liber Landavensis* and the diocese of Llandaff', 56–7, and 'Agweddau', 57–62 and 127–8. Cf. James, 'The Book of Llan Dav and the diocesan boundaries disputes', 333–7.

charters of Brochfael ap Meurig are 'confined to Gwent',[31] and we have no charters of his brother Ffernfael, except for those in which their father Meurig appears (225 and 199bii). Of the places mentioned in the eight charters in the Book of Llandaf which refer to a Meurig who could be Meurig ab Arthfael[32] only one (216b) lies outside Gwent and Ergyng, being thought to refer to a site near Llandaf, but one phrase in which Meurig's name occurs (*& uerbo Mourici regis Morcannuc*) has been dismissed by Wendy Davies as 'an obvious interpolation revealed by the syntax',[33] and a reference to Morgannwg is an anachronism at this date;[34] otherwise Meurig only occurs in 216b's witness list, as *Mouricus rex*, which could also be an addition. The only other charter of the eight to name Meurig's kingdom does so in the phrase *regnante Mourico rege Gleuissicg filio Iudhail* (214), where the patronymic *Iudhail* rather than *Artmail* shows that we have either a corrupt (or forged) charter or else that some other King Meurig is intended;[35] hence this charter cannot be used as evidence.

The available evidence suggests, then, that Meurig ab Arthfael, like his sons Ffernfael and Brochfael, ruled only in Gwent, whereas their contemporary Hywel ap Rhys, the king of Glywysing, held sway (perhaps for a time in conjunction with the mysterious Meurig ab Ithel of 214?) over both Glamorgan and Gwent, to judge by his charters.[36] There is no evidence for the members of the line of HG 29 earlier than Meurig ab Arthfael, partly, no doubt, owing to a chronological lacuna in the Book of Llandaf just before the charters of Meurig and Hywel begin.[37]

The insertion of the name *Mouric* into HG 28, which was suggested as a certain emendation by Phillimore,[38] depends on identifying the earlier part of HG 28 with the earlier part of JC 9. In JC 9 Morgan ab Owain's patrilineage is traced through his grandfather, Hywel of Glywysing (the king mentioned by Asser), back to Tewdrig and beyond. The text of JC 9 begins as follows in Bartrum's edition [his emendations are in brackets]:

Morgant m. Eweint m. Howel m. Rees m. Ar[th]uael m. Gwryat m. Brochuael m. Rees m. Nud hael ['*read* Iudhael'] m. Morgant m. Adroes m. Meuric m. Thewdric m. Llywarch m. Nynnyaw m. Erb ...[39]

---

[31] Davies, *An Early Welsh Microcosm*, 82 and 95.

[32] For these see Davies, *The Llandaff Charters*, 59–62, s.n. *Mouricus*. The places named are marked on her map in *An Early Welsh Microcosm*, 82, which hardly justifies the statement at 95 that Hywel ap Rhys *and* Meurig ab Arthfael 'are called *rex Glywysing* and appear all over the south east'. Cf. below, n. 35.

[33] Davies, *An Early Welsh Microcosm*, 104 n. 2.

[34] See above, 117 n. 4.

[35] Cf. above, 120 n. 20, and cross-references there. Charter 214 is the only evidence for the statement that Meurig ab Arthfael was called *rex Glywysing* (Davies, *An Early Welsh Microcosm*, 95).

[36] See above, 120.

[37] Cf. below, 155.

[38] Phillimore, 'The *Annales Cambriae* and Old-Welsh genealogies', 182 n. 1 (unaware that *Mouric* was also absent from ABT 15(E), discussed below, 132). Similarly Jones, 'The Book of Llandaff', 141, Brooke, *The Church*, 46 n. 118, and Guy, 'Did the Harleian Genealogies draw on archival sources?', 124. Kirby, 'British dynastic history', 87, inserts the name without any indication that it is an emendation, as with the other genealogies he prints.

[39] *EWGT* 45 and n. 2. The emendation of *Aruael* to *Ar[th]uael* makes good sense in view of *Arthwael* in JC 10 and *Arthuael* in JC 12 and 16, but *Ar[tha]uael* is also possible (cf. forms with *-a-* in Table 13.4 below). Syncopated and unsyncopated forms of such names

13. The royal genealogical framework

It will be seen that if we leave aside the proposed emendations, HG 28 and JC 9 overlap below *Teudubric/Thewdric* only insofar as a Morgan ab Athrwys occurs in both. As both name and patronymic are very common ones (and may have been 'leading names' in the dynasty) there is no good reason to identify the two Morgans, especially as it entails emending HG 28 (inserting *Mouric*) to do so.[40] If, then, we take HG 28 and JC 9 as they stand and assume that *Teudubric* and *Thewdrig* are the same person (see above), we arrive at the solution given in Table 13.1, Fig. 1, which may be regarded as preferable to the solution given in Table 13.1, Fig. 2, which takes account of Bartrum's two emendations to produce a single line for five generations. Names found in HG are in **bold**.

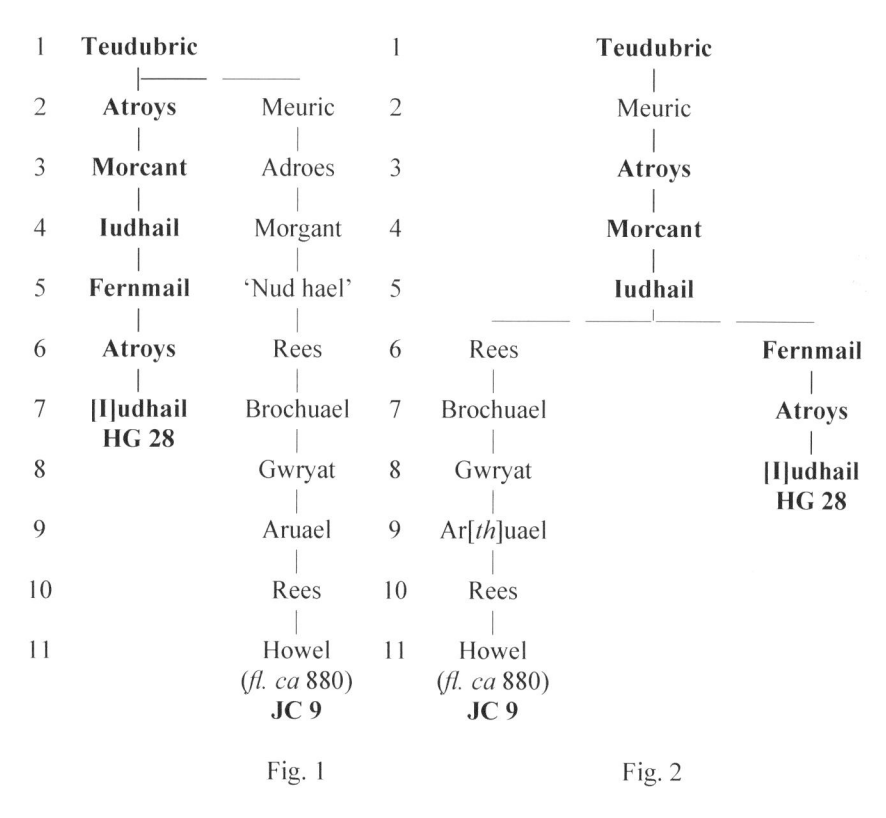

	Fig. 1			Fig. 2	
1	**Teudubric**		1	**Teudubric**	
2	**Atroys**	Meuric	2	Meuric	
3	**Morcant**	Adroes	3	**Atroys**	
4	**Iudhail**	Morgant	4	**Morcant**	
5	**Fernmail**	'Nud hael'	5	**Iudhail**	
6	**Atroys**	Rees	6	Rees	**Fernmail**
7	**[I]udhail** HG 28	Brochuael	7	Brochuael	**Atroys**
8		Gwryat	8	Gwryat	**[I]udhail** HG 28
9		Aruael	9	Ar[*th*]uael	
10		Rees	10	Rees	
11		Howel (*fl. ca* 880) JC 9	11	Howel (*fl. ca* 880) JC 9	

Table 13.1 HG 28 and JC 9 unemended (Fig. 1) and emended (Fig. 2)

---

co-existed (e.g. *Cadfael ~ Cadafael*). See Sims-Williams, *The Celtic Inscriptions of Britain*, 115, 117, 127, and 148. Perhaps *Aruael* should not be emended, however, for *Armael* occurs beside *Arthmael* in the Welsh translations of Geoffrey of Monmouth: <http://www.rhyddiaithganoloesol.caerdydd.ac.uk/cy/wordlist.php?prefix=armael> (6 Sept. 2018).

[40] Sims-Williams, 'The kings', 72. Cf. Bartrum, 'Notes', 69: 'identification of persons cannot always be certain unless the survey gives *at least two generations of ancestors*, and even then there is danger of mis-identification'.

While both solutions are possible, that in Table 13.1, Fig. 1, has the advantage of not requiring the insertion of *map Mouric* in HG 28, since it treats HG 28 and JC 9 as complementary rather than as conflicting pedigrees.[41] It also gives full weight to the early date and generally careful nature of HG.

The emendation of *Nud hael* in JC 9 to *Iudhael* is superficially attractive – misread minims and mistakes in capitals are not uncommon – and has been generally accepted.[42] However, the variant of JC 9 in the sixteenth-century tract *Brenhinllwyth Morganwc*, edited by Bartrum as Miscellaneous Pedigrees 3 (MP 3), gives the name as *Einvdd* (without epithet), as do other late texts.[43] It is difficult to see how this could be a corruption of *Iudhael*, but it could easily be a corruption of *Nud(d)* (without the epithet *hael*), perhaps influenced by the occurrence of the name *Einudd* later in MP 3. It may be suggested, therefore, that the name in JC 9 is correctly given as *Nud*. The epithet *hael* 'generous' is probably a late addition, inspired by the epithet of the literary hero Nudd Hael ap Senyllt in *Trioedd Ynys Prydein* and elsewhere; this would accord with the 'fictional elements' and 'influence of TYP' which Rachel Bromwich detected in the Jesus College genealogies.[44] A similar addition may have occurred in JC 19, where a person called *Neithon map Senill* in HG 4 appears as *Neidaon m. Senilth hael, tryd hael or gogled*, perhaps through confusion with Nudd Hael ap Senyllt.[45] Note also the naming of *Caradawc vreichvras* in JC 9, where the epithet is regarded as a literary-inspired addition.[46]

Bartrum edited MP 3 (*Brenhinllwyth Morganwc*) from three sixteenth-century manuscripts.[47] It gives the patrilineage of Caradog ap Iestyn (*fl.* 1127), a descendant of Hywel ap Rhys (*fl.* 880), back to Tewdrig (who is called not *m. Llywarch* as in JC 9, but *ap Teithvallt* as in the *Vita Cadoci* and other early sources),[48] and thence back to a certain *Kyllin ap Kradoc*; and as the latter is identified with Caradog ap Brân of the tract *Bonedd yr Arwyr*, the compiler finally manages to get back as far as the Trojans.[49] Apart from the difficulty of explaining *Einudd* from *Nud hael*, MP 3 might

---

[41] JC 9's *Meuric* cannot be regarded as an interpolation in view of the evidence in *LL* as well as that of later genealogies for the existence of Meurig ap Tewdrig. For a reference to Athrwys ap Tewdrig in Cardiff, Central Library, MS 3.77, see 132 below.

[42] Anscombe, 'Some Old-Welsh pedigrees', 84; *TYP*[4] 464 (*Iudbail* is a misprint, absent from the first edition); *EWGT* 45 n. 2; Davies, *The Llandaff Charters*, 87 n. 42. The emendation is implied by Lloyd in the passage cited below, 135 n. 103. Cf. HG 28, where the first name (*Iudhail*) is written [ ]uδ hail, arguably with a space before *h* (Phillimore, 'The *Annales Cambriae* and Old-Welsh genealogies', 181 and n. 6; Sims-Williams, 'The kings', 70 n. 13). For a facsimile showing the *Nud hael* of JC 9 see Pearce, *The kingdom of Dumnonia*, pl. 31, or <http://digital.bodleian.ox.ac.uk/inquire/p/d14ae34a-351c-4613-913f-4ea5c9f0dc31> (6 Sept. 2018). The *N* is not one of the red decorated letters – it does not mark the beginning of a pedigree – so it cannot be attributed to a rubricator's mistake, unlike, say, the *L* for *I* in the name *Llud* in JC 3 (cf. *DP* III 233; *EWGT* 44 n. 3). Incidentally, the Old Breton name *Nodhail* is quite distinct (it is cognate with Welsh *nawdd*) and cannot be connected.

[43] *EWGT* 122 (cf. Table 13.4 below); Sims-Williams, 'The kings', 77–8. On MP 3 see below. See also *Iolo Manuscripts*, ed. Williams, 3 and 331 (*Einydd*).

[44] *TYP*[4] 304.

[45] *EWGT* 140. Cf. *TYP*[4] 5–7, 464, and 498; Bartrum, *A Welsh Classical Dictionary*, 586.

[46] *TYP*[4] 304 and *EWGT* 139 (cf. above, 54 n. 29).

[47] *EWGT* 122. On his MS B (Peniarth 138 by Thomas ap Llywelyn ab Ithel) see Bartrum, 'Notes', 81 n. 3 and 'Further Notes', 111. See *ibid.*, 107, for the date of Pen. 178 (MS A).

[48] See Sims-Williams, 'The kings', 74–5.

[49] See *EWGT* 158; also Bartrum, 'Was there a British "Book of Conquests"?', 4–5.

13. The royal genealogical framework

easily be regarded as an expansion and modification of JC 9 itself in the light of other sources, rather than a derivative of a text anterior to JC. But another text suggests that the latter conclusion is the correct one. BL Harley 4181, 37r–39v, contains an account of the ancestors of Morgan Hen ab Owain ap Hywel ap Rhys by Hugh Thomas (*ob.* 1720) which is closely related to MP 3 though, on the whole, much more corrupt.[50] But this account is not a mere derivative of MP 3; it seems to go back to a common source with it. It lacks the Trojan elaboration. Also it contains many notes on collateral lines missing in MP but related to those in JC. These notes (which are corrupt) appear to derive not from JC but from an earlier, and in a few respects better, text. For instance where JC 10 has *Kenedlon merch Biuael* [*sic*] *vrydic*, Hugh Thomas has *Genedlon Daughter to Brianayl Vridig*, which is closer to the correct *Briauael* (*LL* charters 149 and 151b); compare, too, *Brian* with *-r-* in a version of the genealogy in NLW 3067B (Mostyn 212b) by Thomas Jones of Tregaron (*ob.* 1609).[51] The genealogists of the fifteenth to seventeenth centuries do not seem to have had access to JC itself – if they had they would have made obvious use of it – but they occasionally show knowledge of some of its constituent parts.[52] The obvious explanation is that JC is itself a compilation and that some of the shorter texts from which it was compiled survived in independent copies.[53] I would suggest that MP 3 and Hugh Thomas had a common source which descends from a manuscript anterior to JC.[54] Now it is significant that Hugh Thomas has *Enyth*,[55] and that Thomas Jones of Tregaron has *Ainydd*.[56]

An indication that the form *Nud hael* in JC 9 may not be unique to that manuscript is provided by the late-fifteenth- or sixteenth-century tract *Gwehelyth Morgannwg*, §1, edited from two sixteenth-century manuscripts by Ben Guy, who argues that it is not a direct descendant of JC. Here the forms *Haddhail* and *Hyddheyl* clearly correspond to *Nud hael*:

> Morgan Mwynfawr ap Ywain ap Howel ap Rys ap Arthuayl ap Gyriat ap Brochuail [Llanstephan 12 omits *Gyriat ap Brochuail*] ap Meyrig ap Rys ap Haddhail [*Hyddheyl* in Llanstephan 12] ap Morgan ap Adroes ap Meyrig ap

---

[50] This has not been printed apart from Vaughan, 'Welsh pedigrees', 109, and the extract in *EWGT* 139. (See also below, 131.) Hugh Thomas quotes a manuscript by Richard Williams (*fl.* 1645) as his source. On him see Bartrum, 'Further notes', 117–18. Although Hugh Thomas knew JC itself (*EWGT* 41) he has not used it to correct Richard Williams it seems. On Hugh Thomas see Jones, 'An approach', 421–8. He has the same material in Harley 6831, 197r. Guy, 'Medieval Welsh genealogy', II 329 n. 46 notes that *Gwehelyth Morgannwg* §5 (see below) has *Briauayl*.

[51] *EWGT* 139–40. The Mostyn 212b material is also in Cardiff, Central Library, 2.16 (RWM 59), pp. 38–9 (1611), on which see Davies, *The National Library of Wales Catalogue of Manuscripts*, I 123.

[52] *EWGT* 41; Bartrum, 'Notes', 64–5; Sims-Williams, 'The kings', 77.

[53] This explains, for instance, why JC 33–34 alone appear in NLW 3042B (Mostyn 134), fo. 15 (early seventeenth century). See Bartrum, 'Notes', 64–5. In the manuscript JC 33–34 are separated from JC 32 and JC 35 by blank lines, which might suggest an independent origin, but see Guy, 'Medieval Welsh genealogy', I, 53 and 73–4.

[54] NLW 3067B (Mostyn 212b) (mentioned above) may also go back to a common source with Hugh Thomas and MP 3; for another point of contact see *EWGT* 141 on JC 20, and below, 129 n. 67.

[55] BL Harley 4181, 39v, and similarly 6831, 197r. Cf. Vaughan, 'Welsh pedigrees', 109.

[56] NLW 3067B (Mostyn 212b), p. 57.

Tewdrig, y gwr a seiliodd eglwys Llandaf ag a roes iddi y harglwyddayth a brainiay.[57]

The simplest way to explain the variation in the pedigree represented by JC 9 is to suppose that the original name was either *Nud* or *Einud*, that this was transmitted in one branch of the tradition as *Einudd* as in MP 3 (*Enyth* in Hugh Thomas, *Ainydd* in Thomas Jones) and in the other as *Nud* and then (under the influence of the famous character's epithet) as *Nud hael* as in JC 9 and, corrupted, as *Haddhail/Hyddheyl* in *Gwehelyth Morgannwg*. There is no reason to suppose that *Iudhael* was the original reading in JC 9, other than a wish to equate it with HG 28.

I have suggested elsewhere that the prestigious pedigree of Morgan ab Owain underlying JC 9–16, MP 3, and the other late sources may have been created by or for Morgan's descendant Caradog ap Iestyn ap Gwrgan ab Ithel (*fl.* 1127), with whom MP 3 begins. His father and grandfather appear in the Book of Llandaf itself, and he retained power in western Glamorgan despite the Norman advance.[58] The patrilineage honours Caradog's ancestor Morgan ab Owain ap Hywel ap Rhys, whose line is notably absent from HG, by linking him to Morgan ab Athrwys ap Meurig ap Tewdrig in the Book of Llandaf, a possible source for these four names in JC 9 and the rest. It is perhaps significant that most of the above texts include Briafael ap Llywarch, a person otherwise only known from *LL*, and that *Gwehelyth Morgannwg* connects Tewdrig with the foundation of Llandaf. A hint that the patrilineage in JC 9 and related texts was not at first authoritative is the fact that a quite different version of the patrilineage is given in the pedigree of Caradog's son, Morgan ap Caradog ap Iestyn ap Gwrgan (*ob. ca* 1208).[59]

Bartrum's emendation of the probably Gwent pedigree, HG 29 in *EWGT* (quoted above) depended for its validity on the correctness of his emendation of *Nud hael* in JC 9 to *Iudhael*, and, moreover, carried the argument still further. He identified the *Ris map Iudhail map Morcant* of HG 29 with the *Rees m. Nud hael m. Morgant* of JC 9, and took the *Artmail map Ris* of HG 29, to be the same person as the *Ar*[*th*]*uael m. Gwryat* of JC 9 and related pedigrees. These identifications led him to insert two generations into HG 29 between *Artmail* and *Ris*, namely Gwriad and Brochfael, whom he took from JC 9. These names were presumably supposed to have been lost from HG 29 by homoioteleuton (. . . *mail* . . . *mail*), just as homoioteleuton presumably has to explain the omission of *Gyriat ap Brochuail* in the Llanstephan 12 copy of *Gwehelyth Morgannwg*, unless that omission was due to collating some other text.[60]

---

[57] '... the man who founded the church of Llandaf and gave it its lordship and privileges'. Text in Guy, 'Medieval Welsh genealogy', II, 336 (from NLW, Brogyntyn I.15, pp. 396–7, and Llanstephan 12, pp. 81–5), and discussion in I, 87–9. *Gwehelyth Morgannwg* is more systematic than JC 9–16: Morgan Mwynfawr's female ancestors are given in a logical (albeit impossible) order, i.e. mother (§2), grandmother (§3), great-grandmother (§4), and great-great-grandmother (§5). Dr Guy emphasises to me that a textual connection between JC 9, MP 3, and *Gwehelyth Morgannwg* is especially indicated by their spellings of the name Athrwys.

[58] Sims-Williams, 'The kings', 77–8. Gwrgan ap Ithel's genealogy, very similar to MP 3, appears in NLW 3067B (Mostyn 212b), pp. 57–9.

[59] See below, 132, on ABT 15(E).

[60] Guy, 'Medieval Welsh genealogy', II 335, suggests that Llanstephan 12 was influenced by ABT 15 (on which see below).

13. The royal genealogical framework

Bartrum's restoration of Gwriad and Brochfael from JC 9, coupled with his emendations to HG 28 and JC 9 (already discussed), resulted in the scheme in Table 13.2, Fig. 1 (HG names are in **bold**).

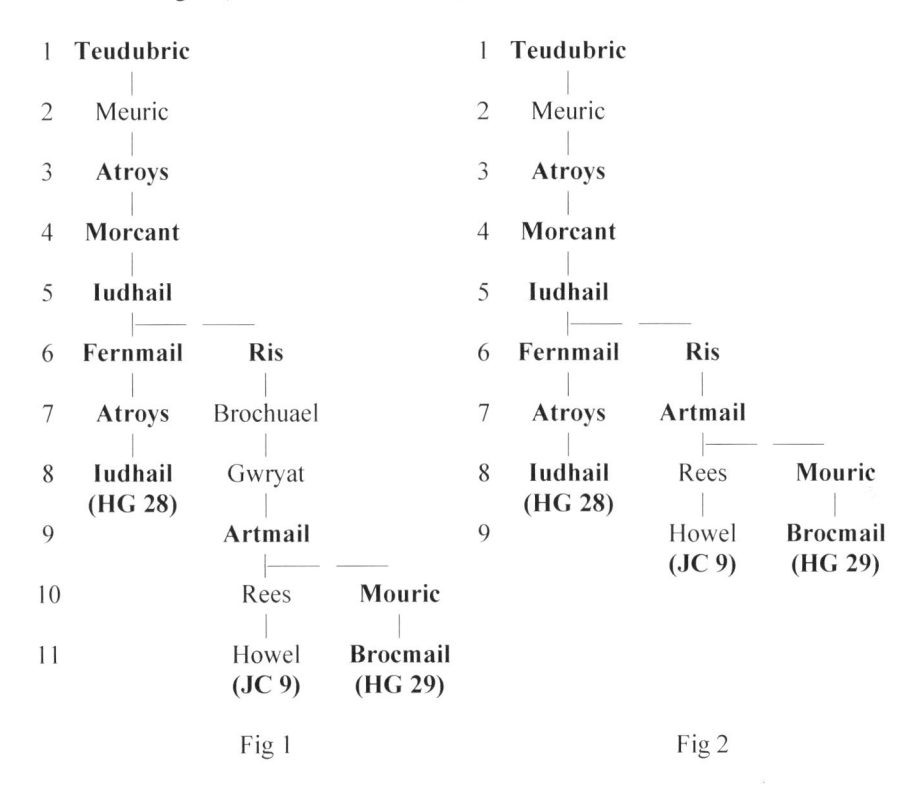

```
1   Teudubric                           1   Teudubric
    |                                       |
2   Meuric                              2   Meuric
    |                                       |
3   Atroys                              3   Atroys
    |                                       |
4   Morcant                             4   Morcant
    |                                       |
5   Iudhail                             5   Iudhail
    |_____                                |_____
6   Fernmail    Ris                     6   Fernmail    Ris
    |           |                           |           |
7   Atroys      Brochuael              7   Atroys      Artmail
    |           |                           |           |_____
8   Iudhail     Gwryat                  8   Iudhail     Rees        Mouric
    (HG 28)     |                           (HG 28)     |           |
9               Artmail                 9               Howel       Brocmail
                |_____                                (JC 9)      (HG 29)
10              Rees      Mouric
                |         |
11              Howel     Brocmail
                (JC 9)    (HG 29)

        Fig 1                                   Fig 2
```

Table 13.2 The genealogies according to *EWGT* (Fig. 1) and according to Bartrum's 'Corrections' (Fig. 2)

An alternative consequence of the proposed identifications, which was adopted by J. W. James, was to regard *Gwryat m. Brochuael* in JC 9 as an interpolation which must be deleted in order to square JC 9 with HG 29.[61] His interpretation resulted in a scheme similar to that shown in Table 13.2, Fig. 2. (I have added generation numbers for comparison with Table 13.2, Fig. 1). Bartrum's 1993 'Corrections', in which he suggested deleting his inserted '[*map Guriat map Brocmail*]' in HG 29, comes to the

---

[61] James, 'Chronology', 138 and 142 n. 74 (rejected by Davies, *The Llandaff Charters*, 87 n. 42, who assumes that the *Artmail* of HG 29 is the *Ar[th]uael* of JC 9). James also thought that HG 28 and JC 9 (which he equates in the same way as other scholars) both left out several generations and that the *Morcant* son of *Atroys* and the *Morcant* father of *Iudhail* at generation 4 of Table 13.2, Figs. 1 and 2 are different people. This is an entirely separate matter and depends not on textual considerations but on an interpretation of the chronology of *LL* which I believe to be erroneous. See below, 150 n. 179.

same thing, and was followed by Charles-Edwards in 2013.[62] By contrast, in 2012 Ben Guy – without mentioning Bartrum's 1993 'Corrections' – retained a preference JC 9 over HG 29, and made the novel suggestion that HG 29 was created by someone who went through some of the charter collections later used in *LL* – specifically Wendy Davies's Groups C and F – and failed to include the generations *map Guriat map Brocmail* owing to these names' absence from Groups C and F; in addition, the compiler of HG 29 'must have made a leap of faith in assuming that Arthfael was the son of Rhys'.[63]

The identifications and emendations accepted by most scholars are of more than minor textual interest, for if they are correct they mean that the whole of south-east Wales was dominated by a single dynasty.[64] They are questionable, however, since they involve equating only very common names. Thus there is no strong reason for identifying the *Ris map Iudhail map Morcant* of HG 29 with the *Rees m. Nud hael m. Morgant* of JC 9 – and the identification is, of course, impossible unless one emends *Nud hael* to *Iudhael*. Similarly the *Iudhail map Morcant* of HG 29 cannot be assumed to be the same person as the *Iudhail map Morcant* of HG 28, although they could be. (If they are identical the *Brocmail* in HG 29 must probably belong to an earlier generation than the one contemporary with Hywel ap Rhys who is mentioned by Asser, unless one inserts some generations into HG 29, as Bartrum did, or takes two out of JC 9, as James did.) Again, it is quite possible that *Brocmail map Mouric* and *Howel m. Rees* both had grandfathers called Arthfael without supposing that the two grandfathers were one and the same person. The relationship between *Howel m. Rees* and *Brocmail*'s father *Mouric*, which has been suggested by Bartrum and James on the basis of an *LL* charter (212) is quite uncertain. According to this charter *Houel ... regem Gleuissicg filium Ris* undertook penance *consilio patruelis sui Mourici*.[65] Bartrum comments that '"Patruelis" means literally "descended from a father's brother", generally cousin, but uncle might be allowable' and goes on to identify this *Mouric* with *Brocmail*'s father, *Mouric map Artmail*.[66] Really, however, we have no means of telling who this *patruelis* was, and the identity of names is too slight a basis for an identification. One is thus led to conclude that although the proposed genealogical association of the Gwent and Glywysing dynasties, and the emendations of the Harley genealogies which it

---

[62] Bartrum, 'Corrections', 171; Charles-Edwards, *Wales and the Britons*, 252 n. 32 and 253.

[63] Guy, 'Did the Harleian Genealogies draw on archival sources?', 130. On Groups C and F see above, ch. 9.

[64] For example, Charles-Edwards, *Wales and the Britons*, 19, 125, 253, 495 n. 126, and 505. Similarly see Davies, *The Llandaff Charters*, 74 and 76, *An Early Welsh Microcosm*, 17, 65, and 102, and *WHEMA* IX 8–9. In *The Llandaff Charters*, 87 n. 42, and *An Early Welsh Microcosm*, 95 and 102 n. 2, she accepts Bartrum's equation of JC 9 and HG 29 and his emendations.

[65] Davies, *The Llandaff Charters*, 119, and *An Early Welsh Microcosm*, 180, thinks that this Narration is unlikely to be an original part of the charter.

[66] 'Some studies', 284, and *Welsh Genealogies*, I, chart [17] – similarly James, 'Chronology', 134, and Guy, 'Did the Harleian Genealogies draw on archival sources?', 123 and 127. See also Davies, *An Early Welsh Microcosm*, 102 n. 2, where a different identification (wrongly attributed to James) is quoted, viz. identification with the obscure Meurig ab Ithel of charter 214 and 120 n. 20 above, presumed to be a grandson of Hywel's grandfather Arthfael. *Patruelibus* is glossed *ceintiru* ('first cousins') in Old Welsh: Charles-Edwards, 'Some Celtic kinship terms', 107; cf. *idem*, *Early Irish and Welsh Kinship*, 171 and 185.

13. The royal genealogical framework

entails, are quite possible, they are not necessarily correct, and the two families may be unconnected. (See Table 13.5 below.)

The south-eastern female lines in the Jesus College genealogies

Table 13.3 attempts to show how Bartrum in his edition harmonises the three genealogies discussed above (HG 28, HG 29, and JC 9) and also three more genealogies of Morgan Hen in the Jesus College collection which trace his descent through female lines (JC 10, 12, and 14). I have not shown the earliest generations. Square brackets denote Bartrum's editorial additions; note also that he emends 'Nud hael', 'Arbeth', and 'Eleothen' to 'Iudhael', 'Arb' for 'Erb', and 'Clothen' respectively. The = sign denotes 'marries' and the boxes indicate the identifications assumed by Bartrum. JC 16 refers to Morgan, but is omitted as being so corrupt as to be unusable. It is possible that JC 20 ('Morgant; Nest oed y vam ef') refers to Morgan's descent through his mother Nest from Rhodri Mawr, who is the subject of JC 20, and I include this in Table 13.5, adopting Bartrum's suggestion that JC 20 meant to list Morgan as Rhodri's *grandson*, as explicitly stated by later genealogists, not as his *son*.[67] Historically, of course, this is most unlikely, especially in view of Morgan's family's exclusion from HG, originally compiled in Gwynedd.

I have already discussed the first three columns of Table 13.3, casting doubt on the insertions of *Mouric*, *Brocmail*, and *Guriat* and the emendation of 'Nud hael' to *Iudhael* and questioning the identifications in generations 2–9 marked by boxes. The remaining three columns provide no evidence for the male line above Arthfael, as may be seen. JC 14 connects Arthfael with the royal line of Buellt through his wife Brawstudd (whom later texts make Rhys ab Arthfael's wife),[68] while JC 12 connects him with the royal line of Dyfed through his mother *Ceingar* (whom later texts make Hywel's wife).[69] JC 10 is clearly corrupt; it makes *Kenedlon* Arthfael's mother, which conflicts with JC 12. Later texts makes her Rhys ab Arthfael's mother,[70] which is equally unsatisfactory chronologically. JC 10 is several generations too short compared to JC 9, since its 'Arbeth' is presumed to be the same person as *Erb* in JC 9: *Pibiawn glawrawc m. Arbeth* is identified with the king *Peipiau clauorauc filius Erb* of the allegedly early charters in *LL*, which seem to place him four generations before Meurig ap Tewdrig;[71] moreover *LL* makes St Dyfrig's mother Efrddyl the

---

[67] See *EWGT* 141; Sims-Williams, 'Historical need', 12–13 and 25 n. 85. To the sources cited add *Gwehelyth Morgannwg*, §2 (ed. Guy, 'Medieval Welsh genealogy', II, 336).

[68] Cf. *Historia Brittonum*, §49, printed in *EWGT* 8, for the Buellt line, and cf. *DP* III 223 n. 2. According to Thomas Jones of Tregaron (*ob.* 1609), 'mam Howel ap Rys oedd Brawst verch Klouydd ap Basgen Byellt' (NLW 3067B (Mostyn 212b), p. 59); *Gwehelyth Morgannwg*, §4, agrees (*Brawst*), as does Harley 6831, 197r.

[69] Cf. HG 2, etc. In *Gwehelyth Morgannwg*, §3, *Gaingar* (daughter of Maredudd, *ob.* 796) is the grandmother of Morgan (*ob.* 974), clearly impossibly. Harley 6831, 197r, is similar.

[70] *Gwehelyth Morgannwg*, §5; NLW 3067B (Mostyn 212b), p. 59.

[71] *LL* 72a and p. 78 etc. Meurig's wife is the daughter of Gwrgan (140), who seems to be Erb's great-grandson (144). See below, 146–9 and Table 13.5. In *Gwehelyth Morgannwg*, §3 (ed. Guy, 'Medieval Welsh genealogy', II, 336), *Gaingar*, daughter of Maredudd, is the mother of Owain (generation 12 of Table 13.3), which is chronologically worse than JC 12, while §4 makes 'Brawst' the mother of Hywel (generation 11), not Rhys as in JC 14, and §5 makes 'Geneddlon' the mother of Rhys (generation 10), not Arthfael as in

	HG 28	HG 29	JC 9	JC 10	JC 12	JC 14
1			Erb	'Arbeth'	Kyngar	Gwidawl
	Teudubric		Nynnyaw	Pibiawn	Peder	Gwrtheyrn
				glawrawc		gwrthenev
			Llywarch	Tewdwr	Arthur	Pascen
			Thewdric	Llywarch	Nennue	Riagath
2	[Mouric]		Meuric	B[r]i[a]uael	'Eleothen'	Idnerth
				Vrydic		
3	Atroys		Adroes [=]	Kenedlon	Cathen	Pawl
4	Morcant	Morcant	Morgant	[Morgant]	Gwgawn	Elaed
5	Iudhail	Iudhail	'Nud hael'	[Iudhael]	[Rein]	Morvo
6	Fernmail	Ris	Rees	[Rees]	Teudos	Gwedgad
7	Atroys	[Brocmail]	Brochuael	[Brochuael]	Maredud	Pascen Buellt
8	[I]udhail	[Guriat]	Gwryat =	[Gwryat]	Ceingar	Gloud
9		Artmail	Ar[th]uael	Arthuael	Arthuael =	Braustud
10		Mouric	Rees	Rees	Rees	Rees
11		[B]rocmail	Howel	Hewel	Hoel	Howel
12			Eweint	Eweint	Eweint	Ewein
13			Morgant	Morgant	Morgant	Morgant

Table 13.3   The female lines in the Jesus College genealogies

13. The royal genealogical framework

daughter of *Pepiau nomine clauorauc*[72] which doubtless agrees with a corrupt part of JC 10 ('Pibiawn glawrawc .m. Arbeth .m. Deuric sant. merch Peibiawn') which may be corrupted from something like: 'Pebiaw glawrawc mab Erb et m[ater] (or m[am]) Deuric sant [oed] merch Peibiaw'.[73] The two sons of Erb, *Nynnyaw* (JC 9) and *Pibiawn*, are no doubt to be connected with *Nynhyaw a Pheibyaw, a rithwys Duw yn ychen am eu pechawd* ('Nynnio and Peibio, whom God transformed into oxen for their sin') in the tale *Culhwch ac Olwen*.[74] Another indication that several generations are missing from JC 10 is the probability that its *B[r]i[a]uael vrydic m. Llywarch* is the same person as the *Briauail* (or *Briuail*) *filius Lumarch* who appears in *LL* charters in the time of Meurig ap Tewdrig and Morgan ab Athrwys.[75] Most probably, then, the lacuna in JC 10 is of *about* five generations between *Arthwael* and *Kenedlon*.[76] If so *Kenedlon* was probably supposed to have married the *Adroes* of JC 9, unless the generations were out of step as often happens.[77] Thus the missing generations in JC 10 can be tentatively restored from JC 9, following Bartrum, who suggests that a manuscript line in an exemplar may have got lost. My only point of difference (for reasons already given) would be over the restoration of *Iudhael* where JC 9 has *Nud hael*; it is a great pity that the lacuna in JC 10 and later related texts has deprived us of further evidence on that vexed reading. As it is, the three pedigrees JC 10, 12, and 14 provide us with no help in handling HG 28–29 and JC 9. Their main value is in reinforcing the impression that the genealogies for Morgan ab Owain in JC and related later texts were inspired by a knowledge of the Book of Llandaf, or a similar text, making *LL*, or a congener, a likely source for the sequence *Morgant m. Adroes m. Meuric m. Thewdric* in JC 9.

In effect, what these texts do is create an artificial bridge – Arth(a)fael back to Nudd/Einudd – between the historically attested Morgan ab Owain ap Hywel ap Rhys and the above ancient sequence in *LL* (Morgan ab Athrwys ap Meurig ap Tewdrig). It may well be significant that the dynastic marriages in JC 10, 12, and 14 are not attached to Morgan ab Owain's immediate forebears, as one would expect

---

JC 10. Hugh Thomas agrees: Harley 4181, 39v, and 6831, 197r. *Pepiau* king of Ergyng also appears in Rhygyfarch's *Life of St David*; see above, 51, on him and his epithet *clauorauc*. Anscombe, 'Some Old-Welsh pedigrees', 78 and 81, unconvincingly posits a distinction between Peibio ab Erb and Peibio grandfather of Dyfrig. His proposed identification of Peibio's *socer* Constantinus *rex* in *LL* no. 72a is mere speculation, although Wade-Evans agrees in 'The Llancarfan charters', 163.

[72] *LL* p. 78. A later addition (printed on p. 337) makes Peibio himself the father of Dyfrig (incestuously?).

[73] See the note in *EWGT* 140, and emendations on p. 45. Dr Guy will be publishing a new interpretation of this crux.

[74] *Culhwch and Olwen*, ed. Bromwich and Evans, lines 599–600.

[75] See below, 147 and 149–50; *EWGT* 140; Davies, *An Early Welsh Microcosm*, 114 and 119; and Guy, 'The *Life* of St Dyfrig', 31 n. 89.

[76] The late texts quoted in *EWGT* 139 are of no help since they also show a lacuna (similarly *Gwehelyth Morgannwg*, §5, has 'Geneddlon' marrying Arthfael – possibly confused with Athrwys?). That in Harley 4181, 39v, which I have consulted, is an impossible rehash of the marriages in JC: it is not Arthfael but his son Rhys who married Brawstudd, and it is Rhys's son Hywel, not Gwriad, who marries *Ceingar*. *Gwehelyth Morgannwg*, §§3–4, agrees.

[77] The name of a wife of Meurig ap Tewdrig is known from *LL* (*Onbraus(t)*); see below, 143 and 147–9. *EWGT* 140 (cf. Davies, *An Early Welsh Microcosm*, 114 n. 1) notes that *LL* charter 190b gives Morgan ab Athrwys a wife *Ricceneth*; however, I take this Morgan to be not the one in JC 9 but the one in HG 28 (see below, 151 and Table 13.5).

in a 'status genealogy',[78] but to his remoter male ancestors, especially those in the 'bridge', as if these required additional validation. Moreover, there is a suspicious similarity between the names of the wives *Kenedlon* (JC 10), *Ceingar* (JC 12), and *Braustud* (JC 14) and three wives in the *LL* charters: *Ricceneth*, wife of Morgan [ab Athrwys] (190b), *Ceincair*, wife of Ffernfael ab Ithel (207), and *Onbraust*, wife of Meurig ap Tewdrig (140, also p. 132).

Achau Brenhinoedd a Thywysogion Cymru 15

Another later medieval pedigree (see Table 13.4) presents a different picture from the ones discussed above: Bartrum's *Achau Brenhinoedd a Thywysogion Cymru 15* (ABT 15).[79] This is obviously written in the interests of Morgannwg families who claimed descent from Morgan Hen (*ob.* 974). ABT 15 is the pedigree Morgan ap Caradog (*ob. ca* 1208), the son of the Caradog who is the subject of MP 3 (see above).[80] ABT 15 is first found in fifteenth-century and later manuscripts, but the relevant part (p. 75) of one of these, Bartrum's MS E ('Cardiff 25' i.e. Cardiff, Central Library, MS 3.77), by John Jones of Gelli Lyfdy (1640), is the sole known copy of the lost vellum manuscript 'Y'.[81] A tantalising point of interest in MS E is that in it alone Morgan ap Caradog's mother is referred to in the present tense (*yw*, not *oedd*): 'Gwladus ferc Gruffud ap Rys ap Teudur yu mam forgant'.[82] This agrees with Bartrum's opinion that 'Y' reflects early-thirteenth-century material.[83]

In view of its importance, the readings of MS E are given separately in Table 13.4 as 'ABT 15(E)'.[84] The great interest of ABT 15(E) is that Tewdrig's son is *Arthrwys/Arthwys* (or similar), as in HG 28, not Meurig (as in JC 9 etc.), which supports the reconstruction of the Glywysing pedigree given in Table 13.1, Fig. 1 above. In the manuscript (Cardiff 3.77, p. 75) John Jones copied the relevant lines as follows:

ap Morgant ap Art[*space*] ap Teu=
drig ap Teitfalt, ap Nynyau
ap Irb[*space*] ap Ebig ap Meurig
ap Efynny. ~/

---

[78] e.g. HG 1–2 and JC 17–23. In *Gwehelyth Morgannwg* and related texts the marriages are duly rearranged so as to apply to Morgan's mother, grandmother, etc. (see above, 126 n. 57).

[79] *EWGT* 105, under the title 'Gwehelyth Morganwc', but I do not use that title for ABT 15 to avoid confusion with the aforementioned tract edited by Guy.

[80] See Maund, *Ireland, Wales, and England*, 192–3 and 203, and Sims-Williams, 'The kings', 78.

[81] See Guy, 'A lost medieval manuscript', 72 (correcting the suggestion in *EWGT* 76–7 and 79 n. 1 that 'Y' was Hengwrt MS 141). Guy, 'Medieval Welsh genealogy', I, 110, argues that it 'does not seem possible to assign a date to Y any more precise than "pre-1450", although a date in the fourteenth or even thirteenth century is not out of the question'. 'Y' is otherwise known only from some quotations by Robert Vaughan in Peniarth 283 (see *EWGT* 78 n. 2, and Guy, 'Medieval Welsh genealogy', I, 107–9); this has only the heading 'Jestyn ap Gwrgant' on its otherwise blank 27r.

[82] Cardiff MS 3.77, p. 75. Oddly, this sentence was not collated in *EWGT* 105. For the pedigree see Bartrum, *Welsh Genealogies*, III, s. Iestyn 1–2.

[83] *EWGT* 78. Guy, 'Medieval Welsh genealogy', I 168, narrows this to 1215×23.

[84] Under-dotted *t* and *u* represent standard *th* and *w*.

13. The royal genealogical framework

There is only enough space for the end of the name *Arth*[(r)wys], which was presumably partly illegible in Jones's evidently damaged medieval exemplar; there is not enough room for the patronymic *ap Meurig* as well. Elsewhere Jones has left spaces that evidently correspond in size to the damage in his exemplar.[85] While it is undeniably possible that Jones or his exemplar omitted the name *Meurig* before *ap Tewdrig* by a haplography identical to that usually ascribed to the scribe of HG 28,[86] it is also possible that all the other manuscripts of ABT 15 have added it, for example under the influence of the tradition represented by *LL*, JC 9, MP 3, etc. Whereas John Jones was a copyist, many of the other ABT 15 manuscripts are associated with Gutun Owain, who was a learned compiler and collator. Bartrum noted that his MSS FHJ descended from a 1497 manuscript of Gutun Owain, which he later identified as Manchester, John Rylands Library, Welsh MS 1 (which has the reading 'ap me6ric' at 5r),[87] and MS C is an earlier compilation by Gutun Owain. Bartrum's remaining two ABT manuscripts, which agree on *ap Meurig* – MS C′, by Ieuan ap Madog ap Rhys, and MS G, by Thomas ap Ieuan ap Deicws – descend from a branch of the ABT stemma that is distinct from 'Y'.[88] It is quite possible that this branch 'restored' Meurig's name and was followed in MS C and the Manchester manuscript by Gutun Owain, whom Guy rightly characterises as:

> an enterprising textual scholar of the humanist mode, who sought out many early copies of the texts that he was editing in order to facilitate effective textual criticism. It seems unlikely that many early copies of the [ABT] genealogies survived the fifteenth century without having passed through Gutun Owain's hands at some point.[89]

Guy notes a clear example in the Manchester manuscript of Gutun improving his text of ABT 15 after collating another manuscript.[90] Thus we may have a simple choice between John Jones's copy of 'Y' in ABT 15(E) and the partly conflated and 'improved' text in all the other ABT 15 witnesses, in which the famous Meurig ap Tewdrig has been 'restored' in generation 4 of Table 13.4.

Clearly, as Table 13.4 shows, ABT is two or three generations shorter than JC 9 and MP 3 is two longer. At first sight ABT (but not MP 3) supports James's emendation of JC 9 (cf. Table 13.2, Fig. 2). Yet in *EWGT* Bartrum took it that ABT independently left out *Gwryat m. Brochuael* in just the same way that he supposed HG 29 had left them out.[91] On this view, on the one hand, ABT 15's reading *Ith(a)el* (the later form of *Iudhael*) would confirm the correctness of emending *Nud hael* in JC 9 to

---

[85] 'Irb[*space*]' in ABT 15(E) is perhaps for *Irbeth* (cf. 'Arbeth' in JC 10).
[86] Bartrum, 'Some studies', 283 n. 2.
[87] *EWGT* 79–80; Bartrum, 'Notes', 64, and 'Further notes', 104–5 and 111. I used the photostat, NLW MS 11114B.
[88] As shown by Guy, 'Medieval Welsh genealogy', I, 108. He collates as MS L another manuscript from the same branch of the stemma (NLW 732B), and this also includes Meurig's name (*ibid.*, II, 341 and 368), as do Peniarth MS 177 (mentioned in *EWGT* 79–80, and Guy, 'Medieval Welsh genealogy', I, 127–28), p. 215, and Guy's MS S = NLW 21001Bii, 199v.
[89] Guy, 'Medieval Welsh genealogy', I, 117.
[90] *Ibid.*, I, 116.
[91] See his emendation of ABT 15 in *EWGT* 105, also 'Some studies', 283 n. 2. He changed his mind in 'Corrections', 171.

The Book of Llandaf as a Historical Source

Iudhael (supported by *Haddhail/Hyddheyl* in *Gwehelyth Morgannwg*). In MP 3, on the other hand, Bartrum takes it that *Mevric ap Arthvael* has been wrongly inserted from HG 29.[92] (In MP 3, as noted above, the reading *Einvdd* does *not* support the emendation of *Nud hael* in JC 9 to *Iudhael*.) While Bartrum's is a perfectly possible explanation it is not the only one.

HG 28	HG 29		JC 9	Gwehelyth Morgannwg	ABT 15(E)		ABT 15[93]	MP 3
								Tewdric
				Tewdric				Mevric
Teudubric		1	Thewdric	Meyrig				Adros
Atroys		2	Meurig	Adroes				Morgan
Morcant		3	Adroes	Morgan			Teudric	Einvdd[94]
Iudhail		4	Morgant	Haddhail[95]	Teudrig		Mevric	Rys
Fernmail		5	Nud hael	Rys	Art[ ]		Athrawes	Arthvael
Atroys	Morcant	6	Rees	Meyrig	Morgant		Morgan	Mevric
[I]udhail	Iudhail	7	Brochuael	Brochuail[96]	Itael		Ithel	Brochuael
	Ris	8	Gwryat	Gyriat[97]	Rys		Rrys	Gwraidd
	Artmail	9	Ar[th]uael	Arthuayl	Artafael		Arthavael	Arthavael
	Mouric	10	Rees	Rys	Rys		Rrys	Rys
	[B]roc-mail	11	Howel	Howel	Howel		Howel	Howel
	(*fl. ca* 880)	12	Eweint	Ywain	Ewein		Ywain	Owain
		13	Morgant (*ob.* 974)	Morgan Mwynfawr	Morgant maur		Morgan mawr	Morgan mwynvawr

Table 13.4 Conflicting patrilineages

Let us suppose that ABT 15(E) is superior to the rest of ABT 15 and that it was compiled *ca* 1200 when the available early genealogies resembled those in HG and JC. The compiler of ABT 15(E) may have had a source which only went back as far as Arth(a)fael in the ninth generation, perhaps being defective thereafter (like JC 10 and 16) or only continuing in the female line (like JC 12).[98] He may have then turned to a version of HG 29 to supply three more names, to take him from Arth(a)fael back to Morgan in the sixth generation. (Thus the *Iudhail* of HG 29 would be the source of his *Ithael* and need not affect the crucial *Nud hael* question.) Finally some other source, similar to HG 28, would serve to enable the compiler to proceed back beyond Morgan to Tewdrig, thereby providing Morgan ap Caradog (*ob. ca* 1208)

[92] *EWGT* 158. *Gwehelyth Morgannwg* complicates this view.
[93] As in *EWGT* 105, but omitting his insertion of [*Gwriad ap Brochwel*].
[94] Cf. *Enyth* in Hugh Thomas and similar forms discussed above.
[95] *Hyddheyl* in Llanstephan 12.
[96] Llanstephan 12 omits *Brochuail*. On the omission of *Gyriat ap Brochuail* see 126 above.
[97] Llanstephan 12 omits *Gyriat*.
[98] Although not recorded in Asser and *LL*, it may have been general knowledge that Hywel ap Rhys's grandfather was called Arth(a)fael.

13. The royal genealogical framework

with an impressive patrilineage composed only of the most venerable names (unlike his father's one in MP 3).

The compilers of the late pedigrees may also have had defective materials and have been given to 'improving' them, as already seen in the case of ABT as opposed to ABT(E). Thus the compiler of MP 3 may have had a source similar to JC 9 but have interpolated *ap Mevric ap Arthvael* between *Brochuael* and *Rys*, perhaps owing to some knowledge of the *Brocmail map Mouric map Artmail map Ris* in the Gwent line (HG 29), as Bartrum suggested.[99] The insertion of *Meyrig* as the father of *Brochuail* in *Gwehelyth Morgannwg* (in the sixth generation) could also be due to a memory of the Gwentian *Brocmail map Mouric.*

These considerations underline the disquieting possibility that there were in circulation texts which did not show Morgan Mawr as the direct descendant in the thirteenth generation of Tewdrig, but showed a break of several generations between, say, Arthfael in the ninth generation and Morgan Mawr's namesake Morgan ab Athrwys ap Meurig ap Tewdrig in the fourth. The possibility is disquieting in that we have no earlier source than JC 9 for some of these middle generations (which unfortunately fall *between* Wendy Davies's Sequences ii and iii in the Book of Llandaf).[100] It is therefore not impossible that what we have in JC 9 is an artificial backwards extension of a genuine short patrilineage for Morgan Mawr (*ob.* 974), intended to affiliate his line with an early branch of the dynasty which claimed descent from Tewdrig. The absence of any genealogy for Morgan's family from HG could be regarded as an indication that they were comparatively recent upstarts for whom a distinguished pedigree had not yet been created when the relevant HG pedigrees were recorded towards the end of the reign of Rhodri Mawr (*ob.* 878).[101] Lloyd went so far as to describe Hywel ap Rhys as 'of quite uncertain pedigree'[102] and to add that in JC 9 'he is connected with Ithel[103] ap Morgan, but the pedigree is a generation or two too long and its details are not attested by other authorities'.[104] Later scholars have been much less cautious.[105]

---

[99] *EWGT* 158.

[100] See the discussion below, 135. The lack of overlap between the names in JC 9 and those in *LL* is noted by Guy, 'Did the Harleian Genealogies draw on archival sources?', who draws the opposite conclusion to mine. Preferring the testimony of JC 9 to the earlier HG, he suggests that HG 28–29 were put together on the basis of some of the charters now surviving in *LL*.

[101] For this date see above, 118. Lloyd, *A History*, I 275 n. 262, however, suggests that 'The pedigree of Hywel ap Rhys is not to be found in Harl. MS. 3859, probably because Owain ap Hywel Dda [*ob.* 988] was unwilling to recognise the rights of the family'. Cf. Sims-Williams, 'The kings', 75–6. Note that in JC 12 Hywel ap Rhys is linked to Owain ap Hywel via a common Dyfed ancestor Maredudd (cf. HG 2 etc. and Table 13.5 below).

[102] Similarly Lewis, 'Agweddau', 129.

[103] Lloyd is tacitly emending 'Nud hael' in JC 9.

[104] *A History*, I 275 and n. 262. Cf. Jones, 'The Book of Llandaff', 141, Table, where the joining of Brochfael and Ffernfael, sons of Meurig, to the earlier line, via Meurig ab Ithel ap Morgan, is very questionable: see above, 120 n. 20.

[105] E.g. Davies, *An Early Welsh Microcosm*, 65 and 102 ('It is perfectly clear that the single dynasty of Meurig ap Tewdrig dominated the area from the mid-seventh until the late eleventh century'), and James, '*The Book of Llandav*: the church and see of Llandav', 9 ('Mouric ... founded a dynasty which persisted for 500 years, and whose last representative was alive in 1070').

The usually accepted emendations of HG 28–29 and JC 9 combine to produce a genealogy like that in Table 13.2, Fig. 1. The drift of this chapter so far has been that the emendations are uncalled for, that the probably Gwent genealogy in HG 29 can plausibly be regarded as a quite separate line, and that the Glywysing pedigrees HG 28 and JC 9 can be understood as they stand, giving two separate lines descending from Tewdrig (if we identify *Teudubric* and *Thewdric*, as in Table 13.1, Fig. 1), with the claims to that illustrious descent for Hywel ap Rhys (*fl. ca* 880) in JC 9 being more suspicious than those for his predecessor Ithel ab Athrwys (*ob.* 848?) in HG 28.[106]

I am doubtful whether Hywel ap Rhys's ancestry was remembered much further back than his grandfather Arth(a)fael, and suspect that all the elaborations in JC are part of an attempt by twelfth-century descendants of Hywel's grandson Morgan (*ob.* 974) to provide Morgan with a 'status genealogy' – that is, one with impressive connections through male and female lines.[107] It now remains, however, to test JC's plausibility, and the plausibility of the conservative view of HG presented above (and in Table 13.6 below), against the evidence provided by the *Annales Cambriae* and the Book of Llandaf.

In Table 13.5, I have supplemented HG 28–29 (unemended) and JC 9 with some names from the Book of Llandaf (in *italics*), to clarify the ensuing discussion, and with the marriages into the royal families of Dyfed and Buellt from JC 12 and 14. To provide a chronological control some names for the Dyfed and Buellt lines have been taken from the Harley genealogies and *Historia Brittonum* §49 respectively.[108] I have also added part of the Brycheiniog line from HG 15 and JC 8. People who occur in HG or (in the case of the Buellt dynasty) in the *Historia Brittonum* are printed in **bold type**. Starred names, and all those in italics, occur in *LL*. Most names have been modernised in spelling, but the only emendations accepted are: Erb for 'Arbeth' in JC 10 and Bartrum's insertion of five generations in JC 10, resulting in the possible marriage between Cenedlon and Athrwys in generation 3.[109] (His emendation of the Brycheiniog pedigree JC 8 is not accepted.[110]) The synchronism of Ithel ap Morgan and Æthelbald of Mercia (716–57) comes from *LL* (charter 192). The 829 *floruit* for Ffernfael of Buellt is based on the *Historia Brittonum*[111] and that of *ca* 880 for Brochfael, Ffernfael, Hywel, Hyfaidd, and Elise is based on Asser's *Life of King Alfred*. The obits of Maredudd of Dyfed and his descendants are taken from the *Annales Cambriae*,[112] and other obits marked with question marks are taken from the same source. Dates marked with ? are solely to elucidate the discussion of *Annales Cambriae* and are not advanced as necessarily likely.

---

[106] Although these are not provable either; see Sims-Williams, 'The kings', 74–5. On the 848 date see below.

[107] *Ibid.*, 76–8. On 'status genealogies' see Charles-Edwards, *Wales and the Britons*, 363–4 and 473–5.

[108] See *EWGT* 9–10 (HG 2, cf. Charles-Edwards, *Wales and the Britons*, 662) and 7–8 (*HB* 49).

[109] See above, 129–31.

[110] Bartrum, 'Noë, king of Powys'. Cf. Dumville, 'Late-seventh- or eighth-century evidence', 48–51; Bartrum, *A Welsh Classical Dictionary*, 509.

[111] Cf. *DP* III 223 n. 2.

[112] 'Offa rex merciorum & morgetiud rex demetorum morte moriuntur. . . . Eugem [*read* Eugein] filius margetiud moritur' (ed. Phillimore, 'The *Annales Cambriae* and Old-Welsh genealogies', 162–3).

13. The royal genealogical framework

Absolute chronology

An often underestimated problem in using the *Annales Cambriae* is the identification of the persons whom they mention without reference to place or kingdom. Entries which *may* be relevant to the present purpose are as follows. Years are mostly given as in Phillimore's edition; even though they may be slightly out in some cases (e.g. 885 for 886, etc.), such variation is of negligible importance here.

> 612 Conthigirni obitus et Dibric episcopi.
> 665 Morcant moritur.
> 775 Fernmail filius Iudhail moritur.
> 848 Gueit Finnant Iudhail . rex Guent . a uiris Broceniauc occisus est.
> 849 Mouric occisus est a Saxonibus.
> 873 Nobis et Mouric moriuntur.
> 885 Higuel in Roma defuntus est.
> 974 Morgan obiit.[113]

The only one of these persons about whose identity we can feel certain is St Dyfrig in 612, and in this case we can put little faith in the date (which is also given in *LL*), since his name may be a mere addition to an earlier annal giving Kentigern's obit.[114] Ffernfael son of Ithel in 775 is often identified with the one with this patronymic in HG 28 and the Book of Llandaf,[115] but in view of the commonplace nature of both names one cannot be absolutely sure, plausible though it is. The Morgan of 665 could, at a great stretch, be the generation 3 grandfather of this Ffernfael (see Table 13.5)[116] or the generation 4 grandson of Meurig — or neither. He could also be the Morgan ap Gwrgan of *LL* charter 163b.[117] The Ithel of Gwent slain in 848 can hardly be identified with the Ithel ap Morgan in the Gwent genealogy HG 29, whose great-great-grandson, Brochfael ap Meurig, was living *ca* 880; Lloyd and others prefer to

---

[113] All entries from Phillimore, 'The *Annales Cambriae* and Old-Welsh genealogies' (adding capitalisation), except the last which is from *Annales Cambriae*, ed. Williams Ab Ithel, 19.

[114] Hughes, *Celtic Britain*, 70. Cf. J. R. Davies, 'Bishop Kentigern among the Britons', 68–71, also 'Cathedrals', 111. While Doble, *Lives*, 65 n. 17, and 180, and Jones, 'The Book of Llandaff', 131, state that the date 612 in *LL* p. 84 was taken from the *Annales Cambriae*, it is possible that the writers drew on a common source. See also above, 52.

[115] Kirby, 'British dynastic history', 88; Davies, *The Llandaff Charters*, 76 and 164, and *An Early Welsh Microcosm*, 18; similarly *DP* III 270 n. 1, Lewis 'Agweddau', 129, and Charles-Edwards, *Wales and the Britons*, 358. But Bartrum rejected the identification in *EWGT* 189 s.n. *Ffernfael*; and in *EWGT* 129 and 'Some studies', 283 and 288, he suggested that the Ffernfael ab Ithel who died in 775 was an otherwise unknown *great-grandson* of the person of this name in HG 28, i.e. a son of the Ithel ab Athrwys in HG 28. This is impossible if one accepts *LL* 192, which associates Æthelbald of Mercia (716–57), Bishop Berthwyn, and a king Ithel who (in view of the reference to Berthwyn) must be Ithel ap Morgan, the father of the Ffernfael ab Ithel of HG 28. See below, 152. Bartrum changed his mind in *A Welsh Classical Dictionary*, 264.

[116] Lloyd, *A History*, I 274 n. 257 rejects this on the grounds that 665–775 is too great a span for grandfather to grandson. See also Davies, *The Llandaff Charters*, 87 n. 40, James, 'The "Book of Llan Dav" and Bishop Oudoceus', 35, and 'Chronology', 130, and Guy, 'The *Life* of St Dyfrig', 28–30.

[117] Below, 148, and Table 13.5.

Custennin ERGYNG *Erb*

N == =*Peibio* Nynnio

Gwyddgi Tewdwr Llywarch

DYFED

Efrddyl *Cynfyn* *Gwrgan* *Nowy* *Llywarch* *Gwrgan magnus* 1 *Tewdrig*

Dyfrig ob. 612? JC 10

Morgan *Caradog* Cloten *Briafael* Onbrawst =2= *Meurig*
d. 665?

Cathen Cenedlon = ====?==== =3= =*Athrwys*   GLYWYSING
JC 10

Cadwgon   4 *Morgan*   Ffriog   *Athrwys*
                                     d. 665?
                                                  Idnerth   Guallunir *Morgan* = Ricceneth
BRYCHEINIOG   ob. 665?

Awst *Rhain*   5 Nudd (hael) Rhys   *Ithel*
                                                                           (temp. Æthelbald)
JC 8   Rhodri   Guednerth Meirchion
                                                                                    Ffernfael =*Ceincair*
Elwystl *Tewdwr* Tewdws   6 Rhys   ob. 775?
                                                              Meurig   Athrwys
                                                   Gwrgafarn   &   GWENT
Nowy   Maredudd   7 Brochfael   BUELLT   ?Arthfael   Morgan
            ob. 796   Pasgen   Meurig   Gwrgan
                                                                                    Athrwys   Ithel

                                                                                    Ithel
                                                                                    ob. 848?
                                                                                    HG 28

	Gruffudd HG 15	**Owain** ob. 811	**Rhain** ob. 808	Ceingar JC 12	=8=	= Gwriad	Gloud	**Tewdwr**	Rhys
	Tewdwr	**Tangwystl**	**Tryffin** ob. 814 HG 13						*Arthfael
9	*Elise fl. ca 880	**Hyfaidd** fl. ca 880. ob. 892				Arthfael = 	= Brawstudd JC 14	**Ffernfael** fl. 829 HB 49	
10	JC 8	HG 2				*Rhys			*Meurig ob. 849/874?
11						*Hywel fl. ca 880.	ob. 885?	GWYNEDD Rhodri ob. 878	Ffernfael *Brochfael fl. ca 880 HG 29
12						*Owain ==	===?===	=== Nest JC 20	
13						*Morgan ob. 974 JC 9			

Table 13.5 The genealogists' scheme

identify him with the Ithel ap Athrwys of HG 28,[118] which is plausible, although of course some other Ithel could be meant. Peter Bartrum and Wendy Davies identify the Meurig ab Arthfael in HG 28 with the Meurig of 873 (*recte* 874),[119] though the Meurig of 849 would also seem to be possible; yet in the absence of any localisation in the *Annales* both identifications must be regarded with caution.[120] The Hywel of 885 (*recte* 886) has often been identified with Hywel ap Rhys. Lloyd thought this identification 'very unlikely' because the Book of Llandaf associates him with Bishop Cyfeilliog, who was alive in 914 according to the *Anglo-Saxon Chronicle*, and (more dubiously) died in 927 according to the lists of consecrations and obits in the Book of Llandaf and related texts.[121] Yet Wendy Davies has rightly pointed out that Lloyd's objection is not insuperable, since Cyfeilliog may have had a very long episcopate.[122] Nevertheless, in view of the common nature of the name Hywel, the identification can only be treated as a possibility. Finally, the 974 obit has always been taken to refer to Morgan Hen of Morgannwg, and it is certainly at about the right period, since the Book of Llandaf makes Morgan Hen a contemporary of Edgar (957–75) and Bishop Gwgon (963/72–982);[123] nevertheless it could refer to some other Morgan.

The *Annales Cambriae* prove, then, to be a treacherous guide by which to check the chronology of the genealogies. It seems safer to adopt instead as a fixed point for the eleventh generation in Table 13.5 the *floruit* of *ca* 880 which may be deduced from Chapter 80 of Asser's *Life of King Alfred*.[124] Some dates marked on Table 13.5 harmonise fairly well with it. Even the dubious obit of 612 for Dyfrig in generation 1 agrees: if we assign Dyfrig a *floruit* of 600, between him and Hywel there are ten generations of twenty-eight years each, which is an acceptable figure; and a historically more acceptable *floruit* of 550 would give the equally acceptable average of thirty-three years.[125] The generation averages between Hywel and the dated Dyfed and Buellt persons in the seventh to tenth generations are less acceptable, and the same applies to the averages between Hywel and Ithel ab Athrwys in the seventh generation and Ffernfael in the fifth. The figures can be improved, however, if one or

---

[118] See above, 137 n. 29, and 137, for the suggestion that his family ruled in Gwent. The site of the 'battle of *Finnant*' is uncertain: see Jones, *Brut y Tywysogyon: Peniarth MS. 20 Version*, 135. See also Sims-Williams, 'The kings', 73–5.

[119] Bartrum, *EWGT* 129; Davies, *The Llandaff Charters*, 76 and 87 n. 44, and *An Early Welsh Microcosm*, 19 and n. 1. The *Nobis* of the annal is usually identified with one of the bishops of this name (e.g. Jones, 'The Book of Llandaff', 137, cf. below, 169–70 nn. 93 and 95), in which case its *Mouric* may also be a churchman.

[120] Some very late manuscripts of *Brut y Tywysogion* assign the Meurig of 849 to Gwent, perhaps merely influenced by the reference to Gwent in the previous year. See Jones, *Brut y Tywysogyon: Peniarth MS. 20 Version*, 4 n. 5. Bartrum, 'Some studies', 286 and 288, identified the Meurig of 849 and Ithel of 848 with the Meurig ab Ithel of *LL* charter 214 and his father. Cf. above, 120 n. 20, and below, 155 n. 215. Charles-Edwards, *Wales and the Britons*, 358, says simply 'a common name in the Gwent dynasty'.

[121] Lloyd, *A History*, I, 327 n. 29.

[122] *WHEMA* IV 62; Davies, *The Llandaff Charters*, 88 n. 45 and 155. See below, 171, on Cyfeilliog's dates.

[123] *LL* charter 240. Cf. *WHEMA* IV 62–3 and 68; Davies, *The Llandaff Charters*, 80; Keynes, 'Welsh kings', 112–13.

[124] On the date see Keynes and Lapidge, *Alfred the Great*, 262–3.

[125] On problems of generation counting in general see Miller, 'Date-guessing and pedigrees' and 'Date-guessing and Dyfed', and Jones, 'An approach', 415. On the dates of Dyfrig see above, 51–3.

13. The royal genealogical framework

two generations in the middle of JC 9 are held to be the result of interpolation or of the splicing of unconnected pedigrees (see above).

Other considerations raise more serious problems. In Table 13.5 Brochfael ap Meurig in HG 29 is aligned, inevitably, with Hywel ap Rhys in JC 9, his contemporary in Asser. This makes it impossible to equate Morgan at the head of HG 29 with Morgan ab Athrwys in HG 28 and, more seriously puts Brochfael ap Meurig at an impossibly large number of generations after Ithel ap Morgan in HG 28, who was contemporary with Æthelbald (*ob.* 757) according to *LL* 192. This again suggests strongly that JC 9 has too many generations, as Lloyd stated, and is probably one of the factors that eventually persuaded Bartrum and others that Brochfael and Gwriad in generations 7 and 8 of JC 9 should be omitted.[126] If they are omitted the generations align better: Ithel ap Morgan in HG 28 can be more nearly contemporary, if not identical, with Ithel ap Morgan in HG 29, and can be contemporary with Æthelbald; and Ithel's son Ffernfael can easily be identical with the one who died in 775. Moreover, the chronological disparity with the Dyfed kings disappears along with Gwriad and his alleged marriage to *Ceingar* (JC 12).

Personally, I would go further and reject rather than emend JC 9 and all the other late genealogies which attempt to trace Hywel ap Rhys's ancestry back to Tewdrig. If all the generations from his father Rhys (or perhaps his grandfather Arthfael) back to Morgan ab Athrwys in generation 4 are dismissed as spurious, we can arrange the relevant lines in HG, *LL*, and Asser as shown in Table 13.6.[127] Names in *LL* starred.[128]

Comparison of LL and VC with the genealogies

The charters in the Book of Llandaf and in those attached to the *Vita Cadoci* in Cotton Vespasian A.xiv are regrettably unhelpful on the crucial points that might have enabled one to decide between Tables 13.2 and 13.6. Although they are compatible with the emendations to the genealogies which result in Table 13.2, they do not require these emendations to be made as seems often to have been assumed.[129] It will be necessary to present all their genealogical evidence at length in order to demonstrate this. Because the present order of the charters in the Book of Llandaf is demonstrably anachronistic I shall treat them in the order in which most of them can be rearranged, in their three sequences,[130] mentioning the charters that lie outside those sequences at the appropriate places. To avoid charges of circular argument it must be emphasised that the order of charters in the three sequences are founded on the internal evidence of the charters (in particular their witness lists), and not on a comparison with the genealogies. The *VC* charters will be dealt with at the points rendered appropriate by comparison with the Llandaf witness lists.

---

[126] Lloyd, *History*, I 275 n. 262. See the pedigree in Charles-Edwards, *Wales and the Britons*, 253, where Gwriad ap Brochfael is omitted, following Bartrum, 'Corrections', 171.

[127] Cf. Sims-Williams 'The kings', 81, Fig. 4. Some *Annales Cambriae* dates are adjusted by a year.

[128] Both men called Morgan ab Athrwys are starred as it is not clear which is meant e.g. in 145 and the witness list of 147 (see below, 150). Power may have swung from one side of the dynasty to the other (see below).

[129] See e.g. Jones, 'The Book of Llandaff', 141; Brooke, *The Church*, 46 n. 118.

[130] Following Davies, *The Llandaff Charters*, 35–7, 41–53, and 59–69, except for Sequence i, for which see ch. 4 above.

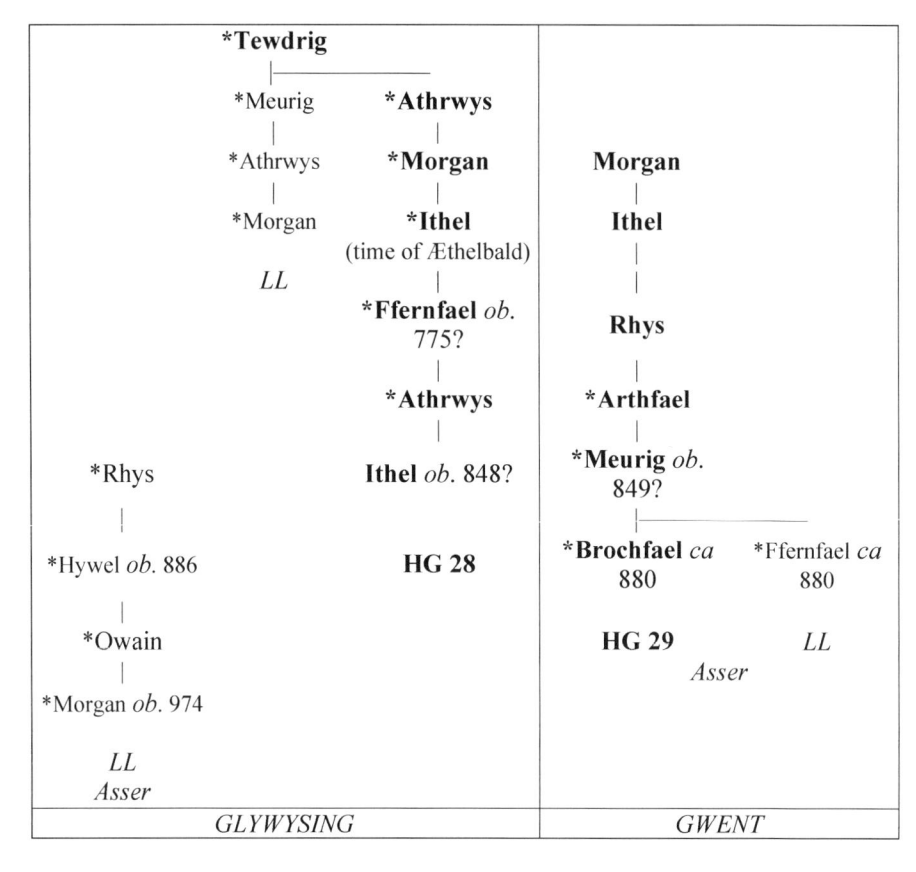

	*Tewdrig	
	*Meurig *Athrwys	
	*Athrwys *Morgan	Morgan
	*Morgan *Ithel	Ithel
	(time of Æthelbald)	
	LL	
	*Ffernfael *ob.* 775?	
		Rhys
	*Athrwys	*Arthfael
*Rhys	Ithel *ob.* 848?	*Meurig *ob.* 849?
*Hywel *ob.* 886	**HG 28**	*Brochfael *ca* 880 *Ffernfael *ca* 880
*Owain		HG 29 LL
*Morgan *ob.* 974		Asser
LL		
Asser		
GLYWYSING		GWENT

Table 13.6   A possibly historical scheme

Initially, the *LL* and *VC* must be regarded as two twelfth-century witnesses, containing material of disputable antiquity, which can be used to check the *textual* accuracy of the genealogies in the Harley collection of *ca* 1100 and later collections. The *historical* accuracy of the genealogies is a further question which is not to be settled simply by comparison with the charters, for the simple reason that the writers and revisers of the charters arguably referred to genealogies, as Brooke maintained.[131] Brooke suggested that the apparently early charters (those of Sequence i) reflected 'a pedigree of the kings of Erging, ... which is otherwise unknown, but probably authentic – Morcant map Gurcant map Cinuin map Peipiau map Erb'[132] and that the slightly later group (Sequence ii) was controlled by the author of the *LL* by the use of HG 28 and JC 9.[133] Certainly, even if one accepts the basic authenticity of the Llandaf charters, it

---

[131] Brooke, *The Church*, 33–4 and 46–7. Note also the converse in Guy's question 'Did the Harleian genealogies draw on archival sources?', mentioned above, 30 n. 44.

[132] Brooke, *The Church*, 47. One might question its authenticity, however. It could be part of a hagiographical genealogy related to Dyfrig, Custennin at Welsh Bicknor (charter 72a), and others.

[133] *Ibid.*, 34 and 46.

13. The royal genealogical framework

would be difficult to deny that many of them may have been expanded by scribes with an eye on genealogies:[134] In charter 140, for instance, the genealogical detail in the reference to *Mouric rex Morcanhuc filius Teudiric & uxor eius Onbraust filia Gurcanti magni* may be as much an addition as the anachronistic reference to the kingdom of Morgannwg.[135] (Compare the reference in the *Vita Oudocei* to *Rex Mouricus cum duobus filiis suis & uxore sua Onbraus filia Gurcanti magni.*)[136] Again in charter 149 the grandfather's name in the reference to *Morcant rex ... super sepulchrum Mourici regis iacentis Landauiæ aui sui* could be as much an addition as is the presumably anachronistic claim to royal burial at Llandaf.[137] The doublets 73b/163a and 175/186b include the same genealogical information respectively, but word it differently. The authentic (but admittedly non-royal) charters in the Lichfield Gospels are free from any genealogical material other than simple patronymics.[138] One is therefore tempted to regard the presence of any genealogical elaboration with suspicion, like allusions to historical events in Anglo-Saxon charters;[139] nevertheless, though genealogical elaboration may cast doubt on the authenticity of a charter in its present form, it may shed useful light on the text of the genealogy which the writer of the charter used in order to add a spurious chronological accuracy or historical authenticity to his text.

Sequence i

Sequence i in the Book of Llandaf introduces us to early members of the Ergyng dynasty (cf. Table 13.5) and other south-eastern rulers whose family relationships cannot be established, plus Nowy ab Arthur of Dyfed in a charter of very dubious authenticity (77).[140] According to the genealogies (HG 2, etc.), Nowy was the great-great-great-great-great-grandfather of Maredudd of Dyfed, who died in 796 (*Annales Cambriae*); working on a thirty-year generation average Nowy's death could be placed

---

[134] For instance when inserting formulae of royal consent. Cf. Davies, *An Early Welsh Microcosm*, 104, and above, 109. Thus *uerbo et consensu regis Rotri filius Iudhail* occurs in 210b but not the doublet *VC* 66.

[135] See above, 117 n. 4.

[136] *LL* p. 132.

[137] Cf. *LL* pp. 132–3, where Euddogwy's privilege gives Llandaf the bodies of the kings of Deheubarth, which Jones, 'The Book of Llandaff', 134, rightly detects as an anachronism, 'an usurpation perhaps from the great Glamorgan monasteries'. Cf. Lloyd, *A History*, I, 276, who suggests Llantwit (cf. below, 154 n. 208), and Davies, *An Early Welsh Microcosm*, 132 n. 2, for Llancarfan. Davies, *The Llandaff Charters* 99, thinks the reference to Llandaf in charter 149 just possibly original, 'if the witness list reference is to Llandaff rather than to Llanddowror'. On the latter reference (*Saturn principis Taui urbis*) cf. *EA* I, 184, James, 'The "Concen charters"', 94, and 'The Book of Llan Dav and the diocesan boundaries disputes', 340, Davies, *An Early Welsh Microcosm*, 135–6, and above, 29 n. 36.

[138] Davies, *WHEMA* IX 10 n. 17, notes that all the 'Chad' charters are non-royal. On their dates see *ibid.*, 6 n. 8.

[139] Cf. Stenton, *The Latin Charters*, 27.

[140] Davies lists 77, the grant by Nowy, as i.2, but as she rejects its witness list this placing within Sequence i is arbitrary: *The Llandaff Charters*, 38 and 95 (see also 39, 75, and 86 n. 35). The remark on Nowy in Jones, 'The Book of Llandaff', 130, contains two misidentifications (inspired by Phillimore, 'The *Annales Cambriae* and Old-Welsh genealogies', 175 n. 5) and must be ignored. *DP* I 246 n. 1 (and III, 201 n. 2 and 266 n. 1, also IV 429) is also in error. See Bartrum, 'Noë, king of Powys'.

The Book of Llandaf as a Historical Source

in 616, which would indeed make him a contemporary of Dyfrig, if one accepted the 612 obit for Dyfrig in the *Annales Cambriae* and the Book of Llandaf itself (cf. Table 13.5). Nowy's grant to Dyfrig may therefore have seemed quite credible to the writers of the charter, if not to us.[141] Since St Davids had charters referring to Nowy and his father,[142] Nowy was an appropriate name for Llandaf polemicists to pick.

Leaving aside charter 77, I shall deal with Sequence i in the order given in Chapter 4 above: 166, 121, 122, 72a, 76a, 72b, 73a, and 73b/163a (Bishop Arwystl), 162b (Bishop Aeddan), 76b, 160, 161, 162a (Bishop Ufelfyw), 163b and 164 (Bishop Inabwy), 165 (Bishop Cyfwyre), and 75 ([Bishop?] Elhaearn).

Charters 166, 121, and 122 are granted by *Idon rex filius Ynyr Guent* (121) either to Arwystl, Dyfrig's disciple according to the *Vita Dubricii* (*LL* p. 80), or to St Teilo, Dyfrig's alleged disciple and successor. Iddon appears as a contemporary of Cadwallon ap Cadfan of Gwynedd (*ob.* 634) in the Welsh *Life of St Beuno*,[143] so he might reasonably be regarded as a contemporary of St Teilo, the supposed disciple of a saint who died in 612. According to charter 123, which is omitted from Sequence i because it contains no witness list:

Tempore predicti regis Idon uenerunt Saxones in regionem suam depredari, et ipse cum suo exercitu secutus est illos.

In the time of the aforesaid King Iddon the English came into his country to plunder, and he pursued them with his army.

This correlation with English attacks – presumably on Gwent, for Iddon reaches Llanarth in his pursuit – suggests that Iddon flourished not much before the beginning of the seventh century, in view of the usual chronology of the *adventus Saxonum*.[144] No more is heard of Iddon ab Ynyr Gwent in *LL*, and he is absent from all the early genealogical collections. It would seem that his dynasty was eclipsed in Gwent by that of Tewdrig (see below).

The next seven charters (72a, 76a, 72b, 73a, 73b/163a, and 162b) introduce us to Dyfrig's contemporary *Peipiau rex filius Erb* (72a, etc.), who is once styled king of Ergyng (163a), and to his two sons, *duo filii Pepiav Cinuin uidelicet & Guidci*

---

[141] Cf. *DP* IV 429. The *Vita Oudocei* in *LL* 133 makes the saint and Meurig ap Tewdrig contemporary with a Cadwgon of Dyfed, presumably Nowy's great-grandson (see Table 13.5); cf. *DP* III 224 n. 1 and 270 n. 1. Davies, *An Early Welsh Microcosm*, 158 n. 1, regards the contemporaneity of Meurig and Cadwgon as credible, but really there is no evidence for or against it. Cadwgon is three generations before Maredudd (*ob.* 796) and Meurig is three before Ffernfael (*ob.* 775) according to Tables 13.5 and 13.6, or four according to Table 13.2. On the Dyfed rulers in *LL* see Guy, 'The *Life* of St Dyfrig', 10 n. 31.

[142] An alleged charter of Nowy was extant at St Davids in the sixteenth century, and Leland saw a charter referring to Nowy's father Arthur. See above, 14–15.

[143] *Buchedd Beuno*, ed. Sims-Williams, §20, etc. See above, 53.

[144] Cf. Davies, *The Llandaff Charters*, 75 and 86 n. 32, and *An Early Welsh Microcosm*, 17 and n. 1 and 93, where she draws attention to the *Anglo-Saxon Chronicle*, s.a. 577, in which the Anglo-Saxons have not yet encroached on the borders of Wales (similarly Bartrum, *A Welsh Classical Dictionary*, 379). Cf. Sims-Williams, *Britain and Early Christian Europe*, II 33–4. An undated attack on Worcester by 'the long-haired men of Gwent' is mentioned in *Legendary Poems from the Book of Taliesin*, ed. Haycock, no. 14, lines 23–4.

13. The royal genealogical framework

(73b, etc.).[145] By charter 72a Peibio grants to his cousin Inabwy and to St Dyfrig *Lann Custenhinngarthbenni* (Welsh Bicknor), the eponym of which, *Constantinus rex*, is said to be Peibio's father-in-law (*socer*).[146] In charters 163a and 162b, Peibio has been succeeded by one or both of his sons: *Cinuin rex et Guidci frater eius filii Peipiau clauorauc*.

The next charter (76b), which is placed here in the Sequence only because of [Bishop] Ufelfyw's attestation, grants Bishopston in Gower to 'Archbishop' Dyfrig, *regnante Merchguino filio Gliuis*.[147] This king may be the same as the *Meirchyawn* named among the sons of Glywys, the eponym of Glywysing, in JC 5, despite the difference in spelling. Bartrum suggests that JC's *Meirchyawn* is an error for *Merchwyn*,[148] but possibly the error is the other way round, with *Merchion* or similar (< *Marcianus*)[149] having been replaced in the charter by *Merchguinus* under the influence of the name of its clerical witness *Merchguinus*, who recurs in the list of Dyfrig's disciples (*LL* p. 80). The relative chronology of the persons mentioned in the Book of Llandaf and the children of Glywys is, however, too obscure for any comment on the plausibility of Merchwyn's appearance to be ventured.[150] Possibly the charter is a genuine Gower charter which has been completely rewritten in favour of 'Archbishop' Dyfrig and Ufelfyw in order to support Llandaf's claims to Bishopston. Some authentic basis is suggested by the name of the lay witnesses *Lugobi* (nominative) and *Luuaet*, early forms of the Irish names *Luigbe* and *Lugaed*; also *Garu*, which may reflect Irish *Garb*.[151]

The next charter is a grant of *Lann Sulbiu* (Llancillo, Herefordshire) by a mysterious *rex Mouricus* (160). It is assigned to this place in the sequence only because it shares (Bishop) Ufelfyw with the Merchwyn charter just discussed and the two Gwrfoddw charters discussed next; otherwise its witness list is exiguous

---

[145] *Cinust* in 76a is probably an error for *Cinuin* (Davies, *The Llandaff Charters*, 94).

[146] See Doble, *Lives*, 77 and 78 n. 62, and above, 131 n. 71. He takes *suo* in *suo consobrino* to refer to Peibio, as does Guy, 'The *Life* of St Dyfrig', 24 n. 66.

[147] Davies, *The Llandaff Charters*, 81, regards the reference to Dyfrig as an error but the position of the charter in *LL* shows that the compiler accepted it. It is clear that he regarded 72a–77 as belonging to Dyfrig's time, not noticing that 74 is really a variant of 171b and belongs near the start of Sequence iii (see Davies, *WHEMA* II 343). The difficulty of placing 76b in sequence is emphasised by Davies, *The Llandaff Charters*, 40.

[148] *EWGT* 138 and *A Welsh Clasical Dictionary*, 472. On Glywys see Davies, *An Early Welsh Microcosm*, 99 and n. 1, Sims-Williams, 'A Turkish–Celtic problem', and Charles-Edwards, 'Dynastic succession', 73–5. Glywys seems to have a 'West Glamorgan focus', as Davies says; *LL*'s focus may be more easterly, despite the constant references to Glywysing.

[149] Possibly identical with the *Meirchiaun, rex Glatmorcanensium*, of *Vita Iltuti* (*VSB*, 194–233), §17 (cf. §§8–10, 18, 20–1, and 26) and the *Meirchiawn* of *VC* 57, who is arguably a king (see Doble, *Lives*, 103, and Bartrum, *A Welsh Classical Dictionary*, 465).

[150] The complex of persons and characters grouped about Glywys is closely bound up with the legend of St Cadog (cf. Brooke, 'St Peter of Gloucester', 301–3, shortened in his *The Church*, 83–4), and the compilers of *LL* wisely made no attempt to fit any Cadog material into their own chronology; Cadog himself is not even mentioned, except when referring to the 'altar of Cadog' (Llancarfan), etc.

[151] Rhys, 'The Kilmannin ogam', 65; Uhlich, *Die Morphologie*, 271–2; Sims-Williams, *The Celtic Inscriptions of Britain*, 282, 290–1, and 293–4. As *Garw* is not a known Welsh name, Irish *Garb* seems more likely. Cf. below, 160 n. 20. An Irish lay witness in a later charter is *Maildun* in 231, which concerns an unidentified location (Coe, 'The place-names', 436).

and therefore suspicious.[152] In the absence of a patronymic, there is no sure way of identifying its *rex Mouricus* (but see on 165 below). He could be the *Mouricus rex* who, in the distorted chronology of *De Primo Statu Landauensis Æcclesiæ* (*LL* pp. 69 and 71), consents to the foundation of Llandaf by Germanus, Lupus, and Dyfrig (in the fifth century!) and grants Mochros (Moccas, Herefordshire) to Llandaf.[153]

In the next charters a *Gvoruodu rex Ercyng regionis*, of unknown ancestry, and his son *Eruic* intrude (161 and 162a), making grants in Ergyng to Bishop Ufelfyw. Like Iddon, Gwrfoddw is said to have fought against the English (161), which suggests a seventh-century (or later) date for him in reality or at least in the mind of the writer of the charter.[154] *Eruic* may be the *Erbic* who had attested one of Iddon's charters (121).[155]

The next two charters (163b and 164), granted to Bishop Inabwy (cf. 72a above),[156] return to the dynasty of Peibio with *Gurcant rex Ercicg filius Cinuin*, the witness list of 163b supplying us with the names of *filii eius Morcant et Caratauc* (cf. Table 13.5). *Gurcant rex* may well be the *Gurcantus magnus* who is named as the father-in-law of Meurig ap Tewdrig in Sequence ii (140, also p. 132). This is not certain, however, so they have been kept apart in Table 13.5.

165 is a grant of estates in Chepstow and in Herefordshire to Bishop Cyfwyre, formerly abbot of Mochros (see 163b), by *Athruis rex Guenti regionis ... pro anima patris sui Mourici*. It seems plausible that the *Mouric* mentioned here is the mysterious king of 160, who is connected with Mochros in *De Primo Statu*. Wendy Davies considers the possibility that 165 could be a very early grant by the Athrwys ap Meurig who appears in Sequence ii (see Table 13.5),[157] but also makes the suggestion that the name of Athrwys ap Meurig may have been erroneously coupled with a genuine Sequence i witness list.[158] An element of confusion if not fabrication seems likely: in 165 Athrwys of Gwent's father Meurig is already dead, whereas in Sequence ii both father and son issue charters (see below), and furthermore there is no other example of a person who spans Sequence i and Sequence ii.[159] The notion that there was a *Mouricus rex* in the Sequence i period may be due to the misplacing in that period of charter 74, a doublet of 171b (iii.5), which belongs to the time of

---

[152] 160's lay witness *Cinuin* could be King Peibio's son, *Cinuin rex* in 162b, but this is unlikely unless he suffered a demotion to sub-king. 'Cu [*space*] abbas' in the 160 witness list could be the *Cuelinus* of 76b, and 'Iohannes ... cum clericis suis' may refer to *Iouan* in 72a–72b. See above, 34 n. 12.

[153] *De Primo Statu* is translated in Birch, *Memorials*, 21–3.

[154] Anscombe, 'Some Old-Welsh pedigrees', 80, identified him with Arthur's uncle *Gorbothu Hen* in *Culhwch and Olwen* (ed. Bromwich and Evans, lines 252 and 1164); see *ibid*, 88, also *Legendary Poems from the Book of Taliesin*, ed. Haycock, no. 14, line 29 and note. For the name see Lloyd-Jones, *Geirfa*, 701.

[155] On equating *Erbic* and *Eruic*, cf. above, 34 n. 17.

[156] In 72a Inabwy, cousin of King Peibio, may be abbot of *Garthbenni* (Welsh Bicknor); by the time of 163b and 164 the abbot is *Guenuor* or *Guernabui*.

[157] Davies, *The Llandaff Charters*, 37, 38, 40, 58, 75, 86 n. 33, 105–6, and 149, and *An Early Welsh Microcosm*, 17 and 171. The map on p. 78 of *An Early Welsh Microcosm*, shows the grants of the Athrwys of Sequence i (no. 165) and those of the Athrwys of Sequence ii without distinction. They are also equated by Guy, 'The *Life* of St Dyfrig', 27–31.

[158] Davies, *The Llandaff Charters*, 105–6.

[159] Cf. Davies, *The Llandaff Charters*, 37 and 40 (*Gurcon/Guidcon* is noted as a possibility).

13. The royal genealogical framework

Meurig ab Arthfael (*ob.* 849?), who was indeed connected with Gwent, as Asser confirms.

75, the last charter of Sequence i, is a grant to St Dyfrig by *Erb rex Guenti & Ercic*, witnessed by *Pepiau* among others. The early grantor is not credible, but the witness lists include credible names, enough to place it here in the sequence. Erb's presence is incompatible with the statement in the *Vita Dubricii* in the Book of Llandaf, and the implication in JC 10, that Erb was Dyfrig's great-grandfather;[160] Dyfrig is already styled *archiepiscopus* in the grant! This is a clear indication that the redactors of the charters and the final Llandaf compilers had incompatible ideas about chronology.

So far as one can tell, then, the kings of Sequence i hang together reasonably well, apart from the appearance of Erb in 75 and the problematic *rex Mouricus* of 160 and 165. But their real or supposed absolute chronology is very obscure, and the approximate dates suggested by Wendy Davies should be treated with extreme caution.[161] The most that one can say is that, prior to the fantastic chronology of *De Primo Statu Landauensis Ǽcclesiæ*, the charters in Sequence i were felt to belong in the seventh century.[162] They cover at least three generations of rulers of Ergyng – Peibio, Cynfyn, and Gwrgan – with Iddon in Gwent perhaps being contemporary with Peibio, Gwrfoddw intruding in Ergyng between Cynfyn and Gwrgan, and Gwrgan the Great ruling in Gwent as well as Ergyng. The merger between Gwent and the *Dunsætan* of Ergyng and Anergyng, remembered *ca* 994 in the Old English tract on the *Dunsætan*,[163] may go back to the time of Gwrgan.

The time lapse, if any, between Sequence i and ii is obscure. On the one hand, if 160 and 165 indeed refer to Meurig and his son Athrwys (generations 2–3 of Table 13.5), the last charters of Sequence i will overlap with the first ones of Sequence ii. On the other hand, if one understands 140 (and *LL* p. 132) to mean that Meurig ap Tewdrig of Sequence ii married the daughter of the Gwrgan ap Cynfyn of Sequence i (Onbrawst), Sequence ii will begin about a generation after the end of Sequence i. The latter interval is also indicated in JC 9–10, where Meurig ap Tewdrig and Briafael ap Llywarch (who attests charters of Meurig and Morgan ab Athrwys between ii.3 and ii.17) are four generations after their common ancestor Erb (see Table 13.5).[164] Possibly *LL* and JC elongated the chronology so as to create a long gap between the time of St Dyfrig and Peibio and the time of Meurig ap Tewdrig.[165] It is difficult to be sure, however, and the possible appearance in both 160 and 165 of Meurig and Athrwys is an uncertain basis for proposing a tighter chronology.

---

[160] See above, 129–31.
[161] Davies, *The Llandaff Charters*, 74–5 and passim. She herself says they are approximate (±fifteen years) on pp. 79 and 146.
[162] See ch. 6 above.
[163] See Charles-Edwards, 'The Three Columns of Law', 59 and nn. 19–20; also *Wales and the Britons*, 422–3 and 513.
[164] The marriage between Cenedlon and Athrwys implied in JC 10 cannot be cited, of course, as it is editorial, designed to fit the above chronology (see *EWGT* 139).
[165] Guy, 'The *Life* of St Dyfrig'.

Sequence ii

Sequence ii of the Llandaf charters begins with those of Meurig ap Tewdrig, who is clearly to be identified with the person of this name in JC 9, in the second generation of Tables 13.5 and 13.6. Charter 141, a very dubious charter which Davies excludes from her sequences because it contains no witness list, presumably precedes Sequence ii, since in it *rex Teudiric* is still alive and active in his retirement.[166] It refers to his death at the time of English incursions across the Wye, which is another indication that we have reached the seventh century, if not later. The supposed recipient is Bishop Euddogwy (*Oudoceus*), as in the first eighteen charters of Sequence ii (and also the thirtieth, 158, a clear interpolation). It is unlikely, however, that he was bishop as early as Tewdrig's day, as that would make his episcopate span four royal generations. Three other charters which should also precede Sequence ii are *VC* 64, 65, and 68, the second of which is witnessed by Bishop *Eudoce* (i.e. Euddogwy).[167] Of these three grants, *VC* 64 is by a certain *Terengual, pro anima sua et pro anima Morcant* – neither of whom are necessarily members of a royal family; *VC* 65 describes transactions involving *Andres* or *Andrus* (Athrwys) son of *Morcant* and *Mouric* and his son *Iudnerth*, and its lay witness list is headed by *Mouricus et filii eius*; and *VC* 68 involves *Mouricus rex* and his sons, clearly the Meurig ap Tewdrig of *LL* and JC 9 – his sons included Idnerth, according to charters in Sequence ii discussed below (cf. Table 13.5). The *Mouric* of *VC* 65 is clearly the same king.[168] Bartrum identified the *Morcant* of *VC* 64–65 with Morgan ap Gwrgan ap Cynfyn in charter 163b (cf. Table 13.5), which is unprovable.[169]

The first two charters of Sequence ii are full of genealogical information. The first, 144, belonging to *tempus Athruis filii Mourici*, concerns a grant *de manu Athruis Gurcanti magni nepotis*, and is attested by *rex Mouricus super filium suum Athruis*. The second, 140, is a grant by *Mouric rex Morcanhuc filius Teudiric & uxor eius Onbraust filia Gurcanti magni* and is attested by *Muricus rex, uxor eius Onbraust, filii sui Athruis et Idnerth*. The information may be set out as follows:

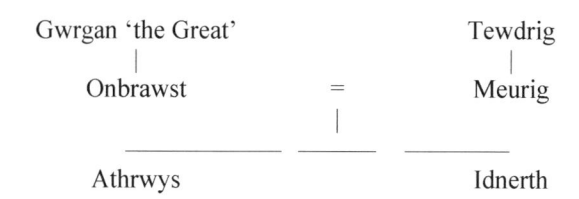

```
     Gwrgan 'the Great'              Tewdrig
            |                           |
       Onbrawst        =             Meurig
                       |
        ─────────────────────────
            |                           |
         Athrwys                     Idnerth
```

---

[166] Davies, *The Llandaff Charters*, 79. Jones, 'The Book of Llandaff', 135, rightly describes it as 'more of a legend . . . than a diplomatic instrument'. It is translated by Birch, *Memorials*, 96–8.

[167] See above, 40–1. The identity of the *Eudoce* of *VC* 65 with the *Oudoceus* of *LL* was convincingly elucidated by Doble, *Lives*, 213–16, but, as he says, there is no internal or other evidence to enable one to date him (p. 216). Jones, 'The Book of Llandaff', 134, says 'sometime in the ninth century', a century too late in view of the association between his successor Berthwyn and Æthelbald of Mercia, discussed below, 152–3.

[168] Charles-Edwards, *Wales and the Britons*, 287–8.

[169] 'Some studies', 288 (Table II); similarly Wade-Evans, 'The Llancarfan charters', 163. Davies, *WHEMA* IX 10 n. 17, discusses which of the *VC* charters are royal.

13. The royal genealogical framework

The *Gurcantus magnus* of Sequence ii is quite likely to be the same person as the *Gurcant rex Ercicg filius Cinuin* of Sequence i (163b–164); there is no absolute proof of this equation, however, which is a pity, since it would provide a link between the two Sequences.[170] The two men have been kept apart in Table 13.5. It may well be that the marriage between Meurig and Onbrawst in *LL* was invented in order to justify his dynasty's control over Ergyng.[171] A similar function is fulfilled in JC 9 by his descent from Nynnio, Peibio ab Erb's brother, and by the marriage between his dynasty and Cenedlon, a great-great-granddaughter of Peibio, in JC 10.

In Sequence ii.3–4 there follow two more Meurig charters (143 and 147), the second of which refers to his killing of a certain *Cynuetu* and is attested by *Mouric rex cum filio suo Frioc et nepote Morcant filio Athruis*, thus adding to Table 13.5 a name not in the genealogies (Ffriog). Since *nepos* is ambiguous, the Morgan mentioned could be either Meurig's grandson (JC 9) or his nephew (HG 28/ABT 15(E)). In 143 Briafael [ap Llywarch] makes his first appearance in a witness list; he is in the same generation of descent from Erb as Meurig, according to the scheme in JC 10 (Table 13.5),[172] which, for what it is worth, might seem to favour identifying Morgan in 147 with Meurig's nephew (HG 28) rather than his grandson in the following generation. Against this, however, is the fact that Briafael ap Llywarch definitely attests at least one charter of Meurig's grandson (149). This stretches the generations uncomfortably, suggesting that Briafael's descent from Peibio in JC 10, like his daughter Cenedlon's marriage into Meurig ap Tewdrig's line, may be another invention designed to link the two dynasties.[173] That Briafael has an alliterating epithet *Brydig* 'valiant, eager'[174] in JC and related texts suggests that he was the subject of legend.

In the next three charters (152, 155, 151b) *Morcant rex Athruis filius* appears (*cum senioribus Morcannuc* in 152), and in the first two it is said that he killed his paternal uncle (*patruus*) *Frioc* son of *Mouric*. This shows that we have to do now with the Morgan who was the grandson of Meurig (JC 9), not the grandson of Tewdrig (HG 28/ABT 15(E)), and that is confirmed by the next charter (149) which refers to *Morcant rex* and *sepulchrum Mourici regis iacentis Landauiæ, aui sui*. Next come two problematic grants concerning adjacent estates, near or at Llandaf, by a *Guedguenus Brochmaili filius* (151a), who was perhaps a king, and *Brochmail filius*

---

[170] In *LL* p. 118 the Sequence i *Gurcant* may be meant by *Gurcant maur*. Their identity was accepted by Bartrum, 'Some studies', 284, who described it as 'very reasonable'. Davies, *The Llandaff Charters*, 170 s.n. *Gurcant*, queries it but apparently accepts it in *An Early Welsh Microcosm*, 65 and 94. Wade-Evans, 'The Llancarfan charters', 162–3, identifies both *Gwrgan*s with the *Wrgannus Varius/Vawr* of the *Vita Cadoci*, §24. There were various characters of this name: Sims-Williams, 'Did itinerant Breton *conteurs* transmit the *matière de Bretagne*?', 99–100.

[171] Cf. Guy, 'The *Life* of St Dyfrig', 27 n. 75, and 30–1.

[172] See above, 131.

[173] *Gwehelyth Morgannwg*, §5 (ed. Guy, 'Medieval Welsh genealogy', II, 337), adds a generation between Peibio and Tewdwr; this eases the problem but lacks authority. For a different approach see Guy, 'The *Life* of St Dyfrig', 31 n. 89. Rejecting Gwrgan's status in *LL* as Meurig's father-in-law, he argues that Gwrgan, grandson of Peibio, in Sequence i (163b–164), was contemporary with the Athrwys ap Meurig of Sequence ii, so that Briafael, great-grandson of Peibio (JC 10), could well be contemporary with Morgan ab Athrwys ap Meurig. This argument depends on the doubtful equation between the Athrwys ap Meurig of charter 165 and the Athrwys ap Meurig of Sequence ii. See above, 146.

[174] A rare adjective: Lloyd-Jones, *Geirfa*, 80.

Guidgentiuai [*sic*] (159b), who has been regarded as the former's son though they may well be identical.[175] The next charter, which is regarded as very suspicious by Wendy Davies,[176] is a grant in Glamorgan to Bishop Euddogwy by an otherwise unknown *Ivdhail rex, Athruis filius* (157). Compare an eleventh-century charter, 259, referring to land rights existing *a tempore Iudhail regis Morcannuc filii Athruis contemporanei Oudocei episcopi*. He could be a son either of Athrwys ap Meurig (JC 9) or of Athrwys ap Tewdrig (HG 28/ABT 15(E)) – or of neither – which is why he had to be left out of Table 13.5. Davies then lists two charters of Awst, king of Brycheiniog (146 and 154), in favour of Bishop Euddogwy, but points out that their witness lists are simply lifted from the preceding charter in the sequence (157).[177] With the next charter (148) we return to Morgan ab Athrwys ap Meurig ap Tewdrig: *Morcant rex filius Athruis ... pro ... anima Mourici aui sui filii Teudiric*. The bounds refer to the *uilla* 'in qua occidit Mouric Cynuetu' (cf. charter 147 above).

In the next charter we seem to have a glimpse of a separate dynasty and a further echo of the name of the *Cynuetu* slain by Meurig: *Iudic rex filius Nud & Cinan filius Cinuedu ambo reges* grant land to Bishop Euddogwy (150b). The many unique lay witnesses are presumably the new kings' henchmen. *Cinan* disappears again, but the next charter (which could equally well precede 150b) is a grant by *Movricus rex simul & Iudic filius Nud* to Bishop Euddogwy (150a). *Movric(us)* is probably a slip for *Morcant*, since the charter's witness list has *Morcant rex, Iudic hereditarius filius Nud*.[178] We then have a charter of *Morcant rex Morcannhuc filius Athruis* in which Briafael [ap Llywarch] attests for the last time (145) and a charter of *Morcant rex Gleuissic* (156), in which Bishop Euddogwy appears for the last time (excepting the interpolated 158). It is always assumed that the king *Morcant* (*filius Athruis*) of these charters is the grandson of the Meurig ap Tewdrig of JC 9 and earlier charters; however, he could equally well be the grandson of Tewdrig in HG 28, since the kingship of Glywysing may have swung from one branch of the family to another, and from one Morgan to another.[179]

The charters of Bishop Euddogwy's successor[180] Berthwyn begin with one in which a king *Clotri*, who is said to have killed a king *Iudguallaun*, is associated with

---

[175] The witness list of 151a reads 'De laicis. Rex solus. Guidgen cum suis', which may make *Guidgen* a king (cf. 59 n. 4), despite Doble, *Lives*, 76. See the discussion of 151a and 159b by Phillimore, *DP* III 285; Wade-Evans, 'The Llancarfan charters', 158; Doble, *Lives*, 76 and 228; and Davies, *The Llandaff Charters*, 100, 103, and 167. *Guedgen filius Brocmail* appears in *VC* 68.

[176] Davies, *The Llandaff Charters*, 83 n. 16 and 102. James, 'The "Concen charters"', 82, 84, and 88, treats charter 157 (his no. 15) as if it were a grant by Ithel ap *Morgan* – one of several errors. Jones, 'The Book of Llandaff', 133 and 135, wrongly takes 259 to refer to the Ithel ab Athrwys [HG 29] 'who died about 848'.

[177] Davies, *The Llandaff Charters*, 43, 55–56, 81, 83 n. 16, 98, and 101. On Awst's charters see above, ch. 6.

[178] Davies, *The Llandaff Charters*, 99. On Iddon and Iddig see *eadem*, *An Early Welsh Microcosm*, 45.

[179] James, 'The *Book of Llan Dav* and Bishop Oudoceus', 34–7, and 'Chronology', 131–2 and 138, argues that the Morgan charters of the episcopates of Euddogwy and Berthwyn refer to two different Morgans, separated by a century: Morgan ab Athrwys and Morgan father of Ithel. His argument depends on his theory that Berthwyn was not Euddogwy's successor, which is contradicted by charter 180b and the evidence of the witness lists (despite *idem*, 'The "Concen charters"').

[180] Cf. charter 180b.

13. The royal genealogical framework

Morcant rex (176b) and with one in which *Morcant rex* consents to a grant by *Rotri* (183b), almost certainly a slip for *Clotri*, as the witness list shows. It is clear which *Morcant* is meant since 176b names his son as *Ithail* (see HG 28). The next grant, moreover, which is one of *Morcant filius Athruis* attested by *Iudhail* (174b), has an appendix relating how *Ithail rex filius Morcant* returned the land to Berthwyn after it had been appropriated. Thus we have to do with the line of HG 28 now, not that of JC 9, where Morgan's son is *Nud* ('Nud hael'). A later charter of Hywel ap Rhys refers back to 174b as *tempore Morcanti regis Gleuissicg filii Athruis contemporanei Berthguin episcopi Landauiæ* (229b).[181] There follows another charter *Morcanti & filii eius Ithail* (176a), the doublet of which names Morgan's wife as *Ricceneth* (190b).[182] While 176a is attested by *Guednerth frater Morcanti*, 190b has *Gaidnerth filius* [sic] *Morcanti frater*; perhaps he was a brother[183] of *King* Morgan or, more likely, his nephew.[184] (Wendy Davies's next charter [ii.24], in which a *Brochuael rex* appears [205], probably belongs much later, in the episcopate of Tyrchan.)[185] The last charter of *Morcant rex* now follows (180b). It refers to *Guidnerth* (the *filius Morcanti frater* mentioned above, it seems) who had killed *fratrem suum Merchion* in a dynastic dispute (*causa contentionis regni*) during the episcopate of Euddogwy.[186] *Iudic filius Nud* (who was *rex* in 150b) witnesses for the last time. There is a variant version of this charter in *VC* 67,[187] which is attested by *Marcant*, who is presumably King Morgan, though he is given no title. Another charter which belongs about here, to judge by its witness list is *VC* 62, which specifically mentions the title of *Morcant rex*.[188]

We now come to the charters of Ithel ap Morgan and his sons. The first of these, which belongs to the episcopate of Berthwyn, refers to him in the phrase *uerbo Iudhali* [sic] *regis et consensu* (188b); it has a variant, in which he is not mentioned, in 179a.[189] Wendy Davies's next charter (204b) is probably placed too early, and should belong to the episcopate of Tyrchan.[190] We then have a charter of the time of Bishop Berthwyn, by which *Iuthail rex* grants land previously given him by *Morcant rex* (180a). It is attested by *Iudhail rex cum filiis suis Mouric et Fernuail* (cf. Table 13.5), and also by an abbot *Gnouan* of Llancarfan.[191] We then have two more charters of *Ivthail rex*

---

[181] See Davies, *The Llandaff Charters*, 21 and 122.
[182] Charles-Edwards, *Wales and the Britons*, 306, and above, 97.
[183] So Anscombe, 'Some Old-Welsh pedigrees', 85, and Bartrum, 'Some studies', 288. Cf. *VC* 67/*LL* 180b. Although *Guednerth* may thus be the king's brother, Davies, *The Llandaff Charters*, 167, and *An Early Welsh Microcosm*, 114, 119, and 173, regards him as the same person as *Guidnerth filius Guallonir* who appears in the other charters of Sequence ii.
[184] Cf. Charles-Edwards, *Wales and the Britons*, 306–8, and above, 98.
[185] See above, 33 and n. 6.
[186] Charles-Edwards, *Wales and the Britons*, 306–7.
[187] See above, 99–102.
[188] I agree with James, '*The Book of Llandav*: the church and see of Llandav', 12–13, that *VC* 62 is *not* a variant of *LL* 147. On its date see above, 40.
[189] On the latter see Davies, *The Llandaff Charters*, 79. On p. 45 she wrongly omits Ithel from the table for 188b.
[190] See above, n. 185.
[191] It is possible that the two charters of Paul, abbot of St Cadog's (Llancarfan), *VC* 59 and 61, should be placed shortly before this charter, since in one of them (*VC* 61) *Gnouan* is still merely one of the clergy of the monastery. (Regrettably, neither charter makes specific reference to royalty, but *Guallonir* in *VC* 59 is probably the person mentioned above, n. 183.) This placing depends heavily on the identification of *Gnouan*, but there are some other connections with the witness lists of *LL* and of *VC*'s charters of abbot *Conigc*,

filius Morcanti & filii eius Fernuail et Mouric (179c and 158). The second includes *Episcopus Oudoceus* in its witness list by a clear error.[192] Possibly the adjacent charter in *LL* (159a), which also refers to Bishop Euddogwy, belongs here as well (it has no witness list). It refers to *Ithail rex* without patronymic.[193] In Sequence ii three more Ithel charters follow which add no further genealogical information (187, 190a, and 179b), but the third has a variant (191), which is granted by *Iudhailo rege Gleuissicg & a filiis eius Fernuail et Mourico et Rotri* and is attested by *Iudhail rex et filii eius, Arthuail, Mouric, Rotri, Ris*. Wendy Davies regards *Arthuail* as a slip for the well-known *Fernuail*, who appears in the main text; he could, however, be the ARTMALI commemorated with IUTHAHELO on a cross at Llantwit.[194] The following eleven charters either mention Ithel ap Morgan, often with one or more of his sons, or mention no kings at all (175 = 186b, 183a, 189, 184, 188a, 195, 185, 186a, 178, and 202). 183a is a grant by Ithel and his son Meurig *pro anima Athruis filii*, a son not mentioned elsewhere. In 178 Bishop Berthwyn makes his last appearance, and he is succeeded by Bishop Tyrchan in 202, which includes the final appearance of King Ithel ap Morgan. 204b, a sale by *Iudhailo rege Gleuissicg filio Morcant* in the time of Bishop Tyrchan, placed much earlier by Wendy Davies,[195] really belongs here in all probability.

Charter 192, a memorandum without witness list which Wendy Davies therefore omits from her sequences, deserves consideration here since it provides the main internal indication of the absolute chronology of the charters of Sequence ii, apart from the Euddogwy-Awst synchronism discussed earlier.[196] It belongs to the time of Bishop Berthwyn and a *rex Iudhail*, who can hardly be other than Ithel ap Morgan, whose reign corresponded very closely to Berthwyn's episcopate, as we have seen.[197] Charter 192 begins as follows:

---

discussed below, 154. See Bartrum, 'Some studies', 294–6. I suggested above (41) that the order of abbots of Llancarfan is *Iacob, Concen, Sulgen, Paul, Gnouan, Danoc, Dagan, Conigc*. James, 'The "Concen charters"', 89, identifies *Concen* (= Cyngen) and *Conigc* (= Cynyng), but this philologically and historically unlikely. Abbot *Gnouan* is to be separated from the *Gnauan* of *VC* 11 and 53, on whom cf. *DP* II, 290 n. 3.

[192] As is noted by Jones, 'The Book of Llandaff', 135 and 137, Bartrum, 'Some studies', 281 n. 1, and Davies, *The Llandaff Charters*, 81 and 102. (Differently Anscombe, 'Landavensium ordo chartarum', 273.)

[193] Davies, *The Llandaff Charters*, 79 and 102, makes a different identification: the Ithel of charter 157, discussed above.

[194] *Ibid.*, 113; Redknap and Lewis, *A Corpus*, I, 381. On the cross see below, 154.

[195] See above, 33.

[196] The dates suggested by Davies are uncertain: *The Llandaff Charters*, 76 and passim; her fixed points are the Ithel–Æthelbald synchronism, the 775 obit for Ffernfael, and the Awst synchronism, and both the last two are uncertain, as we have seen, above 137 (Ffernfael) and 49 and 57 (Awst).

[197] In 'Some studies', 283, Bartrum suggested that its *rex Iudhail* was Ithel ab Athrwys, the great-grandson of Ithel ap Morgan in HG 28, and that the references to Bishop Berthwyn are therefore mistakes. These interpretations are only necessary if one accepts his chronology for the charters, which rested heavily on accepting a sixth-century date for the Euddogwy/Oudoceus of the charters and on accepting the authority of one of the 'earliest' charters in the *Vita Cadoci*, which are clearly fabrications. See 'Some studies', 281–2, where the Samson of *VC* 63 is identified with St Samson of Dol (cf. above, 52 n. 18) and its Iacob is identified with the abbot of this name in *VC* 65 (on which see above, 40–1). On these matters see Doble, cited above, 57 n. 45. The late stage at which Euddogwy was made successor to Dyfrig and Teilo is evident from *LL* itself – see Davies, *The Llandaff Charters*, 15 and Brooke, *The Church*,

13. The royal genealogical framework

> Sciendum est quod euenerunt magnæ tribulationes & uastationes in tempore telpaldi & ithaili regum brittanniæ & a saxonica gente infidelissima, & maxime in confinibus britanniæ & angliæ uersus herfordiam intantum quod britanniæ totum confinium fere deletum est, & multum extra confinia ex utraque parte aggliæ & brittanniæ, & circa flumen guy maxime propter bella et sepe facta diurna et noctura inter utrasque. Post tempus sedata pace restituta est ui sua et fortitudine terra sua quamuis deleta et inhabita raro homine & rara peste cuique britanno in illis partibus perpetrato federe. & rex iudhail omnibus superstitibus reddidit patrimonia. quamuis per spatium desolata. & berthguino episcopo sua loca redditit per omnia. ...[198]

Apparently all the lands which King Ithel restored to Bishop Berthwyn were in the Ergyng/Hereford area.[199] Usually and, surely, rightly *telpaldi* is held to refer to Æthelbald of Mercia (read *in tempore* [e]*telpaldi*?), even though the writer of the Book of Llandaf makes him a king of *Britannia* which seems to mean Wales in the context.[200] The fact that Æthelbald claimed the title *rex Britanniae* in his charters[201] may have led to the confusion. As Æthelbald is known to have reigned 716–57 we can say that Ithel ap Morgan's *floruit* lay, or was believed to have lain, *somewhere* within that long period. Such a *floruit* in the first half or middle of the eighth century would fit in well with the identification of his son Ffernfael ab Ithel with the person of that name who died in 775 (*Annales Cambriae*), unprovable though such identifications are.

After the charters of Ithel ap Morgan, Sequence ii continues with a charter mentioning no kings (198a), a charter issued *uerbo et consensu regum Mourici & Ris filiorum Iudhail regis Gleuissicg* and attested by *Mouric rex et frater eius Ris* (204a), and two more charters mentioning no kings (197 and 199a). The brothers

---

47–8. In *A Welsh Classical Dictionary*, 392 and 578–9, Bartrum accepts that Ithel ab Morgan is meant in charter 192 and rejects his own early date for Abbot Samson.

[198] The following paraphrase is given by Bartrum, *A Welsh Classical Dictionary*, 392: 'Let it be known that great tribulations and plunderings occurred in the time of *Telpaldus* and *Ithailus*, kings of *Britannia*, which were committed by the most treacherous Saxon nation, and most of all on the confines of *Britannia* [Wales] and *Agglia* [England] towards *Herfordia* [Hereford], so that all the border country of *Britannia* was nearly destroyed, and much beyond the borders of both *Agglia* and *Britannia*, and especially about the river *Guy* [Wye], on account of frequent daily and nightly encounters between each other. After a time, peace having been established, the land was restored to its owners and its former authority, and an alliance of the Britons [Welsh] formed in those parts. And king *Iudhail* [Ithel] restored to the survivors their patrimony, though for a time destroyed, and likewise restored to bishop *Berthguin* [Berthwyn] eleven estates which had belonged to the church in the days before the troubles'. See also Guy, 'The *Life* of St Dyfrig', 31–2.

[199] Cf. *DP* III, 273 n. 1. For a map see Hughes, 'The Celtic Church', 18, map 3.

[200] The identification is accepted by Phillimore in *DP* III, 271; Bartrum, 'Some studies', 280 and 283; Davies, *The Llandaff Charters*, 76, 86 n. 37 and 113, and *An Early Welsh Microcosm*, 18; and Kirby, 'British dynastic history', 88. In 'Some studies' Bartrum associated Ithel's restoration of land to the church with the victories of the *Dexterales Brittones* noted in *Annales Cambriae* s.a. 722, which is speculative (cf. *A Welsh Classical Dictionary*, 392). – Note also the battle of Hereford s.a. 760, which may have been a Welsh victory for all we know. James, 'Chronology', 133, supposes that Ithel's victory took place at the time of Æthelbald's death (cf. *DP* III, 271–2). Davies, *The Llandaff Charters*, 113, associates the Æthelbald reference with his war against the Britons recorded in the *Anglo-Saxon Chronicle*, s.a. 743.

[201] Stenton, *Preparatory to Anglo-Saxon England*, 53–6.

Meurig and Rhys ab Ithel then disappear from the record for a while and we have seven charters of *Fernuail rex filius Iudhaili* (201, 203a, 198b, 199bi, 203b, 200, and 207), two of which mention Ffernfael's sons *Mouric* and *Gu(o)rcant* (203a and 203b) and one of which mentions his wife *Ceincair* (207).[202] In the last of these seven Ffernfael charters Bishop Tyrchan has been succeeded by Bishop Cadwared, whose episcopate lasts till the end of Sequence ii.[203] Charter 205, a Tyrchan charter, which Wendy Davies places much earlier, at ii.24, belongs somewhere here.[204] It refers to a *Brochuail rex* who cannot be certainly identified elsewhere.[205] He could just possibly be the Brochfael ap Rhys of JC 9 (see Table 13.5), but there is no other evidence that the people around generation 7 in JC 9 – if even historical – were rulers.

Ffernfael ab Ithel now disappears (dying in 775?) and two charters of *regis Rotri filius* [*sic*] *Iudhail* follow (210b and 209b). The first of these has a doublet[206] in *VC* 66, which does not mention Rhodri, but does give Cynyng as a witness. In view of the latter feature, it is probable that two other charters in the *Vita Cadoci* in which Cynyng (abbot of Llancarfan) appears (*VC* 55–56) should be placed about here in Sequence ii, as shown by Bartrum.[207] The first of these (*VC* 55) refers to a *Rodri*, who could be the king, though this is uncertain. It also mentions *Samson, abbas altaris sancti Eltuti*, who may well be the cleric of this name who attests a charter of King Rhodri ab Ithel (209b) and a charter of his brother Rhys ab Ithel (211a), immediately after Bishop Cadwared in both charters. He is likely to be the abbot Samson who erected an extant late-eighth-century(?) cross at Llantwit for the soul of a King Ithel (IUTHAHELO), who could be the father of Rhodri ab Ithel and his brothers.[208] The cross also commemorates an Arthfael (ARTMALI) and a TECANI (genitive). The latter may be the unusually named cleric *Teican* who witnesses 211a along with a *Samson*. The Arthfael could be Ithel's son *Arthuail*, who is named only in 191 as discussed above (p. 152); perhaps he died too young to appear elsewhere in the charters.[209]

Rhodri ab Ithel's two charters are followed in Sequence ii by two charters (211a and 209a) of *Ris filius Iudhail, rex Gleuissicg*, who then disappears. We now move to

---

[202] On her see Charles-Edwards, *Wales and the Britons*, 306.

[203] A note in *LL* p. 206 reads 'Eluogus episcopus sequitur Turchanum episcopum, tempore Mourici, Ris, Fernmail, Rotri, filiorum regis Gleuissicg' (cf. Davies, *The Llandaff Charters*, 21); we have no charters of this bishop. Bartrum, 'Some studies', 285 (cf. 293), notes 'plenty of evidence to show that Cadwared followed immediately after Terchan'. Anscombe, 'Landavensium ordo chartarum', 66, attempted, unconvincingly, to place the charters of Cadwared after those of Bishop Cerennyr (i.e. in Sequence iii). The succession from Tyrchan to Cadwared is clear from the starred names in Davies, *The Llandaff Charters*, 51–3 (see also 57). Cf. Jones, 'The Book of Llandaff', 137.

[204] See above, 151.

[205] Davies, *The Llandaff Charters*, 151, suggests that he is Brochfael ap Gwyddien.

[206] I agree with Brooke, *The Church*, 32, against James, '*The Book of Llandav*: the church and see of Llandav', 15. See discussion of 210b/*VC* 66 in ch. 11 above.

[207] 'Some studies', 294–6. Cf. above, 151 n. 191, and 41, also *WHEMA* IX 6 n. 8. Bartrum, 'Some studies', 288 (Table), suggested that the Tewdwr ap Meurig of *VC* 55 was a son of Meurig ab Ithel ap Morgan (cf. my Table 13.5) but this is quite uncertain.

[208] Sims-Williams, *The Celtic Inscriptions of Britain*, 277–8; Redknap and Lewis, *A Corpus*, I 377–82, no. G65; Charles-Edwards, *Wales and the Britons*, 125, 138, 152, 162, and 626. See above, 57.

[209] Sims-Williams, *The Celtic Inscriptions of Britain*, 278. TECANI may be Irish *Tecán* (ogam TXGANN); see *ibid.*, 52 and 176. Was he the scribe? The spelling *ei* could reflect one Roman-letter equivalent of the ogam X (see Sims-Williams, *Studies*, 133, 143–4, and 152).

13. The royal genealogical framework

the next generation (the sixth[210] in Table 13.5) with two grants made with the consent of *Gurgauarn rex filius Fernuail* (206 and 211b). One suspects that this may be the same person as the *Gu(o)rcant* son of Ffernfael whom we have already met (203a and 203b), even though the names are distinct. Sequence ii ends with two charters of *Athruis rex filius Fernuail* (210a and 208), who is evidently the person of this name in HG 28 (see Table 13.5).

The main evidence for dating Sequence ii is the Ithel ap Morgan/Æthelbald synchronism, supported by the attractive equation between Ffernfael ab Ithel and the person who died in 775 (*Annales Cambriae*), and the approximate late-eighth-century date of the Llantwit cross. Thus the charters of Sequence ii belong to the eighth century, broadly speaking.[211] Sequence ii does not get as far as the generation of Ithel ab Athrwys, the last person named in HG 28. Ithel presumably lived in the ninth century; quite possibly, then, he is the king 'of Gwent' slain by the men of Brycheiniog in 848 according to *Annales Cambriae* ('Gueit Finnant Iudhail . rex Guent . a uiris Broceniauc occisus est').[212] Lloyd deduced that Ithel was the last of his line and that his pedigree (HG 28), 'stopping short with him, implies that he left no descendants'.[213] This is plausible; since HG 29 gets as far as the 880s, some explanation is needed if HG 28 stops some years earlier.

The start of Sequence iii

There is no overlap of names between the end of Sequence ii and the beginning of Sequence iii;[214] thus Sequence iii, which begins with the charters of Meurig [ab Arthfael][215] of Gwent (HG 29) and Hywel ap Rhys of Glywysing (JC 9) is of no help in establishing the date of the end of Sequence ii, except insofar as it provides a *terminus ante quem* in the second half of the ninth century, which is far too late to be helpful. As the dynasts who emerge at the start of Sequence iii did not descend directly from the Athrwys ap Ffernfael (HG 28) who ends Sequence ii, there is no hope of computing this generation gap in absolute terms with any accuracy. Roughly,

---

[210] The five-generation span from generation 2 to 6 agrees reasonably well with the occurrence of four generations of the two families in the lay witness lists by this point. See Davies, *The Llandaff Charters*, 58, also *An Early Welsh Microcosm*, 115 and 118–19.

[211] See above, 54–8. Llandaf lost sight of this when Bishop Euddogwy was made a disciple of Dyfrig rather than the predecessor of Æthelbald's contemporary Berthwyn.

[212] Cf. above, 121 n. 29.

[213] Lloyd, *A History*, I, 274 and n. 260 (cf. Sims-Williams, 'The kings', 73–4 and 75). On the Meurig ab Ithel of charter 214 see below, n. 215.

[214] Davies, *The Llandaff Charters*, 58–9, 84 n. 22, and 85 n. 23. James's suggestion ('Chronology', 133–4) about Bonus in *Historia Brittonum*, which she cites at 84 n. 22, is incredible; on this person see the references given by Fleuriot, 'Old Breton genealogies', 3. Anscombe, 'Landavensium ordo chartarum', 294–5, attempted unconvincingly to connect the witness lists of Sequence ii and Sequence iii.

[215] In Sequence iii a King Meurig appears, interspersed with appearances of Hywel ap Rhys, in many of the first seventeen charters, but not until the twelfth (no. 225) do his two sons Brochfael and Ffernfael occur with him and not until the sixteenth (no. 199bii) is his patronymic *Arthfael* given, thus fixing his identity without doubt. It is therefore possible that the Meurig of some of the charters earlier than 225 is a different Meurig, and this is supported by the patronymic *Ithel* in the tenth (214), if this is not just a slip (*Iudhail* for *Artmail*), as plausibly stated by Davies, *The Llandaff Charters*, 87–8 and 119. Cf. above, 120 n. 20.

though, Sequence ii may have ended *ca* 800, a generation after Ffernfael (*ob.* 775?), and Sequence iii may have begun *ca* 850, a generation before Hywel ap Rhys and Brochfael ap Meurig, who flourished in the 880s (Asser). If the existence of Gwriad ap Brochfael in JC 9 is rejected (see above), the generation gap becomes much shorter than Table 13.5 would suggest.

The preceding pages have attempted to give all the information that can be deduced from the Book of Llandaf about the succession of the early kings and their family relationships. We have seen that this information is perfectly compatible with the conservative view of the texts of the genealogies as set out in Table 13.5, especially if Gwriad and Brochfael are omitted. It must be admitted that it is also compatible with the usual emendations to the texts which lead to Table 13.2, Fig. 1 or, better, Table 13.2, Fig. 2;[216] the Book of Llandaf has nothing to confirm or disprove the existence of the *Atroys map Teudubric* of HG 28 or the *Nud* (*hael*) of JC 9. Nor can it tell us if the dynasties of HG 28 and HG 29 are really one and the same dynasty, since the crucial generations lie in the blank years between Sequence ii and Sequence iii. Thus, in the criticism of HG 28–29 and JC 9 we are thrown back upon the purely textual arguments in the first part of this chapter. It is my submission that the arguments for the usual emendations to the texts of the genealogies are not conclusive and that a textually conservative genealogy like Table 13.5 may better represent what the genealogists had in mind, and may even come closer to historical reality, than do the more usual Table 13.2, Figs 1–2, which depend on emendations to the texts. Table 13.6, however, is probably superior since it omits JC's dubious link between Hywel ap Rhys and Tewdrig.

A possible reconstruction of the reality behind Tables 13.5 and 13.6 is as follows.

The earliest charters (seventh-century) were granted by the kings of a number of regions, but principally by the families of Peibio ab Erb in Ergyng and Tewdrig in the south-east. (Despite the genealogists, there is no good reason to suppose that the two families shared a common ancestor.) Peibio's dynasty died out, but Tewdrig's dynasty split into two. Meurig ap Tewdrig, his son Athrwys ap Meurig, and his grandson Morgan ab Athrwys all made grants, after which nothing is heard of Morgan's descendants for many years. The dynasty of Athrwys ap Tewdrig lasted longer, perhaps down to 848 if Ithel, grandson of Ffernfael (*ob.* 775), was the Ithel 'of Gwent' slain then by the men of Brycheiniog.

Not long afterwards, new rulers appeared: Meurig ab Arthfael, in Gwent, whose dynasty lasted until the 880s, and his contemporary Hywel ap Rhys in Glywysing. Meurig ab Arthfael's ancestry received respectable coverage in the Harley genealogies, but Hywel's was omitted. Only much later did Hywel's grandson Morgan Hen (*ob.* 974) receive two honourable patrilineages, one of which (JC 9) joined his dynasty, artificially perhaps, on to the ancient line of Morgan ab Athrwys ap Meurig ap Tewdrig – a line which could have been known from the Book of Llandaf itself – and the other of which (ABT 15(E)) traced him back to the Morgan ab Athrwys ap Tewdrig known from HG 28. In the charters there is no trace of any of the men in the linking generations 5 to 9 of the JC 9 patrilineage, and it is not impossible that they were invented as late as the twelfth century to satisfy some of Morgan Hen's descendants. The links between Morgan and Tewdrig in ABT 15(E) may be equally artificial, created by splicing together names from HG 28 and HG 29.

---

[216] See pedigree in Charles-Edwards, *Wales and the Britons*, 253, which has a framework similar to Table 13.2, Fig. 2.

14

THE EPISCOPAL FRAMEWORK

The seventh-century Church

The fullest available picture of the southern Welsh churches in the sixth to seventh centuries comes from the Breton-Latin *Life* of St Samson, bishop of Dol (*fl. ca* 561), written about a century after his death (probably) and dedicated to a Bishop Tigernomalus, perhaps a person of this name who died in 707. Though the author writes from a Breton perspective, and follows literary models, including Venantius Fortunatus's *Life* of St Paternus of Avranches (near Dol), he has visited places associated with Samson in Wales and Cornwall and has obtained information from an old man of nearly eighty whose uncle, Henog, a cousin or kinsman of Samson, had obtained information from Samson's mother Anna.[1] Thus the *Life* gives us a rare contemporary glimpse of the seventh-century Welsh Church and offers memories of the sixth century, when monasticism was starting to take hold in Britain, as already seen in the writings of Gildas.[2] It suggests a context for the more austere data in the charters.

According to the *Life*, Samson and his father were from Dyfed and his mother was from the – at that time – adjacent province of Gwent. Both parents were of high status and had fostered kings in their respective provinces (I.1 and 6). Samson's father's name, *Amon*, has been held to suggest sympathy with Egyptian asceticism.[3] He and his wife, Anna, took their first-born, Samson, aged five, together with the customary entry fees (I.9), to 'the school of the famous master of the Britons', Illtud (*Eltutus*), a disciple of St Germanus, who was believed to have been ordained priest in his youth by Germanus himself.[4] The Breton author, who praises Illtud's curriculum,

---

[1] *La vie ancienne de saint Samson*, ed. Flobert. See *St Samson of Dol*, ed. Olson. The author's literary shaping of the historical narrative is also discussed by Krajewski, *Archetypal Narratives*, 95–154. The 'second half of the seventh century' date proposed by Hughes, 'The Celtic Church', 4, remains plausible. Knight, *South Wales*, 39, suggests that Henog (*Henocus*) is the 'possible eponym of Llanhennock [Llanhenwg] near Caerleon'. The Celtic name from *Senacos* was not uncommon, however (see Sims-Williams, *The Celtic Inscriptions of Britain*, 94); derivation from the biblical *Enoch* has also been suggested: J. R. Davies, 'Cathedrals', 110 n. 48.

[2] See Herren, 'Gildas and early British monasticism'.

[3] Morris, *The Age of Arthur*, 356. But Sowerby, 'A family and its saint', 35, views the family's names as more broadly Old Testament and suggests that they adopted them on entering the monastic life.

[4] I.7. If this is placed during Germanus's alleged second visit to Britain in the 440s, the chronology is strained but not impossible. If Illtud was priested by Germanus in 445 at the age of twenty-five, he could have schooled Samson at the age of seven in 500, when he

has visited Illtud's 'magnificent monastery', presumably Llantwit,[5] and has gathered stories about Illtud from the brothers there (I.7–8). Illtud, we learn, arranged for Samson to be ordained deacon and priest by Bishop Dyfrig (*Dubricius*) when he visited; we are not told what see Dyfrig came from, or even that he had one (I.13 and 15), but evidently Llantwit did not have a resident bishop. The only named office is that of *pistor* ('cook' or 'cellarer', I.16), the office occupied by one of Illtud's nephews.[6] The latter and his brother, who was in priestly orders, feared that Samson would gain control of their 'hereditary monastery' and plotted against him (I.14 and 16). So monasteries were clearly embedded in the kindred, as elsewhere in Europe.

Seeking a more ascetic life, Samson moves on to an island monastery recently founded by the priest Piro – presumably Caldy Island (Ynys Bŷr)[7] – which the hagiographer himself has visited (I.20). Samson's parents give away most of their wealth, and, following their example, Amon's brother, sister-in-law, and their three sons pay for the foundation of monasteries, while Anna promises to do similarly (I.30–1). The whole family removes to Piro's island, where Bishop Dyfrig, according to his custom, is residing in his own lodgings for the forty days of Easter (I.33). Dyfrig appoints Samson to the office of *pistor* and supervises Samson's election as abbot, after Piro, inebriated, falls into a pit and dies (I.34–6). Within a year and a half, Dyfrig gives Samson permission to go to Ireland with some Irish scholars returning from Rome. There Samson heals the abbot of a monastery near Howth (*Arx Etri*), and the grateful abbot makes over his monastery to Samson and accompanies him back to Caldy, where Samson's uncle is sent across by Samson to be abbot of the Irish monastery (I.37–40). An ogam stone on Caldy Island reading *MAGL[ ] DUBR[* suggests some connection with Ireland, even if the interpretation 'servant of Dubricius' is uncertain.[8]

Next Samson, his predecessor as *pistor*, the Irish ex-abbot, and his father Amon, move to a *castellum* by the river (*flumen*) Severn, which the hagiographer himself has visited. Samson himself dwells apart in a cave, returning each Sunday to join the other three for mass (I.41–2).[9] A synod summons Samson and appoints him abbot of 'the monastery built by St Germanus', presumably Llantwit (I.42).[10] The bishops are accustomed to meet there annually to consecrate new bishops, and at one such

---

would be eighty, and if Samson himself lived to seventy that would enable him to attend the Council of Paris ca 561.

[5] For detailed arguments in favour of Llantwit see Wooding, 'The representation', 146–9.

[6] For monastic officers in the charters see Davies, *An Early Welsh Microcosm*, 127–8.

[7] Wooding, 'The representation', 147–53, who questions the idea that *insula* can merely mean 'monastery'. (For metaphorical comparisons between churches and islands, which are rather different, see above, 13 n. 42.) *Piro* seems to be a latinisation of Welsh *Pŷr*, which may derive from Gallo-Latin *Porius* or a British cognate. See Sims-Williams, *The Celtic Inscriptions of Britain*, 34, 71, and 283; Schrijver, *Language Contact*, 44. He also gave his name to Manorbier on the mainland (OW *Mainaur Pir*, *LL* pp. 124 and 255): Charles, *The Place-Names of Pembrokeshire*, II, 567 and 697–8.

[8] Edwards, *A Corpus* II, 296–8.

[9] *Flumen* rather than *mare* may suggest that it was on the river Severn rather than the Bristol Channel.

[10] See above for Germanus's supposed connection with Illtud; Germanus has not been mentioned otherwise. Wooding, 'The representation', 154 n. 124, questions the identification with Illtud's monastery. Flobert, *La vie ancienne de saint Samson*, 208 n. 2, anachronistically suggested Llandaf.

14. The episcopal framework

festival three bishops, including Dyfrig, consecrate Samson bishop, with the approval of all the *consiliarii* (I.43–4);[11] that Dyfrig arrives late may suggest that he was not based at Llantwit. The Welsh part of the story ends with Bishop Samson visiting his mother and aunt, consecrating the churches they have built, excommunicating his adulterous sister, and crossing the Bristol Channel (*Habrinum mare*) on his way to Cornwall and, ultimately, to Brittany (I.45).

The *Life* illustrates the international character of monasticism, and its perennial disputes about the ideal degree of asceticism. As well as administering the sacraments, bishops visit monasteries, have a considerable authority over them,[12] and attend synods in them which are attended by *consiliarii*. Aristocratic families found monasteries out of their own resources and, as in the rest of Europe, problems arise when their kinsmen are passed over for high office in what they regard as their inheritance.[13] The importance of the founder's family is underlined by the detail that the hagiographer has often heard Samson's parents' names read out at the saint's altar (I.1). 'The recital of the names of the dead in Gaul in the seventh century', to quote Edmund Bishop, was

> living, intimate, personal ... a prominent feature of the service on those days precisely when the Churches were full, Sundays, feast days ... [T]he 'nomina' prayers in the Gallican missals ... dwell continually on the names of the dead, friends or relatives known to all, 'our dear ones' as the Gallican formulae are never weary of calling them.[14]

The *Life* is frustratingly silent about much of Dyfrig's career, neither confirming nor contradicting his birth in Herefordshire and burial on Bardsey Island, as recounted in the *Vita Dubricii* in *LL*. Dyfrig appears only at Llantwit and Caldy Island – did he travel by sea, like Samson himself? The political geography is also unclear. Was Llantwit in the province of Dyfed rather than Gwent at this period? Was there a period when Gwent reached as far as Caldy?[15] It is impossible to know, and we cannot assume that Dyfrig was bishop of a diocese that corresponded to a secular unit, although the possibility of a sub-Roman diocese based on Carmarthen (*Moridunum*) or Caer-went (*Venta Silurum*) has been suggested.[16]

Most of the grants prefaced to Dyfrig's *Vita* in *LL* are in or near Ergyng, but they conclude with two particularly dubious ones concerning a western area closer to the one in which Dyfrig operates in the *Life* of Samson. Charter 77, which has a fabricated

---

[11] On this passage see Chadwick, 'The evidence of dedications', 173–5.
[12] Hughes, 'The Celtic Church', 4–5. The author, whose work was dedicated to a bishop, may exaggerate this.
[13] Ibid., 5. Cf. Sims-Williams, *Religion and Literature*, 115–43; Davies, *An Early Welsh Microcosm*, 119–30; Flechner, 'Identifying monks', 824.
[14] Bishop, *Liturgica Historica*, 100.
[15] Compare Glywysing, a kingdom carved out of Dyfed, according to the *Vita Cadoci*, and stretching from the Usk at least as far as the Tywi (*VSB* 24; *EWGT* 24; Bartrum, *A Welsh Classical Dictionary*, 288). Glywys's sons rule from Edeligion by the Usk to as far west as Cydweli by the Tywi (cf. Rees, *An Historical Atlas*, plate 22), and we cannot be sure that the unidentified *Crucmetil* was not still further west, although Knight, *South Wales*, 74 (cf. 96), suggests Cantref Bychan.
[16] J. R. Davies, *The Book of Llandaf*, 10. In 'The archbishopric', 296, he notes Caer-went as 'a good guess'. Cf. Knight, *South Wales*, 28.

witness list, purports to be by Nowy ab Arthur, king of Dyfed, and grants Dyfrig three churches associated with St Teilo: Penally, Llandeilo Fawr, and Llanddowror. Nowy was perhaps selected because the three places were in Dyfed and because he would seem to belong to about the same generation as Dyfrig, at least to those acquainted with Dyfrig's 612 obit in *Annales Cambriae* and *LL* itself.[17] Since Penally is on the mainland facing Caldy, it is conceivable that some tradition associated it with Dyfrig as well as Teilo. Such a tradition could have been invented in Llandaf itself, using the geography of the *Vita Samsonis* to boost its claim to these western churches.

The other westerly charter, 76b, is entitled *Porth Tulon* – a place in Gower (possibly Caswell Bay, near Bishopston) claimed by Llandaf and confirmed in the papal privileges.[18] A certain *Guorduc* gives Dyfrig the land along with his daughter, the eponymous *Dulon*, as a nun. (Compare Samson's parents' 'donations' when they send Samson to Illtud.) *Guorduc*'s grant is made in the reign of Merchwyn ap Glywys, probably the *Meirchyawn* named among the sons of Glywys in the Jesus College genealogies.[19] The charter is the only one in *LL* to involve the family of Glywys. Another peculiarity is its lay witness list, which includes some very early forms of Irish names: *Garu* (probably *Garb*), *Lugobi* (later *Luigbe*), and *Luuaet* (an Old Welsh spelling of *Lugaed*).[20] Such Irish names are explicable at a coastal location, and call to mind Caldy's Irish connections in the *Life* of Samson. They are unlikely to have been invented in Llandaf.

Porth Tulon is mentioned again in an early-tenth-century charter (239) by which King Gruffudd ab Owain (ap Hywel ap Rhys) grants properties even farther west on the Gower coast[21] to Bishop Llibio (*ob.* 929) in recompense for royal misdemeanours in Gower, including 'selling *Porth Dulon*, a church of St Dyfrig since the earliest times'. Curiously, the witnesses of this charter include *Mail-brigit sacerdos*, clearly the Irish name *Máelbrigte* 'servant of Brigit' in Welsh dress.[22] Bishop Llibio is elsewhere found in Brycheiniog, operating under the auspices of the bishop of St Davids (charter 237b), and arguably belongs to a different line of bishops from most others in *LL*.[23]

Both 76b and 239, with their unusual Glywysing and Irish personnel and their westerly location, seem to come from a different milieu from the rest of the *LL* charters. Whether they reflect an old tradition about Dyfrig in Gower is unknowable, but is not impossible.

Most other Dyfrig charters of Sequence i are focused on Ergyng,[24] which most modern scholars have regarded as Dyfrig's homeland, following the *Vita Dubricii*

---

[17] See above, 52, and 137. On 77's witness list see above, 33. For an alleged charter of Nowy at St Davids see above, 14. On Teilo's connection with the three places see Doble, *Lives*, 80, 166, 196–7, and 199–200.

[18] See Coe, 'The place-names', 713–14.

[19] See above, 145.

[20] See above, 145. Two of these Irish names predate syncope (conventionally *ca* 550), and syncope is irrelevant to the first.

[21] They seem to be near Paviland (see Coe, 'The place-names', 582–3, 689–90, and 804–5), which was confirmed to Llandaf in the papal privileges (J. R. Davies, *The Book of Llandaf*, 187–8).

[22] *Brigit* given in undeclined form in accordance with Welsh grammar. Cf. *LL* p. 276: *Lannsanbregit.*

[23] See above, 18, 68, and below, 172 and 178.

[24] For maps see Sims-Williams, *Religion and Literature*, 63, and Guy, 'The *Life* of St Dyfrig', 13.

14. The episcopal framework

in *LL*. No manuscript earlier than *LL* connects Dyfrig with Ergyng, however, or mentions his death on Bardsey Island (Enlli).[25] John Reuben Davies has suggested, on the one hand, that Dyfrig's cult was first brought to Ergyng in the second half of the eleventh century, noting the record in *LL* p. 275 that Bishop Herewald consecrated (or reconsecrated?) churches to Dyfrig and Teilo jointly at *Lann Guern* – probably Llanwarne – and at *Henllann*, possibly Hentland (SO542263) a little further south.[26] Ben Guy, on the other hand, is less sceptical, arguing that the *Vita Dubricii* in *LL* is based on a much older lost *vita*, possibly written at Moccas (*Mochros*), one that conceivably concerns a local Dyfrig, different from the Dubricius of the *Vita Samsonis*.[27] The controversy cannot easily be resolved, owing to the lack of relevant texts between the *Vita Samsonis* and *LL*.

As presented in *LL*, most Sequence i charters are grants either to St Dyfrig (those between 72a and 77, which precede the *Vita Dubricii*) or to St Dyfrig and St Teilo jointly (those between 160 and 165). In 164 Teilo is mentioned and then forgotten towards the end of the charter, suggesting that the addition of his name was editorial. An exceptional Sequence i charter, lacking both saints, is 163a, a grant by Peibio's sons *Deo et Elgisto episcopo*, but this does state that the land was formerly granted to Dyfrig. Its doublet, 73a, is a grant by Peibio to Dyfrig, with *Arguistil* as the first witness. This case suggests that the inclusion of Dyfrig, or at least his position in the charter, was to some extent editorial. In a minority of charters Dyfrig heads the clerical witness list (72a, 75, 76a, 76b, 77). If these attestations derive from ancient exemplars of these five charters, they may reflect an old convention like that already seen in the Llandeilo Fawr charters, where *Deus testis* heads a witness list ('Chad 3').[28] From the point of view of the *LL* compilers, however, Dyfrig attested all five in his earthly lifetime, and this is why they are attached to the *Vita Dubricii*, unlike charters placed later in the book, such as 162a which is granted *Deo et sancto Dubricio et suæ congregationi ... & in manu Vuelbiu episcopi* and has a witness list headed by *Vueluiu episcopus*. From our point of view, of course, the charters' earthly recipients are clearly the later bishops, wherever Dyfrig is mentioned in the charters. Compare *Deo et sancto Eliudo* in the above mentioned Llandeilo charter ('Chad 3').

Two Sequence i grants (121 and 122), both by Iddon of Gwent, are to St Teilo, without Dyfrig, and have *Teliaus archiepiscopus* at the head of their witness lists. The *LL* editors probably felt that Teilo was the more appropriate saint to receive grants well west of the river Monnow, especially as Llan-arth (121) and Llandeilo Bertholau (122) were explicitly Teilo churches.[29] Some other Teilo charters have

---

[25] Dyfrig's death on Bardsey is mentioned in the *Life* of Elgar as well as that of Dyfrig, both in *LL*. See Jankulak and Wooding, 'The Life of St Elgar'.

[26] J. R. Davies, 'The saints of south Wales', 373–5, followed by Petts, *The Early Medieval Church*, 73, 163, 167, and 177. On the place-names see Coe, 'The place-names', 361–2 and 425, also *DP* IV 546, and Copleston-Crow, *Herefordshire Place-Names*, 111–13, 151, and 179. *Henllann* (also *LL* p. 80) is problematical, Dixton (cf. charter 183a) and Llanfrother (SO542287) being alternative identifications (see Coe, 'The place-names', 361–3 and 460).

[27] Guy, 'The *Life* of St Dyfrig', esp. 35 n. 102. Dyfrig was not a unique name; cf. the cleric *Dubric* in charters 209b–210.

[28] See above, 11.

[29] Llan-arth is described in charter 123 as Teilo's *podum*. For map, see Hughes, 'The Celtic Church', 16, map 1.

similar characteristics, but have to be excluded from Sequence i as they lack convincing witness lists (123, 125a, 125b, 127a, 127b).[30]

If the sporadic inclusion of Dyfrig and Teilo in their witness lists is ignored, the charters of Sequence i – omitting the obviously forged charter 77 – can be seen to be in favour of six successive seventh-century bishops:[31] Arwystl, Aeddan, Ufelfyw, Inabwy, Cyfwyre, and Elhaearn. Where was their episcopal see, assuming they had one? The distribution of the grants points to Ergyng or nearby. Wendy Davies's plausible candidate is *Garth Benni* (probably Welsh Bicknor), which is called *episcopalis locus* in 72a and is associated there with King Peibio's cousin Inabwy (eponym of Llandinabo), who is also one of the clerical witnesses; *Garth Benni* was thus tied to the royal dynasty.[32] Ben Guy, however, suggests Moccas (*Mochros*), a place of importance in the *Vita Dubricii*.[33] It is possible that both hypotheses are correct: that the bishopric began in Moccas and moved south to Welsh Bicknor, perhaps in response to Anglo-Saxon pressure. Both places were monasteries – their abbots are named in the charters – but this in no way rules out their being bishops' houses simultaneously.[34]

The places granted to Bishop Arwystl by the kings of Gwent and Ergyng are Llangoed in Llys-wen in Cantref Selyf (166),[35] Llan-arth (121), Llandeilo Bertholau (122),[36] Welsh Bicknor (72a), Eaton Bishop (76a),[37] *Lann Cerniu* on the river Dore (72b),[38] Llandinabo (73a), and *Cum Barruc* in the Dore valley (73b/163a).[39] *Mafurn*, yet another place in the Dore valley, is the sole grant to a Bishop Aeddan (162b).[40]

Bishop Ufelfyw is the first clerical witness after Dyfrig in the grant of *Porth Tulon* in Gower discussed above (76b). More credibly, he receives the *podum* of Llancillo (160) – 'Cu [space] abbas' in the witness list is perhaps its abbot and the same person as the cleric *Cuelinus* in 76b, and another witness is a *Iohannes* 'cum clericis suis'. Ufelfyw also receives Bellamore, near Moccas, by charter 161, which is witnessed by a *lector*, the son of a *sacerdos*, and the son of an *equonimus* (the

---

[30] For map see Hughes, 'The Celtic Church', 16, map 1.

[31] For the date see above, ch. 6, for the order of the sequence see ch. 4, and for the episcopal status of the grantees see ch. 7. Elhaearn (75) is not specifically called *episcopus*.

[32] Davies, *A Early Welsh Microcosm*, 130, 134, 145, 150, 152, and 158. On *consobrino suo* see above, 145 n. 146. On the identification of *Garth Benni* see Coe, 'The place-names', 300–1.

[33] Guy, 'The *Life* of St Dyfrig'. That Llandaf used 'a cartulary of Mochros or some other Archenfield centre' was hypothesised by Jones, 'The Book of Llandaff', 136. See also James, quoted below, 177 n. 148.

[34] See below, 164–5.

[35] On the identification see Coe, 'The place-names', 518–19. Cf. Richards, *Welsh Administrative and Territorial Units*, 127, 147, and 251.

[36] 'Ubi Biuan cum quattuor sociis suis iacet' – perhaps the lay witness of this name in another of King Iddon's charters, 166 (differently *DP* IV 376). See above, 34 n. 14.

[37] On this identification rather than Madley see Coe, 'The place-names', 809–10.

[38] Not Dorstone specifically. See *ibid.*, 408–9. Abbey Dore remains a possibility according to Coplestone-Crow, *Herefordshire Place-Names*, 27.

[39] On *Cum Barruc* see Coe, 'The place-names', 200–1, and Coplestone-Crow, *Herefordshire Place-Names*, 85. The latter (pp. 51–2) identifies *Lann Iunabui* (73a) with Bredwardine, but Coe is sceptical (pp. 500–1).

[40] Coe, 'The place-names', 562–3. Perhaps Peterchurch according to Coplestone-Crow, *Herefordshire Place-Names*, 179–80.

14. The episcopal framework

person 'responsible for the economic needs' of a community),[41] and Garway (?), by charter 162a,[42] witnessed by a *summus sacerdos*, a *lector*, and a *sacerdos*.[43]

The next bishop, Inabwy, is presumably the above mentioned eponym of Llaninabo and cousin of the former king, Peibio. Perhaps he was abbot of Llandinabo before becoming bishop. He is granted the *poda* of Llancloudy (163b) and Ballingham (164).[44] The two charters' witness lists include abbots of Moccas, Bellamore, Garway, Much (or Little) Dewchurch,[45] Doward (at Ganarew or Whitchurch),[46] and Welsh Bicknor. The abbot of Doward (Ganarew/Whitchurch) in these charters is called *Bithen*, which is difficult to explain except as the Irish name, *Bithén*.[47] An Irish abbot is not out of place; on the Anglo-Saxon side of the border, before 675, there was an Abbot Colmán at Hanbury, near Worcester, and the eponymous Máeldub at Malmesbury.[48] And there were indigenous Irish in Brycheiniog, at Crickhowell, for instance.[49]

The abbot of Welsh Bicknor in 163b and 164 is accompanied by his *alumnus* Gwrwarwy, and a *magister* appears in 164. Thus the witness lists show us a Church in which the offices of bishop, abbot (*abbas/princeps*), *summus sacerdos*, *sacerdos*, *magister*, *lector*, and *equonimus* existed, and in which signatories could be accompanied by their own *clerici* and *alumni*.

Cyfwyre, the abbot of Moccas in Inabwy's two charters, has become bishop in charter 165. Other important changes in this charter are that Bithén, abbot of Doward (Ganarew/Whitchurch) in 163b–164, is now abbot of Lancaut in Gwent, and that Gwrwarwy, the *alumnus* of the abbot of Welsh Bicknor, is now [abbot of] *Lann Enniaun*, later known as *Lann Oudocui* (Llandogo) after St Euddogwy, subsequently recorded as a large estate 'of some 2,100 acres' on the Wye.[50] These two men's removal down the Wye (under Anglo-Saxon pressure?) suggests that the churches of Ergyng and Gwent were now closely allied, an alliance already anticipated by Iddon of Gwent's grants to Bishop Arwystl (charters 166 and 121–122 above). This Gwent connection is borne out by the content of charter 165. A king of Gwent, Athrwys ap Meurig,[51] grants Bishop Cyfwyre the church of Cynfarch near Chepstow

---

[41] Charles-Edwards, *Wales and the Britons*, 594.

[42] The identification of *Lann Guoruoe/Guorboe* with Garway is accepted by Coe, 'The place-names', 427–8 and 570–1, but remains controversial; the eponym may have given his name to more than one church in the area (cf. Charles, 'The Welsh, their language and place-names', 90; Hughes, 'The Celtic Church', 14 n. 52; Sims-Williams, *Religion and Literature*, 78 n. 92; and Coplestone-Crow, *Herefordshire Place-Names*, 21–3, 92, and 103–4).

[43] On *sacerdos* cf. above, 60 n. 7.

[44] On the latter identification see Coe, 'The place-names', 404. Coplestone-Crow, *Herefordshire Place-Names*, 40–1, argues for Carey in Ballingham.

[45] See Coe, 'The place-names', 415–16. Charles, 'The Welsh, their language and place-names', 90, suggests that the eponym of this and other Dewi churches in the vicinity may be not St David but the *Deui summus sacerdos filius Circan* of charter 162a – his father Circan was a *sacerdos* (161). Contrast Dickins, "Dewi Sant"'.

[46] Both near Great and Little Doward. See Coe, 'The place-names', 418; Coplestone-Crow, *Herefordshire Place-Names*, 102–3.

[47] See Sims-Williams, 'The emergence', 53 n. 5.

[48] Sims-Williams, *Religion and Literature*, 105–9.

[49] Redknap and Lewis, *A Corpus*, I, 72–3 (maps) and 159–62 (no. B2).

[50] Knight, 'Gwent churches', 37–8, and *South Wales*, 81. Attention is drawn to these moves by Coe, 'The place-names', 397 and 418, and Guy, 'The *Life* of St Dyfrig', 21.

[51] On whom see above, 146.

The Book of Llandaf as a Historical Source

(St Kynemark's [ST526942], later a house of Augustinian canons, like some other old *clasau*),[52] and also grants – or, rather reconfirms him in the possession of – the following Ergyng churches: Dewchurch, Llandinabo, Garway, and (in the Dore valley) *Mafurn, Lann Calcuch* (identical with *Cum Barruc*),[53] and *Lann Cerniu*. The valuable seventh- and eighth-century Christian metalwork from St Arvans[54] may be relevant here.

It is conceivable that the earliest Ergyng charters which ended up in the Llandaf archives came down the Wye to Gwent at this period. Such a hypothesis is slightly uneconomical, as it does not explain the transmission to *LL* of the later Ergyng charters of Sequences ii and iii. There may have been more than one Ergyng charter collection, however, and groups of Ergyng charters may have been acquired at various stages.

In 75, the final charter of Sequence i, Elhaearn, who was abbot of Garway in 163b and 165, is probably the charter's bishop, judging by the fact that his attestation follows that of St Dyfrig. The grant concerns *Cil hal*, apparently Pencoyd.[55] The grantor is given as Erb (Peibio's father), which is chronologically impossible,[56] but the title assigned to Erb – *rex Guenti & Ercic* – may be another indication of a close connection between Ergyng and Gwent. It has been suggested that Elhaearn may be identical with the St Aelhaearn of Cegidfa (Guilsfield) in Powys,[57] a saint associated with St Beuno. This is not impossible – Garway is only about eleven miles south-east of Llanveynoe, in Ewias, given to Beuno by Iddon of Gwent's father in the Welsh *Life of St Beuno* – but there is no reason to suppose that Elhaearn moved to Cegidfa, other than his name, which may not in fact be identical with Aelhaearn's, since *El-* was a distinct name element as well as a possible Latinate spelling of *Ael-*.

Most if not all of the places granted in the charters were evidently religious centres, as is indicated by references to abbots in Bellamore, Dewchurch, Doward (Ganarew/Whitchurch), Garway, Lancaut, Llandogo, Moccas, Welsh Bicknor, and Penally[58] and to a nun at *Porth Tulon*, and also probably by the element *Llan-* in some of the place-names, two of which are also described as *poda* (Llan-arth 123, Llancloudy 163b).[59] The presence of an abbot does not rule out the presence of a

---

[52] Coe, 'The place-names', 769–70; Butler, 'St. Kynemark's Priory', 35; Knight, *South Wales*, 80.
[53] Coe, 'The place-names', 405–6.
[54] Redknap, 'Crossing boundaries', 44–5; Knight, *South Wales*, 79–80.
[55] Coe, 'The place-names', 166–7; Coplestone-Crow, *Herefordshire Place-Names*, 178.
[56] See above, 147.
[57] Doble, *Lives*, 71–2; J. R. Davies, *The Book of Llandaf*, 83 n. 49. Cf. Sims-Williams, *Buchedd Beuno*, 37, 46–7, 52, 55, and 83–6, on this Aelhaearn, and 37 and 41–5, on the allusion to Llanveynoe (Llanfeuno) in §4.
[58] Penally has a *princeps* in charter 149.
[59] Petts suggests that *Llan-* names only began after 800 (*The Early Medieval Church*, 124), whereas J. R. Davies suggests that names of the type *Llan-* + saint's name 'had begun by the end of the seventh century' and that names of the type *Llan-* + topographical feature were older still ('The saints of south Wales', 393; cf. Knight, 'Gwent churches', 37). The mostly negative evidence advanced by Petts seems insufficient to invalidate the text of the charters. It is certainly likely, however, that *Lann* sometimes replaced terms such as *merthir* or Latin *podum* in transmission; for such replacement see Davies, *An Early Welsh Microcosm*, 36–8, 121–3, and 134–8, and Parsons, *Martyrs and Memorials*, 3 and 21–2. I am grateful to Dr O. J. Padel for discussing these problems with me.

14. The episcopal framework

bishop, as is shown by the case of Welsh Bicknor which has an *abbas* or *princeps* in 163b and 164 but is called *episcopalis locus* in 72a; compare Dyfrig's presence at monasteries in the *Life* of St Samson.[60]

The background of some of the bishops can be deduced from the witness lists, assuming that we have ordered Sequence i correctly.[61] Ufelfyw had been in second position to his predecessor but one, Arwystl. His successor, Bishop Inabwy, a *presbiter* (73a) related to King Peibio (72a), had been in second position to Ufelfyw, and was presumably the eponymous founder of Llandinabo. Inabwy's succesor, Bishop Cyfwyre, had been in second position to him, and had also been abbot of Moccas (163b, 164). His successor, [Bishop] Elhaearn had been in third position to Cyfwyre, and also abbot of Garway (163b, 165). Only Bishop Aeddan appears from nowhere. His Irish name, *Aedán*, could explain this. He was not necessarily Irish, however, since the name *Aedán* became naturalised in Wales.[62]

Accepting that the recipients of the Sequence i charters are indeed bishops,[63] what seems to be happening in the seventh century is that they are gradually gaining control over originally independent and often 'family' monasteries, just as happened across the border in Worcester diocese.[64] Such a development is consonant with Bishop Dyfrig's activities in the *Life* of St Samson. The charters cannot, unfortunately, reveal anything about any monasteries which remained outside the episcopal orbit. Nor are they concerned with the region around Llandaf!

The eighth-century Church

The Sequence ii charters are dominated by Bishops Euddogwy, Berthwyn, Tyrchan, and Cadwared, who succeed each other in an orderly fashion, each bishop having appeared in the witness lists of his predecessor's charters, often in a high position: Berthwyn is among the *clerici* in Euddogwy's charters (148, 150a, 156);[65] Tyrchan is among the *clerici* in two (dubious) charters of Euddogwy (157 and 148)[66] and in seven charters of Berthwyn (174b, 187, 175/186b, 189, 184, 188a, 185) – he is styled *lector* in 175; and Cadwared is among the *clerici* in six of Tyrchan's charters (204b, 202, 198a, 204a, 197, 200) – he is styled *presbiter* in 198a and 197.

Where were these four bishops based? Their credible grants are concentrated in Gwent and Morgannwg east of the Tywi – or more precisely east of the Neath valley – with some in Ergyng,[67] so it is reasonable to suppose that they were based in

---

[60] See parallels in Davies, *An Early Welsh Microcosm*, 150 n. 1.
[61] See above, Table 4.1.
[62] Sims-Williams, *Irish Influence*, 157 n. 136; *LL* p. 386 s.n. *Aidan*.
[63] See above, ch. 5.
[64] See Sims-Williams, *Religion and Literature*, passim, esp. 144–6, and 63 for a map showing Welsh and English monasteries.
[65] His and Tyrchan's presence in 148 is suspicious according to Davies, *The Llandaff Charters*, 84 n. 17 and 99.
[66] Both uncertain; see preceding note and Davies, *The Llandaff Charters*, 102. Charters 205 and 204b (ii.24 and 27), with Tyrchan already a bishop, probably belong later in Sequence ii than ii.24 and 27; see above, 33.
[67] See maps 2–4 in Hughes, 'The Celtic Church', 17–18. It is uncertain whether Berthwyn's charter (189) relating to *Machinis* refers to a place near Llanelli; see Coe, 'The place-names', 559–60, and J. R. Davies, *The Book of Llandaf*, 181. As befits one of the three

eastern Morgannwg and Gwent. The fact that so many of their grants are attested by abbots of Llantwit, Llancarfan, and Llandough, attesting *en bloc*, points in the same direction. Confirmatory traces of these block attestations occur in the Llancarfan charters, including three charters (*VC* 64, 65, 68) a little earlier than Sequence ii, one of which is actually attested by *Eudoce episcopus* as well as by the abbots of Llandough, Llancarfan, and Llantwit (*VC* 65).[68] Considering the geography, it is possible that Euddogwy and his three successors were based in the vicinity of these three houses, perhaps at Llandough, as suggested by Wendy Davies,[69] or at Llancarfan[70] – or even at Llandaf, despite the near universal scepticism of modern scholars. The Book of Llandaf portrays Euddogwy as acting on behalf of the three abbots, and even interceding to help Llantwit avoid an obligation to render a vessel of honey and an iron cauldron to the king,[71] and in one of Berthwyn's charters the abbots are called '*his* three abbots' (176b).

According to his *Vita* in the Book of Llandaf, Euddogwy retired to *Lann Enniaun* (now Llandogo < *Lann Oudocui*) on the river Wye, granted to him by an otherwise unknown eponymous *Enniaun* (Einion), king of Glywysing.[72] In reality, Llandogo may be where Euddogwy originated, for according to charter 156, from the middle of his episcopate, *Lann Enniaun* was 'restored' to Euddogwy by Morgan, king of Glywysing. We have already noted in charter 165, one of the last charters of Sequence i, that Bithén, the former abbot of Doward (Ganarew/Whitchurch) in Ergyng, has become abbot of Lancaut in Gwent, and that Gwrwarwy, the *alumnus* of

---

Llandaf saints (cf. Dyfrig and Teilo in Hughes, 'The Celtic Church', 16, map 1), and the doctrine of *Vita Oudocei* (*LL*, p. 133), Euddogwy is assigned some grants further afield – a suspicious distribution. Charters 140, 144, 145, and 154 are dubious 'restorations' to Euddogwy of places allegedly granted to Dyfrig and Teilo, and those in 144 are admitted to have been disputed by Llantwit. Charter 146 (Llan-gors) is agreed to be a forgery (see above, 49). The identification of 150b in Llanegwad, Carmarthenshire is uncertain; see Coe, 'The place-names', 812, and J. R. Davies, *The Book of Llandaf*, 175.

[68] On these charters see above, 40. For further confirmation that the attestation of abbots of other named monasteries might be included see *VC* 55, one of the latest Llancarfan charters.

[69] See above, 29, on her and Conway Davies's interpretations of *LL* 180b/*VC* 67 and *LL* 149 respectively. On the archaeological evidence at Llandough see Knight, 'From villa to monastery'.

[70] See below, 175, on charter 243.

[71] Charter 152. Cf. above, 105 n. 17.

[72] *LL* pp. 137–8; translated by Birch, *Memorials*, 93, and Doble, *Lives*, 220–2. Euddogwy may have been made to *retire* to Llandogo because that is where his body lay (though this is not stated). Doble's discussion of the *Vita* is more relevant for present purposes than that of Merdrignac, 'La "Vita Oudocei"'. Doble's attempt to distinguish Bishop Euddogwy and St Euddogwy of Llandogo is unconvincing. His argument that the appearance of a 'stone of Euddogwy' (*Lech Oudoucui*) in the bounds of 156 'shows that the eponym must have lived long before the time of Bishop Oudoceus' (p. 227) overlooks the fact that boundary clauses were regularly added later. Coe, 'Dating the boundary clauses', 37, places 156's in his Periods I ('up to *c*. 930') or III ('*c*. 990–*c*. 1010'). That *Lann Enniaun* was also known as *Lann Oudocui* (Llandogo) is stated both by a gloss in charter 156 and in the text of a tenth-century charter, attested by its abbot, which mentions a synod held there (222). As Doble notes (*Lives*, 222 and 229), there was a St Euddogwy's Well (*Fontem Sancti Eudaci*) in Dixton, further up the Wye. Dixton is probably the place granted to Berthwyn in charter 183a (Coe, 'The place-names', 460).

14. The episcopal framework

an abbot of Welsh Bicknor in Ergyng, has reappeared at *Lann Enniaun* (Llandogo). It may be that Euddogwy started his career at *Lann Enniaun* in this Lower Wye milieu with its Ergyng connections, and was subsequently able to exercise an episcopal role in southern Morgannwg as well as Gwent, owing to the patronage of Meurig ap Tewdrig and his family.[73]

The most notable feature of the episcopates of Euddogwy's successors[74] Berthwyn, Tyrchan, and Cadwared is that while they too receive grants in southern Morgannwg and Gwent, they also receive them further north, in Ergyng.[75] This development must surely be connected by the list in 'charter' 192 of the following Ergyng churches which Ithel ap Morgan restored to Berthwyn, following wars with Æthelbald, king of Mercia 716–57: *Cenubia Colcuch*, *Lann Cerniu*, and *Mafwrn* (all in the Dore valley), Garway (?), Llandinabo, Dewchurch, Moccas, *Lann Ebrdil* (Madley), Bellamore, Llancloudy, and Llangarron.[76] These gains, or recoveries, must have made it possible for bishops to (re)assert their authority over the Ergyng churches. The bishops in question are no longer based in Ergyng, but are further south, under the auspices of kings operating in Gwent and Morgannwg – the old Ergyng dynasty having disappeared – and it is now bishops like Berthwyn who are feasted by the nobles of Ergyng and hold synods and receive grants at *Garth Benni* (Welsh Bicknor), a likely see of the former Ergyng bishops.[77]

Although Sequence ii is dominated by Bishops Euddogwy, Berthwyn, Tyrchan, and Cadwared, we are reminded that other bishops were active in neighbouring areas by charter 167 (mid-eighth-century?), by which Tewdwr, king of Brycheiniog, grants Llanfihangel Tal-y-llyn in Brycheiniog to a Bishop Gwrfan (*Guruan*), who was based at Glasbury (Clas Cynidr ar Wy), in the north-east of his kingdom, assuming that *Gueman* in the list of Glasbury bishops is a mistake for *Gurman*, as suggested by John Reuben Davies. Glasbury would seem to be a rather recent see, as *Gueman* was only its third bishop, after *Brecchert* and the eponymous *Keneder*. The compilers of *LL* do not, of course, accept that the Gwrfan of charter 167 was other than a Llandaf bishop, though elsewhere, in charters 193 and 195, they demote him to the status of a hermit at Clodock in Ewias.[78] Quite likely, as the Herefordshire name Kenderchurch (*Lanncinitir*) suggests, the bishops of *Clas Cynidr*, no doubt supported by the kings of Brycheiniog, competed for influence in Ergyng with Euddogwy and his successors.[79] The latters' lack of influence in Brycheiniog is underlined by the fact

---

[73] For whom see above, 148–55.
[74] That Berthwyn succeeded Euddogwy, despite the order of charters in *LL*, is stated in 180b. See above, 27.
[75] See maps 3–4 in Hughes, 'The Celtic Church, 18.
[76] See above, 56, and 153, and map 3 in Hughes, 'The Celtic Church', 18. On the identifications see Davies, *The Llandaff Charters*, 113–14, and Coe, 'The place-names', passim. Madley is the preferred identification for *Lann Ebrdil* in view of its position in the list. Cf. Coe, 'The place-names', 419.
[77] Charters 176b, 178, and 184. On *Garth Benni* see above, 162, and below, 168.
[78] See above, 20 n. 22, and 66–70. See map 3 in Hughes, 'The Celtic Church', 18, but note that charter 167 should be six miles north-west, at Llanfihangel Tal-y-llyn, not at Llanfihangel Cwm Du (see above, 18 n. 10).
[79] Petts, *The Early Medieval Church*, 167, 170–1, 176, and 181, with map. Herewald consecrated *Lanncinitir* in the time of William the Conqueror (*LL*, p. 277). There was a hermitage of St Cynidr near Bredwardine (Coplestone-Crow, *Herefordshire Place-Names*, 52), and note also Llangynidr near Crickhowell.

that charter 146, granting Euddogwy the royal Brycheiniog monastery of Llan-gors, is so obviously fabricated.[80]

The ninth-century Church

The first half of the century lacks documentation for some reason. Normal service resumed in the second half with Wendy Davies's Sequence iii. Her first bishop is Greciel (iii.1–5), but he was possibly preceded by Bishops Gwyddloyw and Eddylfyw (charters 168 and 169a), whom she places at iii.14–15.[81]

Bishop Greciel (iii.1–5) has grants in Gwent and Ergyng, like Berthwyn, Tyrchan, and Cadwared, but not, unlike them, in Morgannwg.[82] Nudd, a prominent witness in Greciel's charters, where he is twice styled *lector* (169b, 170), clearly succeeds to his bishopric (iii.8ff) and likewise has grants confined, or almost confined, to Gwent and Ergyng.[83] When charter 225 (iii.12) was issued he was residing at Llan-arth, in northern Gwent.[84] Another Nudd charter of this period, 230b (iii.13), which presumably concerns an estate in Ergyng, affords a glimpse of monasteries there, being witnessed by the abbots of Dixton, Sellack, Foy, and *Garth Benni* (probably Welsh Bicknor).[85]

Since the witness lists of the charters of Bishop Cerennyr (iii.9–18 passim) overlap in time with those of Bishop Nudd, Wendy Davies argued that the two bishops were contemporaneous, the difference being that Cerennyr's activities ranged 'over the whole of the South East'.[86] The context for such a scenario is hard to detect. Both bishops are involved with the kings known from Asser – Hywel ap Rhys of Glywysing and Brochfael and Ffernfael of Gwent (and their father Meurig) – and in fact Nudd, despite his Gwent and Ergyng connection, is more especially associated with the Glywysing ruler. Again, Nudd and Cerennyr both have charters attested by Elisedd, abbot of Llantwit in Glywysing.[87] Charles-Edwards agrees with Davies that Nudd and Cerennyr may have been active at the same time, but notes that 'the degree of overlap in [their] households would then indicate that these two bishops

---

[80] See above, 49, 57, 68, and 150.
[81] Davies, *The Llandaff Charters*, 61 (also 71, where she doubts that they really were bishops). See, however, below, 170.
[82] See map 5 in Hughes, 'The Celtic Church, 19. Note that Greciel and Cerennyr are also associated with Cemais in Gwent in charter 183b, a charter which makes it clear that Greciel came long after Berthwyn, despite the final order of bishops in *LL* (see Jones, 'The Book of Llandaff', 136–7).
[83] This is not certain, for Davies, *The Llandaff Charters*, 121, tentatively places *Villa Eliau* (227a) at Splott in Cardiff (cf. map 6 in Hughes, 'The Celtic Church', 19), equating it with *Tref Eliau* (for which see Richards, *Welsh Administrative and Territorial Units*, 207, and Coe, 'The place-names', 822), although Coe, p. 870, thinks somewhere in Gwent more likely on account of 'the associations of its witnesses (predominantly charters 74/171b, 227b, 228, 229b, 230a, and 230b), which are very strongly with places in Gwent' (230b may rather be Ergyng, *ibid.*, 863, and below).
[84] *Ibid.*, 484; cf. charters 121 and 123.
[85] *Ibid.*, 863.
[86] Davies, *The Llandaff Charters*, 71, and *An Early Welsh Microcosm*, 154. See map 5 in Hughes, 'The Celtic Church', 19. Cf. Charles-Edwards, *Wales and the Britons*, 596.
[87] Charters 212, 214, 228, 229b, and 230a (possibly interpolated in 214, cf. Davies, *The Llandaff Charters*, 119, and Charles-Edwards, *Wales and the Britons*, 596 n. 82).

operated out of the same church'.[88] Another way of interpreting the evidence, bearing in mind that the name Nudd was not uncommon, is to suppose that there were *three successive* bishops:

(1) Nudd I (Greciel's former *lector*) in iii.8 and 11–13 (under Hywel ap Rhys and Meurig of Gwent).
(2) Cerennyr in iii.9–10 and 16–18 (under Hywel ap Rhys, Meurig of Gwent, and Brochfael ap Meurig). There is no inherent difficulty in moving Cerennyr's charters 212 and 214 (iii.9–10), to just before iii.16–18.[89]
(3) Nudd II in iii.19–23 (under Hywel ap Rhys).

Nudd II would then be identical with the cleric Nudd, of unspecified status, who attests Cerennyr's last charters (iii.10 and 16–18) either in second position (214,[90] 199bii and 216b) or in third position (216a). That the see should have two bishops of the same name is not unlikely; compare Anglo-Saxon Crediton with three bishops Ælfwold, Dorchester with two bishops Eadnoth, Elmham with two Theodreds and three Ælfrics, Ramsbury with two Ælfrics, Rochester with two Godwines, Selsey with two Æthelrics, Sherborne with three Wulfsiges, two Ælfwolds, two Brihtwines, and two Æthelsiges, Winchester with two Ælfheahs, two Ælfsiges, and two Æthelwolds, Worcester with two Wulfstans, and York with two Wilfrids, two Eanbalds, and two Wulfstans.[91]

There seems to be no way of identifying either Nudd I or Nudd II with Iolo Morganwg's alleged 'Nudh', abbot of Llantwit;[92] they seem to have risen through the ranks.

If Nudd II was formerly subordinate to Cerennyr, as his *lector* or similar rather than his suffragan bishop, who is the *Nouis* whose attestation intervenes between *Cerenhir episcopus* and *Nud* in 216a? Charles-Edwards has made the interesting suggestion that he is the *Nobis episcopus*, assigned no charters, but listed after charter 216b as the nineteenth bishop (*sc.* 'of Llandaf').[93] If so, the correct order may be: (1) Nudd I; (2) Cerennyr; (3) Nobis; (4) Nudd II. Another possibility is that he is none other than Asser's kinsman *Nobis archiepiscopus*, whom Hyfaidd, king of Dyfed, expelled from St Davids;[94] in that case the Llandaf compilers may have misunderstood a record of his temporary sojourn in the episcopal *familia* as a

---

[88] *Wales and the Britons*, 596 (with a parallel at Kildare).
[89] Above, 33.
[90] Assuming the three abbots in 214 are interpolated; see above, 33. Davies, *The Llandaff Charters*, 71, suggests that the cleric Nudd in these four charters is Bishop Nudd, 'with Cerennyr taking precedence', comparing charter 237b, with 'bishop *Lunberth* of St. David's following bishop *Libiau*'. If the cases were exactly comparable, both Cerennyr and Nudd would attest as *episcopi*.
[91] Fryde et al., *Handbook of British Chronology*, 215–16 and 220–4.
[92] See above, 61.
[93] *Wales and the Britons*, 596 n. 82 (seeing him as a 'local bishop'). The name *Nobis/Nouis* seems not uncommon, so he cannot be securely identified elsewhere (cf. Davies, *An Early Welsh Microcosm*, 153, and above, 140 n. 119). The one who died in 873 ('Nobis et Mouric moriuntur') is too early. I have not attempted to modernise the name to *Nyfys*, *Nofis*, or *Nofys*, etc.
[94] *Asser's Life of King Alfred*, §79 (ed. Stevenson, 66). Nobis became bishop of St Davids in 840 (*Annales Cambriae*). If Asser's Nobis witnessed Cerennyr's charter, he cannot be the Nobis of unspecified status who died in 873 (*Annales Cambriae*: 'Nobis et Mouric

record of his episcopate. Yet another possibility is that the *Nouis* of charter 216a is *Nobis, episcopus Teiliav*, who witnesses 'Chad' 3–5 in the 'late ninth century';[95] the Llandeilo Fawr bishop might conceivably have an interest in Llangua, the subject of charter 216a, since it lay on his side of the river Monnow, albeit 75km east of Llandeilo (see below).

Bishops Gwyddloyw and Eddylfyw, two bishops with one charter each, 168 and 169a, placed at iii.14–15 by Wendy Davies, are difficult to fit in chronologically – and also geographically, as the estates mentioned cannot be identified. The former charter is granted, and both are witnessed, by a layman called *Cuchein* son of *Gloiu*. *Cuchein*'s father *Gloiu* may be the layman of this name who attests grants to Greciel in Ergyng and Gwent (74/171b and 173), and possibly his son is the *Cuchein* later found witnessing Bishop Cyfeilliog's charter concerning Matharn in Gwent (235a). Gwyddloyw's charter (168) is witnessed by a layman Abraham, who may be the Abraham who grants Nudd II *villa Branuc* in Ergyng by charter 230b, a charter with which it shares a clerical witness *Conan*, who appears in grants to Greciel in Ergyng (iii.1–4) and to Cerennyr at nearby Llangua (iii.18 = 216a). 168 also shares a clerical witness, *Iudguoret*, with a grant to Nudd I at Caerleon (225), and another, *Dofran*, may be the *Dibran* who attests a grant to Cerennyr at Saint-y-nyll, four miles west of Llandaf (216b). The general orientation of these connections suggests that Bishop Gwyddloyw may have been based in an area within reach of Ergyng and Gwent, perhaps in Ewias – a region with no Nudd or Cerennyr grants – or in Brycheiniog.

Bishop Eddylfyw may have been Gwyddloyw's predecessor or successor. His only grant (169a) is also witnessed by *Cuchein*. The grantors are Gwrgan and Bonus. Bonus appears in Bishop Greciel's Ergyng charters (170, 169b, 171a), and Bonus and the *sons of* Gwrgan are the grantors of the third of these (171a), an *ager* on the river Monnow.[96] Gwrgan would seem, then, to have died *before* the time of Greciel's charters, two more of which are attested by Gwrgan's sons (170 and 169b). The charter of Bishop Cerennyr that concerns the above mentioned Llangua, facing Ergyng across the Monnow, was granted to him by Cynfyn son of Gwrgan (216a). This is the charter in which the attestation of *Nouis* occurs between *Cerenhir episcopus* and *Nud*.

A possible interpretation of the above is that Bishops Gwyddloyw and Eddylfyw were active when Gwrgan was still alive, *before* and perhaps during the episcopate of Greciel, and that their see was at Llangua, a church with sanctuary rights according to charter 216a and later the site of a priory.[97] Their independent episcopate could have come to an end when Gwrgan's son Cynfyn granted Llangua to Bishop Cerennyr. Possibly the unexpected emergence of Bishop *Nobis/Nouis* in the 'Llandaf' succession is connected with his (non-episcopal) attestation of the Llangua charter:

---

moriuntur'), some twenty years before Hyfaidd's death. See further below, 171, on Asser's possible attestation of charter 236 (iii.24).

[95] Date from Jenkins and Owen, 'The Welsh marginalia', 56. The idea that the 'Chad' Nobis was from St Davids (so still Jenkins, 'From Wales to Weltenburg?', 78) was rejected by Charles-Edwards, 'The seven bishop-houses', 257 n. 4. See also J. R. Davies, 'The archbishopric', 299 and 302.

[96] On 171a and 169a see Charles-Edwards, *Wales and the Britons*, 285–6. On J. W. James's ideas about Bonus see above, 155 n. 214.

[97] On Llangua (Llangiwa), already mentioned above, see Lewis, 'A possible provenance', 10–13. The fact that its name is misspelt in *LL* (*ibid.*, 10) may show that Llandaf had lost interest in this distant property, which does not figure in its appeals to the Pope.

14. The episcopal framework

he may have been designated as Cerennyr's successor as part of a deal to merge the two bishoprics.

The fact that the nine *clerici* attesting charter 168 with Gwyddloyw do not reappear in the *familiae* of the later bishops, with the possible exceptions of *Conan*, *Iudguoret*, and *Dofran*, suggests that he ran an independent house. One of his *clerici*, *Guingual*, along with 'his progeny to serve the church ... in perpetuity',[98] is included in *Cuchein*'s grant to Gwyddloyw.

The Book of Llandaf does not trouble to name Eddylfyw's *familia*, simply saying 'Hedilbiu episcopus, cum clericis suis' (169a). It is also vague about the estates granted in the two charters: *Cuchein* grants Bishop Gwyddloyw *uilla uallis*/*Villa hir pant* 'the township of the valley' (168)[99] and, from Gwrgan, Bishop Eddylfyw receives 'part of an *ager* across the road' with 'another *ager* from his *uncia*' from Bonus (169a).[100] The charters may have been absorbed along with their estates, perhaps from Llangua, and escaped later emendation, owing to their uselessness.

Cyfeilliog is the final ninth-century bishop (iii.24–32), and his episcopate lasted into the tenth century. This is true even if we disregard his 927 obit in the lists of consecrations and obits in the Book of Llandaf and related texts,[101] for a secure floruit of 914 is provided by the *Anglo-Saxon Chronicle*'s reference to King Edward paying a ransom of forty pounds following the Vikings' capture of *Cameleac ... biscop on Ircinga felda* ('bishop of/in Archenfield/Ergyng').[102] The Anglo-Saxon king's intervention gives some credence to the consecration lists' claim that Cyfeilliog was consecrated by Æthelred, archbishop of Canterbury 870–89 – no doubt during the period of King Alfred's alliances with the southern Welsh.[103] Cyfeilliog was already active in the late 880s since what is probably his earliest charter (236 = iii.24) is a grant to him – of two serfs and all their progeny – from Alfred's ally, Hywel ap Rhys (*ob*. 886).[104]

Although Cyfeilliog does not appear in any charters before becoming bishop – which leaves open the possibility that he really is the *Camelauc* listed among the abbots of Llantwit, dubious though the source is[105] – he seems to have inherited most of his *familia* from his predecessors to judge by the names *Iudnerth*, *Tuted*/*Tuthed*/*Tuteth*/*Tuteh*, and *Bleinguid* in high position in his earliest clerical witness lists; subsequently these familiar names are replaced by new ones such as *Catgen filius Bleinguid* (presumably following in his father's footsteps), *Aceru*, and *Guinda*. One surprise in the Hywel ap Rhys charter (236), is the name *Asser*, immediately after *Ciuelliauc episcopus* and preceding *Tuthed*, *Bleinguid*, and *Iudnerth*. This intruder

---

[98] The name of Llandaf is, of course, interpolated. Cf. Charles-Edwards, *Wales and the Britons*, 308, where *Guingual* is mistakenly assigned to the lay list.

[99] While *hir* may mean 'long' (Charles-Edwards, *Wales and the Britons*, 285), it is more probably the definite article (Coe, 'The place-names', 878).

[100] See Charles-Edwards, *Wales and the Britons*, 285–6.

[101] See above, 23.

[102] See above, 23–5, and 65.

[103] On which see above, 119–20.

[104] This is Hywel's last charter. 237a (iii.25) is granted by a King Arthfael, probably the one listed among Hywel's sons and daughters in 236. In 236 *et filiorum* is probably a mistake for *et filiarum* (Birch, *Memorials*, 198, and Bartrum, *Welsh Genealogies*, I, chart [43]). Note that one of the daughters has an English name, *Erminthridh*, a symptom of the Anglo-Saxon connection.

[105] See above, 61–6.

could well be the famous Asser.[106] Asser tells us in his Chapter 79 that King Hyfaidd sometimes expelled him from St Davids, like his kinsman Bishop Nobis, and that he spent a whole year sick in Caer-went, apparently in 885–6.[107] Perhaps, then, Asser was temporarily attached to Bishop Cyfeilliog when the latter received the grant from Hywel ap Rhys (*ob*. 886) and was accorded the honour of attesting in first place after the bishop, just as *Nouis* – perhaps Asser's kinsman Nobis – was accorded a high place in Bishop Cerennyr's Llangua charter (216a), discussed above.

Cyfeilliog may well have been based at Caer-went, for all his securely locatable grants are nearby,[108] and most of them are from Brochfael ap Meurig, whom Asser styles king of Gwent. Presumably he was active in Ergyng as well, unless the *Anglo-Saxon Chronicle*'s 914 entry uses 'bishop of Archenfield' in a very vague way or merely means that he happened to be 'in Archenfield' when captured. A further indication that he was active near the English border may be the cipher reading *Cemelliauc prudens prespiter* ... in the Cambridge Juvencus, a manuscript that passed to England in the tenth century and was in Worcester in the eleventh.[109] Cyfeilliog's indebtedness to King Edward could explain the passage of this useful schoolbook.

The tenth-century Church

The consecration lists have Cyfeilliog dying in 927 – rather late for someone consecrated by Archbishop Æthelred in 870×89 – and his successor Llibio dying in 929 after an episcopate of only three years, despite allegedly having also been consecrated by Æthelred.[110] Leaving aside this impossibly early consecration, a floruit in the 920s fits Llibio well, for one of his two grants (239) is from Hywel ap Rhys's grandson, Gruffudd ab Owain (*ca* 928–35), and the other (237b) is from Tewdwr ab Elise of Brycheiniog (*fl*. 934).[111] The former grants Llibio estates in Gower and the latter grants him Llanfihangel Tal-y-llyn in Brycheiniog, the church already granted in the eighth century to Bishop Gwrfan, who may have been based at Glasbury (see above). Llibio may have been his successor in some sense, though not at Glasbury

---

[106] As Egerton Phillimore suggested *apud* Stevenson, *Asser's Life of King Alfred*, lxx. (Stevenson's alternative, the *Asser* of charter 223, is chronologically impossible, as noted by Keynes and Lapidge, *Alfred the Great*, 219 n. 81.) It must be admitted that the *Asser* of charter 236 could be an Old Testament equivalent ('Blessed', cf. Keynes and Lapidge, 49) of the *Guinda* ('Blessed and good') of charters 234, 235a, 235b, 237a, or an error for the *Aceru* (cf. Welsh *agerw* 'fierce') of charters 234 and 235b.

[107] On the chronology see Keynes and Lapidge, *Alfred the Great*, 213 n. 24.

[108] See Hughes, 'The Celtic Church', 19, map 6, and Knight, 'Gwent churches', 39. The placing of 231 at Monmouth is doubted by Coe, 'The place-names', 435–6, and J. R. Davies, *The Book of Llandaf*, 187. Coe, 'The place-names', 118–19, suggests, however, that 237a may refer to a site near Llandaf. For references to Caer-went as a religious centre see Davies, *An Early Welsh Microcosm*, 136, and Sims-Williams, *Buchedd Beuno*, 41–5. J. R. Davies has suggested that it was the site of a sub-Roman bishopric (see above, 159 n. 16). For its archaeology see Edwards, 'Early medieval Wales', 74–5.

[109] McKee, *The Cambridge Juvencus Manuscript*, 27–9 and 34–8.

[110] See above, 23–5.

[111] Gruffudd's father Owain ap Hywel was still king of Gwent in 927 (*Anglo-Saxon Chronicle*) and Gruffudd himself died in 935 (or 934). Cf. Lloyd, *A History*, I, 338 n. 66, who deduces that Gruffudd was king of Gower from *LL* itself. On which Gruffudd is meant see further above, 69 n. 61.

14. The episcopal framework

since he is absent from the Glasbury episcopal list. Possibly he was based between Llanfihangel Tal-y-llyn and Gower, at somewhere like Llandeilo Fawr.[112] It may be significant for such a westerly orientation that Bishop Llunferth of St Davids (*ob*. 944) appears along with him in the Llanfihangel Tal-y-llyn charter, together with an *Eneuris presbiter* who must be Llunferth's successor (*ob*. 946) as bishop of St Davids.[113] Certainly the Llandaf compilers seem to have been uncomfortable with the status of both Gwrfan and Llibio, at one point turning them into two hermits from the cantref of Penychen (around Llandaf), settled at Clodock. This suggests that they were not counted in the regular succession that stretched back to Euddogwy and Berthwyn.[114]

It may be a coincidence, however, that Bishop Llibio's only two charters happen to concern estates more distant from Llandaf than is the norm in Sequence iii. Their witness lists include enough names to enable them to be fitted into Sequence iii as charters iii.33–34.[115] While several of the clerics in Llibio's own entourage do not appear outside the two charters, one finds the priest *Diuin*, the *scriptor Dissaith*, and the clerics *Enim filius Catgen, Marchi filius Catgen*, and *Reuelgur* recurring in the charters of Bishops Wulffrith (*Gulbrit*) and Pater (iii.35–40). *Elstan* (Æthelstan?), one of the lay witnesses of Tewdwr's charter to Llibio (237b), reappears in a charter of Cadwgon ab Owain to Bishop Wulffrith (224 = iii.35), *Branud*, one of the lay witnesses of Llibio's other charter (239), who has already appeared in charters to Bishop Cyfeilliog (iii.25–27), and another lay witness, *Marchi*, reappear in Cadwgon's charter to Bishop Wulffrith (iii.35 = 224), while *Branud*'s son, *Cinuelin* occurs in another of Wulffrith's charters (iii.36 = 222). Thus the witness lists of Llibio's charters show some contact with other *LL* charters, though the lay lists especially are fairly isolated, presumably for geographical reasons. Possibly, then, Llibio did belong to the main line of bishops after all. The similarity between his Llanfihangel Tal-y-llyn charter and that of the more extraneous Bishop Gwrfan[116] could be due to Llibio acquiring Gwrfan's charter along with the church and being influenced by its wording.

The next bishop is Wulffrith (*Gulbrit*), with three grants of places in Morgannwg and Gwent (224, 223, and 222 = iii.35–37) from Hywel ap Rhys's grandsons Cadwgon ab Owain (*ob*. 950) and Cadell ab Arthfael (*ob*. 942).[117] Charter 222 is the record of a synod held at Llandogo following a disturbance at Whitebrook,[118] two miles up the Wye from Llandogo; the abbot of *Lann Enniaun, id est Lann Oudocei* is among the witnesses. Another disturbance in the same area is mentioned in the third of the three charters of Pater, the next bishop (221, 218, 217 = iii.38–40). All three are grants

---

[112] But J. R. Davies, 'The archbishopric', 302 and n. 51, suggests that Llibio is interpolated either in 237b or 239, also that 237b may really be a grant to Llunferth.
[113] Noted by J. R. Davies, 'The archbishopric', 299.
[114] See above, 66–70.
[115] Cf. Charles-Edwards, *Wales and the Britons*, 594–6, who sees a 'succession to a single bishopric ... that ... covered all the south-east' (595).
[116] See above, 67–9.
[117] Hughes, 'The Celtic Church', 9 and 20, map 7. A location at ST104779 near St Bride's-super-Ely is suggested for 224 by Coe, 'The place-names', 855 and 883. Cadwgon was the brother of Llibio's benefactor Gruffudd ab Owain. See Bartrum, *Welsh Genealogies*, I, chart [43]. The bishop's English name *Gulbrit* (Wulffrith), noted by Keynes, 'Welsh Kings', 112, is no doubt due to the fashion for English names at the period.
[118] Coe, 'The place-names', 75.

from Nowy ap Gwriad, an 'intrusive' king in Gwent, *ca* 955.[119] In the third of them Nowy makes amends for despoiling *Arcoit* son of *Dissaith* in the episcopal *podum* of *Mainuon* in *Trilec*; this *podum* was in the area of Trelleck Grange, two miles southwest of Llandogo, and had been granted to bishops Tyrchan and Cerennyr by kings of earlier dynasties (Ffernfael ab Ithel and Meurig ab Arthfael).[120] Charles-Edwards identifies the father, *Dissaith*, with the *scriptor* and *lector* of this name who witnesses this and many other charters of Llibio, Wulffrith, Pater, and Gwgon, quotes Wendy Davies's suggestion that Llandogo 'was the see of these tenth-century bishops' – presumably its roots could go back to Euddogwy, eponym of Llandogo – and himself suggests that their bishopric possibly 'covered all the south-east'.[121]

By the time of Pater (*fl.* 955) and his successor Gwgon (963×72–982),[122] the bishopric seems to have shrunk to Gwent between the Usk and the Wye,[123] perhaps because the powerful and long-lived king Morgan Hen ab Owain (*ob.* 974) preferred to favour religious houses in Morgannwg such as Llantwit, where his grandfather Hywel ap Rhys had erected a cross to commemorate Morgan's great-grandfather, Rhys – Llantwit was evidently important to the dynasty.[124] Perhaps Morgan was also hostile to a line of bishops in Gwent that turned to Canterbury for consecration. Pater's three grants are all from the 'intrusive' Nowy ap Gwriad, whose father may have attended Athelstan's court,[125] and two of Gwgon's three grants (iii.41–43) are from Nowy's son Arthfael (243 and 244). Morgan makes no grants, but is alleged to have *restored* nine churches east of the Usk to Bishop Gwgon at the behest of King Edgar and Archbishop Dunstan.[126] Morgan's son, King Idwallon, does guarantee a

---

[119] See Davies, *An Early Welsh Microcosm*, 84 and 95–6. Charter 218 bears the date 955. Perhaps Nowy's father Gwriad is the *Wurgeat* who attends Athelstan's charters in 928–32. Cf. Keynes, 'Welsh kings', 88–90; Charles-Edwards, 'Dynastic succession', 76.

[120] *LL* 199bi–ii; Coe, 'The place-names', 433.

[121] Charles-Edwards, *Wales and the Britons*, 594–5. Cf. Davies, *An Early Welsh Microcosm*, 154–5. As an alternative to Llandogo, Davies suggests St Maughan's, on which see Knight, 'Gwent churches', 36. For *Dissaith*'s attestations see Davies, *The Llandaff Charters*, 64–6 and 160. The cleric *Catgen filius Dissaith* in 244 may be his son.

[122] Keynes, 'Welsh Kings', 112, notes that the witnesses to his consecration belong in the 960s.

[123] For Pater see J. R. Davies, *The Book of Llandaf*, 185, and Hughes, 'The Celtic Church', 20, map 7 (Pater; charter 221 is omitted as the location is uncertain, cf. Coe, 'The place-names', 122). Gwgon receives two estates near Earlswood (charter 244, see Coe, 'The place-names', 440–1 and 884, and Knight, 'Gwent churches', 42) and the grantor of charter 243 is elsewhere associated with land beside Caer-went (see charter 262, on which see Maund, *Ireland, Wales, and England*, 195, and Coe, 'The place-names', 865). *Villa Seuan* (245) is unidentified: see *ibid.*, 844.

[124] Redknap and Lewis, *A Corpus*, I, 369–73, no. G63. A bishop Ffili may have operated near Ogmore; see *ibid.*, 496, no. G117, and above, 18. It appears from the *Life* of St Samson that Llantwit was the site of annual episcopal synods; see above, 158. Charles-Edwards, *Wales and the Britons*, 595, emphasises the surprising absence from *LL* of charters from Morgan ab Owain, and in 'Dynastic succession', 76, he suggests that 'to some extent, at least, sub-kingdoms each had their own bishop'. Woolf, Review, 161–2, objects to 'a plethora of local bishops'.

[125] See above, n. 119.

[126] 'Charter' 240 (without witness list). For the places see J. R. Davies, *The Book of Llandaf*, 188, and map 7 in Hughes, 'The Celtic Church', 20.

14. The episcopal framework

grant to Gwgon of an unidentified *Villa Seuan* (245), but this was presumably after Morgan's death, when relations may have improved.

According to a peculiar first-person charter in the convoluted style of contemporary Anglo-Saxon charters, witnessed by Bishop Gwgon and the *lector* of Caer-went, Arthfael ap Nowy consented to a grant by one Meirchion ap Rhydderch, who is elsewhere associated with land beside Caer-went.[127] It seems to describe Gwgon as both bishop and 'abbot of Llancarfan by hereditary right'.[128] This may indicate that Gwgon and his episcopal line, though now confined to Gwent, retained aspirations in the heart of Morgannwg.

The Book of Llandaf (*LL* pp. 246 and 252) and the consecration lists plausibly put Gwgon's death in 982, and, impossibly, have Bleddri consecrated by Archbishop Ælfric (995–1005) in 983, evidently regarding Bleddri as in some sense Gwgon's successor, as indeed he is so far as extant charters go.[129] Following Gwgon's obit, however, *LL* has a note that one Marchlwydd was bishop of Llandaf in the time of Morgan Hen's sons, Owain, Idwallon, Cadell, and Cynfyn,[130] and then leaves the rest of the column blank, evidently having no available charters for Marchlwydd. A possible explanation is that the Gwgon and Bleddri charters emanate from their see in Gwent (Llandogo?), whereas Marchlwydd was bishop somewhere in Morgannwg – perhaps already at Llandaf – at a see whose archive did not survive. It is equally possible, however, that he succeeded Pater and Gwgon in Gwent and had even fewer charters than they and his successor Bleddri did.

The eleventh-century Church

The three grants to Bishop Bleddri (*ca* 1000–22) are again restricted to Gwent between the Usk and the Wye.[131] His origins are unknown, owing the lack of late tenth-century charters, no doubt. There is no good reason to identify him with Iolo Morganwg's Abbot Bleddri of Llantwit.[132] A few witnesses in his charters are carried over from Gwgon's charters – understandably few since twenty years has elapsed – and a few continue from Bleddri's charters to those of Bishop Joseph (1022–45).[133] In

---

[127] Charter 243; cf. charter 262, above, n. 123.

[128] On charter 243 see *EA* II 512–13; Davies, *The Llandaff Charters*, 125, and *An Early Welsh Microcosm*, 156; Charles-Edwards, *Wales and the Britons*, 256 and 595; and Keynes, 'Welsh kings', 112. The Caer-went *lector* may be responsible for its unique Anglo-Saxon formulae. The extant text has, of course, been altered in favour of Llandaf, but the odd reference to Llancarfan is presumably original.

[129] Cf. above, 24 n. 11.

[130] *LL* p. 246: 'Marchluid episcopus Landauiæ. tempore filiorum Morcant. Ouein. Idguallaun. Catell. Cinmin.'

[131] Hughes, 'The Celtic Church', 20, map 8 (charters 251, 249b, 246 = iii.44–46). Coe, 'The place-names', 879, does not accept that 249b refers to Undy, but agrees that it must be in Gwent. On Bleddri's charters cf. Maund, *Ireland, Wales, and England*, 184–7.

[132] See above, 61.

[133] The best examples are lay: *Merchiaun et filius eius Gurcant* in 243 and 262 and *Gurcant filius Merchiaun* in 246; and *Gurcinnif . Gurci* (*sic*) in 251 and *Gurcinnif filius Gurci* in 262. Cf. Davies, *The Llandaff Charters*, 66–7 and 85 n. 26, and Maund, *Ireland, Wales, and England*, 184–7. The latter's equation of *Gurci* and *Gurhi* is unlikely. On Joseph's dates see above, 24 n. 11.

the latter category it is significant that the clerical witness list of charter 246 begins: *Bledri episcopus. Ioseb presbiter et decanus Landauiæ*. While 'dean of Llandaf' may be due to 'Hand B' (the 'editor' of the Book of Llandaf, who copied charter 246),[134] it is credible that Joseph had been a priest under Bleddri until his consecration in 1022. While four of his grants are in the same area as Bleddri's, he has more in the area of Llandaf and between the rivers Taf and Thaw. These, taken together with the *EPISCOPI IOSEPH* inscription at Llandaf, give credence to the idea that Joseph transferred (or brought back?) the see to Llandaf, which was perhaps already dedicated to St Teilo, for all we know to the contrary.[135]

Joseph's grants around Llandaf itself must be due especially to his managing to get on good terms with Morgan Hen's grandson, Hywel ab Owain (*ob*. 1043), and with the latter's son, Meurig ap Hywel, and grandson, Cadwgon ap Meurig.[136] Joseph's successor, Herewald, bishop of Glamorgan 1056–1104, continued the same policy, receiving territory adjacent to Llandaf (*Henriu Gunua*) from Cadwgon (267), as well as more distant grants from Cadwgon's cousin Iestyn ap Gwrgan (271), from the 'intrusive' dynast Caradog ap Gruffudd (272), and from Gruffudd ap Llywelyn, 'king of Wales' (269), and Roger fitzWilliam fitzOsbern, count of Hereford and lord of Gwent (274).[137] According to the circumstantial tract in *LL*, Herewald was able to control a large diocese owing to Cadwgon ap Meurig's rule beyond Glamorgan in Gower, Cydweli, and Cantref Bychan, to Caradog ap Gruffudd's rule in Ystrad Yw, Gwent Uwch Coed, and Gwynllŵg, and to Rhydderch ab Iestyn's rule in Ewias and Gwent Is Coed.[138] Gruffudd ap Llywelyn's campaigns in Ergyng and his sacking of Hereford in 1055 also offered Herewald opportunities.[139]

The most significant development in Herewald's time lay in Ergyng. While most bishops between Berthwyn and Cyfeilliog seem to have been active in Ergyng as well as in Gwent, this activity apparently ceased in the time of Wulffrith, Pater, Gwgon, Bleddri, and Joseph, except that Joseph is said to have ordained a priest Idfab at Llangarron.[140] Presumably, after the time of Cyfeilliog, bishops based elsewhere intervened in Ergyng – most likely the bishops of Hereford and the bishops of Glasbury, the last of whom, Tremerin, moved to Hereford to assist Bishop Athelstan of Hereford (1012–56) in his infirmity.[141] The death of Bishop Tremerin

---

[134] J. R. Davies, '*Liber Landavensis*: its date and the identity of its editor', 4–5.

[135] See above, 7; cf. Davies, *An Early Welsh Microcosm*, 155; J. R. Davies, *The Book of Llandaf*, 16–18. For Joseph's charters see Hughes, 'The Celtic Church', 20, map 8, which omits charter 253 (Joseph's privilege) as being suspicious (cf. Maund, *Ireland, Wales, and England*, 188–9, and Charles-Edwards, *Wales and the Britons*, 283).

[136] See Davies, *An Early Welsh Microcosm*, 72 and 86 (map K).

[137] See *ibid.*, 73 and 85–6 (maps J–K). On *Henriu Gunua* see Coe, 'The place-names', 366. Coe, *ibid.*, 876, sites *Villa Gunnuc* (274) at Beiliau, near Llan-gwm (ST 427997). The location of *Pennros* in Gruffudd ap Llywelyn's grant cannot be identified (*ibid.*, 694 and 906).

[138] *LL* pp. 278–9, discussed above, 19.

[139] J. R. Davies, *The Book of Llandaf*, 29.

[140] *LL*, p. 277, quoted above, 20. On map 8 in Hughes, 'The Celtic Church', 20, Joseph seems to have one grant just north the Monnow (264a), due to copying Wendy Davies's grid reference for nearby Llangynfyl (*The Llandaff Charters*, 128); in fact the grant was on the opposite side of the river from Llangynfyl/Llangunville. See Coe, 'The place-names', 150–1.

[141] See above, 20.

14. The episcopal framework

after the sack of Hereford in 1055, followed by the deaths of Bishop Athelstan and his successor Leofgar (both in 1056), must have given the newly elected Herewald prospects in Ergyng.[142] Whether or not he already found the cults of Dyfrig and Teilo there,[143] he certainly propagated them.

As a consequence of the above political and ecclesiastical upheavals, Herewald became involved in some of the Book of Llandaf churches that were most distant from Llandaf. For example, he consecrated four churches in Ystrad Yw, not far south of bishops Gwrfan and Llibio's church at Llanfihangel Tal-y-llyn,[144] and also many of the churches in Ergyng that appear in the Sequence i charters and in some early Sequence iii charters such as those of Greciel. It is tempting to suppose that Herewald himself collected these churches' charters and brought them to Llandaf. While that may be the case, it is also possible that the Ergyng ones had been brought south much earlier, in the seventh to ninth centuries, when the bishops in Gwent still had close ties with Ergyng; and the Llanfihangel Tal-y-llyn charters could have been brought south by Llibio, if he belonged to the main line of south-eastern bishops.

Herewald's final decades, following the deaths of his patrons Rhydderch ap Caradog in 1076 and Caradog ap Gruffudd in 1081, were mired in a dispute with the church of Hereford, which is probably why he was placed under an interdict by Archbishop Anselm.[145] Three years after Herewald's death in extreme old age in 1104, Anselm consecrated Urban – already 'archdeacon of the church of Llandaf', according to *LL* (p. 280) – in his place. Urban attempted to reverse the decline of his diocese in various ways, including summoning witnesses to give oral testimony against St Davids (before 1116) and against Hereford and St Davids in 1129,[146] and enlisting Caradog of Llancarfan and others to produce hagiographical propaganda.[147] The editing of ancient charters played an important part in this programme. While some of them, in particular the charters claiming Teilo churches in the diocese of St Davids, are very dubious, many seem to have an authentic basis, in particular the grants to bishops in Ergyng, Gwent, and Glywysing. Urban's claim to be their direct successor was not implausible, but he discredited it by the further claim that their see had always lain in Llandaf, for it is clear that if there was a single line of bishops, their see must have moved several times before reaching Llandaf. Such moves are quite credible. To quote Wendy Davies, 'changes of see are, after all, recorded in the better-documented course of early English history'.[148] Thus the bishopric of Hereford seems not to have been based at Hereford to start with, and, in Wales, the

---

[142] See above, 20–1.
[143] See above, 161.
[144] *LL* p. 279. See above, 172.
[145] *LL* p. 278; above, 21.
[146] See above, 19.
[147] See especially J. R. Davies, *The Book of Llandaf*, passim.
[148] *An Early Welsh Microcosm*, 156–7. Cf. Fryde et al., *Handbook of British Chronology*. Cuthbert's see at Durham is one example (Stenton, *Anglo-Saxon England*, 433, 435, and 666 n. 2), and this struck J. W. James in his Durham D.D. thesis: 'The circumstances of the early history of Llandaff and of Durham are singularly parallel. In the one case Chester le Street succeeded to Lindisfarne and itself gave way to Durham. In the other Mochros in Hereford yielded first to Llandeilo Fawr in Carmarthen and Llandaff in Glamorgan. ... Durham despite the change of Cathedral site still remains the see of Aidan and Cuthbert. Likewise Llandaff remains the see of Dubricius and Teilo and perpetuates their traditions' ('A history of the origins and development of the Celtic Church in Wales', 233).

bishopric St Davids may originally have been at Henfynyw in Ceredigion;[149] neither bishopric went out of its way to draw attention to such discontinuities of course, and neither did Urban.

Judging by the *LL* charters, the 'Llandaf' line of bishops began in seventh-century Ergyng at Moccas and/or Welsh Bicknor before relocating down the Wye to Gwent, perhaps to Llandogo. In the eighth century, under Bishop Euddogwy and his successors, they extended their authority from Gwent into Glywysing, while retaining an intermittent presence in Ergyng, subject to Anglo-Saxon military opposition from the east and Welsh ecclesiastical competition from the west, apparently from a bishopric at Glasbury, to judge by the charter of a Bishop Gwrfan which somehow found its way into *LL*. In the ninth-century charters there are possible hints of competing bishops at ?Llangua (Gwyddloyw and Eddylfyw), while the (independently attested) importance of Llandeilo Fawr presumably restricted expansion into Ystrad Tywi. The ninth- and tenth-century bishops seem to have been centred on Gwent again, probably at Caer-went and Llandogo, before moving back to Glamorgan, and perhaps specifically to Llandaf, in the eleventh century, about the time of Bishop Joseph, Herewald's predecessor.[150]

We have seen that modern scholars have probably exaggerated the evidence for multiple lines of bishops in the *LL* charters. In particular, the supposed evidence for two contemporaneous bishops Nudd and Cerennyr in the ninth century is better explained by postulating three *successive* bishops: Nudd I, Cerennyr, and Nudd II. The most plausibly extraneous bishops, with only one charter each, are Gwrfan (at Glasbury?) in the eighth century and Gwyddloyw and Eddylfyw (at Llangua?) in the ninth. In modern scholarship Bishop Llibio, who receives two distant grants in Brycheiniog and Gower in the tenth century, has also been regarded as an extraneous bishop.[151] This may be incorrect, however, even though the compilers of *LL* may themselves have formed that impression at one stage, when they downgraded Bishops Gwrfan and Llibio into two brothers from Penychen who were established as hermits at Clodock.[152] Presumably they had copies of the Gwrfan and Llibio charters and were at first uncertain how to explain them. In fact, the compilers of *LL* may well have been in a similar position to ourselves: struggling to make historical sense of a disparate and disordered collection of ancient charters.

---

[149] See references above, 20 n. 22, and 15 n. 59, respectively.

[150] See above, in this chapter, passim. Compare the 'inevitably speculative' reconstruction by Wendy Davies, *An Early Welsh Microcosm*, 158, which is partly dependent on the theory of charter Groups A–J, discussed above, ch. 9.

[151] Davies, *An Early Welsh Microcosm*, 155 n. 1. But cf. above 173 and 177, also 18, and 68.

[152] See above, 66–70.

Appendix I

CONCORDANCE AND CHART SHOWING THE PAGINAL AND CHRONOLOGICAL ORDER OF THE CHARTERS[1]

Paginal order (capital letters refer to Wendy Davies's Groups A–J)

A	72a	i.3		164	i.18		198b	ii.52
	72b	i.5		165	i.19		199a	ii.49
	73a	i.6		166	i.9		199bi	ii.53
	73b	i.7	**E**	168	iii.14		199bii	iii.16
	74	iii.6		169a	iii.15		200	ii.55
	75	i.1		169b	iii.2		201	ii.50
	76a	i.4		170	iii.1		202	ii.45
	76b	i.12		171a	iii.3		203a	ii.51
	77	i.2		171b	iii.5		203b	ii.54
B	121	i.10		173	iii.7		204a	ii.47
	122	i.11		174a	iii.4		204b	ii.27
C	140	ii.2	**F**	174b	ii.21		205	ii.24
	143	ii.3		175	ii.35		206	ii.61
	144	ii.1		176a	ii.22		207	ii.56
	145	ii.17		176b	ii.19		208	ii.64
	146	ii.12		178	ii.44		209a	ii.60
	147	ii.4		179b	ii.33		209b	ii.58
	148	ii.14		179c	ii.29		210a	ii.63
	149	ii.8		180a	ii.28		210b	ii.57
	150a	ii.16		180b	ii.25		211a	ii.59
	150b	ii.15		183a	ii.37		211b	ii.62
	151a	ii.9		183b	ii.20		212	iii.9
	151b	ii.7		184	ii.39		214	iii.10
	152	ii.5		185	ii.42		216a	iii.18
	154	ii.13		186a	ii.43		216b	iii.17
	155	ii.6		186b	ii.36	**G**	217	iii.40
	156	ii.18		187	ii.31		218	iii.39
	157	ii.11		188a	ii.40		221	iii.38
	158	ii.30		188b	ii.26		222	iii.37
	159b	ii.10		189	ii.38		223	iii.36
D	160	i.16		190a	ii.32		224	iii.35
	161	i.14		190b	ii.23	**H**	225	iii.12
	162a	i.15		191	ii.34		226	iii.8
	162b	i.13		195	ii.41		227a	iii.11
	163a	i.8		197	ii.48		227b	iii.19
	163b	i.17		198a	ii.46		228	iii.21

[1] Charters which do not appear in the Sequences are omitted. The Sequences are in Davies's order (cf. above, 32).

179

	229a	iii.20
	229b	iii.22
	230a	iii.23
	230b	iii.13
	231	iii.31
	232a	iii.29
	232b	iii.32
	233	iii.30
	234	iii.26
	235a	iii.28
	235b	iii.27
	236	iii.24

	237a	iii.25
	237b	iii.34
	239	iii.33
J	243	iii.43
	244	iii.42
	245	iii.41
	246	iii.46
	249a	iii.54
	249b	iii.45
	251	iii.44
	255	iii.51
	257	iii.50

258	iii.52
259	iii.55
261	iii.56
262	iii.47
263	iii.53
264a	iii.49
264b	iii.48
267	iii.58
269	iii.57
271	iii.60
272	iii.59
274	iii.61

Chronological order (according to Wendy Davies's three Sequences, i–iii)

i.1	75
i.2	77
i.3	72a
i.4	76a
i.5	72b
i.6	73a
i.7	73b
i.8	163a
i.9	166
i.10	121
i.11	122
i.12	76b
i.13	162b
i.14	161
i.15	162a
i.16	160
i.17	163b
i.18	164
i.19	165
ii.1	144
ii.2	140
ii.3	143
ii.4	147
ii.5	152
ii.6	155
ii.7	151b
ii.8	149
ii.9	151a
ii.10	159b
ii.11	157
ii.12	146
ii.13	154
ii.14	148
ii.15	150b
ii.16	150a

ii.17	145
ii.18	156
ii.19	176b
ii.20	183b
ii.21	174b
ii.22	176a
ii.23	190b
ii.24	205
ii.25	180b
ii.26	188b
ii.27	204b
ii.28	180a
ii.29	179c
ii.30	158
ii.31	187
ii.32	190a
ii.33	179b
ii.34	191
ii.35	175
ii.36	186b
ii.37	183a
ii.38	189
ii.39	184
ii.40	188a
ii.41	195
ii.42	185
ii.43	186a
ii.44	178
ii.45	202
ii.46	198a
ii.47	204a
ii.48	197
ii.49	199a
ii.50	201
ii.51	203a

ii.52	198b
ii.53	199bi
ii.54	203b
ii.55	200
ii.56	207
ii.57	210b
ii.58	209b
ii.59	211a
ii.60	209a
ii.61	206
ii.62	211b
ii.63	210a
ii.64	208
iii.1	170
iii.2	169b
iii.3	171a
iii.4	174a
iii.5	171b
iii.6	74
iii.7	173
iii.8	226
iii.9	212
iii.10	214
iii.11	227a
iii.12	225
iii.13	230b
iii.14	168
iii.15	169a
iii.16	199bii
iii.17	216b
iii.18	216a
iii.19	227b
iii.20	229a
iii.21	228
iii.22	229b

Appendix I

iii.23	230a	iii.36	223	iii.49	264a
iii.24	236	iii.37	222	iii.50	257
iii.25	237a	iii.38	221	iii.51	255
iii.26	234	iii.39	218	iii.52	258
iii.27	235b	iii.40	217	iii.53	263
iii.28	235a	iii.41	245	iii.54	249a
iii.29	232a	iii.42	244	iii.55	259
iii.30	233	iii.43	243	iii.56	261
iii.31	231	iii.44	251	iii.57	269
iii.32	232b	iii.45	249b	iii.58	267
iii.33	239	iii.46	246	iii.59	272
iii.34	237b	iii.47	262	iii.60	271
iii.35	224	iii.48	264b	iii.61	274

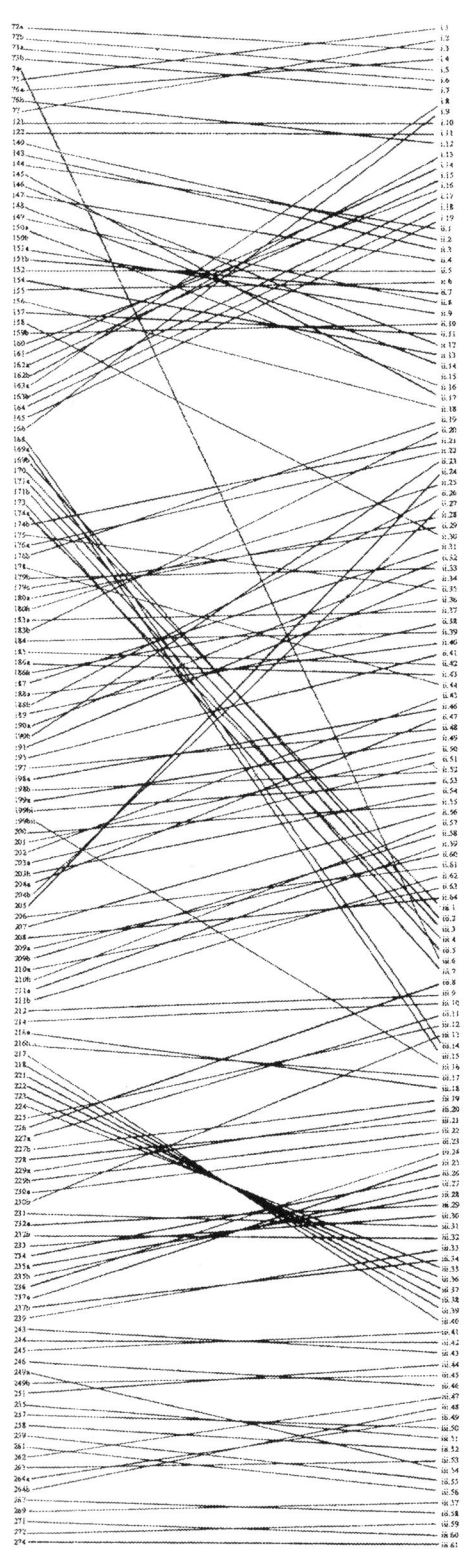

Chart giving a visual impression of difference between the chronological (right) and paginal (left) order of charters

Appendix II

MAPS OF GRANTS TO BISHOPS

Maps 1–8 are from Kathleen Hughes, 'The Celtic Church: is this a valid concept?' (see above, Acknowledgements, viii).

Open (as opposed to solid) symbols indicate approximate locations. Cf. Hughes, 'The Celtic Church', 7.

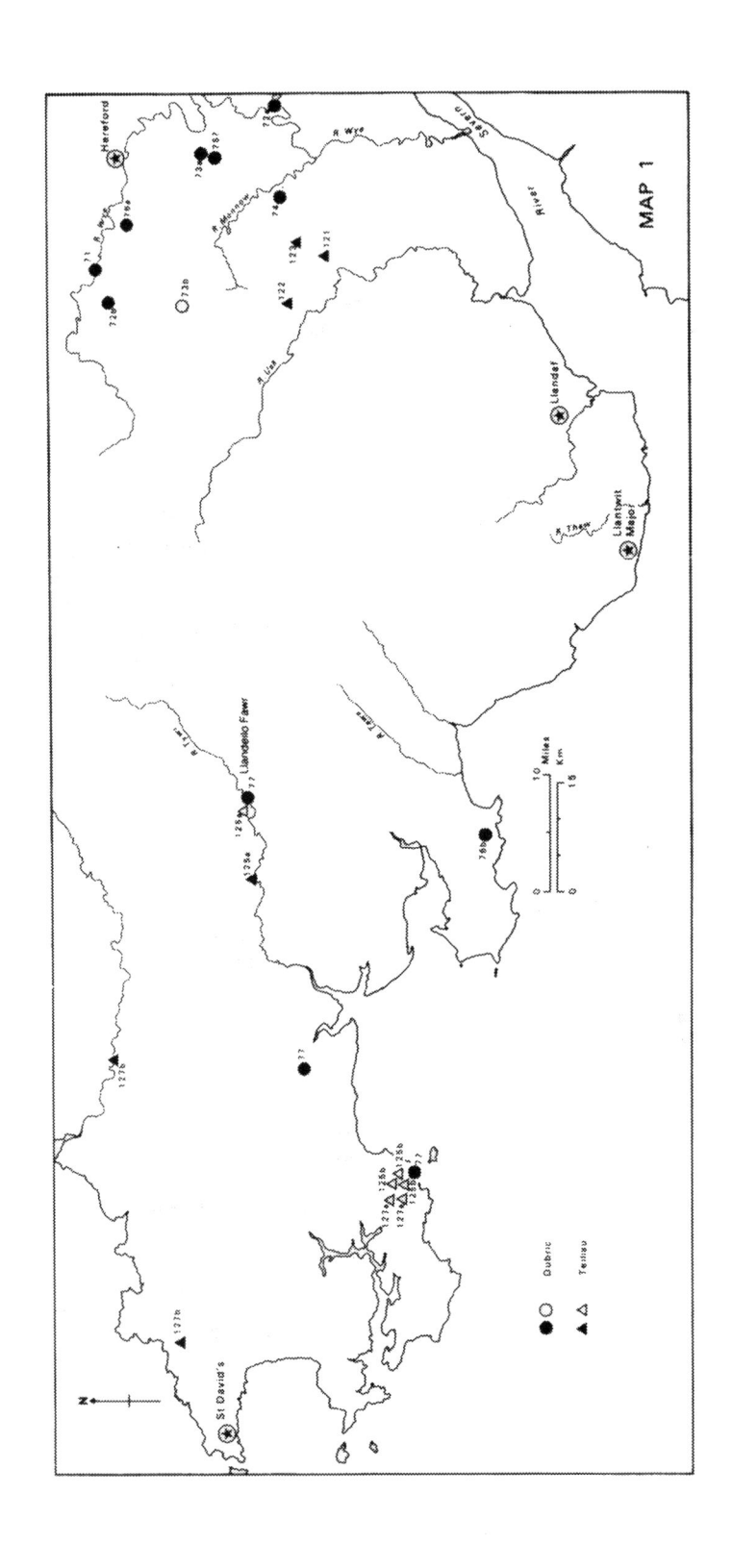

MAP 2

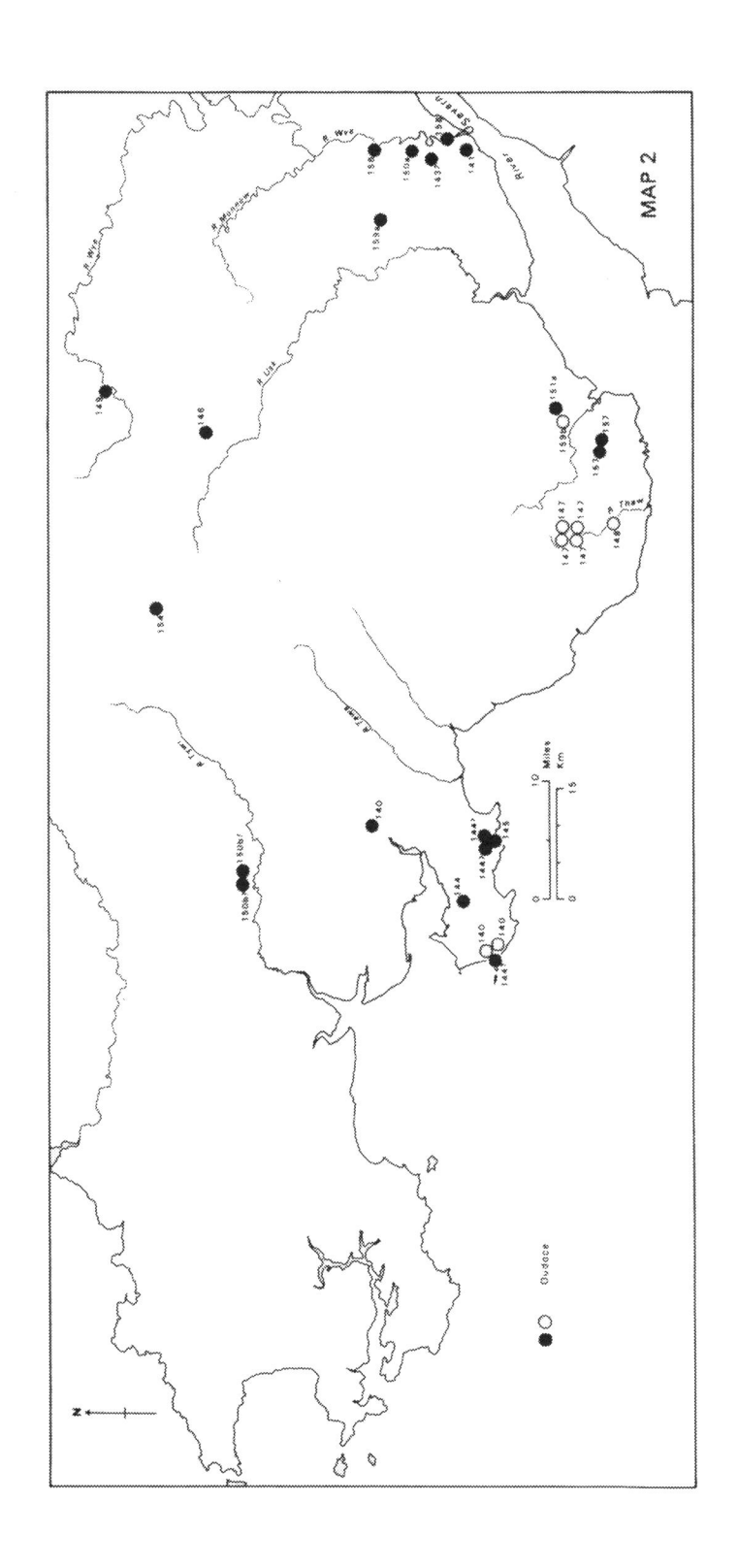

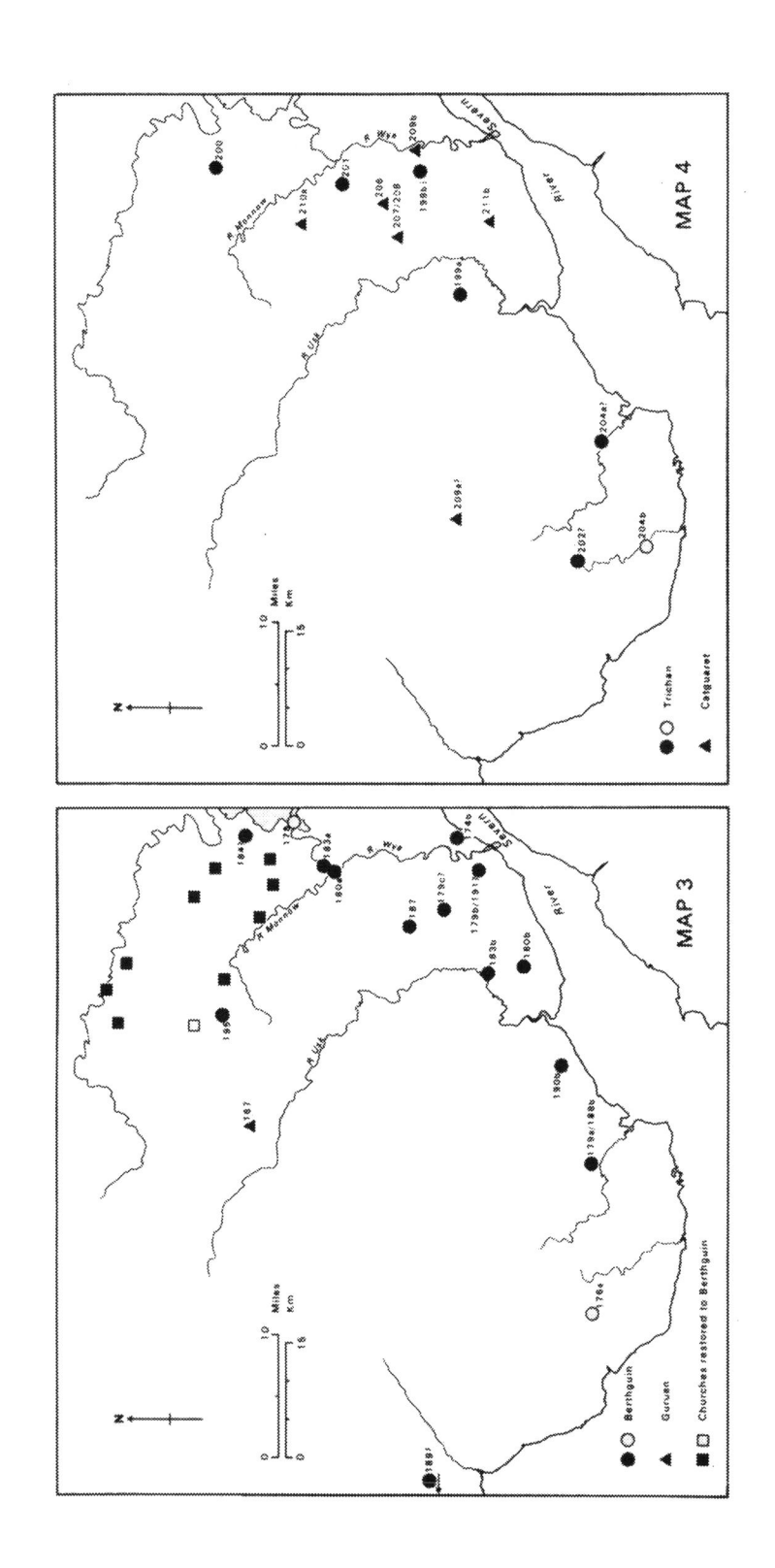

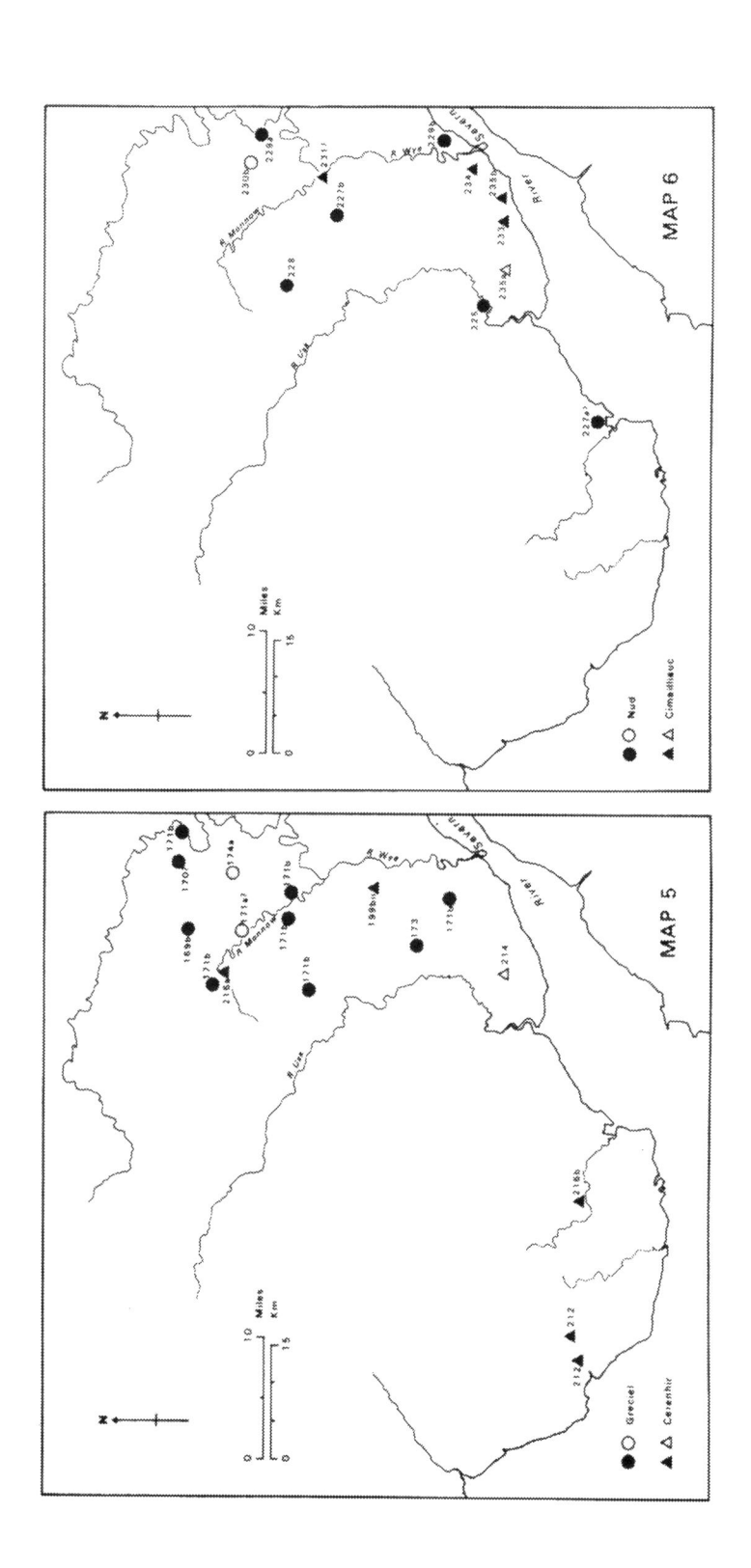

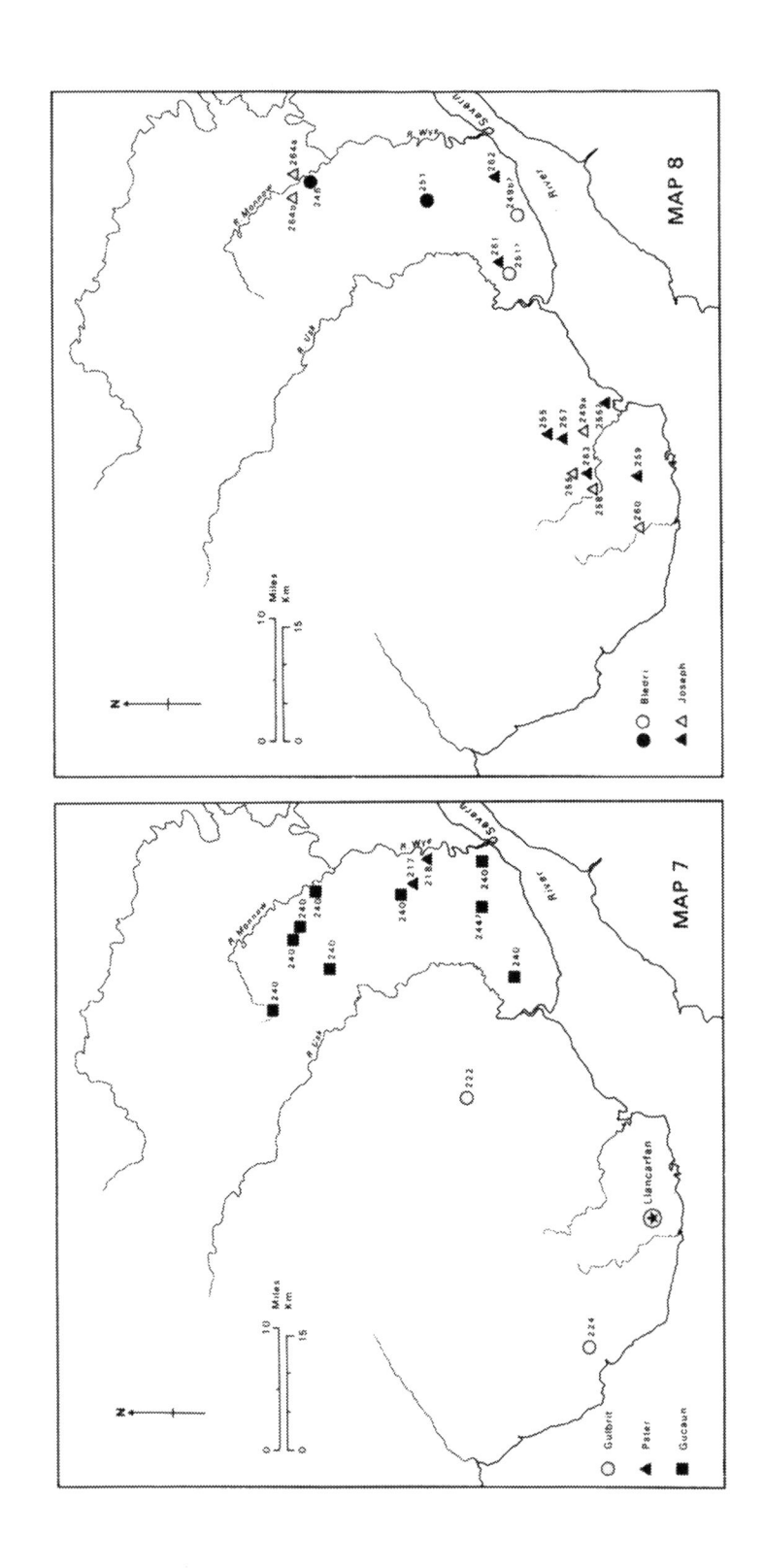

BIBLIOGRAPHY

Abulafia, David, Luscombe, David, and Mayr-Harting, Henry, 'Christopher Nugent Lawrence Brooke 1927–2015', in *Biographical Memoirs of Fellows of the British Academy*, XVI (Oxford, 2017), 239–77.
Anscombe, Alfred, 'Landavensium ordo chartarum', *Celtic Review*, 6 (1909–10), 123–9, 272–7, and 289–95, and 7 (1911–12), 63–7.
—— 'Some Old-Welsh pedigrees', *Y Cymmrodor*, 24 (1913), 74–85.
Atkins, Ivor, 'The church of Worcester from the eighth to the twelfth century: Part II, The familia from the middle of the tenth to the beginning of the twelfth century', *Antiquaries Journal*, 20 (1940), 1–38 and 203–29.
Barrow, Julia (ed.), *English Episcopal Acta VII: Hereford 1079–1234* (Oxford, 1993).
—— (ed.), *St Davids Episcopal Acta 1085–1280* (Cardiff, 1998).
Bartrum, Peter C., *A Welsh Classical Dictionary* (Aberystwyth, 1993).
—— 'Achau Brenhinoedd a Thywysogion Cymru', *BBCS*, 19:3 (1961), 201–25.
—— 'Corrections to *Early Welsh Genealogical Tracts*', *BBCS*, 40 (1993), 171–2.
—— 'Further notes on the Welsh genealogical manuscripts', *THSC*, 1976, 102–18.
—— 'Noë, king of Powys', *Y Cymmrodor*, 43 (1932), 53–61.
—— 'Notes on the Welsh genealogical manuscripts', *THSC*, 1968, 63–98.
—— 'Rhieinwg and Rheinwg', *BBCS*, 24:1 (1970), 23–7.
—— 'Some studies in early Welsh history', *THSC*, 1948, 279–302.
—— 'Was there a British "Book of Conquests"?', *BBCS*, 23:1 (1968), 1–5.
—— *Welsh Genealogies AD 300–1400*, 8 vols (Cardiff, 1974).
Baumgarten, Paul Maria, 'Papal letters relating to England, 1133–1187', *EHR*, 9 (1894), 531–41.
Bieler, Ludwig (ed.), *The Irish Penitentials* (Dublin, 1963).
Birch, Walter de Gray (ed.), *Cartularium Saxonicum*, 3 vols and index (London, 1885–99).
—— *Memorials of the See and Cathedral of Llandaff* (Neath, 1912).
Bishop, Edmund, *Liturgica Historica* (Oxford, 1918).
Bowen, E. G., *The Settlements of the Celtic Saints in Wales*, 2nd edn (Cardiff, 1956).
Boyd, Matthieu, 'The ancients' savage obscurity: the etymology of *Bisclavret*', *Notes & Queries*, 60 (2013), 199–202.
Breatnach, Liam, 'Forms of payment in the early Irish law tracts', *CMCS*, 68 (Winter 2014), 1–20.
Breeze, Andrew, 'Does *scripulum* in the Book of Llandaff mean "piece of gold"?', *THSC*, n.s. 3 (1997), 5–8.
Brett, Caroline, 'Hagiography as charter: the example of the Cartulary of Landévennec', unpublished paper, *Defining the Boundaries of Celtic Hagiography* conference, Dublin, 25 May 2018.
—— 'John Leland, Wales, and early British history', *WHR*, 15:2 (1990), 169–82.
Brett, M., *The English Church Under Henry I* (Oxford, 1975).
Bromwich, Rachel, and Simon Evans, D. (eds), *Culhwch and Olwen* (Cardiff, 1992).
Brooke, Christopher N. L., Review of John Reuben Davies, *The Book of Llandaf and the Norman Church in Wales* (Woodbridge, 2003), in *CMCS*, 49 (Summer 2005), 77–8.
—— 'St Peter of Gloucester and St Cadoc of Llancarfan', in Nora K. Chadwick (ed.), *Celt and Saxon: Studies in the Early British Border*, corrected reprint (Cambridge, 1964), 258–322.
—— *The Church and the Welsh Border in the Central Middle Ages* (Woodbridge, 1986).

Brooks, Nicholas, 'The development of military obligations in eighth- and ninth-century England', in Peter Clemoes and Kathleen Hughes (eds), *England Before the Conquest: Studies in Primary Sources Presented to Dorothy Whitelock* (Cambridge, 1971), 69–84.

Broun, Dauvit, *The Charters of Gaelic Scotland and Ireland in the Early and Central Middle Ages* (Cambridge, 1995).

Brown, Michelle P., 'The Lichfield/Llandeilo Gospels reinterpreted', in Ruth Kennedy and Simon Meecham-Jones (eds), *Authority and Subjugation in Writing of Medieval Wales* (New York, 2008), 57–70.

Butler, L. A. S., 'St Kynemark's Priory, Chepstow', *Monmouthshire Antiquary*, 2 (1965–8), 33–41.

Campbell, James, 'The sale of land and the economics of power in early England: problems and possibilities', *Haskins Society Journal*, 1 (1989), 23–37.

Cane, Meredith, 'Personal names of men in Wales, Cornwall and Brittany 400–1400 AD', Ph.D. dissertation, University of Wales, Aberystwyth, 2003.

Carlisle, Nicholas, *A Topographical Dictionary of the Dominion of Wales* (London, 1811).

Carte, Thomas, *A General History of England*, Vol. I (London, 1747).

Chadwick, Owen, 'The evidence of dedications in the early history of the Welsh Church', in Nora K. Chadwick (ed.), *Studies in Early British History* (Cambridge, 1954), 173–88.

Chaplais, Pierre, 'The origin and authenticity of the royal Anglo-Saxon diploma', in Felicity Ranger (ed.), *Prisca Munimenta: Studies in Archival and Administrative History Presented to Dr A. E. J. Hollaender* (London, 1973), 28–42.

—— 'Who introduced charters into England? The case for Augustine', in Felicity Ranger (ed.), *Prisca Munimenta: Studies in Archival and Administrative History Presented to Dr A. E. J. Hollaender* (London, 1973), 88–107.

Charles, B. G., *The Place-Names of Pembrokeshire*, 2 vols (Aberystwyth, 1992).

—— 'The Welsh, their language and place-names in Archenfield and Oswestry', in *Angles and Britons (O'Donnell Lectures)* (Cardiff, 1963), 85–110.

Charles-Edwards, T. M., 'Dynastic succession in early medieval Wales', in Ralph A. Griffiths and Phillipp R. Schofield (eds), *Wales and the Welsh in the Middle Ages: Essays Presented to J. Beverley Smith* (Cardiff, 2011), 70–88.

—— *Early Irish and Welsh Kinship* (Oxford, 1993).

—— 'Some Celtic kinship terms', *BBCS*, 24:2 (1971), 105–22.

—— 'The seven bishop-houses of Dyfed', *BBCS*, 24:3 (1971), 247–62.

—— 'The Three Columns of Law: a comparative perspective', in T. M. Charles-Edwards and Paul Russell (eds), *Tair Colofn Cyfraith: The Three Columns of Law in Medieval Wales: Homicide, Theft and Fire* (Bangor, 2005), 26–59.

—— *Wales and the Britons, 350–1064* (Oxford, 2013).

Coe, Jonathan Baron, 'Dating the boundary clauses in the Book of Llandaf', *CMCS*, 48 (2004), 1–43.

—— 'The place-names of the Book of Llandaf', Ph.D. dissertation, University of Wales, Aberystwyth, 2001.

Conybeare, W. D., 'Memoir on the history and architecture of the Cathedral of Llandaff', *Arch. Camb.*, 2nd ser., 1 (1850), 24–40.

Coplestone-Crow, Bruce, *Herefordshire Place-Names*, 2nd edn (Almeley, 2009).

Cowley, F. G., 'The Church in medieval Glamorgan', in T. B. Pugh (ed.), *Glamorgan County History*, Vol. III, *The Middle Ages* (Cardiff, 1971), 87–166.

Crouch, David (ed.), *Llandaff Episcopal Acta 1140–1287* (Cardiff, 1989).

Darby, H. C., and Terrett, I. B. (eds), *The Domesday Geography of Midland England*, 2nd edn (Cambridge, 1971).

Dark, K. R., *Civitas to Kingdom: British Political Continuity 300–800* (Leicester, 1994).

Darlington, R. R. (ed.), *The Cartulary of Worcester Cathedral Priory* (London, 1968).

Darlington, R. R., and McGurk, P. (eds), and Jennifer Bray and P. McGurk (transls), *The Chronicle of John of Worcester*, Vol. II, *The Annals from 450 to 1066* (Oxford, 1995).

Davies, Brian, 'Archaeology and ideology, or how Wales was robbed of its early history', *New Welsh Review*, 37 (Summer 1997), 38–51.

Bibliography

Davies, John Humphreys, *The National Library of Wales Catalogue of Manuscripts*, Vol. I (Aberystwyth, 1921).

Davies, John Reuben, 'Bishop Kentigern among the Britons', in Steve Boardman, John Reuben Davies, and Eila Williamson (eds), *Saints' Cults in the Celtic World* (Woodbridge, 2009), 66–90.

—— 'Cathedrals and the cult of saints in eleventh- and twelfth-century Wales', in Paul Dalton, Charles Insley, and Louise J. Wilkinson (eds), *Cathedrals, Communities and Conflict in the Anglo-Norman World* (Woodbridge, 2011), 99–115.

—— 'Church, property and conflict in Wales, AD 600–1100', *WHR*, 18:3 (1997), 387–406.

—— '*Liber Landavensis*: its date and the identity of its editor', *CMCS*, 35 (Summer 1998), 1–11.

—— 'The archbishopric of St Davids and the bishops of *Clas Cynidr*', in J. Wyn Evans and Jonathan M. Wooding (eds), *St David of Wales: Cult, Church and Nation* (Woodbridge, 2007), 296–304.

—— *The Book of Llandaf and the Norman Church in Wales* (Woodbridge, 2003).

—— 'The saints of south Wales and the Welsh Church', in Alan Thacker and Richard Sharpe (eds), *Local Saints and Local Churches in the Early Medieval West* (Oxford, 2002), 361–95.

Davies, W. S., 'The Book of Invectives of Giraldus Cambrensis', *Y Cymmrodor*, 30 (1920) [whole volume].

Davies, Wendy, *Acts of Giving: Individual, Community and Church in Tenth-Century Christian Spain* (Oxford, 2007).

—— *An Early Welsh Microcosm: Studies in the Llandaff Charters* (London, 1978).

—— 'Holding court: judicial presidency in Brittany, Wales and northern Iberia in the early Middle Ages', in Fiona Edmonds and Paul Russell (eds), *Tome: Studies in Medieval Celtic History and Law in Honour of Thomas Charles-Edwards* (Woodbridge, 2011), 145–54.

—— Review of Dauvit Broun, *The Charters of Gaelic Scotland and Ireland in the Early and Central Middle Ages* (Cambridge, 1995), in *CMCS*, 34 (Winter 1997), 115–16.

—— 'Sale, price and valuation in Galicia and Castile-León in the tenth century', *EME*, 11:2 (2002), 149–74.

—— *Small Worlds: The Village Community in Early Medieval Brittany* (London, 1988).

—— *The Llandaff Charters* (Aberystwyth, 1979).

—— *Wales in the Early Middle Ages* (Leicester, 1982).

—— 'When gift is sale: reciprocities and commodities in tenth-century Christian Iberia', in Wendy Davies and Paul Fouracre (eds), *The Languages of Gift in the Early Middle Ages* (Cambridge, 2010), 217–37.

Dickins, Bruce '"Dewi Sant" (St David) in early English kalendars and place-names', in Nora K. Chadwick (ed.), *Celt and Saxon: Studies in the Early British Border*, corrected reprint (Cambridge, 1964), 206–9.

Doble, G. H., *Lives of the Welsh Saints* (Cardiff, 1971).

Dugdale, William, *Monasticon Anglicanum*, 3 vols (London, 1655–73).

Dumville, David, 'Ireland, Brittany and England: transmission and use of the *Collectio Canonum Hibernensis*', in Catherine Laurent and Helen Davis (eds), *Irlande et Bretagne* (Rennes, 1994), 85–95.

—— 'Late-seventh- or early-eighth-century evidence for the British transmission of Pelagius', *CMCS*, 10 (Winter 1985), 39–52.

—— 'The Anglian collection of royal genealogies and regnal lists', *ASE*, 5 (1976), 23–50.

—— 'The "six" sons of Rhodri Mawr: a problem in Asser's *Life of King Alfred*', *CMCS*, 4 (Winter 1982), 5–18.

Dyer, Christopher, *Lord and Peasants in a Changing Society: The Estates of the Bishopric of Worcester 680–1540* (Cambridge, 1980).

Edwards, C. J., 'St Teilo at Llandaff', *JHSCW*, 5 (1955), 38–44.

Edwards, Nancy, 'Early medieval Wales: material evidence and identity', *SC*, 51 (2017), 65–87.

Edwards, Nancy, with Jackson, Heather, McKee, Helen, and Sims-Williams, Patrick, *A*

Corpus of Early Medieval Inscribed Stones and Stone Sculpture in Wales, Vol. II, South-West Wales (Cardiff, 2007).

Edwards, Nancy, with Horák, Jana, Jackson, Heather, McKee, Helen, Parsons, David N., and Sims-Williams, Patrick, *A Corpus of Early Medieval Inscribed Stones and Stone Sculpture in Wales*, Vol. III, *North Wales* (Cardiff, 2013).

Ellis, Henry (ed.), *The Record of Caernarvon* (London, 1838).

Emery, F. V., 'Edward Lhuyd and some of his Glamorgan correspondents: a view of Gower in the 1690's', *THSC*, 1965, 59–114.

Ewert, A. (ed.), *The Romance of Tristan by Beroul*, 2 vols (Oxford, 1963–70).

Falileyev, Alexander, and Russell, Paul, 'The dry-point glosses in *Oxoniensis Posterior*', in Paul Russell (ed.), *Yr Hen Iaith: Studies in Early Welsh* (Aberystwyth, 2003), 95–101.

Finberg, H. P. R., *The Early Charters of the West Midlands*, 2nd edn (Leicester, 1972).

Flechner, Roy, 'Identifying monks in early medieval Britain and Ireland: a reflection on legal and economic aspects', in *Settimane di Studio della Fondazione Centro Italiano di Studi sull'alto Medioevo*, LXIV, *Monachesimi d'oriente e d'occidente nell'alto medioevo* (Spoleto, 2017), 805–44.

Fleuriot, Léon, 'Les évêques de la "Clas Kenedyr", évêché disparu de la région de Hereford', *Études celtiques*, 15:1 (1976–7), 225–6.

—— 'Old Breton genealogies and early British traditions', *BBCS*, 26:1 (1974), 1–6.

Flobert, Pierre (ed. and transl.), *La vie ancienne de saint Samson de Dol* (Paris, 1997).

Flower, Robin, 'William Salesbury, Richard Davies and Archbishop Parker', *NLWJ*, 2 (1941–2), 7–14.

Fryde, E. B., Greenway, D. E., Porter, S., and Roy, I., *Handbook of British Chronology*, 3rd edn (Cambridge, 1986).

Gameson, Richard, 'The insular gospel book at Hereford Cathedral', *Scriptorium*, 56 (2002), 48–79.

Geary, Patrick, 'Land, language and memory in Europe 700–1100', *Transactions of the Royal Historical Society*, 6th ser., 9 (1999), 169–200.

Gibson, Edmund (ed.), *Chronicon Saxonicum* (Oxford, 1692).

Grosjean, Paul, 'Saints anglo-saxons des marches galloises: à propos d'un ouvrage récent', *Analecta Bollandiana*, 79 (1961), 161–9.

Grundy, G. B., *Saxon Charters and Field Names of Gloucestershire*, Part II ([Gloucester], 1936).

Guy, Benjamin David, 'A lost medieval manuscript from north Wales: Hengwrt 33, the *Hanesyn Hên*', *SC*, 50 (2016), 69–105.

—— 'Did the Harleian Genealogies draw on archival sources?', *Proceedings of the Harvard Celtic Colloquium*, 32 (2012), 119–33.

—— 'Gerald and Welsh genealogical learning', in Georgia Henley and A. Joseph McMullen (eds), *Gerald of Wales: New Perspectives on a Medieval Writer and Critic* (Cardiff, 2018), 47–61.

—— 'Medieval Welsh genealogy: texts, contexts and transmission', 2 vols, unpublished Ph.D. dissertation, University of Cambridge, 2016.

—— 'The *Life* of St Dyfrig and the lost charters of Moccas (Mochros), Herefordshire', *CMCS*, 75 (Summer 2018), 1–37.

Haddan, Arthur West, and Stubbs, William (eds), *Councils and Ecclesiastical Documents Relating to Great Britain and Ireland*, Vol. I (Oxford, 1869).

Hall, Antonius (ed.), *Commentarii de Scriptoribus Britannicis auctore Joanne Lelando*, 2 vols (Oxford, 1709).

Hammer, Carl I., 'Land sales in eighth- and ninth-century Bavaria: legal, economic and social aspects', *EME*, 6:1 (1997), 47–76.

Haycock, Marged (ed.), *Legendary Poems from the Book of Taliesin*, 2nd edn (Aberystwyth, 2015).

Hearne, Thomas (ed.), *The Itinerary of John Leland*, 2nd edn, 9 vols (Oxford, 1744).

—— (ed.), *The Itinerary of John Leland*, 3rd edn, 9 vols (Oxford, 1768–69).

Herren, Michael W., 'Gildas and early British monasticism', in Alfred Bammesberger and

Alfred Wollmann (eds), *Britain 400–600: Language and History* (Heidelberg, 1990), 65–78.
Hodge, Arkady, 'When is a charter not a charter? Documents in non-conventional contexts in early medieval Europe', in Jonathan Jarrett and Allan Scott McKinley (eds), *Problems and Possibilities of Early Medieval Charters* (Turnhout, 2013), 127–49.
Howlett, David, *Sealed from Within: Self-Authenticating Insular Charters* (Dublin, 1999).
Hughes, Kathleen, *Celtic Britain in the Early Middle Ages* (Woodbridge, 1980).
—— 'The Celtic Church: is this a valid concept?', *CMCS*, 1 (Summer 1981), 1–20.
—— 'The Welsh Latin chronicles: *Annales Cambriae* and related texts', *PBA*, 59 (1973), 233–58.
Huws, Daniel, *Medieval Welsh Manuscripts* (Cardiff and Aberystwyth, 2000).
Jack, R. Ian, *Medieval Wales* (London, 1972).
Jacobs, Nicolas, 'Clefyd Abercuog', *BBCS*, 39 (1992), 56–70.
—— 'Drysni geirfaol y gwahanglwyf: *claf, clafwr, clawr, clafr*', in Joseph F. Eska, R. Geraint Gruffydd, and Nicolas Jacobs (eds), *Hispano-Gallo-Brittonica: Essays in Honour of Professor D. Ellis Evans* (Cardiff, 1995), 68–78.
—— '*Non, Nonna, Nonnita*: confusions of gender in Brythonic hagionymy', *THSC*, n.s. 23 (2017), 19–33.
James, John Williams, 'A history of the origins and development of the Celtic Church in Wales between the years 450 A.D. and 630 A.D.', unpublished D.D. dissertation, University of Durham, 1931.
—— 'Chronology in the Book of Llan Dav, 500–900', *NLWJ*, 16:2 (1969), 123–42.
—— 'The *Book of Llan Dav* and Bishop Oudoceus', *JHSCW*, 5 (1955), 23–37.
—— '*The Book of Llan Dav* and Canon G. H. Doble', *NLWJ*, 18:1 (1973), 1–36.
—— 'The Book of Llan Dav and the diocesan boundaries disputes, c. 960–1133', *NLWJ*, 16:4 (1970), 319–52.
—— '*The Book of Llandav*: the church and see of Llandav and their critics', *JHSCW*, 9 (1959), 5–22.
—— 'The "Concen charters" in the "Book of Llan Dav"', *THSC*, 1963, 82–95.
—— 'The excommunications in the Book of Llan Dav', *JHSCW*, 8 (1958), 5–14.
Jankulak, Karen, and Wooding, Jonathan M., 'The Life of St Elgar of Ynys Enlli', *Trivium*, 39 (2010), 15–47.
Jenkins, Dafydd, 'From Wales to Weltenburg? Some considerations on the origins of the use of sacred books for the preservation of secular records', in Norbert Brieskorn, Paul Mikat, Daniela Müller, and Dietmar Willoweit (eds), *Vom mittelalterlichen Recht zur neuzeitlichen Rechtswissenschaft* (Padernborn, 1994), 75–88.
Jenkins, Dafydd, and Owen, Morfydd E., 'The Welsh marginalia in the Lichfield Gospels, Part I', *CMCS*, 5 (Summer 1983), 37–66.
Jenkins, Geraint H., Jones, Ffion Mair, and Jones, David Ceri (eds), *The Correspondence of Iolo Morganwg*, 3 vols (Cardiff, 2007).
Jenkins, Philip, 'Regions and cantrefs in early medieval Glamorgan', *CMCS*, 15 (Summer 1988), 31–50.
Johansson, Christer, 'The place-names in a Herefordshire charter', *Studia Neophilologica*, 49 (1971), 185–7.
Johnston, D. R. (ed.), *Gwaith Iolo Goch* (Cardiff, 1988).
Jones, E. D., 'The Book of Llandaff', *NLWJ*, 4:3/4 (1946), 123–57.
Jones, Francis, 'An approach to Welsh genealogy', *THSC*, 1948, 303–466.
Jones, Glanville R. J., 'Post-Roman Wales', in H. P. R. Finberg (ed.), *The Agrarian History of England and Wales*, Vol. I.ii, *A.D. 43–1042* (Cambridge, 1972), 281–382.
—— '"Tir Telych", the Gwestfâu of Cynwyl Gaeo and Cwmwd Caeo', *SC*, 28 (1994), 81–95.
Jones, Owen, Williams, Edward, and Owen Pughe, William (eds), *The Myvyrian Archaiology of Wales*, 2nd edn (Denbigh, 1870).
Jones, Thomas (transl.), *Brut y Tywysogyon: Peniarth MS. 20 Version* (Cardiff, 1952).
Kelly, Fergus, *A Guide to Early Irish Law* (Dublin, 1988).
Ker, N. R., *Catalogue of Manuscripts Containing Anglo-Saxon* (Oxford, 1957).

—— 'Hemming's Cartulary: a description of the two Worcester cartularies in Cotton Tiberius A.xiii', in R. W. Hunt, W. A. Pantin, and R. W. Southern (eds), *Studies in Medieval History Presented to Frederick Maurice Powicke* (Oxford, 1948), 49–75.

Keynes, Simon D., *An Atlas of Attestations in Anglo-Saxon Charters c. 670–1066*, Vol. I, *Tables* (Cambridge, 2002).

—— 'Anglo-Saxon charters: lost and found', in Julia Barrow and Andrew Wareham (eds), *Myth, Rulership and Charters: Essays in Honour of Nicholas Brooks* (Aldershot, 2008), 45–66.

—— 'King Athelstan's books', in Michael Lapidge and Helmut Gneuss (eds), *Learning and Literature in Anglo-Saxon England: Studies Presented to Peter Clemoes* (Cambridge, 1985), 143–201.

—— *The Councils of Clofesho*, Vaughan Paper no. 38 (Leicester, 1994).

—— *The Diplomas of Æthelred 'the Unready' 978–1016* (Cambridge, 1980).

——'Welsh kings at Anglo-Saxon royal assemblies (928–55)', *Haskins Society Journal*, 26 (2014), 69–122.

Keynes, Simon, and Lapidge, Michael (transl.), *Alfred the Great: Asser's 'Life of King Alfred' and Other Contemporary Sources* (Harmondsworth, 1983).

Kirby, D. P., 'British dynastic history in the pre-Viking period', *BBCS*, 27:1 (1976), 81–114.

Knight, Jeremy K., 'From villa to monastery: Llandough in context', *Medieval Archaeology*, 49 (2005), 93–107.

—— 'Gwent churches in the Book of Llandaff', *Monmouthshire Antiquary*, 27 (2011), 35–42.

—— *South Wales from the Romans to the Normans* (Stroud, 2013).

Knight, L. Stanley, 'The Welsh monasteries and their claims for doing the education of later medieval Wales', *Arch. Camb.*, 6th ser., 20 (1920), 257–75.

Koch, John T., 'When was Welsh literature first written down?', *SC*, 20/21 (1985–6), 43–66.

Kölbing, Eugen (ed.), *The Romance of Beues of Hamtoun*, 3 parts with single pagination, Early English Text Society, extra series, 46, 48, and 65 (London, 1885–94).

Krajewski, Elizabeth M. G., *Archetypal Narratives: Pattern and Parable in the Lives of Three Saints* (Turnhout, 2018).

Lewis, Barry J., 'A possible provenance for the Old Cornish Vocabulary', *CMCS*, 73 (Summer 2017), 1–14.

Lewis, Ceri W., 'Agweddau ar hanes cynnar yr Eglwys yng Nghymru', *Llên Cymru*, 6:1/2 (1960), 46–62, and 7:3/4 (1963), 125–71.

—— 'The *Liber Landavensis* and the diocese of Llandaff', *Morgannwg*, 4 (1960), 50–65.

Lloyd, John Edward, *A History of Wales*, 3rd edn, 2 vols (London, 1939).

Lloyd-Jones, J., *Geirfa Barddoniaeth Gynnar Gymraeg*, 2 vols (Cardiff, 1931–63).

Löffler, Marion, with Rhys, Hywel Gethin, 'Thomas Stephens and the Abergavenny Cymreigyddion: letters from the *Cambrian* 1842–3', *NLWJ*, 34:4 (2009), 399–451.

Mabillon, J., *Acta Ordinis Sancti Benedicti*, I (Paris, 1668).

Maund, K. L., 'Fact and narrative fiction in the Llandaff charters', *SC*, 31 (1997), 173–93.

—— *Ireland, Wales, and England in the Eleventh Century* (Woodbridge, 1991).

McGurk, Patrick, *Latin Gospel Books from A.D. 400 to A.D. 800* (Paris, Brussels, Anvers, and Amsterdam, 1961).

McKee, Helen, *The Cambridge Juvencus Manuscript Glossed in Latin, Old Welsh, and Old Irish: Text and Commentary* (Aberystwyth, 2000).

Merdrignac, Bernard, 'La "Vita Oudocei" dans le "Liber Landavensis": traditions "profanes" et littérature hagiographique', *Hagiographica*, 19 (2012), 161–219.

Miller, M., 'Date-guessing and Dyfed', *SC*, 12/13 (1977–8), 33–61.

—— 'Date-guessing and pedigrees', *SC*, 10/11 (1975–6), 96–109.

Morey, Adrian, and Brooke, C. N. L., *Gilbert Foliot and his Letters* (Cambridge, 1965).

Morris, John, Review of Nora K. Chadwick (ed.), *Studies in the Early British Church* (Cambridge, 1958), in *WHR*, 1 (1960–3), 229–32.

—— *The Age of Arthur* (London, 1973).

Naismith, Rory, 'Payments for land and privilege in Anglo-Saxon England', *ASE*, 41 (2012), 277–342.

Bibliography

—— 'The land market and Anglo-Saxon society', *Historical Research*, 89:243 (2016), 19–41.
Nash-Williams, V. E., *The Early Christian Monuments of Wales* (Cardiff, 1950).
Newell, E. J., *Llandaff* (London, 1902).
—— Review of *LL*, in *Arch. Camb.*, 5th ser., 10 (1893), 332–9.
Noble, Frank, *Offa's Dyke Reviewed* (Oxford, 1983).
Nurmio, Silva, 'Middle Welsh -*awr*: the case of the lost plural suffix', *SC*, 48 (2014), 139–70.
Olson, Lynette (ed.), *St Samson of Dol and the Earliest History of Brittany, Cornwall and Wales* (Woodbridge, 2017).
Parsons, David N., *Martyrs and Memorials: 'Merthyr' Place-Names and the Church in Early Wales* (Aberystwyth, 2013).
Pearce, Susan, *The Kingdom of Dumnonia* (Padstow, 1978).
Pearson, M. J. (compiler), *John Le Neve: Fasti Ecclesiae Anglicanae 1066–1300*, IX, *The Welsh Cathedrals* (London, 2003).
Petts, David, *The Early Medieval Church in Wales* (Stroud, 2009).
Phillimore, Egerton, 'The *Annales Cambriae* and Old-Welsh genealogies from Harleian MS. 3859', *Y Cymmrodor*, 9 (1888), 141–83.
Piggott, Stuart, 'The sources of Geoffrey of Monmouth', *Antiquity*, 15 (1941), 269–86 and 305–19.
Pryce, Huw, 'Gerald of Wales and the Welsh past', in Georgia Henley and A. Joseph McMullen (eds), *Gerald of Wales: New Perspectives on a Medieval Writer and Critic* (Cardiff, 2018), 19–45.
—— *Native Law and the Church in Medieval Wales* (Oxford, 1993).
—— 'The church of Trefeglwys and the end of the "Celtic" charter tradition in twelfth-century Wales', *CMCS*, 25 (Summer 1993), 15–54.
Redknap, Mark, 'Crossing boundaries – stylistic diversity and external contacts in early medieval Wales and the March: reflections on metalwork and sculpture', *CMCS*, 53/54 (2007), 23–86.
Redknap, Mark, and Lewis, J. M., with Charles-Edwards, Gifford, Horák, Jana, Knight, Jeremy, and Sims-Williams, Patrick, *A Corpus of Early Medieval Inscribed Stones and Stone Sculpture in Wales*, Vol. I, *Breconshire, Glamorgan, Monmouthshire, Radnorshire, and Geographically Contiguous Areas of Herefordshire and Shropshire* (Cardiff, 2007).
Rees, W. J. (ed. and transl.), *The Liber Landavensis* (Llandovery, 1840).
Rees, William, *An Historical Atlas of Wales from Early to Modern Times*, new edn (London, 1972).
—— *South Wales and the Border in the Fourteenth Century* (map) (Cardiff, 1933).
Rhys, [John], 'The Kilmannin ogam, County Mayo', *Journal of the Royal Society of Antiquaries of Ireland*, 5th ser., 17 (1907), 61–8.
Richards, Melville, *Welsh Administrative and Territorial Units* (Cardiff, 1969).
Richter, Michael (ed.), *Canterbury Professions* (Torquay, 1973).
Robertson, A. J. (ed. and transl.), *Anglo-Saxon Charters* (Cambridge, 1939).
Russell, Paul, 'From plates and rods to royal drink-stands in *Branwen* and medieval Welsh law', *North American Journal of Celtic Studies*, 1 (2017), 1–26.
—— '*Priuilegium Sancti Teliaui* and *Breint Teilo*', *SC*, 50 (2016), 41–68.
—— (ed. and transl.), *Vita Griffini Filii Conani: The Medieval Latin Life of Gruffudd ap Cynan* (Cardiff, 2005).
Salesbury, William (transl.), *Testament Newydd* (London, 1567).
Sayers, William, '*Bisclavret* in Marie de France: a reply', *CMCS*, 4 (Winter 1982), 77–82.
Schrijver, Peter, *Language Contact and the Origins of the Germanic Languages* (Abingdon, 2014).
Seaman, Andy, 'Landscape, settlement and agriculture in early medieval Brycheiniog: the evidence from the Llandaff charters', in Rhiannon Comeau and Andy Seaman (eds), *Living Off the Land: Agriculture in Wales c. 400 to 1600 AD* (Oxford, forthcoming).
Seebohm, Frederic, *The Tribal System in Wales*, 2nd edn (London, 1904).
Sharpe, Richard, 'Gildas as a Father of the Church', in Michael Lapidge and David Dumville (eds), *Gildas: New Approaches* (Woodbridge, 1984), 193–205.

—— 'Which text is Rhygyfarch's *Life* of St David?', in J. Wyn Evans and Jonathan M. Wooding (eds), *St David of Wales: Cult, Church and Nation* (Woodbridge, 2007), 90–105.
Sharpe, Richard, and Davies, John Reuben (ed. and transl.), 'Rhygyfarch's *Life* of St David', in J. Wyn Evans and Jonathan M. Wooding (eds), *St David of Wales: Cult, Church and Nation* (Woodbridge, 2007), 107–55.
Sims-Williams, Patrick, 'A Turkish–Celtic problem in Chrétien de Troyes: the name *Cligés*', in John Carey, John T. Koch, and Pierre-Yves Lambert (eds), *Ildánach, Ildírech: A Festschrift for Proinsias Mac Cana* (Andover, Mass., and Aberystwyth, 1999), 215–30.
—— *Britain and Early Christian Europe: Studies in Early Medieval History and Culture* (Aldershot, 1995).
—— (ed.), *Buchedd Beuno: The Middle Welsh Life of St Beuno* (Dublin, 2018).
—— 'Did itinerant Breton *conteurs* transmit the *matière de Bretagne*?', *Romania*, 116 (1998), 72–111.
—— 'Edward IV's confirmation charter for Clynnog Fawr', in Colin Richmond and Isobel Harvey (eds), *Recognitions: Essays Presented to Edmund Fryde* (Aberystwyth, 1996), 229–41.
—— 'Historical need and literary narrative: a caveat from ninth-century Wales', *WHR*, 17:1 (1994), 1–40.
—— 'IE **peug´-* /**peuk´-* "to pierce" in Celtic: Old Irish *og* "sharp point", *ogam*, and *uaigid* "stitches", Gallo-Latin *Mars Ugius*, Old Welsh *–ug* and Middle Welsh *–y* "fist", Middle Welsh *vch* "fox", and ancient names like *Uccius*', *Transactions of the Philological Society*, 116:1 (2018), 117–30.
—— *Irish Influence on Medieval Welsh Literature* (Oxford, 2011).
—— *Religion and Literature in Western England, 600–800* (Cambridge, 1990).
—— Review of J. Gwenogvryn Evans with John Rhys (eds), *The Text of the Book of Llan Dâv* (reprinted Aberystwyth, 1979), Wendy Davies, *The Llandaff Charters* (Aberystwyth, 1979), and Wendy Davies, *An Early Welsh Microcosm* (London, 1978), in *Journal of Ecclesiastical History*, 33 (1982), 124–9.
—— *Studies on Celtic Languages before the Year 1000* (Aberystwyth, 2007).
—— *The Celtic Inscriptions of Britain: Phonology and Chronology, c. 400–1200* (Oxford, 2003).
—— 'The emergence of Old Welsh, Cornish and Breton orthography, 600–800: the evidence of Archaic Old Welsh', *BBCS*, 38 (1991), 20–86.
—— 'The kings of Morgannwg and Gwent in Asser's *Life of King Alfred*', *CMCS*, 74 (Winter 2017), 67–81.
—— 'The provenance of the Llywarch Hen poems: a case for Llan-gors, Brycheiniog', *CMCS*, 26 (Winter 1993), 27–63.
—— 'The uses of writing in early medieval Wales', in Huw Pryce (ed.), *Literacy in Medieval Celtic Societies* (Cambridge, 1998), 15–38.
Smith, A. H., *The Place-Names of Gloucestershire*, 4 vols (Cambridge, 1964–5).
Smith, J. Beverley, 'The kingdom of Morgannwg and the Norman conquest of Glamorgan', in T. B. Pugh (ed.), *Glamorgan County History*, Vol. III, *The Middle Ages* (Cardiff, 1971), 1–43.
Smith, Joshua Byron, 'Gerald of Wales, Walter Map and the Anglo-Saxon history of Lydbury North', in Georgia Henley and A. Joseph McMullen (eds), *Gerald of Wales: New Perspectives on a Medieval Writer and Critic* (Cardiff, 2018), 63–77.
—— *Walter Map and the Matter of Britain* (Philadelphia, 2017).
Smith, Lucy Toulmin (ed.), *The Itinerary in Wales of John Leland* (London, 1906).
—— (ed.), *The Itinerary of John Leland*, Vol. IV (London, 1909).
Snook, Ben, 'Who introduced charters into England? The case for Theodore and Hadrian', in Bruce O'Brien and Barbara Bombi (eds), *Textus Roffensis: Law, Language, and Libraries in Early Medieval England* (Turnhout, 2015), 257–89.
Snyder, Christopher A., *An Age of Tyrants: Britain and the Britons A.D. 400–600* (Stroud, 1998).
Sowerby, Richard, 'A family and its saint in the *Vita Prima Samsonis*', in Lynette Olson (ed.),

Bibliography

St Samson of Dol and the Earliest History of Brittany, Cornwall and Wales (Woodbridge, 2017), 19–36.
Spelman, Henry, *Concilia, Decreta, Leges, Constitutiones, in re Ecclesiarum Orbis Britannici*, I (London, 1639).
Stenton, F. M., *Anglo-Saxon England*, 3rd edn (Oxford, 1971).
—— *Preparatory to Anglo-Saxon England* (Oxford, 1970).
—— *The Latin Charters of the Anglo-Saxon Period* (Oxford, 1955).
Stevenson, William Henry (ed.), *Asser's Life of King Alfred*, new impression (Oxford, 1959).
Stillingfleet, Edward, *Origines Britannicae, or, The Antiquities of the British Churches* (London, 1685).
Strype, John, *The Life and Acts of Matthew Parker in Four Books*, 3 vols (Oxford, 1821).
Suggett, Richard, 'Iolo Morganwg: stonecutter, builder, and antiquary', in Geraint H. Jenkins (ed.), *A Rattleskull Genius: The Many Faces of Iolo Morganwg* (Cardiff, 2005), 197–226.
Thornton, David E., 'Some Welshmen in Domesday Book and beyond: aspects of Anglo-Welsh relations in the eleventh century', in Nick Higham (ed.), *Britons in Anglo-Saxon England* (Woodbridge, 2007), 144–64.
Thorpe, Lewis (transl.), *Gerald of Wales: The Journey Through Wales and The Description of Wales* (Harmondsworth, 1978).
Tinti, Francesca, 'The reuse of charters at Worcester between the eighth and the eleventh century: a case study', *Midland History*, 37:2 (2012), 127–41.
Uhlich, Jürgen, *Die Morphologie der komponierten Personennamen des Altirischen* (Witterschlick and Bonn, 1993).
Ussher, James, *Britannicarum Ecclesiarum Antiquitates* (London, 1687).
Vaughan, Henry F. J., 'Welsh pedigrees', *Y Cymmrodor*, 10 (1890), 72–156.
Vincent of Beauvais, *Bibliotheca Mundi Vincentii Burgundi Praesulis Bellovacensis*, Vol. IV, *Speculum Historiale* (Douai, 1624).
Wade-Evans, A. W., 'The Llancarfan charters', *Arch. Camb.*, 87 (1932), 151–65.
Wareham, Andrew, 'The redaction of cartularies and economic upheaval in western England, c. 996–1096', *Anglo-Norman Studies*, 36 (2013), 189–219.
Whitelock, Dorothy (ed.), *English Historical Documents c. 500–1042*, 1st edn (London, 1968).
Wilkins, David (ed.), *Concilia Magnae Britanniae et Hiberniae* (London, 1737).
Williams, David, *The History of Monmouthshire* (London, 1796).
Williams, G. J., *Iolo Morganwg: Y Gyfrol Gyntaf* (Cardiff, 1956).
Williams, Hugh, *Gildas*, 2 vols (London, 1899–1901).
Williams, Ifor, 'claforawg', *BBCS*, 7:3 (1934), 277–8.
—— 'The Ogmore Castle inscription', *Arch. Camb.*, 87 (1932), 232–8.
Williams, Taliesin (ed. and transl.), *Iolo Manuscripts* (Llandovery, 1848).
Williams Ab Ithel, J. (ed.), *Annales Cambriae* (London, 1860).
Willis-Bund, J. W., 'The Teilo churches', *Arch. Camb.*, 5th ser., 10 (1893), 193–217.
Wooding, Jonathan M., 'The representation of early British monasticism and *peregrinatio* in the *Vita Prima S. Samsonis*', in Lynette Olson (ed.), *St Samson of Dol and the Earliest History of Brittany, Cornwall and Wales* (Woodbridge, 2017), 137–61.
Woolf, Alex, Review of T. M. Charles-Edwards, *Wales and the Britons, 350–1064* (Oxford, 2013), in *EHR*, 129 (2014), 160–2.
Wormald, Francis, 'The Sherborne "Chartulary"', in D. J. Gordon (ed.), *Fritz Saxl 1890–1948: A Volume of Memorial Essays* (Edinburgh, 1957), 101–19.
Wormald, Patrick, 'Celtic and Anglo-Saxon kingship: some further thoughts', in Paul E. Szarmach with Virginia Darrow Oggins (eds), *Sources of Anglo-Saxon Culture* (Kalamazoo, 1986), 151–83.
—— Review of J. Gwenogvryn Evans with John Rhys (eds), *The Text of the Book of Llan Dâv* (reprinted Aberystwyth, 1979), Wendy Davies, *The Llandaff Charters* (Aberystwyth, 1979), and Wendy Davies, *An Early Welsh Microcosm* (London, 1978), in *History*, 66 (1981), 113–14.
—— *The Making of English Law: King Alfred to the Twelfth Century*, Vol. I, *Legislation and its Limits* (Oxford, 1999).

INDEX

Abbey Dore 162
Abraham, layman 170
ABT (*Achau Brenhinoedd a Thywysogion Cymru*) 53, 122, 126, 132–5, 149, 156
Aceru 172
Aedán 165
Aeddan 23, 34, 43, 144, 162, 162, 165
Ælfric, archbishop 24, 61, 175
Aelhaearn 164
Ælnoth 24
Aergol 35, 53
Æthelbald 27, 56, 91, 136, 137, 141, 148, 152, 153, 155, 167
Æthelnoth 24
Æthelred, archbishop 24–5, 68, 171, 172
Æthelred, ealdorman 119–20
Æthelred, the Unready 48, 60, 85, 112
ager 46
Aidan *see* Aeddan
Aircol *see* Aergol
Alfred 25, 68, 119–20, 171
alumnus 163
Amon 157–8
Anergyng 46–7, 147
Anglian genealogies 119
Anglo-Saxon Chronicle 20, 23, 25, 46, 49, 50, 56, 60, 62, 65, 69, 117, 140, 144, 153, 171, 172
Anna 157–8
Annales Cambriae 4, 8, 15, 23, 24, 51–3, 56, 57, 68, 69, 121, 122, 136–8, 140, 141, 143–4, 153, 155, 160, 169
Anselm 7, 8, 21, 177
Arb, *Arbeth* 129, 133, 136
Archenfield *see* Ergyng
Arguistil *see* Arwystl
Ariconium 117
Arthauael 122
Arthfael ap Hywel 171

Arthfael ab Ithel 57, 152, 154
Arthfael ap Nowy 174–5
Arthfael ap Rhys 30, 128
Arthfael, grandfather of Hywel ap Rhys 134–6, 141
Arthur ap Pedr 15, 144
Artmail *see* Arthfael
Aruael 122–3
Arwystl 23, 26, 34–5, 43, 90, 93, 144, 161, 162, 163, 165
Arx Etri 158
Asser 26, 30, 50, 59, 68–9, 117–21, 128, 136, 140, 141, 156, 169, 170, 171–2
Athelstan, bishop 20, 176–7
Athelstan, king 48, 69, 174
Athruis rex Guenti 55
Athrwys ab Ithel 152
Athrwys ap Ffernfael 121
Athrwys ap Ffernfael 155
Athrwys ap Meurig 32, 55, 146, 147, 149, 156, 163
Athrwys ap Morgan 148
Athrwys ap Tewdrig 132, 156
Augustine of Canterbury 9, 17
Augustinian canons 164
Avranches 157
Awst 49, 57, 66, 150, 152

Ballingham 163
Bardsey Island 8, 159, 161
Bath Abbey 48
Bavaria 115
Beachley-Aust crossing 48, 60
Beiliau 176
Bellamore 162, 163, 164, 167
Bernard, bishop 7, 9, 19
Bernard of Neufmarché 21
Berthwyn (*Berthguin*) 16, 22–3, 27, 28–9, 33, 39, 44, 45, 46, 55, 56, 60, 61, 67, 85–90, 100, 102, 107, 108, 112, 137,

148, 150–1, 152, 153, 155, 165, 166, 167, 168, 173, 176
Beuno 12–13, 106–7, 164
Beuno, *Life* of *see* Buchedd Beuno
bisclavret 51
bishop-houses 85
Bishopston 18, 69–70, 145, 160
Bishton 29, 99, 112
Bithén 34, 163, 166
Biuan 34, 40, 162
Biuon *see* Bywon
Biuone *see* Bywonwy
Bleddri 23–5, 62, 65, 66, 175–6
Bleiddudd 24
Blethuth 24
Bodmin Manumissions 13
Bonedd yr Arwyr 124
Bonus 155, 170–1
Book of Deer 13
Book of Kells 13
Book of St Beuno 12–13
Book of St Chad *see* Lichfield Gospels
bounds 17, 19, 20, 47–8, 49, 51, 84, 91, 93, 94, 97, 98, 100, 103, 150, 166
Boverton 64
Braint Teilo 23, 62, 106, 116
Bramail 41
Brawstudd/Brawst 129, 131, 132
Brecchert 167
Bredwardine 162, 167
Briafael 41, 125, 131, 147, 149, 150
Britannia 153
Brittany 10–12, 16, 51, 84, 100, 105, 115, 159
Britcon 26, 94
Brochfael ap Meurig 29–31, 50, 59, 117–22, 136, 137, 141, 155, 168–9, 172
Brochfael ap Rhys 154
Brochmail filius Guidgentiuai 60, 149–50
Brychan Brycheiniog 67, 118
Brycheiniog 18, 19, 35, 46, 49, 57, 66, 67–9, 119–20, 136, 150, 155, 156, 160, 163, 167–8, 170, 172, 178
Buchedd Beuno 53–4, 106, 144, 164
Buellt 129, 136, 140
Bywon 66
Bywonwy 40

Cadell ab Arthfael 24, 173
Cadell ap Morgan 175

Cadien 40
Cadog 13, 28, 92, 100, 118, 145
Cadwallon 54, 107, 144
Cadwared 23, 27, 28–9, 55, 56, 90, 91, 102, 107, 110, 154, 165, 167, 168
Cadwgon ab Owain 173
Cadwgon ap Cathen 144
Cadwgon ap Meurig 19, 176
Cadwgon *Tredicil* 53
Caerleon 170
Caernarfon 12
Caerurgorn 63
Caer-went 117, 159, 172, 174, 175, 178
Caldy Island 8, 158–60
Calixtus II 8, 9
Camden, William 63
Camelauc, Cameleac *see* Cyfeilliog
Canterbury 7, 8, 9, 17, 24–5, 60, 68, 111, 118, 171, 174
Cantref Bychan 19, 159, 176
Cantref Selyf 68, 162
Caradog ab Ynyr Gwent 54
Caradog ap Brân 124
Caradog ap Gruffudd 19, 21, 176, 177
Caradog ap Iestyn 126
Caradog Freichfras 26, 54, 124
Caradog of Llancarfan 7, 9–10, 71, 177
Cardiff 7, 29, 51, 168
Carey in Ballingham 163
Carlisle, Nicholas 64
Carmarthen 159
Carte, Thomas 63
Cartulary of Landevennec 14
Cartulary of Redon 112
Caswell Bay 160
Catgen *see* Cadien
Catguaret *see* Cadwared
Catthig 40
Cegidfa 164
Ceincair 132, 154
Ceingar 129, 131, 132, 141
Cemais 121, 168
Cemelliauc prudens prespiter 172
Cenedlon (*Kenedlon*) 129, 131, 132, 136, 147, 149
Cennit/Kennit (Cenydd) 61, 63, 64–5
Cenubia Colcuch *see* Lann/Cenubia Calcuch/Colcuch
Cenydd *see* Cennit/Kennit
Ceredigion 69, 178

Index

Cerennyr (*Cerenhir*)   22, 23, 33, 49, 110, 154, 168–9, 170, 174, 178
Cetnig/Cethig   29, 40
'Chad'   *see* CHARTERS
CHARTERS
   'Chad' **1**   10, 84
   'Chad' **2**   25, 103, 115
   'Chad' **3**   11, 26, 87, 103, 161, 170
   'Chad' **4**   103, 170
   'Chad' **5**   13, 15, 116, 170
   LL **72a**   16, 33, 34, 36, 42–3, 131, 142, 144, 145, 146, 161, 162, 165
   LL **72b**   34, 36, 42–3, 47, 83, 144, 162
   LL **73a**   34, 36, 42–3, 78, 83, 90, 144, 161, 162, 165
   LL **73b**   22, 26, 34, 36, 42–3, 45, 59, 75, 89, 90, 93–4, 103, 111, 143, 144, 162
   LL **74**   26, 44, 59, 75, 77, 83, 90, 93, 94–6, 103, 106, 110, 111, 145, 146, 168, 170
   LL **75**   33, 34, 36, 42, 45, 78, 144, 147, 161, 162, 164
   LL **76a**   33, 34, 36, 42–3, 45, 47, 78, 109, 144, 145, 161, 162
   LL **76b**   34, 36, 42–3, 59, 83, 144, 145, 160, 161, 162
   LL **77**   33–4, 36, 39, 42–3, 44, 60, 81, 83, 143–4, 159–60, 161, 162
   LL **121**   34, 36, 42–3, 83, 144, 161, 162, 163, 168
   LL **122**   34, 36, 42–3, 83, 144, 161, 162, 163
   LL **123**   83, 112, 144, 162, 164, 168
   LL **125a**   35, 83, 112, 162
   LL **125b**   35, 51, 53, 83, 112, 162
   LL **127a**   35, 53, 59, 112, 162
   LL **127b**   35, 53, 59, 83, 110, 112, 162
   LL **140** [ii.2]   40, 41, 66, 129, 132, 143, 146, 147, 148, 166
   LL **141**   55, 112, 148
   LL **143** [ii.3]   40, 41, 83, 109, 111, 149
   LL **144** [ii.1]   40, 41, 66, 80, 83, 112, 148, 166
   LL **145**   38, 66, 150, 166
   LL **146**   49, 57, 68, 150, 166, 168
   LL **147** [ii.4]   40, 112, 149, 150, 151
   LL **148**   109, 150, 165
   LL **149** [ii.8]   29, 40, 143, 149
   LL **150a** [ii.16]   41, 109, 150, 165
   LL **150b** [ii.15]   40, 83, 150, 166
   LL **151a** [ii.9]   59, 60, 107, 149
   LL **151b** [ii.7]   40, 149
   LL **152** [ii.5]   40, 80, 83, 105, 112, 114, 149
   LL **154**   49, 57, 68, 83, 150, 166
   LL **155** [ii.6]   40, 149
   LL **156**   150, 165, 166
   LL **157**   30, 49, 112, 150, 152, 165
   LL **158** [ii.30]   41, 44–5, 87, 109, 148, 150, 152
   LL **159a**   83, 152
   LL **159b** [ii.10]   59, 60, 107, 150
   LL **160**   34, 36, 42, 144, 145–6, 147, 162
   LL **161**   34–5, 36, 42, 80, 88, 112, 144, 146, 162
   LL **162a**   34–5, 36, 42, 60, 144, 146, 163
   LL **162b**   34, 36, 42, 94, 144, 162
   LL **163a**   22, 26, 34, 36, 42–3, 45, 59, 75, 89, 90, 93–4, 103, 111, 143, 144, 161
   LL **163b**   34, 36, 42–3, 62, 137, 144, 146, 163, 164, 165
   LL **164**   34–5, 36, 42, 62, 144, 146, 161, 163, 165
   LL **165**   32, 34, 36, 42–3, 62, 83, 93, 144, 146, 147, 163, 164, 165, 166
   LL **166**   34, 36, 42–3, 68, 144, 162, 163
   LL **167**   20, 35, 57, 67, 68, 112, 167
   LL **168** [iii.14]   33, 107, 168, 170–1
   LL **169a** [iii.15]   33, 107, 168, 170, 171
   LL **169b** [iii.2]   26, 168, 170
   LL **170** [iii.1]   26, 111, 168, 170
   LL **171a** [iii.3]   107, 170
   LL **171b**   26, 44, 59, 73, 75, 77, 90, 91, 93, 94–6, 103, 106, 110, 111, 145, 146, 168, 170
   LL **173**   73, 170
   LL **174a** [iii.4]   107, 170
   LL **174b**   48, 87, 88, 151, 165
   LL **175**   44, 45, 48, 75, 81, 84, 87, 88–90, 91, 93, 96–7, 99, 103, 111, 143, 152, 165
   LL **176a** [ii.22]   29, 48, 75, 87, 88–90, 91, 93, 97–8, 102, 103, 108, 109, 111, 151
   LL **176b**   73, 88–9, 91, 151, 167
   LL **178** [ii.44]   73, 88, 91, 107, 152,

167
LL **179a**   23, 35, 75, 87, 88–90, 91, 93, 98–9, 107, 111, 151
LL **179b**   73, 75, 87, 88, 90, 91, 93, 99, 103, 106, 108, 109, 111, 152
LL **179c** [ii.29]   39, 41, 73, 88, 152
LL **180a** [ii.28]   41, 27, 28–9, 35, 39–40, 41, 66, 75, 80, 88, 90, 91, 93, 99–102, 151
LL **180b** [ii.25]   40, 102, 103, 111, 112, 114, 151
LL **183a**   87, 88, 152, 161, 166
LL **183b**   22, 23, 35, 88, 151, 168
LL **184** [ii.39]   88, 107, 152, 165, 167
LL **185**   80, 87, 88, 107, 114, 115, 152, 165
LL **186a** [ii.43]   45, 80, 87, 88, 91, 107, 152
LL **186b**   44, 75, 84, 87, 88, 90, 91, 93, 96–7, 99, 103, 111, 143, 152, 165
LL **187**   87, 88, 91, 152, 165
LL **188a** [ii.40]   88, 91, 107, 109, 152, 165
LL **188b**   35, 75, 87, 88–90, 91, 93, 98–9, 110, 111, 151
LL **189**   88, 91, 152, 165
LL **190a**   87, 88, 91, 114, 152
LL **190b** [ii.23]   48, 75, 87, 88, 90, 91, 93, 97–8, 103, 104, 107, 108, 109, 111, 132, 151
LL **191** [ii.34]   75, 87, 88, 90, 91, 93, 99, 103, 106, 107, 108, 111, 115, 121, 152, 154
LL **192**   27, 80, 88, 91, 93, 97, 112, 137, 141, 152, 153, 167
LL **193**   23, 87, 88, 91, 112, 167
LL **195**   87, 88, 91, 109, 111, 121, 152, 167
LL **196**   23, 87, 91, 110, 112
LL **197** [ii.48]   87, 107, 110, 153, 165
LL **198a** [ii.46]   13, 87, 107, 110, 153, 165
LL **198b**   114, 121, 154
LL **199a** [ii.49]   107, 109, 111, 153
LL **199bi**   22, 121, 154
LL **199bii**   22, 120, 122, 155, 169
LL **200** [ii.55]   41, 154, 165
LL **201** [ii.50]   107, 115, 154
LL **202** [ii.45]   41, 107, 115, 152, 165
LL **203a** [ii.51]   107, 115, 154, 155

LL **203b** [ii.54]   107, 115, 116, 154, 155
LL **204a**   121, 153, 165
LL **204b** [ii.27]   33, 39, 55, 80, 87, 107, 110, 115, 116, 151, 152, 165
LL **205**   33, 39, 60, 87, 110, 151, 154, 165
LL **206**   155
LL **207**   109, 132, 154
LL **208**   155
LL **209a**   109, 154
LL **209b** [ii.58]   87, 104, 107, 115, 154, 161
LL **210a**   155, 161
LL **210b**   29, 39, 40, 41, 66, 75, 77, 80, 84, 90, 91, 93, 102, 110, 111, 143, 154
LL **211a**   38, 154
LL **211b** [ii.62]   55, 110, 155
LL **212**   80, 128, 168
LL **214** [iii.10]   33, 38, 120, 122, 128, 140, 155, 168, 169
LL **216a**   169, 170, 172
LL **216b** [iii.17]   106, 114, 122, 169, 170
LL **217**   173
LL **218** [iii.39]   44, 87, 105, 106, 114, 173
LL **221** [iii.38]   106, 173, 174
LL **222**   24, 166, 173
LL **223**   24, 80, 172, 173
LL **224** [iii.35]   106, 173
LL **225** [iii.12]   83, 106, 122, 155, 168, 170
LL **227a**   51, 168
LL **227b**   51, 168
LL **228**   106, 168
LL **229a**   75
LL **229b**   48, 109, 121, 151, 168
LL **230a**   168
LL **230b**   168, 170
LL **231**   145, 172
LL **233**   80, 115
LL **234** [iii.26]   172, 173
LL **235a**   170, 172
LL **235b** [iii.27]   172, 173
LL **236**   170, 171
LL **237a** [iii.25]   83, 171, 172, 173
LL **237b** [iii.34]   67–8, 80, 160, 172–3
LL **239** [iii.33]   67, 69, 80, 109, 160,

Index

LL 240   172–3, 174
LL 243   166, 174, 175
LL 244   106, 174
LL 245   174–5
LL 246   83, 176
LL 247   22
LL 249b   175
LL 253   35, 176
LL 255   114
LL 257   80
LL 258 [iii.52]   107
LL 259   30
LL 261   19
LL 262 [iii.47]   72, 107, 109, 110, 174, 175
LL 263   49
LL 264a   49, 109, 176
LL 264b   109
LL 267   19, 83, 176
LL 269   35, 176
LL 271 [iii.60]   83, 107, 176
LL 272   19, 83, 176
LL 274   49, 110, 176, 176
Sawyer **60**   44
Sawyer **205**   72
Sawyer **215**   82
Sawyer **216**   82
Sawyer **610**   48
Sawyer **913**   60
Sawyer **1260**   90
Sawyer **1426**   48
Sawyer **1430**   90
Sawyer **1432**   90
Sawyer **1462**   13
Sawyer **1469**   13
Sawyer **1540–1602**   103
Sawyer **1555**   48
VC **55**   15, 39, 40, 41, 43, 57, 154, 166
VC **56**   13, 39–40, 41, 154
VC **57**   40, 145
VC **59**   41, 151
VC **60**   39
VC **61**   41, 151
VC **62**   39–40, 41, 55, 107, 151
VC **63**   152
VC **64**   40, 41, 148, 166
VC **65**   29, 40–1, 61, 148, 152, 166
VC **66**   29, 39–40, 41, 55, 66, 75, 80, 84, 90, 92, 93, 98, 102, 110, 111, 143, 154
VC **67**   28–9, 39–40, 41, 46, 61, 66, 75, 80, 90, 92, 93, 99–102, 103, 111, 112, 151
VC **68**   29, 40, 41, 55, 92, 148, 150, 166
VC **69**   92
Chepstow   146, 163
Childebert   52
Cil hal   164
Cimeilliauc   see Cyfeilliog
Cinan filius Cinuedu   150
Cinuarch   see Cynfarch
Cinuin   see Cynfyn
Cinuur   see Cynwr
clafhorec   51
Clas Cynidr/Clas-ar-Wy   see Glasbury
clasau   164
clauorauc   51, 129, 131
Clodock   66–70, 91, 167, 173, 178
Clothen   129
Clotri   150–1
Clydog   67, 87
Clynnog   12, 53–4, 87, 106
Codex Wintoniensis   44
Collectio Canonum Hibernensis   12, 106
Collier, Jeremy   63
Colmán, abbot   163
Comereg   see Cyfwyre
comites   4, 114
Conan   170–1
Conbran   43
Concen   see Cyngen
Concuun   see Cuncuan
Conguarui   see Cynwarwy
Conigc   see Cynyng
consecrations   17, 19, 20, 21, 23–5, 46, 52, 61, 66, 68–9, 80, 81, 86, 140, 171, 172, 174, 175, 176
consiliarii   159
Constantinus rex   131, 145
Conuc   55
Conuelin   55
Conuil   55
Conybeare, W. D.   2
Cornwall   10, 19, 51, 157, 159
Cors   55
Crickhowell   163
Crucmetil   159
Cuchein   170–1

Cuhelin 15
Culhwch ac Olwen 51, 131, 146
Cum Barruc 162, 164
Cuncuan/Concuun 39–40
Custennin 142, 145
Cuthbert 177
Cydweli 117, 159, 176
Cyfeilliog 23–5, 46, 49, 61, 62–3, 65, 68–9, 110, 115, 140, 170, 171–2, 173, 176
Cyfelach 65
Cyfwyre 23, 34–5, 43, 62, 144, 146, 162, 163, 165
Cynesige 19
Cynfarch, disciple of Dyfrig 43, 163
Cynfarch, father of Urien Rheged 54
Cynfyn ap Gwrgan 170
Cynfyn ap Morgan 175
Cynfyn ap Peibio 35, 59, 144–5, 147
Cyngen 41, 92, 152
Cynidr (*Keneder*) 20, 167
Cynuetu 149–50
Cynwarwy 43
Cynwr 67, 69–70
Cynyng (*Conigc*) 15, 38–9, 41, 151, 152, 154

Daan (*Dagan*) 41, 92, 152
Danog (*Danoc*) 39, 41, 152
David (Dewi) 51, 53, 60, 163
Davies, Richard 14
De Primo Statu Landauensis Æcclesiæ 23, 26, 52, 83, 146, 147
degion 115
Deheubarth 19, 143
Deowiesstow 48, 60
Deui filius Circan 163
Dewchurch 51, 164, 167
Dewi *see* David
Dewstow 21, 60
Dibran 170
Dilwyn 13
Din Birrion/Borrion 102
Dingestow 51
diplomatic 1, 13, 17, 25, 27, 67, 71–7, 78–85, 86, 89, 93–103, 106, 108, 109, 110, 148
Dissaith 174
Dixton 161, 166, 168
Dofran 170–1

Dol 100, 157
Domesday Book 20, 47, 50
Dore 93, 94, 162, 164
Dorstone 47, 162
Doward 163, 164, 166
Dubricius see Dyfrig
Dugdale, William 2, 62
Dulon 59, 160
Dunsæte/Dunsætan 48, 147
Dunstan 174
Durham 177
Dyfed 33, 35, 53, 57, 117, 119–20, 129, 136, 140, 141, 143, 144, 157, 159–60, 169
Dyfrig 8, 10, 17–18, 22–3, 26, 33–4, 39, 41–3, 47, 50, 52–3, 54, 78, 81, 88, 90, 93, 96, 116, 131, 137, 140, 142, 144, 145, 146, 147, 152, 155, 158–62, 164, 165, 166, 177
Dyrham 50

Eadred 119
Eadwig 48
Earlswood 174
Eaton Bishop 47, 93, 162
Eddylfyw 23, 33, 168, 170–1, 178
Edeligion 159
Edgar 140, 174
Edilbiu see Eddylfyw
Edward IV 12
Edward the Elder 25, 171, 172
Edwin ab Einion 13, 20
Einion 166
Einudd 30, 124, 134
Elbod 61–2, 65
Eleothen 129
Elffin 55, 91
Elgist(us) (Arwystl) 23, 26, 93, 161
Elgistus (Elwystl) 90
Elguoredus 43
Elhaearn 34, 43, 144, 162, 164, 165
Elifled 61–2, 64
Elise *see* Elisedd
Elisedd ap Tewdwr 57, 119–20, 136
Elisedd, abbot 168
Elnodd 24
Eltutus see Illtud
Eluogus 23, 91,
Elwystl ab Awst 57, 67, 154
Eneuris 173

Enlli *see* Bardsey Island
Enniaun 166
Enynny 26, 54
Enyth see Einudd
equonimus 162–3
Erb 34, 45, 52, 54, 129, 136, 147, 164
Erbic 34, 55, 146
Eres 109
Ergyng 8, 17, 19–21, 23, 25, 26, 46–7, 51, 54, 55, 85, 90, 93, 114, 117, 121, 122, 143, 146, 147, 149, 153, 156, 159, 160–2, 163, 164, 165, 166, 167, 168, 170, 171, 172, 176–7, 178
Erminthridh 171
Eruic 34, 146
Euddogwy 8, 9, 17–18, 23, 26–7, 39, 40–1, 44, 45, 46, 49, 53, 55, 57, 59, 61, 66, 68, 78, 81, 87, 88, 92, 100, 107, 112, 116, 143, 148, 150, 151, 152, 155, 163, 165–7, 168, 173, 174, 178
Eudeyrn 40
Eudoce see Euddogwy
Eugenius III 53
Ewias 19, 66, 164, 167, 170, 176

Fairwater 98
Ffernfael ab Ithel 56, 107, 121, 132, 137, 140, 141, 144, 151–2, 152, 153, 154, 155, 174
Ffernfael ap Meurig 50, 117–22, 136, 155–6, 168
Ffernfael of Buellt 136
Ffili 18, 174
Ffriog 149
Fidelis 35
Finnant 140, 155
finnaun i cleuion 51
Foy 168

Gaidnerth filius Morcanti frater 151
Ganarew 163, 164, 166
Garb 145, 160
Garth Benni *see* Welsh Bicknor
Garu 145, 160
Garway 43, 163, 164, 165, 167
Geneddlon *see* Cenedlon
Geoffrey of Monmouth 27, 30, 52, 57
Geoffrey Stephen 10
Gerald of Wales 24, 52, 53, 65, 114
Germanus 9, 17, 52, 146, 157–8

Gildas 12, 13, 157
Glamorgan, diocese and lordship 7, 18, 19, 20, 25, 117, 118, 126, 176
Glasbury 18, 20–1, 25, 49, 60, 68, 167, 172–3, 176, 178
Gloiu 170
Gloucester 1, 10, 21, 28
Glywys 54, 97, 117, 145, 159, 160
Glywysing 117, 118–22, 128, 132, 136, 145, 150, 153, 154, 155, 156, 159, 160, 166, 168, 177, 178
Gnauan 152
Gnawan 41
Gnouan 41, 151, 152
Gorbothu Hen 146
Gospels of Gildas 86
Gower 17–19, 38, 61, 66, 67, 68–9, 117, 145, 160, 162, 172, 173, 176, 178
Great Doward *see* Doward
Greciel 22, 23, 26, 91, 96, 168–9, 170, 177
Gruffudd ab Owain 69, 160, 172, 173
Gruffudd ap Cynan 118
Gruffudd ap Hyfaidd 69
Gruffudd ap Llywelyn 20, 35, 176
Gruffudd ap Rhydderch 48
Guadan sacerdos 60
Guallonir/Guallunir 151
Gucaun see Gwgon
Guedg(u)en(us) see Guidgen
Guednerth frater Morcanti 151
Gueman 20, 67, 167
Guengarth 39–41
Guenuor 146
Guernabui 146
Guidcon 146
Guidgen/Guedg(u)en(us) see Gwyddien
Guidnerth filius Guallonir 151
Guidnerth see Gaidnerth
Guilsfield 164
Guinda 172
Guingual 171
Gulbrit see Wulffrith
Guodloiu see Gwyddloyw
Guoidnerth see Gwyddnerth
Guorduc 59, 160
Gurai 48, 97
Gurcant see Gwrgan
Gurceniu 55
Gurcon 146
Gurgauarn filius Fernuail 121, 155

205

Gurguare see Gwrwarwy
Gurhi 175
Gurtauan 35
Guruan see Gwrfan
Guruodu see Gwrfoddw
Guruthon son of *Mabon* 35
Gutun Owain 133
Gwehelyth Morgannwg 125–6, 129, 132, 134–5, 149
Gwent 8, 30, 46, 54, 117, 118–22, 126, 128, 135, 136, 140, 144, 147, 155, 156, 157, 159, 162, 163, 164, 166, 167, 168, 170, 172, 174, 175, 177, 178
Gwent Is Coed 19, 176
Gwent Uwch Coed 19, 176
Gwgan of Llancarfan 7, 9
Gwgon 23–5, 140, 174–5, 176
Gwrfan 18–19, 20, 23, 43, 67–70, 167, 172–3, 177, 178
Gwrfoddw 145–6, 147
Gwrgan ab Ithel 126
Gwrgan ap Cynfyn 55, 59, 146, 147, 149
Gwrgan ap Ffernfael 154, 155
Gwrgan i.e. Urban 7
Gwrgan the Great 55, 129, 143, 146, 147–9
Gwrgan, ninth-century grantor 170
Gwriad/*Wurgeat* 174
Gwriad ap Brochfael 30, 126–9, 133, 134, 141, 156
Gwrinydd 97
Gwrthefyr 54
Gwrtheyrn 54
Gwrwarwy 163, 166–7
Gwyddgi ap Peibio 59, 144–5
Gwyddien (*Guedgen/Guidgen*) 55, 60, 149–50
Gwyddloyw 23, 33, 168, 170–1, 178
Gwyddnerth (*Guoidnerth*) 28–9, 39
Gwynedd 118, 144
Gwynllŵg 19, 176
Gŵyr *see* Gower

Hanbury 163
Hedilbiu see Eddylfyw
Hemming's Cartulary 14, 60, 71, 72
Henfynyw 15, 178
Henllann 161
Henog 157
Henriu Gunua 176

Henry, Robert 63
Hentland 161
heredes 104, 108, 109
hereditarii 99, 104, 108, 109
Hereford 1, 8, 13, 20–1, 56, 65, 153, 176–8
Hereford Gospel Book (Cambridge, Pembroke College 302) 20
Hereford Gospels 12–14
heres see heredes
Herewald 8, 9, 10, 17–21, 22, 23, 25, 26, 35, 46, 49, 50, 61, 67, 69, 80, 86, 161, 167, 176–8
Higueid 69
Honorius II 52, 53
Howth 158
Hyfaidd 69, 119–20, 136, 169, 170, 172
Hywel (*ob.* 885/6) 137, 140
Hywel ab Owain 176
Hywel ap Rhys 50, 59, 117–22, 131, 135, 136, 137, 140, 141, 151, 155–6, 168–9, 171–2, 173, 174

Iacob, abbot 40, 41, 92, 152
Iacob filius Mabsu 39–40
Iddon ab Ynyr Gwent 53–4, 144, 146, 147, 161, 162, 163, 164
Idnerth ap Meurig 41, 148
Idwallon ap Morgan 174, 175
Iestyn ap Gwrgan 126, 132, 176
Ieuan ap Madog ap Rhys 133
Ilias 91
Iliuc 26
Illtud 52, 61, 64, 65, 66, 157–8, 160
Inabwy 23, 34–5, 43, 62, 144, 145, 146, 162, 163, 165
Innocent II 9
Insula Teithi 17
Iolo Goch 12
Iolo Morganwg 2, 61–6, 169, 171, 175
Irb(eth) 133
Ireland/Irish 10–13, 17, 51, 57, 86, 106, 115, 145, 154, 158, 160, 163, 165
Isanus 61, 65
Ithel ab Athrwys 30, 121, 136, 137, 140, 150, 152, 155, 156
Ithel ap Morgan 56, 57, 67, 153, 107, 109, 135, 136, 137, 141, 150, 151–2, 153, 155, 167
Ithel of Gwent (*ob.* 848) 121, 137, 155,

156
Iudguoret 170–1
Iudhael see Ithel
Iudic filius Nud 150, 151
Iudnerth see Idnerth
Iunabui see Inabwy

Jesus, witness 14, 26
John of Worcester 25, 48
Jones, John, of Gelli Lyfdy 132–3
Jones, Thomas, of Tregaron 125, 129
Joseph, bishop 7, 8, 18–20, 23–5, 35, 46, 49, 81, 175–6, 178
Joseph, 'archbishop' of St Davids 8
Juvencus Manuscript 172

Kenderchurch (*Lanncinitir*) 20, 167
Keneder see Cynidr
Kenedlon see Cenedlon
Kennit see Cennit
Kentigern 52, 137
Kidwelly see Cydweli
Kildare 169
Kilmannin 145
Kyllin ap Kradoc 124

Lancaut 48, 163, 164, 166
Lann Bocha/Mocha 94
Lann/Cenubia Calcuch/Colcuch 93, 164, 167
Lann Cerniu 47, 162, 164, 167
Lann Cinith 61
Lann Custenhinngarthbenni 145
Lann Dewi 51
Lann Ebrdil 167
Lann Enniaun 16, 166–7, 173
Lann Guern 161
Lann Guoruoe/Guorboe 163
Lann Merguall 38
Lann Oudocui see Llandogo
Lanncinitir see Kenderchurch
Lannsanbregit 160
Lech Oudoucui 166
lector 162–3
Ledbury 21
Leland, John 15, 61, 144
Leofgar 20, 177
Liber Vitae 13
Liber Wigorniensis 78
Libiau see Llibio

librae 116
Lichfield 10, 13
Lichfield (or Chad/Llandeilo) Gospels 4, 10–16, 25–6, 27, 32, 93, 104, 105, 108, 143
Life of Beuno see *Buchedd Beuno*
Life see *Vita*
Lifris of Llancarfan 13, 28, 46
Little Dewchurch 163
Little Doward see Doward
LL see CHARTERS
llan 164
Llan Sanfrigt / Llanfride 15
Llan-arth 144, 161, 162, 164, 168
Llancarfan 4, 7, 9, 12, 13, 15, 27, 28–9, 32, 38–9, 40–1, 45, 46, 55, 66, 78–9, 90, 92, 100, 102, 107, 121, 143, 145, 151, 152, 154, 166, 175
Llancarfan Gospel 13
Llancillo 145, 162
Llancloudy 163, 164, 167
Llanddeti 60
Llanddowror 33, 143, 160
Llandeilo Bertholau 161, 162
Llandeilo Fawr 4, 9, 10–11, 33, 35, 103, 160, 161, 170, 173, 177, 178
Llandeilo Gospels see Lichfield Gospels
Llandeilo near Abergavenny 8
Llandeilo'r-fân 68
Llandinabo 162, 163, 164, 165, 167
Llandogo 9, 26, 163, 164, 166–7, 173–4, 175, 178
Llandough 28–9, 40, 55, 90, 100, 166
Llanegwad 166
Llanelli 165
Llanfeuno see Llanveynoe
Llanfihangel Cwm Du 18, 167
Llanfihangel Tal-y-llyn 18–19, 67–9, 167, 172–3, 177
Llanfrother 161
Llangadwaladr 28–9, 99–100, 112
Llangarron 20, 167, 176
Llangiwa see Llangua
Llangoed 68, 162
Llan-gors 49, 68–9, 166, 168
Llangua 170–2, 178
Llangunville 176
Llan-gwm 176
Llangyfelach 65
Llangynfyl 176

Llangynidr   167
Llanhennock/Llanhenwg   157
Llantwit (Llanilltud)   8, 29, 39, 40, 55, 57, 61–6, 84, 143, 152, 154–5, 158, 166, 168, 169, 171, 174, 175
Llanveynoe   164
Llanwarne   161
Llibio   18–19, 23–5, 67–70, 160, 172–3, 174, 177, 178
Llunferth (*Lunberth*)   24, 68, 169, 173
llystin   102
Llys-wen   162
Louan   43
Lugaed   145, 160
Lugobi/Luigbe   145, 160
Lunberth   *see* Llunferth
Lupus   52, 146
Luuaet   145, 160
Lydbury North   21

Mabillon, Jean   61
Machinis   165
Madley   47–8, 93, 167
Madrun   54
Máelbrigte   160
Máeldub   163
Maelgwn Gwynedd   53, 92
maenawr   46
Maerun   48, 97
Mafwrn   94, 162, 164, 167
magister   163
Mail-brigit   160
Maildun   145
Malmesbury   163
Manorbier   158
MANUSCRIPTS
   BL Cotton Vespasian A.xiv   10, 13, 22, 28–9, 34, 38–41, 51, 54, 66, 83, 91–2, 93, 94, 141
   BL Harley 3859   29–31, 45, 52, 118–56
   BL Harley 4181   125, 131
   BL Harley 6831   125, 129, 131
   Cambridge, Corpus Christi College, 114   15
   Cambridge, Corpus Christi College, 286 [St Augustine's Gospels]   14
   Cambridge, Pembroke College 302 [Hereford Gospel Book]   20
   Cardiff, Central Library, 1.185   64
   Cardiff, Central Library, 2.16   125
   Cardiff, Central Library, 3.77   124, 132–5
   Cardiff, Central Library, 3.704   64
   Cardiff, Central Library, 4.409   64
   Douai, Bibliothèque Municipale, 322   20
   Dublin, Royal Irish Academy, 12.N.4   62–4
   Hereford, Cathedral Library, P.i.2   12–14
   Lichfield, Cathedral Library, 1   *see* Lichfield Gospels
   Manchester, John Rylands Library, Welsh MS 1   133
   NLW 732B   133
   NLW 3042B (Mostyn 134)   125
   NLW 3067B (Mostyn 212b)   125–6, 129
   NLW 11114B   133
   NLW 13089E   62, 63, 65
   NLW 13098B   62
   NLW 13100B   62
   NLW 13114B   61–6
   NLW 13116B   61–6
   NLW 13153A   61–6
   NLW 13158A   62, 63
   NLW 17110E [*Liber Landavensis*], codicology and palaeography of   1, 9–10, 19, 22, 24, 48, 52, 83, 91, 97, 103, 175, 176
   NLW 21001Bii   133
   NLW Brogyntyn I.15   126
   NLW Llanstephan 12   125–7, 134
   NLW Peniarth 138   124
   NLW Peniarth 177   133
   NLW Peniarth 178   124
   NLW Peniarth 283   132
   Oxford, Jesus College, 20   30–1, 57, 118–56, 160
   Oxford, Jesus College, 112   62
   see also Book of Deer, Book of Kells, Book of St Beuno, Cartulary of Landevennec, Cartulary of Redon, Codex Wintoniensis, Hemming's Cartulary, Juvencus Manuscript, *Liber Wigorniensis*, Llancarfan Gospel, Offa Bible, Redon Cartulary, Sherborne Cartulary

Marcant   *see* Morgan

Index

Marchlwydd (*Marchluid*) 23–4, 175
Maredudd of Dyfed 53, 57, 129, 135, 136, 143, 144
Margam 84
Marshfield 48, 97
Matharn 99, 170
Maximus 54
Meirchion ap Rhydderch 175
Meirchyawn 145, 160
meliores 114
Merchguin *see* Merchwyn
Merchwyn, cleric 34, 43, 145
Merchwyn ap Glywys 145, 160
Mercia 119–20
Mergualdus, Merewald / Merewalh 38
merthir 164
Merthyr Mawr 18
Meurig (*ob.* 849) 137, 140
Meurig (*ob.* 873/4) 137, 140, 169
Meurig ab Arthfael 26, 50, 120–2, 128, 140, 155–6, 168–9, 174
Meurig ab Enynny 26, 54
Meurig ab Ithel 120–2, 140, 151–2, 153–4, 155
Meurig ap Ffernfael 154
Meurig ap Hywel 49, 176
Meurig ap Tewdrig 55, 124, 129, 131, 132–3, 135, 143, 144, 146, 147, 148, 149, 150, 156, 167
Meurig, obscure king 26, 145–7
Moccas/Mochros 62, 146, 161, 162, 163, 164, 165, 167, 177–8
modius 102
monasterium 46
Monmouth 10, 48, 92, 96, 172
Monnow 170
Morcant *see* Morgan
Morgan (*ob.* 665) 137
Morgan (*ob.* 974) 137, 140
Morgan ab Athrwys 107, 117, 120–1, 123, 126, 127, 131–2, 135, 141, 143, 149, 150, 151, 156, 166
Morgan ab Owain 17, 30, 117, 118, 122, 125, 126, 129, 131, 132, 135, 140, 156, 174
Morgan ap Caradog 126, 132, 134
Morgan ap Gwrgan 137, 148
Morgan Hen/Mawr *see* Morgan ab Owain
Morgan *nepos* of Meurig 149
Morgannwg 17–18, 19, 21, 30, 67, 117, 118, 120, 122, 143, 150
Moridunum 159
Mouric *see* Meurig
MP 3 (*Miscellaneous Pedigrees* 3) 124–6, 133–4
Much Dewchurch 163

nant y clauorion 51
Nest ferch Rhodri 129
Nichol(l)s, David 61–6
Nobis (*ob.* 873) 137, 140, 169
Nobis 23, 140, 169–70, 172
Nodhail 124
Noe *see* Nowy
Nouis 169–71
Nowy ab Arthur 14–15, 33, 53, 60, 143–4, 160
Nowy ap Gwriad 174
Nudd, bishop 23, 33, 49, 62, 65, 66, 110, 168–9, 178
Nudd (hael) 30, 124–6, 128, 129, 131, 133–4, 151, 156
Nynnio 131, 149

Offa Bible 14
Offa's Dyke 48
offere 67
Ogmore 78, 97, 174
Old Cornish Vocabulary 51
Onbrawst 131–2, 143, 147, 148, 149
Oudoce(us) *see* Euddogwy
Outegurn *see* Eudeyrn
Over in Almondsbury 48, 60
Owain ap Hywel 117, 135, 172
Owain ap Morgan 175

Paris, Council of 52, 158
Parker, Matthew 14–15, 26
Pater 23–5, 110, 173–4, 176
Paternus 157
patruelis 128
Paul 41, 151, 152
Paviland 69, 160
Peibio 34, 51, 52–3, 59, 129, 131, 144–5, 147, 149, 156, 161, 162, 163, 164, 165
Penally/Penalun 8, 9, 33, 35, 160, 164
Pencoyd 164
Pennros 176
Penychen 67, 173, 178
Pepiau *see* Peibio

209

Peter, St   8, 9, 17
Peterchurch   162
Piro   61, 65, 158
pistor   158
podum   46, 164
Pope   1, 7, 8, 9, 17, 47, 52, 53, 60, 62, 106, 160, 170
Porth Tulon   59, 160, 162, 164
Powys   118, 164
presbiter   38
Price, Thomas   2
princeps   29, 38, 143
Priuilegium Sancti Teliaui   116

Redon Cartulary   84
Rees, W. J.   2
Rhain ap Brychan   57
Rhain ap Cadwgon   57
Rhodri ab Ithel   39, 107, 121, 143, 154
Rhodri Mawr   118–20, 135
Rhydderch ab Iestyn   117
Rhydderch ap Caradog   19, 21, 177
Rhygyfarch   51, 59, 131
Rhys ab Arthfael   129, 131, 141, 174
Rhys ab Ithel   30, 121, 153–4, 154
Ricceneth   131–2, 151
Ris   see Rhys
Robert of Gloucester   7
Rodri   see Rhodri
Roger fitzWilliam fitzOsbern   110, 176
Rome   9, 19, 158
Rotri   see Rhodri
Rumceneu   40

sacerdos   38, 60, 162–3
Sadwrn   28, 100, 143
Saint-y-nyll   170
Salesbury, William   14–15, 26
Samson, abbot   39, 57, 152–3, 154
Samson, St   8, 52, 53, 61, 65, 66, 100, 152, 157–60
Saturn   see Sadwrn
Saturnbiu   15
Sawyer   *see* CHARTERS
scripula   115
Sedbury   48
Segin   61, 64–5
Selden, John   62
Sellack   168
seniores   4, 114, 121

senscríbend deodae   86
Senyllt   124
Severa   54
Sherborne   68
Sherborne Cartulary   4, 14
Sigginston   64
Sigin   62, 64
solus   60, 107, 150
Spain   116
Spelman, Henry   2, 62–4
Splott   51, 168
St Arvans   164
St Augustine's Gospels   14
St Bride's-super-Ely   173
St Davids   1, 3, 7, 8, 9, 12, 14, 17, 19, 25, 26, 33, 52, 60–1, 65, 68, 90, 144, 160, 169, 170, 172, 173, 177–8
St Dogwyn's   *see* Llandough
St Ishmael's   15
St Kynemark's   164
St Maughan's   19, 94, 174
Stephens, Thomas   2
Stillingfleet, Edward   61, 63, 64
Stradling, Edward   63
Sulien (*Sulgen*)   39–40, 41, 92, 100, 152
Synodus II S. Patricii   12

Tatheus, St   54
Taui urbs   29, 143
Tecán   57, 154
Teican   154
Teiliau   see Teilo
Teilo   8, 9, 10–13, 17–18, 23, 25–6, 27, 33, 35, 41–3, 53, 54, 59, 78, 81, 88, 100, 116, 144, 152, 160–2, 166, 176, 177
Teithi, insula   17
Teithvallt   124
Tenby   51
Tewdrig of Brycheiniog   120
Tewdrig of Glywysing   30, 55, 119–20, 122–3, 126, 136, 141, 144, 148, 150, 156
Tewdwr ab Elise(dd)   67, 69, 172–3
Tewdwr ap Meurig   154
Tewdwr ap Peibio   149
Tewdwr ap Rhain   57, 67, 167
Tewkesbury   1, 9
Thomas ap Ieuan ap Deicws   133
Thomas ap Llywelyn ab Ithel   124
Thomas, Hugh   57, 125, 131

Tidenham 48
Tigernomalus 157
Tir Conloc 47, 93
Tirchan see Tyrchan
Tomre 61, 65
Tramerin, bishop St Davids 24, 61
Tref Eliau 168
Trefeglwys 10, 11
Trefesgob see Bishton
Trefwyddog 11
Trelleck Grange 174
Tremerin/Tremerig 20–2, 25, 49, 60–1, 176
Tresigin 64
Trichan see Tyrchan
Trunci 19
Tucker, Henry 64
Tull Coit 98
Twrog, St 12
Tyrchan 22, 23, 27, 33, 38, 39, 46, 55, 60, 87, 90, 91, 107, 110, 151, 152, 154, 165, 167, 168, 174

Ufelfyw (*Ubelbiu*) 23, 34–5, 43, 144, 145, 146, 161, 162, 165
uilla uallis 171
uncia 45, 116
Undy 175
Urban, bp 7, 8–10, 17–21, 25, 47, 67, 68, 71, 86, 106, 115, 177–8
Urien Rheged 54
Ussher, James 2, 61

vallis leprosorum 51
Vaughan, Robert 61, 62, 132
VC see CHARTERS
Venantius Fortunatus 157
Venta Silurum 117
villa 46
Villa Branuc 170
Villa Conuc 48, 97
Villa Eliau 168
Villa Gunnuc 176
Villa hir pant 171
Villa Seuan 174–5
Vincent of Beauvais 61

Vita Cadoci 13, 28, 32, 38, 41, 54, 78, 86, 91–2, 114, 124, 141, 149, 152, 159
Vita Clitauci 66, 91
Vita David 51, 59, 131
Vita Dubricii 22, 23, 26, 33, 48, 51, 53, 84, 111, 144, 147, 160, 161, 162
Vita Elgari 161
Vita Gildae 13
Vita Griffini 118
Vita Iltuti 145
Vita Oudocei 23, 29, 40, 53, 84, 106, 112, 143, 144, 166
Vita Samsonis 8, 52, 60, 61, 65, 105, 116, 161, 165, 174
Vita Tathei 54
Vita Teiliaui 23, 35, 53, 84, 111, 112
Vortigern 54
Vortimer 54
Vuelbiu see Ufelfyw

Webtree 47
Welsh Bicknor 21, 142, 145, 146, 162, 163, 164–5, 167, 168, 178
Weltenburg 13
Wharton, Henry 2
Whitchurch 163, 164, 166
Whitebrook 173
Wilfred, bishop 7, 19
Wilkins, David 2, 62
Williams, David 61, 63, 64
Williams, Edward see Iolo Morganwg
Williams, Richard 125
Worcester 7, 14, 16, 44, 71, 78, 82, 83, 90, 115, 144, 163, 165, 172
Wrgannus Varius/Vawr 149
Wulffrith 23, 24, 110, 173–4, 176
Wurgeat 174
wynepwerth 115

Yellow Plague 53, 54
York 19, 21
Ynyr Gwent 54
Ynys Bŷr 8, 158
Ystrad Tywi 117, 178
Ystrad Yw 19, 67, 176–7

STUDIES IN CELTIC HISTORY

Already published

I · THE SAINTS OF GWYNEDD
Molly Miller

II · CELTIC BRITAIN IN THE EARLY MIDDLE AGES
Kathleen Hughes

III · THE INSULAR LATIN GRAMMARIANS
Vivien Law

IV · CHRONICLES AND ANNALS OF MEDIAEVAL IRELAND AND WALES
Kathryn Grabowski and David Dumville

V · GILDAS: NEW APPROACHES
M. Lapidge and D. Dumville (ed.)

VI · SAINT GERMANUS OF AUXERRE AND THE END OF ROMAN BRITAIN
E.A. Thompson

VII · FROM KINGS TO WARLORDS: THE CHANGING POLITICAL
STRUCTURE OF GAELIC IRELAND IN THE LATER MIDDLE AGES
Katharine Simms

VIII · THE CHURCH AND THE WELSH BORDER
IN THE CENTRAL MIDDLE AGES
C.N.L. Brooke

IX · THE LITURGY AND RITUAL OF THE CELTIC CHURCH
F.E. Warren (2nd edn by Jane Stevenson)

X · THE MONKS OF REDON
Caroline Brett (ed. and trans.)

XI · EARLY MONASTERIES IN CORNWALL
Lynette Olson

XII · IRELAND, WALES AND ENGLAND IN THE ELEVENTH CENTURY
K.L. Maund

XIII · SAINT PATRICK, AD 493–1993
D.N. Dumville and others

XIV · MILITARY INSTITUTIONS ON THE WELSH MARCHES:
SHROPSHIRE, AD 1066–1300
Frederick C. Suppe

XV · UNDERSTANDING THE UNIVERSE IN SEVENTH-CENTURY IRELAND
Marina Smythe

XVI · GRUFFUDD AP CYNAN: A COLLABORATIVE BIOGRAPHY
K.L. Maund (ed.)

XVII · COLUMBANUS: STUDIES ON THE LATIN WRITINGS
Michael Lapidge (ed.)

XVIII · THE IRISH IDENTITY OF THE KINGDOM OF THE SCOTS
IN THE TWELFTH AND THIRTEENTH CENTURIES
Dauvit Broun

XIX · THE MEDIEVAL CULT OF ST PETROC
Karen Jankulak

XX · CHRIST IN CELTIC CHRISTIANITY: BRITAIN AND IRELAND
FROM THE FIFTH TO THE TENTH CENTURY
Michael W. Herren and Shirley Ann Brown

XXI · THE BOOK OF LLANDAF AND THE NORMAN CHURCH IN WALES
John Reuben Davies

XXII · ROYAL INAUGURATION IN GAELIC IRELAND *c.*1100–1600:
A CULTURAL LANDSCAPE STUDY
Elizabeth FitzPatrick

XXIII · CÉLI DÉ IN IRELAND: MONASTIC WRITING AND IDENTITY
IN THE EARLY MIDDLE AGES
Westley Follett

XXIV · ST DAVID OF WALES: CULT, CHURCH AND NATION
J. Wyn Evans and Jonathan M. Wooding (ed.)

XXV · SAINTS' CULTS IN THE CELTIC WORLD
Steve Boardman, John Reuben Davies and Eila Williamson (ed.)

XXVI · GILDAS'S DE EXCIDIO BRITONUM
AND THE EARLY BRITISH CHURCH
Karen George

XXVII · THE PRESENT AND THE PAST IN MEDIEVAL IRISH CHRONICLES
Nicholas Evans

XXVIII · THE CULT OF SAINTS AND THE VIRGIN MARY
IN MEDIEVAL SCOTLAND
Steve Boardman and Eila Williamson (ed.)

XXIX · THE TRANSFORMATION OF THE IRISH CHURCH
IN THE TWELFTH CENTURY
Marie Therese Flanagan

XXX · HEROIC SAGA AND CLASSICAL EPIC IN MEDIEVAL IRELAND
Brent Miles

XXXI · TOME: STUDIES IN MEDIEVAL CELTIC HISTORY AND LAW
IN HONOUR OF THOMAS CHARLES-EDWARDS
Fiona Edmonds and Paul Russell (ed.)

XXXII · NEW PERSPECTIVES ON MEDIEVAL SCOTLAND, 1093–1286
Matthew Hammond (ed.)

XXXIII · LITERACY AND IDENTITY IN EARLY MEDIEVAL IRELAND
Elva Johnston

XXXIV · CLASSICAL LITERATURE AND LEARNING
IN MEDIEVAL IRISH NARRATIVE
Ralph O'Connor (ed.)

XXXV · MEDIEVAL POWYS:
KINGDOM, PRINCIPALITY AND LORDSHIPS, 1132–1293
David Stephenson

XXXVI · PERCEPTIONS OF FEMININITY IN EARLY IRISH SOCIETY
Helen Oxenham

XXXVII · ST SAMSON OF DOL AND THE EARLIEST HISTORY OF
BRITTANY, CORNWALL AND WALES
Lynette Olson (ed.)

Printed in the United States
By Bookmasters